# Putting Expert Systems into Practice

# Putting Expert Systems into Practice

Robert G. Bowerman, B.Sc.
and
David E. Glover, Ph.D.

VNR VAN NOSTRAND REINHOLD COMPANY
New York

Library of Congress Catalog Card Number 87-13296
ISBN 0-442-20842-1



Printed in the United States of America

Van Nostrand Reinhold Company Inc.
115 Fifth Avenue
New York, New York 10003

Van Nostrand Reinhold Company Limited
Molly Millars Lane
Wokingham, Berkshire RG11 2PY, England

Van Nostrand Reinhold
480 La Trobe Street
Melbourne, Victoria 3000, Australia

Macmillan of Canada
Division of Canada Publishing Corporation
164 Commander Boulevard
Agincourt, Ontario M1S 3C7, Canada

16 15 14 13 12 11 10 9 8 7 6 5 4 3 2 1

**Library of Congress Cataloging-in-Publication Data**

Bowerman, Robert G., 1956-
Putting expert systems into practice

Bibliography: p.
Includes index.
1. Expert systems (Computer science) 2. Management information systems. 3. Computer integrated manufacturing systems. I. Glover, David E. II. Title.
QA76.76.E95B68 1988 006.3'3 87-13296
ISBN 0-442-20842-1

*This book is dedicated to all those at the top of the computer profession, that they may take the knowledge contained in this book to heart and put it into practice.*

# Foreword

The commercialization of artificial intelligence (AI) and expert systems technologies has been filled with misconceptions, overstated claims, and not a little marketing hype. Academicians tend to speak a different language from the systems professionals. Product marketing departments tend to employ a third language, and in the case of AI have often misunderstood and not connected with the computer professionals, the academicians, or the end users. It is only within the past few years that systems professionals in companies as dissimilar as American Express, Coopers & Lybrand, DEC, and DuPont have gained enough experience with both the promises and shortcomings of applied expert systems technology to begin to see through the smoke and behind the mirrors. To the newcomer, AI is often presented as a single entity or magical product; rather it is simply a collection of software engineering tools that make some difficult programming tasks easier and other seemingly impossible ones approachable. The major distinction between conventional systems and AI-based systems is that they address more abstract symbolic problems and are able to cope with uncertain or conflicting data to infer useful solutions.

From the point of view of the typical system developer or manager it's important to recognize that the introduction of expert systems is not a new phenomena in the history of software engineering. Just as high-level languages and relational databases emerged from computer science research to become part of the system developer's standard tool kit, so are expert systems just now entering the mainstream of software engineering. The passage of time and experience should make the use of tools such as inference engines, object-oriented programming, and frame based reasoning no more unusual than data dictionaries or transaction processing.

A few points of practical advice directed to the system development professional. These points have grown out of my experience in coordinating the AUTHORIZER'S ASSISTANT expert system for Travel Related Services division of American Express, and are also echoed well within this book.

- Don't use expert systems tools for their own sake. The technology is very seductive, however, business needs should always drive the selection of expert systems as an appropriate technology.
- Never underestimate how good people are at handling what seem like trivial problems. Real "common sense" is not so common.
- Be pragmatic. Pick small and well-defined problems to start with.
- Choose applications that are important to the business and interesting to the expert—without a dedicated champion, a long-term project will never succeed.
- Be willing to accept the experimental nature of projects. Not all will succeed, but something important will be learned from each one.
- Don't underestimate the difficulties of systems integration. Begin planning for connectivity as soon as the data and communications requirements are clear.
- Expect to find frustrations and not a lot of practical experience in moving from the prototype to the integrated delivery system. This caution is especially true if an expert system is to be joined with existing applications in a conventional mainframe environment. (Also be cautious with beware of expert systems targeted to run on mainframes—adequate response times are by no means guaranteed for non-trivial expert systems).
- Don't discard the skills of a lifetime of software project management! Expert systems frequently require incremental prototyping as part of the development cycle in order to understand the problem and its solution, but that doesn't mean that schedules and deliverables are cast aside.

The good news for the pioneering companies is that expert systems techniques have already been used successfully to increase productivity and profitability in a wide variety of environments. The AUTHORIZER'S ASSISTANT, for example, leads to a higher percentage of charges being authorized while at the same time reducing the number of overdue collections. It has condensed the six inch thick Authorization Manual, together with the expertise of the best and most experienced authorizers, to a set of 800 rules, resulting in a less stressful job for the operator (previously they had to study 16 screens of data in just 90 seconds), together with improved consistency—24 hours a day, 7 days a week, around the world. It also has provided American Express with a permanent retention of the company's expertise, a competitive differentiation, and a proof of concept for other expert systems project at American Express. This book, which highlights many of the pitfalls found by early leaders together with pragmatic ways to navigate around them, should be a useful starting point for the MIS or CIM system professional approaching the challenges of expert system development and wishing to build systems which follow in the footsteps of the success stories.

Ted Markowitz
Director—Technology Strategy
American Express Company
Chairman of SMART-F$
(Society for the Management of AI Resources and Technology—Financial Services).

# Preface

This book is directed to those executives, project managers, and software engineers who have read about expert systems and now want to put the theory and technology into practice. Although expert systems have received a great deal of coverage in the trade press, at the time of this writing the total number of shell products sold is well under 20,000. We feel that a reasonable amount of practical guidance is all that is needed to move expert systems shells to a market position similar to database managers, where each major vendor has sold in excess of 100,000 copies of its product into mainstream corporate environments.

Expert systems are likely to be the next popular productivity tool in business and industrial environments, following the approach of database managers, spreadsheet calculators, word processors, and business graphics. We feel the guidance presented in this book will provide a catalyst to help an emergent trend reach fruition, that is, to put expert systems theory and technology into practice. Industry observers have noted that relational database management systems (RDBMS) moved from development into the mainstream around 1983. Three years later, even small corporations had taken advantage of RDBMS technology to replace various manual systems. Expert systems now show signs of following a similar pattern.

*Putting Expert Systems into Practice* discusses strategies and tactics for creating robust production applications. It addresses those general principles for success that will not become outdated as new products are released and application areas expand. Strategies and guidelines are emphasized rather than extensive documentation of existing implementations. The discussion includes a broad analysis of leading and emergent shell tools, tool sets, environments, and symbolic programming languages within the context of examining generic expert system development tool features. This *feature-oriented* approach has two benefits: (1) the knowledge presented will not age so quickly as the emerging field continues to develop rapidly, and (2) the reader will acquire greater facility in analyzing new offerings. The book emphasizes that system designers and implementers must base their creations on sound, stable software engineering and knowledge engineering principles.

The discussion throughout the text concentrates on creating production application in two mainstream corporate environments: Management Information Systems (MIS) for business and Computer-Integrated Manufacturing for industry. Care has been taken to present the material in a terminology and style accessible to readers from traditional commercial and industrial computing backgrounds. Detailed academic programming issues are omitted in favor of strategic design and planning issues.

After an introduction to establish the pragmatic approach, the sequence of chapters follows the expert systems development life cycle, phase by phase, from conception to completion. Chapter 1 introduces the basic knowledge necessary for understanding expert systems, including the artificial intelligence terminology used in expert systems work, the various dimensions involved in implementing expert systems, and an overview of the benefits and limitations of the current technology. Chapter 2 expands on the limitation theme through a common-sense, philosophical discussion of why there is no real "intelligence" in expert systems. Chapters 3 through 9 follow the stages in developing expert systems. Chapter 3 covers *application selection* presenting the general criteria for reviewing the feasibility and cost-effectiveness of candidate applications. The key element is recognizing types of knowledge suitable for expert systems applications. *Application quantification,* the demands for knowledge-representation schemes, inferencing mechanisms, user interfaces, and knowledge-acquisition aids, are addressed in Chapter 4. The requirements of the application, including such traditional issues as machine requirements, size of systems, pricing, and availability must be identified and quantified so appropriate tools can be selected. Chapter 5 addresses the fundamentals of expert system *shell tool set selection.* It analyzes the feature requirements examined in Chapter 4 for nearly 30 expert systems shell building tools, to illustrate the process of selecting the most appropriate tools for the job at hand.

Chapter 6 covers the broader issues of *configuration selection,* outlining the needs for and disadvantages of using specialized programming environments, AI languages, support tools, and shell tools. Strategies and procedures for acquiring knowledge from experts, *knowledge acquisition,* is covered in Chapter 7. This stage is critical to the success of the project and usually requires intensive time and prototyping iterations. Before the new expert system can become a productive part of an enterprise, it must be integrated with a corporation's existing systems.

Issues of *systems integration* are addressed in Chapter 8. With increasing frequency integrated, rather than stand-alone, hardware/software systems are being required by MIS and CIM directors. *System startup* and *management*, or people roles, are the two themes of Chapter 9. People issues are central in moving the completed development into the daily production of a corporation, and this chapter discusses the roles of knowledge engineers, domain experts, consultants, managers, and knowledge-base administrators and support staff, which are at the heart of any project's success. Finally, Chapter 10 addresses some of the issues influencing future trends, in both the short and long terms, in expert systems and Al developments.

Although broad similarities between the structure and use of the expert systems technology and traditional software tools exist, various differences are critical. This distinction is most clearly illustrated by the expert system development life cycle, which may involve a series of prototypes and several iterations through the knowledge-acquisition loop. Some of the principles and strategies presented are common in standard software-engineering practices. We have tried to distinguish those development features and practices peculiar to expert systems developments, while maintaining an appropriate view of software development as a whole. This perspective is often manifested as additional knowledge needed to transform traditional systems analysis into *knowledge engineering*. Building successful applications is based on a clear understanding of the philosophical and practical distinctions between expert systems technology, traditional software systems, and the capabilities of real human experts.

Judging from the literature and our own observations, we believe too many corporations have restricted their expert systems technology to toy problem prototypes using simplistic shells on small computers. Corporations do want more robust and effective results, but may lack the knowledge of where to start or how to proceed. The limited features of small PC-based shells cannot be expected to produce applications with the capabilities of such large expert systems as PROSPECTOR, DENDRAL, XCON, or DRILLING ADVISOR. For many serious production applications, we argue, the developer may have to reject small PC shells and select something more capable running on a larger machine, such as a DEC VAX or IBM mainframe. Fortunately, this process is being facilitated by an increasing number of shell tools ported from AI LISP environments to traditional languages like C, so they can run on general-purpose hosts and be integrated into mainstream environments. What is next needed to generate real-world production-quality systems is knowing how to select the application and the appropriate tools, how to size and specify the configuration, and how to proceed with knowledge capture, codification, testing, and system integration. *Putting Expert Systems into Practice* addresses these strategic issues and introduces computer executives, project managers, and software engineers to the principles required for a successfully fielded implementation.

We thank the numerous academicians and computer industry leaders who have inspired us and helped us complete this work. Special acknowledgment is due Maharishi Mahesh Yogi (the best knowledge engineer we ever met), John Hagelin, Bruce Lester, Robert Fertig, David Rosenbloom, Dave Nelson, Jeffrey Perrone, Jon Cooper, Ella Pappius, Donna Goldin, Steven Olmstead, Robert Baron, Ray Ford, Paula Baudoux, Alex Green, John Sorflaten, Su Bowerman, Tom Miller, Paul Brook, and our many friends among vendors.

Robert G. Bowerman and David E. Glover, Ph.D.
Heliosoft, Inc.
P.O. Box 1205
Fairfield, Iowa 52556
(515) 472-2185

# Contents

# Putting Expert Systems into Practice

# Chapter 1
# Understanding Expert Systems: Technology and Capabilities

SECTION HEADINGS



## OVERVIEW

This introductory chapter of *Putting Expert Systems Into Practice* provides two functions. First, it introduces the key concepts and the discipline's terminology. Second, it presents an overview of the book's major thesis—the creation of robust, expert system production applications. Throughout, the discussion focuses on the process of recognizing strategies and tactics for getting expert systems up and running as integral components in an enterprises' business or manufacturing systems.

## 1-1. EXPERT SYSTEMS: FROM AI RESEARCH TO PRODUCTION APPLICATIONS

What is an expert system? An *expert system* is a system of software or combined software and hardware capable of competently executing a specific task usually performed by a human expert. Expert systems are highly specialized computer systems capable of simulating that element of a human specialist's knowledge and reasoning that can be formulated into knowledge chunks characterized by a set of facts and heuristic rules. *Heuristic rules* are rules of thumb accumulated by a human expert through intensive problem solving in the domain of a particular task, usually over a period of years. The problem-solving capacity of expert systems developed to date is usually limited to a single, narrow field of technical expertise.

Expert systems have been developed for a variety of complex applications, including diagnosing blood infections (MYCIN, Shortliffe, 1976), configuring computer systems (XCON, McDermott, 1982), inferring the structure of unknown chemical compounds (DENDRAL, Buchanan and Feigenbaum, 1978), planning gene-cloning experiments (MOLGEN, Stefik, 1981*a,b*), monitoring and controlling computer operating systems (YES/MVS, Griesmer et al., 1984), troubleshooting telephone networks (AT&T's ACE, Vesonder et al., 1983; Wright et al., 1984), assisting managers in computer systems manufacturing environments (IMACS, O'Connor, 1984), and consulting mineral exploration geologists (PROSPECTOR, Duda and Reboh, 1984).[1]

The number of successfully fielded expert systems has mushroomed since 1984, as high-level development tools have become widely available. For example, Elf-Aquitaine (France) uses a drilling advisor developed with the Teknowledge, Inc. (Palo Alto, California), KS300 Shell (a precursor to S.1); General Research (McLean, Virginia) has a VAX operating system tuner built around the TIMM shell; Texas Instruments (Dallas, Texas) troubleshoots its 990 minicomputers with a tool structured from Radian Corporation's (Austin, Texas) Rulemaster; and Campbell Soup Company has captured sterilizer troubleshooter expertise in "Aldo in a Box," an expert system developed with Texas Instruments' Personal Consultant expert system shell.

Expert system technology is one of the most immediately promising engineering outgrowths of artificial intelligence research (AI). *Artificial intelligence* specializes in understanding intelligent systems—particularly the human system—and simulating intelligent activity in machines. The primary thrust of AI research has been to develop theories, models, and computed-based prototypes of intelligent entities. In recent years some of the research results have begun to move from the laboratory to real-world applications. The conception of intelligence traditionally embraced by the AI community has been behavioral in character. Thus, a machine or program is said to be "intelligent"—in the AI sense—if it exhibits external behavioral characteristics usually associated with an intelligent biological entity. Primarily, two perspectives have been investigated in AI for achieving simulated intelligence. The first uses the human brain, mind, and nervous system as its primary model to be emulated in developing intelligent systems. The human cognitive system or the visual system, for example, might be considered basic computational architectures to be replicated. The second perspective considers the intelligence function to be more important than the computational form. This less restrictive approach opens the door to any internal means of producing the desired behavioral result, regardless of whether the internal mechanisms used are human-like.

Research in artificial intelligence over the last 25–30 years has attempted to produce intelligent systems in vision processing, game playing, theorem proving, natural language understanding and synthesis, robotics, and simulating the knowledge and reasoning capacities of human experts. Some of the specific problems studied, such as kinematics, machine vision, and building-block world planners, have yielded significant solution techniques that are now applied in limited areas. With the aid of AI techniques, robotic arms can now catch bouncing Ping-Pong balls or sort a pile of wrenches into a neat array. Solid modelers, which provide the spearhead of the design process in computer-integrated manufacturing (CIM), derive much of their power from building-block representations invented in the AI laboratories of the 1970s.

In applied AI technologies, the *knowledge-engineering* tools at the basis of the expert system technology hold great immediate and future promise. Work on *knowledge-based* expert systems evolved from the early programs for game playing (e.g., Samuel's checkers player, Samuel, 1963) and theorem proving (e.g., the Logic Theorist, Newell et al., 1963). These programs, with other generalized problem-solving and planning programs of the 1960s and early 1970s (e.g., the General Problem Solver (GPS) (Newell and Simon, 1963) and STRIPS, a blocks world planner (Fikes and Nilsson, 1971)), focused on problem-solving abilities in simplified, limited, "toy problem" domains. Although some successes were achieved in these task domains, the results were generally disappointing when the researchers attempted to scale the systems up to a level of sophistication necessary to handle real-world problems. It is thus important to distinguish between experimental problem-solving techniques used in limited, isolated laboratory settings and those robust techniques and technologies capable of producing consistent, high-quality results in the complex and demanding environment of applied production.

In general, codifying the knowledge that a human brings to a particular problem-solving situation and localizing that knowledge in a computer program was found to be no simple task. AI researchers of the

1960s and early 1970s found, much to their disappointment, an inverse relationship between *breadth of coverage* and *depth of ability* in these programs. The problem-solving programs had increasing difficulty in finding good solutions to particular problems as more generalized problem-solving ability was incorporated. Unfortunately, the great speed and accuracy of computing machinery did not alleviate the problem. The combinatorial explosion experienced in attempting to evaluate all possible solution points in a *search space* of all possible solutions quickly brought even the fastest of computers to its knees. The brute-force approach of evaluating all possible alternatives was quickly shown to be ineffective for areas where the alternatives were not bounded and limited. The so-called weak methods of AI, e.g., depth-first search, hill climbing, and means-end analysis,[2] appeared by themselves to be inadequate for most real-world problems. Obviously, something was wrong with the basic approach.

While some AI researchers were rethinking the basic premises employed in problem-solving strategies, other AI investigators were examining new representation and reasoning schemes. Sophisticated problem-solving representations based on *rules*, *frames*, and *semantic* or *associative networks* evolved. These representations allowed designers of intelligent systems to formulate specific *inference* or *reasoning mechanisms* based on the relationships between the symbols representing the elements of *knowledge* in the *knowledge base*. These systems, which appeared in the mid- and late 1970s, were called *knowledge-based systems*.

Because the domain-independent, general problem-solving systems did not exhibit the robust capacity needed for real-world problem solving, researchers decided that more limited *domain-specific* strategies should be tried. The approach made sense. In addition to the ability to focus deeply in a specific problem domain, the key component for a successful knowledge-based system was the body of knowledge encapsulated in the system. Although this narrow-but-deep knowledge approach has been successful, it should be understood that the original goal of AI researchers—to emulate or capture general intelligence capabilities—has been replaced by a more immediate goal of generating narrow-capacity, marginally "intelligent" machines.

The paradigm shift from brute-force approaches to knowledge-based approaches exemplifies the trend in the western world toward "working smarter," rather than "working harder," to accomplish a task. Before the age of scientific discovery, power was usually equated with military strength. But later, as the age of science and reason dawned, the pen became "mightier than the sword." More recently, data processing and computing technology has shown the immense power contained within information storage, retrieval, and management systems. A still newer

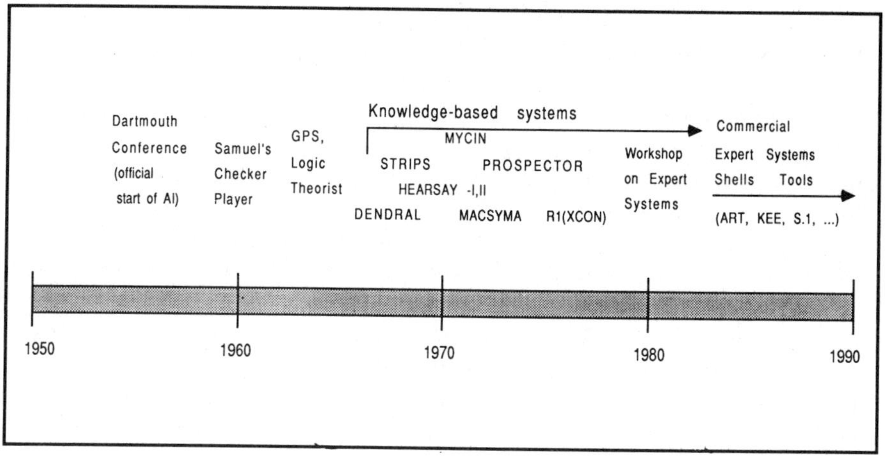


Fig. 1-1. A selected history of the development of expert systems technology.

principle, expounded in information theory and demonstrated by current expert systems technology, is expressed as "knowledge is power" or *knowledge has organizing power.* Not only does knowledge provide the necessary depth and power for a simulated intelligent system, but the structure of the knowledge has an inherent *organizing power* critical to accessing and using the knowledge base. It is not the speed of human information processing and decision making that produces intelligent behavior or expertise, but rather the organization, access, and utilization of knowledge.

The so-called knowledge-based systems of the 1970s were the first generation of expert systems. Each system was custom-built to perform a human expert's task or to assist the human expert in his or her work in a complex, problem-solving task domain. For instance, MYCIN diagnosed blood infection diseases, and PROSPECTOR assisted geologists in finding ore deposits. The success of these systems was based on an appropriate combination of a knowledge base and *inference* or *search strategies.* The inferencing strategy in the expert system is incorporated in the *inference engine*—that element of the expert system that accesses and uses the knowledge base to implement the reasoning process. The knowledge base comprises facts and heuristics, or rules of thumb, gleaned from the expert human problem solver, which were encoded in symbolic knowledge representations.

In 1979, a group of the knowledge engineers responsible for the early expert systems converged at a workshop on expert systems, chaired by Waterman and Hayes-Roth, to organize and codify their collective experience. The resulting landmark text, *Building Expert Systems* (Hayes-

Roth et al., 1983), laid a solid foundation for *knowledge engineering*, the process of designing and constructing expert systems. This publication, along with a similar volume, *Expert Systems in the Micro-Electronic Age*, edited by Michie of the University of Edinburgh, Scotland (Michie 1979), presented for the first time a body of applied expert systems engineering principles. Thus the experiences from earlier work on knowledge-based systems, reported throughout the 1970s and early 1980s in such publications as the *International Joint Conference on Artificial Intelligence* (IJCAI) and the *Proceedings of the National Conference on Artificial Intelligence* (AAAI), had been officially codified and retitled expert system development tools and strategies. Through this process, AI leaders—e.g., Hayes-Roth, Michie, Waterman, Feigenbaum, Lenat, Duda, and others—were able to slowly bring the newly born applied knowledge of expert system technology into the realm of accepted applied computer science. Figure 1-1 provides a brief synopsis of this development history.

This codification of knowledge-engineering techniques and principles has resulted in an increasing number of second-generation expert systems. There are basically five potential routes for acquiring an expert system today:

1. Generate a fully custom implementation using AI symbolic programming languages, e.g., LISP, PROLOG, SMALLTALK,
2. Use an expert system "shell" extracted from first-generation systems, e.g., EMYCIN from MYCIN and KAS from PROSPECTOR,
3. Use expert systems "shells" produced by commercial vendors, e.g., M.1 from Teknowledge, Inc., ART from Inference Corporation (Los Angeles, California), or KEE from Intellicorp (Mountain View, California),
4. Purchase a self-contained expert system with vendor-provided knowledge bases, e.g., OPTIMED from The Health Data Institute (Lexington, Massachusetts) for hospital preadmission certification or SpinPro for selecting ultracentrifuge methods from Beckman Instruments, Inc. (Palo Alto, California).
5. Generate a fully custom implementation using general-purpose programming languages, e.g., C, PASCAL, PROGRESS, and MANTIS.

Expert systems technology comprises the first four alternatives. Out of this range of methods, the open-market availability of expert system shells or building tools presents the possibility for wide-scale, relatively low-cost, commercial use of expert systems technologies in the data-processing (DP), management information systems (MIS), engineering, scientific, and computer-integrated manufacturing (CIM) environments of today. This book provides implementation guidelines and a practical view of the essential knowledge necessary to understand and implement expert systems in common work environments.

## 1-2. THE COMPONENTS OF EXPERT SYSTEM TECHNOLOGY

What are the basic elements used in constructing expert systems for the production environment? In this section the basic terminology will be laid out, and these fundamental components or features will be analyzed in more detail in Chapter 4.

From the definition of an expert system presented earlier, it is apparent that an expert system is defined in terms of its function, rather than its underlying programming and representational structures. One could construct a system that would capture the expert's knowledge in languages such as FORTRAN or COBOL, but the lack of symbolic representational and reasoning structures would make programming unnecessarily complex or infeasible. Expert system technologies tend to be different from conventional DP programs in their extensive use of *heuristics*, *symbolic manipulation*, and *inferencing mechanisms* to represent and extract knowledge from a large knowledge base. In DP programs the basic unit of storage in large databases is the data element, which is then accessed and manipulated by well-defined, repetitive, deterministic algorithms. Expert systems operate heuristically, i.e., according to codified rules of thumb, traversing *inference nets* to deduce a result based on the current set of domain facts and rules existing in the knowledge base. Processing and reasoning based on the use of simple or complex symbol structures, rather than numbers, is at the core of these AI systems.

An idealized modular expert system is shown in Fig. 1-2. The *domain-specific knowledge module* and the *domain-independent knowledge module* are the two key defining components of an expert system. The *domain-specific knowledge* comprises the expert's factual and heuristic, rule-oriented, and structure-oriented knowledge. The *domain-independent knowledge* represents general problem-solving strategies applicable to any set of domain-specific knowledge (within the applicable expert system scheme) built into the system. This domain-independent problem-solving ability is based on an *inference engine* that can deduce various results based on input facts and the expertise captured in the knowledge base. The engine is usually composed of an *interpreter*, which analyzes the current state of the inference process (e.g., a rule interpreter), and a *scheduler*, which sequences the actions taken by the inference engine. The inference mechanism employed in the expert system must, of

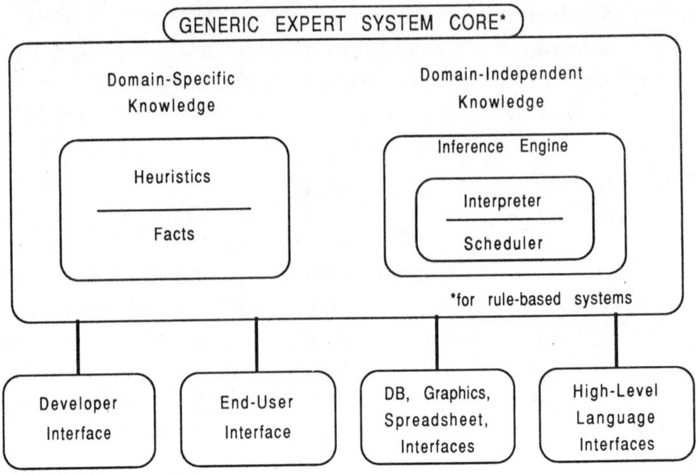


Fig. 1-2. The basic components of an expert system.

course, be compatible with the data structure form used to represent the domain knowledge. One of the key features of expert systems technology is the distinct separation of the domain-dependent and domain-independent aspects of knowledge, allowing much greater ease in updating or modifying the knowledge base.

Two primary knowledge-representation schemes are currently widely used in expert systems work. The first is called *rule-based representation* and is illustrated in Fig. 1-3 by a rule from MYCIN.

A rule representation is usually a modified form of the grammar-based *production rules* used in some first-generation expert systems. The

IF (1) The strain of the organism is grampos, and
(2) The morphology of the organism is coccus, and
(3) The growth conformation of the organism is chains

THEN There is suggestive evidence (0.7) that the identity of the organism is streptococcus.

Fig. 1-3. A rule from the MYCIN Expert System (Shortliffe, 1976).

rules are typically written in a simple "IF/THEN" or "IF/THEN/ELSE" syntax. If a rule *premise*, i.e., the set of conditions specified in the "IF" part, is true, which implies that the conditions are consistent with the current set of facts in the knowledge base, then the *conclusion*, i.e., the group of conditions associated with the "THEN" part, is executed, often adding new facts to the knowledge base. Inference or deduction in the rule-based system is generally in the form of either *forward-chaining* or *backward-chaining*. Forward-chaining is reasoning from input data, often requested by the program and supplied interactively by the user, to a final conclusion moving forward through a rule chain as noted above; i.e., if the premise of a rule is satisfied, then perform the conclusion. With the MYCIN rule, forward-chaining can be used to reason from input symptoms, or facts, to the actual blood infection disease. Backward-chaining starts with a final conclusion, or *goal*, and attempts to determine a set of facts contributing to that goal by working in the reverse direction. It starts with rules containing the final goal in their conclusions, i.e., the conditions associated with the "THEN" or "ELSE" parts, and checks the premises of these rules to see if the truth of the premises can be deduced from facts in the knowledge base. Proving premises, which are often conclusions of other rules in the rule tree, results in a recursive search back through the rule chain. The above MYCIN rule could be used in this mode for medical student training by starting with a particular disease (goal) and querying students for relevant facts leading backward through rule chains to expected symptoms. The MYCIN example presents only a very simplified rule form. Production-quality expert systems may require much more complex rule forms to represent the degree of required knowledge.

"Probability like" *certainty factors* are usually associated with rules. The certainty factor or reliability measures indicate the degree of confidence associated with the facts used in the rule or the results inferred from the rule's logic. The ability to represent and manage the propagation of such uncertainty through the use of specialized non-Boolean logics is the hallmark of expert systems technology. Some systems use *inexact reasoning* methods, perhaps based on Bayesian statistics, to manage this numerical uncertainty. Others employ a form of *fuzzy logic*, where such qualitative expressions as *large*, *small*, *high*, *low*, and *near* are used to express inexact facts. The fuzzy logic inference mechanism is then able to deduce based on these facts.

The second representation scheme, called *frame-based*, or *schema*, representation, localizes an entire body of expected knowledge and actions into one structure. In this sense, the frame is similar to an entire COBOL block or PASCAL record data structure. One frame is made up of many slots. The number of frames and slots per frame is a function of the application. Each *slot,* or field, in the frame contains facts, rules, procedures, or links to other frames in a network of frames. Frame rules are generally of the IF/THEN type, but are not chained together as in the traditional rule-based system. *Procedural attachment* allows entire blocks of traditional programming code to be attached to a frame slot. The procedure is activated if the conditions associated with the slot are met. Similarly, *demons*, or *methods*, are access triggers associated with slots that are automatically fired, often in the background, if some particular event occurs. Demons are always active, but attached procedures are usually only executed when their frame is invoked. Thus a frame contains both data and instructions for the manipulation of data, making it more like a SMALLTALK object (to be discussed in Chapter 6) than a simple data structure.

The primary strength of the frame-based representation is the ability to characterize the structural and, often, spatial arrangement of knowledge. Various forms of symbolic relationships can be used to link frames

Obstructive Airways Disease (OAD) Prototype

| SLOT | VALUE |
|---|---|
| **Author:** | Aikins |
| **Date:** | 27 OCT-78 17:13:29 |
| **Source:** | Fallat |
| **Pointers:** | (degree MILD-OAD) (degree MODERATE-OAD) . . .<br>(subtype ASTHMA) (subtype EMPHYSEMA) . . . |
| **Hypothesis:** | There is Obstructive Airways Disease. |
| **If Confirmed:** | Deduce the degree of OAD<br>Deduce the subtype of OAD |
| **Action:** | Deduce any findings associated with OAD<br>Print the findings associated with OAD |
| **Fact Residual Rules:** | RULE157, RULE158, . . . |
| **Refinement Rules:** | RULE036, RULE038, RULE039, . . . |
| **Summary Rules:** | RULE053, RULE054, RULE055, RULE083, . . . |
| **Components:** | |
| **Total Lung Capacity** | Plausible Values: >100<br>Importance Measure: 4 |
| **Reversibility** | Inference Rules: RULE019, RULE020, RULE022, RULE025<br>Importance Measure: 0 |

Fig. 1-4. A frame for Obstructive Airways Disease (OAD) from the CENTAUR Expert System (Aikins, 1983).

into either *frame hierarchies* or *frame heterarchies.* Inference, or deduction, is accomplished by (1) rule or procedure activation, (2) inheritance of facts, properties, or features within a frame hierarchy, or (3) generalized deduction through traversing frame network links. A frame from CENTAUR, a pulmonary infection diagnosis expert system, illustrates many of these concepts in Fig. 1-4.

The *associative or semantic network,* sometimes noted as a third representation scheme in expert systems literature, can be considered a special case of the frame network described above. The basic limitation is that an associative network *node* generally represents a single concept or simple object, rather than a complex battery of declarative and procedural knowledge associated with a frame. Properties and relationships between concepts are expressed in terms of arcs or links between the simple knowledge objects. Deduction, or inference, is accomplished by traversing the inference net in approximately the same manner as mathematical graph traversal. Property inheritance may be structured into an inheritance heirarchy as noted above.

These data structures and inference schemes, with further AI knowledge-structuring and programming strategies (e.g., PROLOG-like *logic programming, LISP programming, object-oriented programming, access-oriented programming, constraint-oriented programming,* and *blackboard architectures*), will be examined in more detail in Chapter 4. Other important tools that can be used in the expert systems building-and-use environment, e.g., knowledge-acquisition tools, editors, debuggers, database interfaces, graphics interfaces, etc., will also be discussed there.

## 1-3. THE GOALS OF EXPERT SYSTEM IMPLEMENTATION

The emerging, expert systems, software engineering technology can provide a range of benefits in various applications if properly employed. The capture of a specialist's knowledge is the primary justification for an expert system implementation. Approaching such a task using FORTRAN or COBOL may be unthinkable, but the existence of expert systems shell tools and specialized symbolic AI languages can make the task feasible. Ease of development and maintenance may provide a second justification. If the MIS or CIM problem has suitable characteristics, encoding in the expert systems technology may be simpler than in conventional languages. Nevertheless, systems managers and software engineers should avoid the compulsion to jump on the bandwagon and make every programming project an expert systems project just because a new software technology is available. The project team has to learn to design and program with the new knowledge-based, inference-driven paradigm before the technology can provide a simpler solution path than the traditional, familiar software engineering methods. The inference/knowledge paradigm has wide applicability, and the technology should win broad market acceptance once appropriate user approaches have been established.

What else can be said for goals and rationale for expert system implementation? The primary goals are summarized in the following points:

- **Capture of expertise**—As noted above, this benefit is the result of condensing the specific, domain-dependent problem-solving knowledge of an expert or group of experts into a computerized system. The system can then be queried for knowledge facts like a database system. It can be asked to make inferences based on the knowledge in the knowledge base and to produce justifications of the "reasoning" strategies and decision paths used in reaching a conclusion.
- **Codifying expertise**—Experts frequently perform their jobs intuitively, sometimes with little awareness of the logical thought sequence in their thinking and decision-making processes. This apparent lack of strategy greatly inhibits solution explanations, justification, and the training of others. Expert systems do not comprehend such subtleties as intuition and hunches, so the expertise must be delineated in terms of logically linked facts, rules, and heuristics. This codification helps formalize the expert's knowledge, making it available to a wider audience. Knowledge codification also contributes to the repeatability and reliability of the judgments of one expert or to produce consistency among a group of experts.
- **Duplication and transfer of expertise**—How many managers have wished they could multiply their expensive specialists or experts at a fraction of the duplication cost? An expert system can be one way to accomplish this goal. Corporations with geographically distributed offices, often on a global scale, frequently need to communicate guidelines and procedures to all branches. With the appropriate expert system, the expert's knowledge can be multiplied and transferred across time and space boundaries. Portable expert systems also allow transfer of expertise to hostile or remote environments, such as an unmanned probe for investigating ocean depths or the surface of another planet.
- **Saving the expert's time**—Frequently experts spend a large portion of their time doing only moderately specialized, routine work. Codifying the routine aspects of expertise into a stand-alone or assistant capacity expert system can free much more of the experts' time. As a consequence the experts can spend most of their time on the creative and unique aspects of problem solving, making the best use of the specialized

capabilities of human intelligence. The routine decisions are delegated to the machine, and the exceptional situations the machine can't manage can be singled out for specialist attention.

- **Savings on maintenance and update of the knowledge base**—It is well documented that software maintenance is responsible for more than 50% of the cost of a software system over its lifetime (e.g., Boehm 1981). Much of the programming time and effort is absorbed in comprehending and compensating for modification side effects on other program code, for the affected code may be scattered throughout numerous modules in a complex project. In spite of the increased emphasis on structured analysis and programming techniques in software-development environments, managerial, deadline, and financial pressures still thwart the goals of the structured approaches. Not infrequently less than ideal code is generated, and updating this code is extremely problematic. The clear distinction of facts, heuristics, and inferencing (deduction) knowledge in knowledge-based systems reduces maintenance and update costs because the effects of changes are restricted to particular knowledge chunks in the knowledge base. The XCON expert system takes advantage of this benefit—managing VAX configuration change repercussions was not possible with conventional programming technologies.

These benefits translate directly into time and cost savings for software-development departments and corporations as a whole. A corporation's competitive edge may be based entirely on such savings. Cost benefits provide one major justification. The capture of an expert's knowledge in an automated system that would be impractical if not impossible to capture any other way provides another. Last, the expert system approach may provide a simpler way to organize problem information than traditional techniques. This is particularly true if the problem is better suited to symbolic rather than numeric processing.

It is important to note that the goal of expert systems development is not to replace every expert by a software system. In a few highly specialized, logic-oriented domains, e.g., theorem proving, this may be possible. But in most cases, the intelligent abilities the expert brings to bear on a problem are far beyond what can be inculcated into a machine at this time. Most commercial expert systems will be designed as advisors or consultants to assist the domain expert. This advisory status may also be required socially. If an independent, active-agent expert system made one wrong decision in a million, who is liable for the damage? Comprehensive liability insurance standards in modern business may end up restricting the independent capacity of expert systems as the technology continues to advance.

## 1-4. "WHAT" VERSUS "HOW": ABSTRACTION AND POWER

Since the advent of computer languages, language designers have looked for ways to humanize the process of storing and manipulating data and information. In the 1940s and 1950s, few programmers took pleasure in the tedious complexity of programming storage and logical/arithmetic execution sequences in binary codes. When machine language programming was replaced by assembly language programming in the 1960s, the level of power, ease, and conceptual sophistication of programming increased. This advance was based on the use of mnemonics, standardized preprogrammed subroutines for memory operations, I/O, and so forth. The problem-solving tools developed by the systems analyst could be more easily and directly represented and implemented in these language constructs. The higher level languages of the late 1960s and early 1970s (e.g., FORTRAN, COBOL, ALGOL, APL) carried this process one step further by including higher level programming constructs, such as predefined routines for loops, automatic storage management, and subroutine generation. This pattern of high-level advancement has continued with the recent development of fourth-generation languages (4GLs), such as PRO IV, RAMIS, NOMAD, and PROGRESS. The trend is to attend to "what" the programmer or systems analyst desires and needs in the programming environment, leaving the implementation "how" to the program itself. This tendency in 4GLs is found in automatically generating constructs and appropriate representation schemes for high-level functional descriptions based on execution times, frequency of construct use, and other statically or dynamically determined properties. The tools have allowed the developer's attention to move from the new system's internal structures and routines to the user interface and other external characteristics. Personal computer software based on icons, windows, pull-down menus, and pop-up messages can be seen as direct outcomes of these trends.

Increasing the level of abstraction or *indirection* in programming is a natural outgrowth of machine functioning more closely aligned with human cognitive and information-processing structures. The ultimate "how" for a computer is the machine level of bits and hard-wired encodings. This corresponds to the level of sensory input in the human system. At the other extreme, the ultimate "what" is the symbolic/verbal framework exhibited in the high-level human cognitive system. The increasing degree of abstraction found in traditional computer languages and AI tools reflects the attempt to capture more the highly evolved and refined information-processing capabilities embodied in the

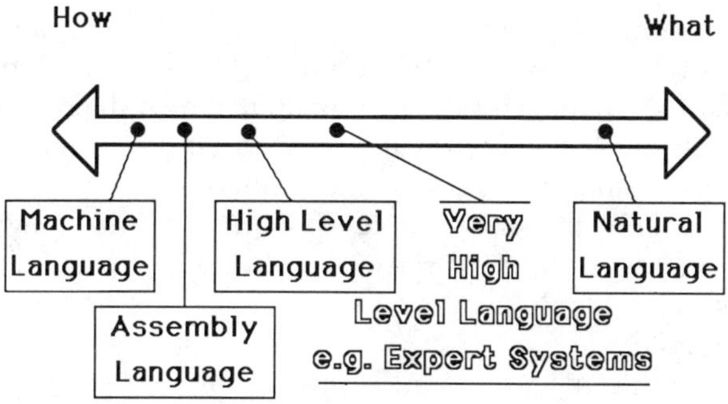


Fig. 1-5. The continuum of "How" and "What".

human nervous system. Expert systems technology, as illustrated in Fig. 1-5, is at the forefront of the "how-what" continuum. By focusing on the essential features of the expert's knowledge, in terms of facts and heuristic rules for performance, the "what" aspect of the human logic thought process can begin to be encoded into a viable, useful body of expertise. The rule-based iconic or natural-language user interfaces typically found in expert systems tie the user more directly to the "what" of a problem situation.

Figure 1-6 shows the abstraction layering structures of the human information-processing system, comparing it with AI computer systems levels. At the lowest level, the human information-processing machine collects massive amounts of incoherent random data through the senses. In the vision system, for example, individual "bits" of color and intensity information are transmitted from the retina rods and cones to the lateral geneculate, via the optic nerve, and then on to the primary visual and

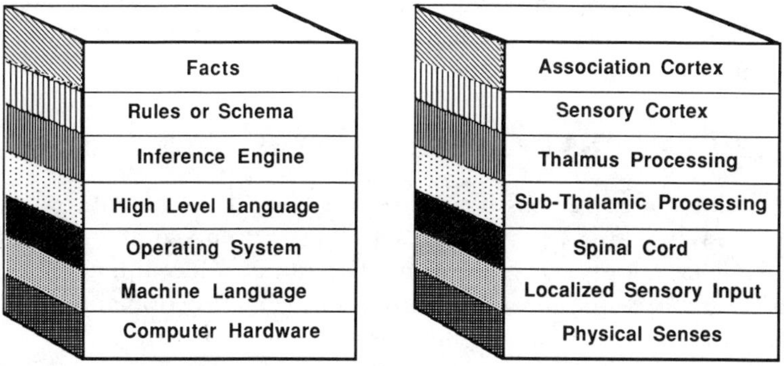


Fig. 1-6. Layers of abstraction in human and machine information processing.

association cortex. These data are processed, compacted, and organized through several layers of brain functioning. This information processing is not consciously managed by the individual. The individual consciously perceives only the final results in the association cortex, recognizing objects, colors, shapes, textures, and motion as specific entities of interest. Essentially, the conscious component of human consciousness is concerned only with the final result, the "what," of the vision-information-processing system, and not the "how," relating how such information was attained.

The end result of human information processing is in terms of function (what is perceived), rather than form (how the information is gained and organized). Comparatively, the highest level of the machine is its user interface. Direct interaction with a high-level symbolic/verbal user interface gives the user a greater feeling of freedom and ease. Expert systems are designed more directly to operate on this level of knowledge. The high level of abstraction or indirection increases the level of power available to the user by freeing him or her from low-level, detailed representational or programming distractions. Layers of indirected software support this increasing abstraction, so internal "how" considerations can be hidden and transformed into an appearance of "what." Concealing internal details from the user is not an easy process, so multiple *layers* are usually employed. The Open Systems Interconnect (OSI) reference model, for example, uses seven layers (American National Standards Institute, 1980). A fully functioning production expert system often requires a similar number of layers (e.g., machine language, assembler, operating system, LISP, LISP dialect, inference engine, knowledge structures). The ideal, which is coming closer to achievement through successive generations of computer interfaces, is to liberate the user so that he can communicate in a symbolic/language conceptual system closely aligned with his own natural thinking process. Externally, computers are evolving to work the way we would like them to, rather than forcing users to adapt to a less efficient, lower-level conceptual communication.

## 1-5. LIMITATIONS OF EXPERT SYSTEMS

The discussion so far has been directed toward the benefits of expert systems. What are the limitations of the current commercial expert systems technology? For the production system developer, the limitations should receive thorough attention. In what task domains do expert systems not perform well? The answers must be carefully reviewed, given the sometimes overly optimistic claims made by AI researchers and expert system products manufacturers. Expert systems technology is still in its infancy, and debate continues over the power and appropriate role of the expert systems technology in the marketplace. This debate is rooted in the "man as machine" versus "man as spirit" controversy and will be examined, in terms of the relationship between artificial intelligence and real or natural intelligence in Chapter 2.

Although expert systems are meant to capture the knowledge of human experts, only certain aspects of human intelligence functioning can currently be simulated by such programs. The focus of expert systems knowledge is on the logical level of human reasoning. Obviously, no one expects that all the human capacities and functions relating to human intelligence will be modeled in the expert system. A strong dose of skepticism is healthy and welcomed in this regard, for it promotes a balanced understanding of what expert systems technology can and cannot do. The following points identify some of the limitations of current applied expert systems (and AI) technologies:

- **Cognitive versus other human tasks**—Expert systems function in the domain of extracted, cognitive, logical thinking processes. They are generally not adept at managing highly sophisticated sensory input or mechanical motor output, although specialized interfaces are beginning to appear in commercial products. Designers considering applications where the human expert performs manual tasks, as well as cognitive thinking, may be ahead of expert systems' capacities unless good interfaces can be defined between the expert system and the work environment.
- **Narrow versus general intelligence simulation**—Expert systems exhibit a narrow band of simulated intelligence based on a narrow range of codified-domain, heuristic knowledge (i.e., a single task). Current expert systems cannot tackle broad, multiple-direction problem spaces. In addition, only knowledge that can be derived from the expert and implanted into the system can be used. The actual intelligence of the expert has not been somehow miraculously transferred to the machine; only certain limited aspects of the logical thinking process have been extracted and distilled. The domain-specific knowledge is only a very small part of the total knowledge available to the expert, but it is all that is available to the automated system. To quote a group of pioneering knowledge-engineering experts: ". . . today's expert systems fall well short on dimensions requiring general intelligent behavior. They are more akin to *idiot savants* than to real human experts."[3] If the expert's reasoning process involves more than logical thinking, the system manager should carefully review the project before embarking on an implementation.
- **Error exception and recovery**—Due to the narrow range of knowl-

edge incorporated in expert systems, these machine experts typically do not respond well to situations outside their range of expertise. Performance degradation is almost immediate and total in such situations. This limitation can be a major, project-halting catch, as it is often only the difficult exceptions that are brought to the expert in the first place.

- **Common sense knowledge**—To a great degree, the flexibility of human problem solving is based on a broad background of ill-defined *common sense knowledge*. Common sense is found to be important when performing cognitive operations in either familiar or unfamiliar situations and tends to play a greater role in the familiar areas, the very field of the expert's specialty. This type of knowledge is difficult to codify, even if its influences are understood. Judgment, the final stage in human decision making, is based on a range of contextual information including social surroundings, random memories, feelings, emotions, and other nonrational information. Common sense knowledge and broad-ranging contextual information are not available in the typical expert system of today. In contrast, the social-cultural-mental environment provided by such knowledge is intimately interwoven into the fabric of human consciousness, giving rise to intelligent thought and action.
- **Qualitative simulation**—Humans reason extremely well with inexact, context-sensitive concepts, such as *large*, *small*, *near*, *far*, and *almost*. This type of *qualitative simulation*, in deference to quantitative reasoning, is intimately related to our ability to make decisions based on common sense knowledge. Computers, however, deal most effectively with specific, concrete numerical values for comparison and judgment. Although AI research has produced some *inexact* or *fuzzy logics*, expert systems technologies are currently quite limited in their ability to perform the kinds of qualitative simulations that humans spontaneously employ when reasoning and making decisions.
- **Intuition**—A deeper level of the judgement value is found in the concept of *intuition*. Humans spontaneously draw from subconscious reservoirs of creativity and insight, which profoundly affects decision making and the knowledge available to the individual. It should be apparent that if an expert system is not good at common sense knowledge or qualitative simulation, it will be completely in the dark when it comes to intuition. Decision makers often go more by hunches than by proven facts or logical arguments and thus operate in a cognitive domain that is generally beyond the reach of current expert systems technology.
- **Learning**—Automated learning processes are hard to come by in expert systems, especially compared with the great ease with which humans learn from experience. If learning occurs in an expert system, it will tend to come from the hand of the user or the knowledge

engineer, not spontaneously from within the system. Some adaptive systems are capable, however, of acquiring rudimentary knowledge or modifying their behavior in a way that resembles learning.

• **Self-knowledge**—Some of the human higher level cognitive capabilities stem from the ability to step back and see our "system" running as a whole. Typically expert systems lack such self-awareness and self-analysis tools. Introspection—observing one's own processes of deriving, refining, and optimizing valid knowledge—is not available in a non-self-referral system. A human can be aware of himself and adaptively modify his functioning or behavior; most of today's expert systems cannot.

In summary, expert systems are capable of performing within a specific, logical-oriented realm of expertise. The deeper values of human consciousness, interwoven as they are into the phenomenon and expressions of human intelligence, however, are beyond the range of anything currently available in AI. Some of these limitations are current AI research topics, but one might rightfully expect some time to pass before robust capabilities for managing these as-yet unknowns in expert systems technology are available for production applications. Given the limitations of current expert systems technology, we can see that perhaps the first critical aspect of application development is choosing a problem of appropriate degree of difficulty.

## 1-6. DATA, INFORMATION, SYMBOLS, AND KNOWLEDGE

The term *data*, as used in the early data-processing field (DP), refers to numeric or alphanumeric strings held as fields on such limited media as 80-column punched cards. The ASCII (American Standard Code for Information Interchange) or EBCDIC (Extended Binary Coded Decimal Interchange Code) codes are used to encode each character as a set of seven or eight bits. Generally, data processing is limited to various sorting, filtering, and collating operations preformed on these elementary data fields.

It was not until the mid-1970s that the term *information*, as in management information systems (MIS), came into popular usage. Although the terms DP and MIS are often used interchangeably, the key distinction between data and information is that the latter is data that are organized and meaningful to the person receiving them. When the right data are in the right place at the right time, they become information. In the late 1970s there was a drive, largely unfulfilled at that time, to make MIS encompass other categories of information, including voice, business graphics, video, and office automation. Such MIS-inspired levels of integration have not generally been achieved on the level of information. Instead, a higher level of processing, known as *symbolic processing*, has been needed to integrate disparate forms of information.

Computer systems have been developed for one primary reason: the organization and use of human knowledge. Masses of data by themselves have little or no value until they are organized by human awareness. This organizational process starts with elementary data items, which have little significance individually. Only in the context of other data items arranged in accepted patterns do data items take on the structure of meaning, the quality of information. Human vision, as noted earlier, performs this same function, where such individual data items as color and intensity in the retina are filtered and grouped to produce the various macroscopic visual elements of object color, shade, contours, intensity, shape, and texture.

The input to the visual cortex may be in the form of information, but the conscious cognitive level of human intelligence quickly transforms this information into a set of interconnected *symbols* that capture the essence and value of the qualities expressed in the information. Information by itself is lifeless and has little inherent value. Human information processing arises from the power of man's consciousness to perceive the information patterns and form them into the symbolic/verbal icons—the normal mode of human qualitative reasoning. As is said, a picture is worth a thousand words. The interactions of these symbols and the qualities they represent can give rise to the experience of *knowledge*. In human experience, knowledge can be characterized in terms of three aspects: the *knower*, the *known*, and the *process of knowing*. Knowledge arises as the interaction of the knower, the object of knowledge and the process of knowing, and is a living, dynamic experience within the fabric of human consciousness. Human subjectivity, as the knower and director of the process of knowing, is at the basis of the experience we call knowledge. Without the knower, the subjective element, there is no knowledge as we experience it, but merely unconnected objects.

Where are the symbol and knowledge levels in commercial computer programs? The data and information levels are well established in traditional computer applications. High-level symbolic processing, however, is also becoming entrenched in conventional programming environments. Word-processing systems provide the classic example. The symbols are the words, and the rules of operation of the system are located in the word-manipulating routines, which are derived from the English language. The greater the number of English language rules embodied in the word processor, the easier it is to use. Similarly, in decision-support systems, graphics package routines manipulate charts

| Class of Software Tool | Symbol | Rules |
|---|---|---|
| Spread Sheet Calculator | Cells in Rows & Columns | Formulas which link Cells together |
| Database Management System | Data Elements in Relations (Tuples) | Relational Operators (e.g. Join, Project) |
| Word Processor | Letters, Words & Sentences. | Editing Rules, Grammar, Spelling |
| Business Graphics | Pie, Bar, Column Scatter Graphs | Graphing Rules Map numbers onto graphical shapes |
| Draw / Paint Tool | Graphical Objects or Image Bit Maps | Graphical Editing Technical Drawing |
| Project Planner | Tasks, Milestones Costs, Budgets | Critical Path, Sequencing |
| Expert System | IF / THEN Rules (or Frames) | Inference by Chaining |

Fig. 1-7. Examples of symbol/rule sets.

and graphs, relational database programs manipulate tables, and spreadsheet calculators manage cells. In each case, a class of symbols is referenced and manipulated according to a specific set of rules. This pairing of symbols and manipulations is reminiscent of the combination of knowledge-base facts and heuristics in the expert system.

Figure 1-7 illustrates some of the layers of symbols and rule sets employed in standard decision-support systems—best understood as high-level symbolic processing systems. The structure of symbolic processing, as used in expert systems, is a key to integrating different kinds of information. As an example of AI symbolic processing, the Symbolics, Inc. (Cambridge, Massachusetts) LISP Machine uses a 36-bit word in its computer systems: 32-bits for the value and 4 bits to indicate the symbol type. Once the symbol has been identified, the correct set of manipulation rules can be invoked. This mechanism prevents such errors as multiplying sentences or verifying the spelling in a table of numbers.

Locating the layer or level of knowledge in computer systems is not so simple. First, the concept of knowledge per se is not directly recognized in traditional MIS or DP programs, except perhaps in context of the "knowledge" embodied in a system as a whole. Some researchers, such as AI's Alan Newell, however, assert that the knowledge aspect of a computer program is equivalent to the program's "symbol structure plus its processes."[4] Machine knowledge in expert systems technology is explicitly expressed as a set of interconnected symbols, where the

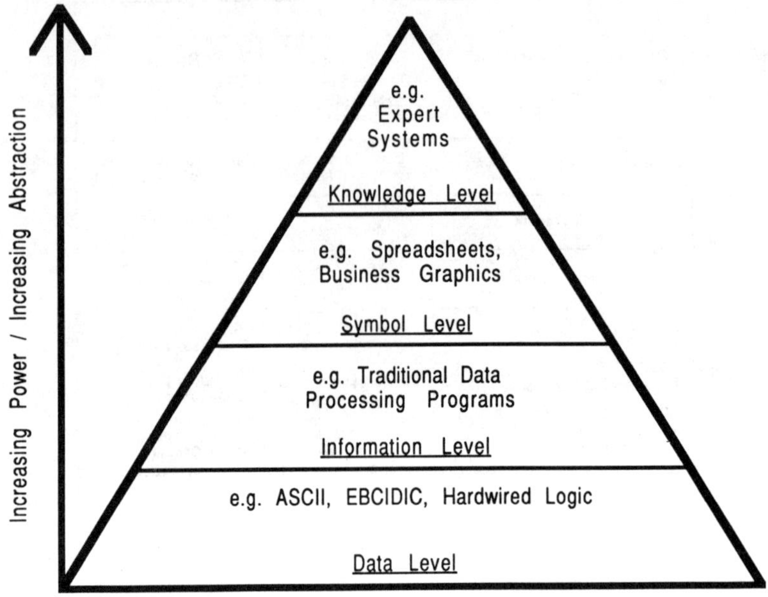


Fig. 1-8. Four levels of abstraction in AI or computer systems.

elements of knowledge are each powerful symbols arranged in specific structural or procedural representations. These primitive symbols and combinations of symbols represent either facts or heuristics. Rules bind the symbols together in such a way that the resulting *inference net* can be used to simulate a chain of action expressed in the knowledge structure. The reality of expert systems' knowledge is nothing more than this appropriate organization of facts, rules, and inferencing mechanisms. The central element in the human knowledge experience—the knower, the subjective element—is not to be found. This machine knowledge is therefore rightly called *shallow knowledge*. The levels of abstraction expressed by the knowledge model are shown in Fig. 1-8. Each successive or higher layer is built upon the preceding or lower one.

The levels of power in the system and the level of abstraction or indirection expressed by the corresponding symbol/rule system are directly correlated. Symbolic processing provides more power than traditional DP or MIS programming structures due to the inherent qualities ascribed to the symbol itself. As the symbol set and operations that can be performed on it become more abstract, the capacity for simulating the characteristics of human information processing, shallow knowledge, and intelligent functions increases.

## 1-7. DEEP KNOWLEDGE, SHALLOW REASONING, AND COMMON SENSE

It is apparent from the above discussion that knowledge, in the sense we know it as humans, is something more than the collection of individual symbols and their interactions. We look to our own experience and validate the nature of our own knowledge. Understanding arises directly from the organization of the objects of knowledge by the knower. This *self-referral* quality of the observer is not available in expert systems technology.

As AI work proceeded in the 1960s and 1970s, it became increasingly obvious that an understanding of human information processing, which humans take for granted, was woefully lacking. It is one thing to develop a psychological, mental model that describes and perhaps predicts some of the behavioral artifacts of human intelligence functioning, but it is another thing to attempt to build such models into viable working systems. Externally derived descriptive models based on observed functions are not prescriptive constructive models. If it were necessary to single out one contribution AI has made to the study of cognitive science, it would probably be the identification of multiple dimensions of ignorance existing in our own self-knowledge.

Human problem solving is based on *deep knowledge* of a situation. This deep knowledge structure is an experience humans have (recall the triangle of knowledge, known, and process of knowing, touched on above, and discussed in more detail in Chapter 2). Deep knowledge is based on a completely integrated, cohesive body of human consciousness that includes the totality of all aspects of cognitive processes, emotions, intellect, common sense, intuition, and so on. This type of knowledge is difficult to codify, even if its influences are understood. Judgment, the final stage in human-decision making, is based on a huge variety of sensory, cognitive, emotional, and associatively accessed memory information. Expert systems do not have this type of integrated consciousness.

The use of explanation facilities, one of the most common types of self-knowledge found in expert systems, illustrates one of the common shortcomings of expert system knowledge. The end user of an expert system, e.g., the domain expert or a novice, typically queries the system to determine the path of reasoning leading to a conclusion. In many cases, the explanation facility will simply backtrack through the set of rules from the conclusion to the original starting point, listing the activated rules as it goes. The problem, however, is that the set of rules, expressed in symbolic or mathematical (probabilistic) terms, may have little meaning to the novice or even to the domain expert. It is often necessary that this shallow model of expertise be supplemented by another set of reasoning explanations, attached to each rule, to make the rules more understandable. This attachment, however, does not remove the problem, for the shallow model is used only for representational and inference purposes and may have little to do with the way the expert actually views and understands his domain. In such a case, a second, deeper, more human-oriented model may also be needed to provide appropriate explanations.

To construct deep models of knowledge, scientists or engineers must have a profound understanding of the primitive elements and their interactions produced by the laws of nature operating in a particular discipline. Today's electronically based society would be impossible without knowledge of the electron and its motion through conducting metals. Atomic power remained hidden until the laws of nature governing the interactions inside the atomic nucleus were understood. Expert systems and other AI, knowledge-based programs can only express the degree of intelligence simulation associated with the laws of nature actually known and documented at science's current level of understanding. This is the technology's fundamental limitation.

Until scientific investigation has revealed the laws of nature governing the interacting aspects of human consciousness, the goal of producing machines that simulate intelligence functioning is likely to remain unattainable. The shortcomings of expert systems in common sense, intuition, qualitative simulation, and qualitative reasoning are due in part to a lack of real understanding of the knowledge mechanisms that support such phenomena in humans. This is not to say that other means cannot be found to organize such intelligence-related mechanisms in machines. But until deep understanding can be achieved in such areas, expert systems will continue to be more in the "idiot savant" class and less in the genuinely intelligent dimension.

## 1-8. WHERE THE PROBABILITIES COME FROM

One of the important features of expert systems technology is the ability to manage life's uncertainty to a limited degree. When a rule is encoded for a knowledge base, it often has an associated probability-like certainty factor. This measure quantifies the reliability of the result, given that all the input data are completely valid. In addition, facts and other categories of input data can also have certainty factors. The combination of the *unreliability* of rules and *uncertainty* of facts means that the inference engine has to propagate levels of combined certainty factors through the search space as it moves toward a conclusion. If two conclusions are reached and there is more evidence for one of them, i.e., the certainty or reliability of the end result is higher, then this rule is usually favored. Although in most systems the certainty measures associated with rules are not real probabilities, they do convey the sense of the likelihood of the statement being true. Due to the central role of these uncertainties in expert systems, it is important to ask why uncertainty is necessary. Where do the uncertainties come from? Why are they necessary?

Uncertainty seems to be a characteristic of our perception of the real world, where noisy, inconsistent, and inaccurate data constantly impinge upon our senses. In the human sensory system many levels of precognitive processing occur. Eventually, after numerous transformations, impulses reach our conscious awareness. Fortunately, the nervous system has the capability of filtering out noise and focusing attention on the dominant underlying patterns. We are not constantly aware of the shirts on our backs or the shoes on our feet, unless that information is needed, even though that information is constantly available. If this filtering process did not occur, experience would be chaos. Human awareness, through the visual and associative cortexes, is able to recognize patterns and faces or friends, even though they may have changed their appearance. The image of a distant object seen in dim light may appear to be either a deer or a calf, but eventually enough visual cues are received to resolve the uncertainty and perceive the correct animal.

This phenomenon can be clarified from the perspective of *coherence* in information theory. Coherence between two points $X$ and $Y$ is defined as the amount of signal that can be passed from $X$ to $Y$. The complement of coherence (1 − coherence) is then seen as the degree of noise that has crept into the signal path as the signal moves from $X$ to $Y$. The field of signal processing, which is applied information theory, contains a battery of techniques for separating signals from noise, or, in expert system terms, for reducing the uncertainties. Is this uncertainty a fundamental property of the objects of observation, or is it a characteristic associated with the observer?

A short digression into the realm of modern physics can shed some light on this question. In physics, one interpretation of *quantum mechanics* theory (QM) (the Copenhagen School) depicts uncertainty as a fundamental property of the universe. Quantum mechanics explains that all objects and forces and their expressions in the universe are actually localized expressions of underlying, unbounded, abstract *wave functions*. The ability to localize one of these wave functions and describe it in nonprobabilistic mathematics occurs only when the perceiver freezes the observation by using classical measurement techniques. This event is known as the *collapse of the wave function*, where an unbounded, probabilistic, unmanifest form collapses into a concrete, deterministic, classical observation. Since 1930, Schroedinger's Copenhagen School has provided the leading interpretation of QM, which teaches that the universe's basic reality is only probabilistic. The unmanifest level of quantum mechanical existence, the *vacuum state* of the quantum field, is seen as a parallel reality that coexists with the gross level of observation. A dual coexistence of wave and particle is the logical outcome of this school of thought, which has been accepted by the majority of physicists for 50 years. Some physicists have difficulty accepting this dualistic view. Einstein, for instance, said, "I shall never believe that God plays dice with the world" and spent some 20 years of his life in search of a Unified Field Theory that transcended the wave function uncertainty represented by the Copenhagen School.

In the early 1980s a mathematically more complete refinement and interpretation of QM emerged and by 1986 came to the forefront of physics. New *Unified Field* theories (UF) provide a deeper interpretation of QM, explaining that probabilities are not actually basic to existence, but rather, arise from lack of knowledge. The UF approach describes all phenomena covered by the earlier QM, plus many newer experimental results that perplexed the Copenhagen School. The Heterotic Super String Theory of Extended *Supergravity* is currently the most advanced UF theory capable of explaining such phenomena as proton and neutron decay, the quantity of neutrinos radiated from the sun, the movement of stars in globular star clusters, and the monojet events seen in the world's largest particle accelerators.[5] Unified Field theory describes how the underlying field is the true reality, as all manifest forms are expressions of it. Particles are just ripples in the field where the radius of field curvature is a little tighter than the neighboring space. The underlying field is also in a constant state of liveliness, technically referred to as *Zitterbewegung*, which is German for "jitterbugging." Fluctuations of the field, which are going on spontaneously all the time, create temporary or virtual particles in exactly determined and well-ordered distributions. All grosser levels are seen as a direct effect and manifestation of the subtlest level. When a classical observation is made, the clumsiness of the measuring apparatus is able to perceive only a snapshot of the multiple variant forms of the field, and thus a localized particle is seen where there is really only an unbounded, unmanifest wave. The snapshot also blurs the deterministic liveliness, giving rise to a perception of randomness or probability. These physics theories show the universe to be in essence nonprobabilistic, where uncertainty arises only because of the observer's limited capabilities. From Einstein's viewpoint of the deeper aspects of nature, God does not play dice.

Even though the universe is not fundamentally random, noisy partial observations mean that a high degree of uncertainty has to be handled in life. Improving the measuring apparatus, and even the observer, can decrease the uncertainties. With everyday observations, however, the uncertainly spreads from the sensory level, to the experiential level, and into the internalized, personal qualitative concepts, or knowledge. As a consequence AI researchers are hard pressed to represent even a limited degree of knowledge in machines. Common sense knowledge and the qualitative simulation reasoning process in humans manage to work around and through the uncertainties to come to conclusions. Something of a regression technique seems to be used in the brain to find the best-fit solution given the input data. The probability-like measures used in expert systems technology, although nowhere near the sophistication of the brain's constructs, are currently the easiest means to manage uncertainty. The new area of non-algorithmic *neurocomputing* may also provide some solutions to these problems.

Returning from this brief tour of the quantum mechanical world, we can sum up its implication for building expert systems: in a knowledge-based system, the more complete, accurate, and reliable the domain facts and heuristics are, the less uncertainty needs to be represented in the system. Vague, noisy domain facts and heuristics must be represented with greater uncertainty. Increasing the degree of certainty results in logic closer to the standard Boolean logic, rather than inexact reasoning based on fuzzy or probabilistic logics. For instance

IF *a* (1.0) AND *b* (1.0), THEN *c* (0.6)

indicates that if both *a* and *b* are known to be certain (i.e., certainty of 1.0), then *c* can still be concluded to be true only with a 0.6 likelihood or certainty. A more complete understanding of the domain elements and the rules operating in the problem domain might give rise to a modified rule such as

IF *a* (1.0) AND *b* (1.0) AND *d* (1.0) AND *e* (1.0), THEN *c* (1.0)

based on the added certain information presented by *d* and *e*. This example shows one of the primary mechanisms of decreasing knowledge uncertainties, namely, by adding more clauses to a condition premise. Theoretically, it should be possible to transform a heuristic model into an exact algorithm by adding enough conditional clauses. A key factor for successful expert systems development is to constrain and limit the uncertainties as much as possible. Even though expert system technology allows for uncertainties, almost by definition, a knowledge engineer should be concerned with limiting their use and removing them whenever possible.

## 1-9. POSITIONING EXPERT SYSTEMS BETWEEN SOFT SCIENCES AND HARD SCIENCES

One of the curious things about AI is that as soon as a difficult "intelligent behavior" problem is solved, the behavior is no longer considered "intelligent." Understanding demystifies the problem, and the magic of intelligence is replaced by standard engineering techniques. As soon as the knowledge of laws of nature guiding an area is revealed, the mystery is removed. Metascience becomes science.

All sciences display this characteristic. The scientific paradigm, the systematic investigation of knowledge based on repeatable experimentation, is the dominant methodology used in all types of learning today. Humans seek hard, objective validation of theories to remove the element of uncertainty in life.

Each scientific discipline attempts to codify knowledge within a particular area of life. The so-called hard sciences, e.g., physics and chemistry, had their beginning just some 400 years ago, with the advent of the scientific revolution. In just four centuries the hard sciences have developed to a high level of precision in predicting the structure and behavior of reality at various levels. In contrast, the "soft" sciences, e.g., psychology, sociology, management science, anthropology, are newer fields of scientific investigation, less highly developed, that rely on statistical tools to cope with the imprecision present within their areas of

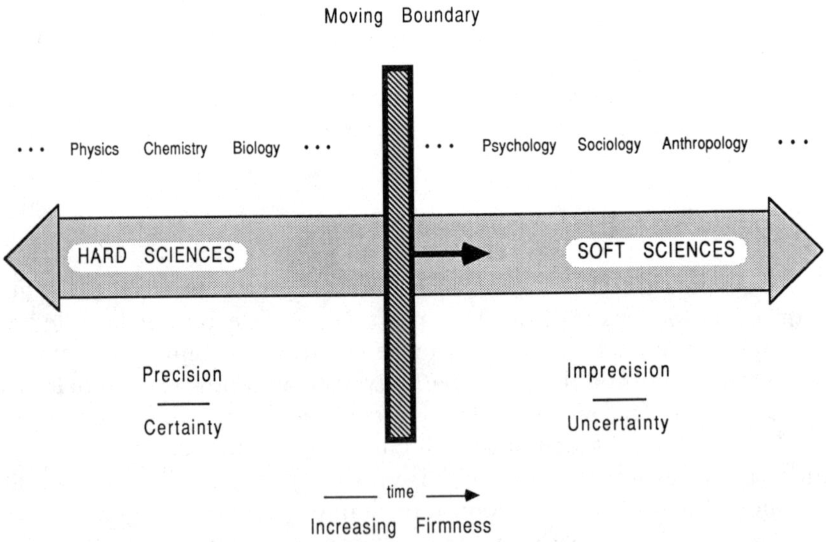


Fig. 1-9. The development of sciences.

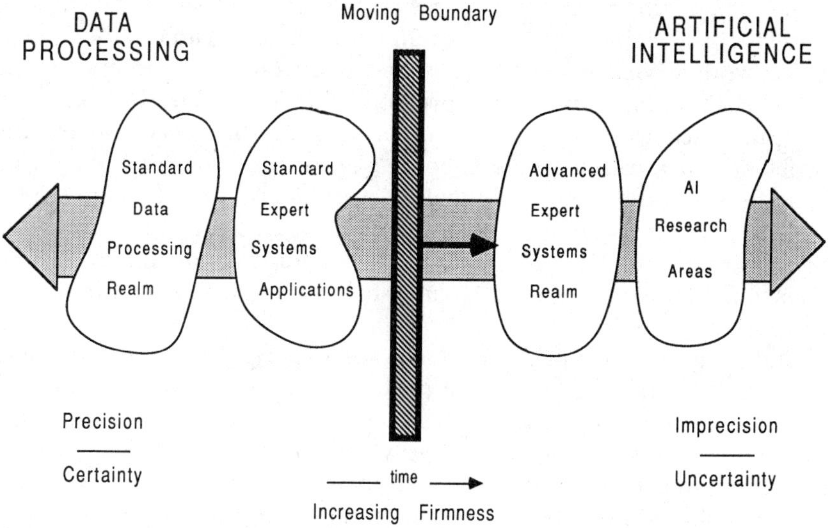


Fig. 1-10. The development of AI technology.

investigation. The different sciences can be laid out in a soft-to-hard continuum, as shown in Fig. 1-9.

The history of science shows that time firms up the knowledge of the sciences. The lack of precision found in psychology, for instance, has decreased as the discipline has matured. Put another way, the predictive value of the collected developments in psychology has increased as new discoveries have been made. The degree of uncertainty in a science can be seen as a function of the complexity of the area combined with the firmness of other supporting disciplines. Changes in the way scientists view physics or chemistry may provide new insights for sociological systems analysis. For example, Wilson's *Sociobiology* (Wilson, 1977) explains many sociological events in terms of underlying biological mechanisms. Figure 1-9 shows a conceptual advancing frontier moving disciplines out of the zone of softness into the area of hard or well-established sciences. It is interesting to observe that the borderline disciplines, in striving to become firmer, frequently add the word *science* to their names. For instance business management, military tactics, and computers are frequently marketed as management science, military science, and computer science.

Figure 1-10 relates the soft/hard science spectrum to identifying applications for expert systems in the real world. Basically, that realm near the junction between soft and hard, where an embryonic discipline is in the throes of becoming a well-established science, is where expert system technology can often be best applied. AI, as the fledgling "intelligent machine" arm of computer science (CS), can also be seen as a very young science in its early stages of firming. At one end of the CS/AI continuum there are the problems that are well under control in computer science, while at the other end of the spectrum are the problems, such as humanoid robots, that are still science fiction. From firm to soft are seen traditional DP problems, well-defined expert systems areas, experimental expert systems areas, current AI research projects, such as common sense and reasoning, and at the far end science-fiction-type research goals, such as invincible computerized weapons systems.

Choosing an appropriate problem for expert systems development may be difficult. In general, the problems suggested for business and industry should not overlap with areas covered by AI research. If the problem is well understood and easily solved by standard data processing or engineering techniques and tools, however, then simple approaches should probably be used instead. An appropriate application is one that is manageable with the current level of expert systems technology, but is infeasible or not practical to manage using conventional CIM or MIS technologies. A possible exception would be if the expert system technology provided greater returns on investment than other techniques, due to its provision of a more comprehensive solution. If the difficulty of the problem is too far to the right of the current level of firmness (the vertical bar in Fig. 1-10), the need for uncertainty will be much greater due to the sparsity of deep fundamental knowledge in that area.

## 1-10. SYSTEM DEVELOPMENT LIFE CYCLES

The best way to learn about putting expert systems into practice is to build them. Construction must be preceded by instruction to familiarize builders with the basic concepts of AI and expert systems development. Short of this hands-on experience, a simulated strategy test run is a good learning vehicle. This book has therefore been structured around the body of a recommended expert systems development *life cycle*. The reader is invited to view the reading of Chapters 3 through 9 as a trial run through the phases of this life cycle, keeping favorite unsolved problems in mind.

There are many different life cycles available for computer and engineering developments, and therefore it is important to select an appropriate one for the task. The first split in conventional software life cycle types is into *custom system* and *product* life cycles. In custom system development, usually only a single occurrence of the system is to be built, and the proposed users are clearly identified. Future system users can thus be interviewed and their requirements taken as the foundation for designing the custom system. In product-development life cycles, however, many copies are to be produced, making it no longer possible to identify all future users, and not even conceivable to incorporate all of their different views into the design. Marketing techniques have to be used to select features. A custom system development life cycle can thus proceed with the following sequence of steps

1. Inception and planning phase
2. Analysis and modeling phase
3. Functional specification phase
4. High-level design phase
5. Low-level design phase
6. Implementation and unit test phase
7. Integration and system test phase
8. Parallel running and handover phase
9. Maintenance and evolution phase

A product development life cycle, however, requires two parallel tracks, one of marketing and one of engineering. More life-cycle variants exist for product development, but a proven condensation of many candidates has been described by Cooper (1983). This optimized product model contains seven steps, each with technical/production activities and market activities

1. Idea phase
2. Preliminary assessment phase
3. Concept phase
4. Development phase
5. Testing phase (sometimes called alpha test)
6. Trial phase (sometimes called beta test)
7. Launch phase

The majority of readers will be applying expert system technology to single-copy custom systems, as opposed to multiple-copy commercial products. Certainly anyone considering a product development would be wise by starting with a single-copy system development. In fact, it is often true that successful products appear only after the team has created several successful one-off systems. Custom systems are easier to develop than products and in addition provide an excellent way to learn about the market while remaining in a low-risk environment.

Based on the nine-step, custom system development life cycle outlined above, many variants have evolved to suit specific applications and technologies. For instance, if the project has no old system to replace, then the analysis/modeling phase for understanding the old system can be consolidated with the functional specification phase. Another simplification occurs when high-level software tools are used for implementation. Relational database management systems (RDBMSs), when combined with certain nonprocedural fourth-generation languages, allow the functional specification to be implemented directly, bypassing the design stages. To a large extent, expert system shells can also provide this streamlining, as they work more with the "what" of the problem than the "how." Sophisticated, real-time embedded systems, however, tend to require both high- and low-level design phases to ensure that the functional requirements are correctly mapped into the implementation facilities. The Department of Defense work on Ada and its supporting development environment (Wasserman and Freeman, 1983) illustrates a comprehensive methodology for such implementation complexites as real-time embedded code.

Another approach to life cycles for single-customer developments has been that of fast, or rapid, *prototyping*. Such traditional tools as APL or those comprising the UNIX environment are able to mock up possible requirements in a fraction of the time of low-level languages, then modify and expand on them as the user wishes. Such fast prototyping is usually at the expense of execution efficiency and has its limitations for many classes of problems. As an approach, however, it is especially suited for situations where the functional requirements are not or cannot be well known in advance. In effect the analysis/modeling and functional specification phases are omitted. An interative sequence of implementation and review takes their place. Some software departments employing fast prototyping consider it to be an alternative to the life cycle itself.

Software-development life-cycle experts have been quick to offer alternative models (e.g., McCracken and Jackson, 1982; Gladden, 1982; Blum, 1982). The general conclusion drawn from the life-cycle debate is that various sets of phases and models of progression from phase to phase are definitely appropriate for different projects. Ultimately managers have to devise the most appropriate life cycle for the project at hand. The basic principles of good software engineering should not be ignored, but if the manager has sufficient knowledge, then a custom life cycle can be superior to an off-the-shelf one. The points established in the above discussion, coupled with the experience of the authors, have resulted in the life cycle presented in this book which is appropriate for most expert system developments.

Although a large array of expert systems building tools are available on the market, an expert system designer should resist the temptation to purchase a tool and then find a problem to solve with it. This temptation to spend time developing toy prototype expert systems for oversimplified problem domains with tools that cannot be used in industrial-strength problems should be avoided. Choose the application first, then the tool. Selecting the application first provides several practical advantages. For instance, the application can be carefully evaluated to see if it would be better solved using a high-level or fourth-generation language or to see if the problem is too complex for the level of sophistication currently available in expert system tools. To determine the feasibility of a particular tool for a certain application, rapid prototyping of subsets of a problem with the candidate tool or tools is frequently the most powerful approach. The expert system cycle is similar to, but subtly different from, the standard DP cycle, and it may or may not include prototyping.

The following seven-phase life cycle is recommended. The seven phases are expanded upon, one phase per chapter, in Chapters 3 to 9

1. Application qualification phase
2. Application quantification phase
3. Tool set selection phase
4. Configuration selection phase
5. Knowledge acquisition phase
6. Systems Integration phase
7. Startup and Management phase

Phase 1, *application qualification,* is covered in Chapter 3, "Recognizing Knowledge In Order To Select An Application." In this phase the candidate applications have to be reviewed for feasibility and cost-effectiveness. Underlying this qualification process, which is akin to a salesman's qualification of prospects, are the fundamentals of recognizing the types of "knowledge" suitable for expert systems applications. The outcome of this phase could be described as the functional specification.

Phase 2, *application quantification,* is described in Chapter 4, "Features to Look for When Selecting Expert System Tools." The various requirements of the application have to be identified and quantified, so that the appropriate tool or tools can be selected for the job. Demands for knowledge representation, inferencing mechanisms, user interfaces, and knowledge-acquisition aids revelant to the development of an expert application must be examined. Such traditional issues as machine requirements, size of systems, pricing and availability, and characteristics of expert systems vendors are also vital to this design phase.

Phase 3, *tool set selection,* is the topic addressed in Chapter 5, "Expert System Shell Tools—Product Analysis by Feature." The feature requirements delineated by Phase 2 and explained in Chapter 4 are analyzed for nearly 30 expert systems shell building tools. All the tools on the market have some value. What is necessary is to make an educated selection of the most appropriate tool for the job at hand.

Phase 4, *configuration selection,* is covered in Chapter 6, "Specialized Hardware and Programming Environments for Expert Systems." It can happen that no expert system shell on the market meets the needs of even a cut-down version of the chosen application. In this case specialized programming environments, AI languages, or tools will have to be considered. Even if such AI environments as LISP are not needed, the analyst has to round out the tool selection to ensure that a complete hardware/software configuration is specified for the project.

Phase 5, *knowledge acquisition,* is discussed in Chapter 7, "Knowledge Capture and Codification." Once the tool set has been acquired, it is still an empty shell waiting to be filled with specific application knowledge. In this phase expertise is gleaned from the expert or team of experts. Correctness of the knowledge must be ensured. This stage is critical to the success of the system, but there is no absolute magic for getting it right the first time. Thus prototyping iterations are usually required.

Phase 6, *systems integration,* is addressed in chapter 8, "Integrating Expert Systems into MIS and CIM Environments." Before the new system can become a productive part of the enterprise as a whole, it has to be integrated with the corporation's existing systems. Even if there are no electronic links, procedural connections must be established. With increasing frequency, however, integrated hardware/software systems are being required by MIS and CIM directors, so this phase becomes of strategic importance.

Phase 7, *startup and management,* is the central topic of Chapter 9, "People Roles in Creating the Production Expert System." A key principle of the life cycle expressed in this book is that expert systems technology has to move from the laboratory into the day-to-day production environment if it is to become profitable. People issues are central to this final phase of moving the completed development into the daily production of the corporation. The roles of knowledge engineers, domain experts, consultants, managers, and knowledge-base administrators and support staff are central to this success.

As can be seen, the nature of the new knowledge-based tools necessitates steps of progress markedly different from the standard software-development life cycles. If an inappropriate framework is used in planning, frequently the result will be inappropriate—too time-consuming or too expensive. For this reason, the importance of the appropriate life cycle for successful planning should not be underestimated.

## 1-11. KNOWLEDGE HAS ORGANIZING POWER

Looking at the overall strategy for putting expert systems into production, it is important to recognize that a central feature of human knowledge is its organizing power. The goal of the seven steps of implementation is to increase the enterprise's organizing power. In addition, understanding the fundamentals of expert systems technology enhances the designer's own organizing power. This knowledge is necessary to successfully implement an expert system of appropriate scope and magnitude for the current state of the technology. Information theory makes the point: the greater the degree of knowledge captured, in terms of "negative entropy," the greater the degree of organizing power available to accomplish the task. The work of Nobel laureate in chemistry and nonequilibrium thermodynamics, Ilya Prigogine of Brussels Free University, has established the principle that knowledge is or has organizing power. This organizing power is fundamental to living systems (Prigogine, 1968).

One goal of this book is to enable existing developers to add organizing power to their current knowledge-engineering efforts. Several thousand expert system shells have been sold to people who, according to the literature, seem to have been experimenting and learning with them, rather than building robust production applications. The industry and trade press do contain increasing reports of research or test-stage expert systems, but the number reported to be in production is a small percentage of the whole. Thus, as an alternative to selecting an application that has never been implemented before, as discussed in Chapter 3, many readers are likely to find candidate applications in various states of completion already existing in their corporations. Any application, whatever its current state of completion, should be reviewed thoroughly for viability before further investments are made. Unsuccessful expert systems developments have often begun with an inappropriate application and continued with mismatched tools. There is no one solution to all the problems, but the strategies outlined throughout this book can go a long way to rectifying common mistakes. Successful expert systems, such as PROSPECTOR and XCON, have demonstrated that potential paybacks from this new technology can be large.

The implication of the formula "knowledge has organizing power" for company directors is that the fruit of successful expert system implementation is increased corporate organizing power. A central goal for all corporations is to help organize society, by increasing the order in the marketplace. In return society gives to the corporation, in the form of payment for goods and services, and profits are made. Thus, it can be seen that the knowledge owned by the corporation is at the basis of its success. The purer the knowledge base, i.e., the more orderly it is in information theory terms, then the greater its organizing power. Purity, not just quantity of knowledge, is the key to increasing organizing power. Developers therefore have to be most systematic in their work, so as not to create disorder and in turn decrease the organizing power of the resultant implementation. Taking the information theory philosophy and equations to their limit, we can infer that a perfectly (infinitely) orderly system would have infinite organizing power. A future filled with highly ordered expansive knowledge bases could significantly help make society function more smoothly and coherently.

## 1-12. MAIN POINTS: UNDERSTANDING EXPERT SYSTEMS—TECHNOLOGY AND CAPABILITIES

In this chapter, we have outlined some of the key points of expert systems theory and practice. We have been careful to paint a realistic picture of the potential uses of the technology by noting its limitations. The non-AI reader has been introduced to AI expert system teminology in reference to conventional computer science jargon.

Before expanding on the ideas expressed in this chapter, in Chapters 3 to 9, Chapter 2 presents a brief digression into the concept of intelligence in machines. The intent is to demystify the AI paradigm and the potential for machine intelligence so that concrete, practical application advances can be made based on the reality of the technology. This exploration will provide further background for expanding the reader's knowledge of AI capabilities and should enhance the basis for efficiently and effectively choosing candidates for expert systems development.

- Knowledge-engineering research of the 1970s gave birth to the expert systems approach of the 1980s, with fielded applications beginning to be significant and widespread in the years 1984 to 1986.
- Expert system shells, or development tools, usually provide faster development times than symbolic programming languages, at the expense of flexibility.
- The principle components of an expert system are its inference engine, knowledge base, and interfaces. The knowledge base comprises domain-specific facts and heuristics.
- The main knowledge-representation approaches are (1) rules, and

(2) frames, or schemas, sometimes called semantic or associative networks.

• Expert systems can provide a good means for saving an expert's time by capturing, documenting, duplicating, and transferring expertise.

• Increasing levels of abstraction, or indirection, are used in these layered software systems to deliver higher levels of power to the user.

• Some of the things expert systems are not good at include noncognitive tasks, general intelligence, exception handling, common sense, qualitive reasoning, intuition, learning, and self-knowledge.

• Four levels of machine functioning, in historical sequence, are data, information, symbol, and knowledge. Human information processing follows a similar layered approach.

• Knowledge in humans can be seen as arising from the interaction of the knower, the process of knowing, and the object of knowledge. Without some form of consciousness or real intelligence, expert systems can be expected to forever be more like idiot savants.

• The universe, according to the latest developments in physics, has certainty at its basis. Expert system probabilities arise from lack of knowledge and should be constrained for successful implementations.

• A fruitful area for applying expert systems is that zone where soft sciences are maturing into hard sciences.

• A sensible approach for the qualified project manager is to construct a development life cycle matching the application and tools.

• The raison d'être for embarking on expert system development is that knowledge has organizing power.

## NOTES

[1] For an extensive review of expert systems in various stages of development circa 1984, see Waterman's *Guide to Expert Systems,* 1986.

[2] See Rich (1983) for a discussion of these domain-independent techniques.

[3] Hayes-Roth et al. (eds.), *Building Expert Systems,* p. 55.

[4] See "The Knowledge Level" by Alan Newell (1982), p. 113.

[5] For a layman's introduction to Super String Theory, see *Discover Magazine,* Oct. 22, 1986.

## FOR FURTHER READING

### Artificial Intelligence in General

Charniak, E., D. McDermott (1985). *Introduction to Artificial Intelligence.* Reading, MA: Addison-Wesley.

Hunt, D. V. (1986). *Artificial Intelligence and Expert Systems Sourcebook.* New York: Chapman & Hall.

Rich, E. (1983). *Artificial Intelligence.* New York: McGraw-Hill.

Winston, P., K. A. Prendergast (1986). *Commercial Uses of Artificial Intelligence.* Cambridge, MA: MIT Press.

Yazdani, M. (1986). *Artificial Intelligence: Principles and Applications.* New York: Chapman & Hall.

## Expert Systems Technology and Applications

Forsyth, R. (ed.) (1985). *Expert Systems: Principles and Case Studies.* New York: Chapman & Hall.

Jackson, P. (1986). *Introduction to Expert Systems.* Reading, MA: Addison-Wesley.

Klahr, P., D. A. Waterman (1986). *Expert Systems: Techniques, Tools, and Applications.* Reading, MA: Addison-Wesley.

Silverman, B. (1987). *Expert Systems in Business.* Reading, MA: Addison-Wesley.

# Chapter 2
# Why AI Expert Systems Do Not Have Intelligence

## SECTION HEADINGS



## OVERVIEW

Before embarking on the expert system development life cycle in the following chapters, we will clarify the distinction between artificial intelligence and natural intelligence. Most of the expert systems literature tends to rate the software as something markedly different from the bulk of common computer programs. This common view is in part due to the mystique surrounding the word *intelligence*. Understanding human intelligence as an attribute of the holistic functioning of human consciousness, based on the subjectivity of the experiencer, puts the potential of current AI and expert systems technology into proper perspective. Expert systems do not provide human intelligence and thus cannot be expected to act as human surrogates. Choosing an inappropriate implementation, based on an incorrect understanding of basic expert systems capabilities, does not lead to success. The pragmatic conclusion of this common-sense, but philosophical chapter is that expert systems technology can be best understood and utilized in the same light as other familiar classes of software systems.

## 2-1. THE REDUCTIONISTIC PARADIGM

Although the potential for applying expert systems commercially is great, confusion has existed over the real and immediate versus the imagined capabilities of this technology. This confusion arises from four sources:

1. a misunderstanding of the relationship between AI and expert systems
2. excessive claims made by AI proponents and vendors
3. the connotations of the phrase *artificial intelligence*
4. the lack of a firm scientific understanding of the fundamentals of *natural intelligence*.

The relationship between AI and expert systems technologies was outlined in Chapter 1 along with some of the strengths and limitations of the applied technology. It was noted that the goal of AI, as a research discipline, is to investigate, model, and build computer systems displaying intelligent-like characteristics. Expert systems technology, however, is an engineering application of certain AI principles geared to the representation, access, and use of knowledge derived from very narrow cognitive/logical domains of human expertise. This applied technology has both great potential and severe limitations, compared with human experts. Understanding the power of expert systems rests on understanding the concepts and constraints associated with the scientific investigation of artificial intelligence and natural intelligence. These concepts are further elaborated in this chapter.

Part of the mystery and misunderstanding about expert systems, as an artificial intelligence technology, stems from its very name. The phrase *artificial intelligence*, inadvertently coined in 1956 by one of AI's founders, John McCarthy, is a misnomer. The intent of AI study, according to McCarthy's statement 30 years ago, ". . . is to proceed on the basis of the conjecture that every aspect of learning or any other feature of intelligence can in principle be so precisely described that a machine can be made to *simulate* it [italics added]."[1] A more suitable term for such a study is *machine intelligence*, but this expression still leaves the uninitiated with the impression that something magical occurs within the computer to make it come alive with "intelligence." A more accurate depiction of McCarthy's original intention would be found in the descriptive title *simulated intelligence*.[2] The title AI, however, with all its potential misunderstandings, appears to be here to stay.

When AI researchers describe a computer system as "intelligent", they are using a behavioral definition. If a system behaves in a manner that would be called intelligent had the behavior been performed by a biological entity, then the system is called *intelligent.* This definition is based on the simulated intelligent behavior, not the internal operation or knowledge of the system. This classic behavioral view of intelligence was immortalized by an early computer scientist, Alan Turing, in a 1950 paper entitled "Computing Machinery and Intelligence."[3] The so called Turing test placed a human in one room, a sophisticated present or future "intelligent" computer in another room, and a second human "interrogator" in a third room. The interrogator does not know which room contains the machine and which the human. He directs questions, via teletype, to both rooms. Both the computer and the person respond as humans. If the interrogator cannot distinguish between the human's and the computer replies, then the computer must be considered "intelligent" in the same way the human is. The "existence" of intelligence in a machine has been confused with the concept of "displaying intelligent behavior" since Turing proposed this provocative thought experiment.

McCarthy's early definition of AI is characteristic of the Western scientific *reductionistic paradigm,* which operates under the assumption that knowledge and operation of a system as a whole are nothing more than the sum of the operations of its parts and their interactions. Two additional founders of AI, Alan Newell and Herbert Simon, crystallized this theme of "parts summing to the whole" in terms of a *physical symbol system hypothesis.* They argued that a physical symbol system has the necessary and sufficient means for general intelligent action.[4] This thesis has yet to be proven, and it may not in fact be amenable to proof or disproof on the level of logic. Although this view may be useful to describe physical systems, its applicability to natural intelligence is questionable. An analysis of human intelligence and associated functions suggests that *the whole is greater than the sum of its parts.*

The physical symbol system hypothesis has been carried one step further in Alan Newell's description of the "knowledge level" of a generalized intelligent agent, as shown in Fig. 2-1. Each component of the knowledge level, notably agents, actions, knowledge, goals, and the principle of rationality, has a corresponding representation in the symbol level of the system. The totality of an intelligent agent is purportedly reduced to appropriate symbol-level components and operations. The rationalistic/logical principle is the sole guiding force responsible for motivating and directing the intelligence agent's actions.[6] The symbol system hypothesis applied to expert systems is shown in Fig. 2-2. This may be an appropriate model to use for a starting point in developing intelligent machines, but current implementations do not begin describing the complexity of elements giving rise to human

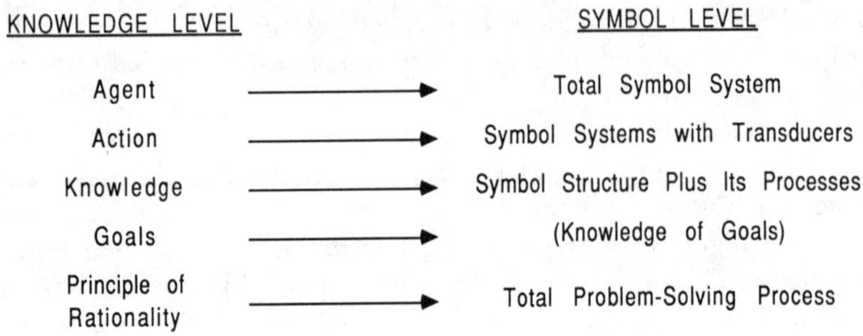


Fig. 2-1. Newell's knowledge and symbol levels for an intelligent agent (Newell, 1982).

intention, knowledge, motivation, desire, emotion, and so on that lead to final thought and action.

Regardless of its validity when applied to natural systems, this hypothesis has become the guiding light of current AI research. Unfortunately, enthusiastic AI public relations specialists often elevate the hypothesis to the level of absolute truth. For instance in 1965, early AI enthusiasts claimed that by 1985, machines would be capable " . . . of doing any

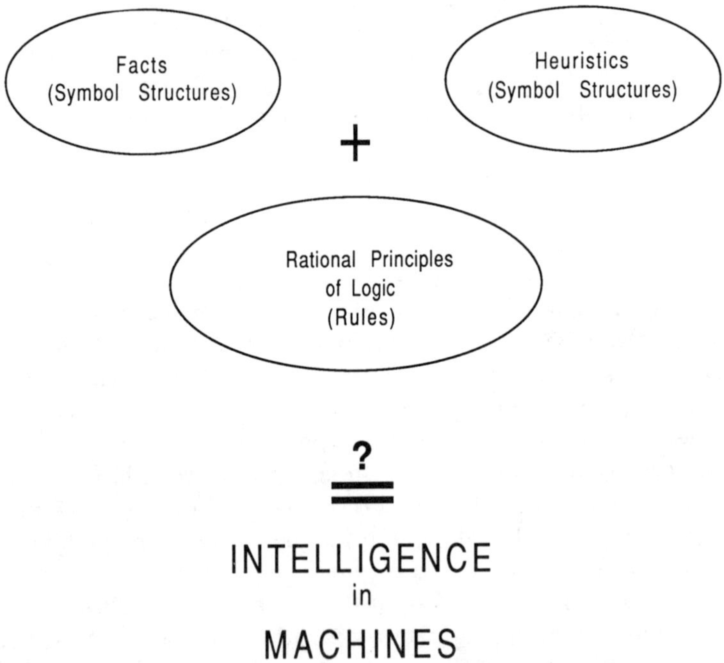


Fig. 2-2. The physical symbol system hypothesis for expert systems.

work that a man can do."[5] There is no real evidence to support the assumption that the phenomenon we call intelligence is generated solely by a society of symbols interacting according to a set of specified rules. AI promoters like to play on the element of intelligence in AI systems, for such statements humanize the technology and imply a problem-solving power usually associated only with human intelligence. Such sensational statements tend to only confuse and mislead the public.

## 2-2. SYNTHESIS REQUIRES COMPLETE KNOWLEDGE OF THE SUBSTANCE

The physical symbol system hypothesis and the "knowledge level" concept presuppose that intelligence is in fact decomposable. Such decomposition would require that intelligence can be known by analyzing its component parts and then synthesized by constructing a suitable symbol system. As a step to analyzing this basis of AI, assume for now that the decomposition statement is true. Further assume that the primary AI interest is synthesizing intelligent behavior or simulated intelligence, rather than creating in the machine the type of intelligence usually associated with biological entities. What then are the basic building blocks necessary to construct intelligent behavior?

To approach the possible synthesis of intelligence, it is useful to look at the experience gained through chemistry and other physical sciences. In chemistry the point is clear: synthesis of a substance requires complete knowledge of the substance. The necessary knowledge includes the constituent elements and their interactions. For a chemist to produce vanilla, he must have complete knowledge of the molecular makeup of vanilla, as well as knowledge for combining appropriate base atoms to produce the molecule. Deviation from the chemical formula will produce something perhaps similar, but subtly different from vanilla. Even though some of the attributes of the real vanilla and imperfect clone may be similar, other aspects of the imperfect version could be very different, perhaps producing dangerous side effects. Possibly only through extensive longitudinal studies on users of the products would the variety of possible harmful side effects resulting from incorrect synthesis show up. Examples of negative side effects in pharmaceuticals and food additives, for instance, appear never to end. Clearly, a substance and its close imitation are not identical in properties or effects. The parallel question in AI relates to the synthesis of simulated intelligence. How can such a synthesis take place without a clear understanding of what real intelligence is. Unfortunately, progress in the cognitive- and neurosciences has been slow and has not yet produced deep, verifiable knowledge of the basic formula for human intelligence.

Another important and closely related principle, essential in all scientific disciplines, is the concept of a ground state. Identifying and understanding the ground state are critical in transforming a soft science into a hard science. The quantum mechanical description of this principle can be effectively stated as follows: if full knowledge of the *ground state* of a system's primitive elements and interactions is available, then all the various layers of *excited states* of the system and their properties can be deduced. The principle has been named the *reconstruction theorem* and is generally recognized as a necessary condition to be satisfied by all advances in such fields as physics and chemistry. In atomic theory, knowledge of the periodic table of the elements stems from understanding the hydrogen atom. Before the structure of the simplest atom—hydrogen—was understood, it was not possible to predict the behavior of the more complex atoms. In contrast, once quantum theory had formulated a successful model of the hydrogen atom, the same ground rules were found to explain all the higher order elements of the table. The property is not restricted to atoms. Quantum fields behave such that the properties of the excited states are direct functions of the properties of the ground state wave functions.

Other examples of this principle abound in the sciences. The entire field of mathematics, according to set theory, rests on comprehending the null set or empty set generator—equivalent to 0 in the natural numbers. The entire spectrum of modern mathematics, from counting numbers to the set of all sets, is generated from the ground state null set and its self-interacting dynamics. In the physiological sciences the DNA is the ground state element, the blueprint of the organism found in every cell. DNA contains within it the knowledge for generating all the parts of the organism's physiology, the "excited states" or states of fully developed potentials. As illustrated by DNA, once the ground state is known it can be seen that *the whole is in every part.*

These and other fields of study have shown that only when the ground state of the field, the basic field of primitives and the axioms or rules governing their interactions, is known can the activities of the higher level diversified states be understood. Assuming that the same principle applies to human intelligence, to understand and then simulate the "excited states" of everyday human intelligence and its extensions into action-oriented thought and behavior, this ground state knowledge of intelligence must be available.

AI researchers, as noted in Chapter 1, tend to be divided into two camps on how to approach intelligence. The first group typically uses the human neural or cognitive system as a model for synthesizing intelligent systems. The second group examines any potential hardware/software organization that will produce the desired result or function, regardless of whether the internal workings of the system are consistent with our knowledge of the human information processing system. Feigenbaum (1984) has summed up this second approach with his phrase "intelligence is as intelligence does."

A human-based model suggests a variety of potential information-processing levels. Should the investigation focus on the neural level, the lower brain, the brain cortex, or the cognitive functioning experiental level? All these levels combined comprise the range of cognitive science studies. Do any of the various cognitive psychological or physical system models available represent a ground state set necessary, or necessary and sufficient, to generate intelligent behavior that could rival the level of human functioning in some specific domain? Unfortunately, the answer appears to be no—although much work is being done on understanding adaptive, learning, dynamical systems (e.g., Grossberg, 1982). Could any machine or network of machines built on such principles effectively pass the Turing test? Even if such a system did pass the test, would it really be considered intelligent?

Obviously, there are more questions here than answers. One thing is certain: AI research does not yet have an irrefutable ground state set of tools for building intelligent systems. Until one or more of the AI "hydrogen atoms" are known, the "vanilla" AI researchers desire to produce will be likely to remain far more imitation than real.

## 2-3 NATURAL INTELLIGENCE: NATURE'S BEST KNOWN AND BEST KEPT SECRET

Human beings have the ubiquitous experience of embodying the phenomenon of natural intelligence without really knowing what it is or how it works. Investigating the display or behavior of intelligence is one thing; understanding and creating technologies using the actual stuff of intelligence is another.

As noted in the previous section the objective scientific research method has disclosed little knowledge of the foundations and structural mechanisms of man's intelligence. The results of most studies into the nature and substance of intelligence, e.g., cognitive psychology and mental modeling, have revealed little more than a poignant awareness of our own ignorance. Although AI implementations are an outgrowth of concrete computer science principles, the knowledge of the phenomenon of intelligence that AI seeks to simulate remains a chimera, somewhere just beyond reach, a curious state because it is intelligence which seeks to know itself. Is it possible to build intelligent systems when the true nature of intelligence remains unknown?

Intelligence, as we view it in the human species, appears to be far more than an isolated ability to perform a specific task or solve a particular problem. The mystery of the phenomenon we call intelligence is embedded in the holistic functioning of human consciousness, where all aspects of perception, thought, memory, intellect, emotion, intuition, ego, and so on are integrated into a supremely correlated whole. The superficial extraction of a few of the externally visible artifacts from this unified field of consciousness is not likely to recreate the whole of natural intelligence. The whole may well be different from, as well as more than, the sum of the parts, even if the parts were known. The elementary building blocks sufficient to reconstruct intelligence are most likely the fundamental building blocks of human consciousness itself, whatever they may be. Using anything less than models based on these deep primitives of human consciousness will probably continue to produce shallow, weak, and superficial simulations in machine intelligence.

The AI perspective of human intelligence, based on the premise that these subtle qualities can somehow be re-created from an interacting set of symbolic structures, springs from the reductionistic paradigm noted earlier. This paradigm that has dominated objective Western scientific thought for the last 400 years. The objective reductionistic methodology locates the fundamentals in an area of investigation through analysis, with the hope that synthesis can then proceed based on that knowledge. This technique has worked remarkably well in the physical sciences, as our current state of technology shows. Human intelligence, in contrast, is intimately connected with *subjectivity,* a personal feeling of "I" and "my," which is an *experiential* phenomenon that cannot be completely known through external objective observation. It is known as it is experienced. The subjective element of consciousness unifies all awareness and experience, creating holistic knowledge and understanding. It is emminently reasonable that this subjective value of experience and intelligence will have to be investigated by a form of *subjective science,* as well as by objective science, to get at the deep knowledge desired.

The question of pure subjectivity and valid subjective experience has always intrigued philosophers. One of the major topics of philosophy is ontological status, i.e., distinguishing between what really exists and what only appears to exist. Through the technique of the dialectic, Plato and his school were able to experience this quiet state of perfect self-reflection, the "Good," pure subjectivity, where the mind is fully awake in its own state of pure intelligence without any objects of perception. Descartes and Kant described similar experiences. Other philosophers, such as the empiricist Hume, doubted the existence of such a state, due to their apparent inability or lack of a technique to experience and understand it clearly.

Western scientists have not always excluded subjective experience as a means of gaining valid knowledge. Newton, for example, stated that time had two aspects, one subjective and one objective. Objective time marched by as determinately and precisely as inches are marked on a ruler. Subjective time, however, was determined by the flow of attention, moods, and emotions. William Blake, the English poet, described this type of subjective time in the phrase "To see . . . eternity in an hour." Subjective time is just one element of internal experience. Other experiential knowledge includes cognitive processes, emotions, feelings, and other elements resulting in deep insights, such as intuition or cognitions. Many leading scientists have claimed that they "see" the inner workings of nature in their mind's eye during quiet reflective periods or even sleep. This type of deeper intuition is then validated in mathematical theory and later laboratory experimentation, leading to such diverse discoveries as the chemical structure of the benzene ring, DNA, and the theories of relativity and quantum mechanics. Certain innovative people seem to have an internal window in consciousness that opens onto the field of nature's inner workings.

It is likely that future developments in the science of mind and intelligence will draw more strongly on such subjective methods of gaining knowledge. If such subjective techniques can be cultivated then they should yield a true science of a subjective means of gaining knowledge on a equal status with the objective techniques already in use. The problem has been the lack of repeatably verifiable experimentation, which, since the time of Freud and James, has caused Western science to avoid such introspective methodologies. The primary objection to subjective investigation has been the lack of systematic, consistent protocols for discerning repeatable, valid internal experience. "Thought experiments", structured in mathematics and guided by intuition, are now required for modern physics studies, because material accelerators to create sufficient energy to experimentally validate the latest theories can no longer be built. For Einstein, discovery was first a matter of deep cognition within the realm of consciousness, followed by external verification. It is likely that the deep inner workings of intelligence embedded in consciousness can be discovered only by subjective consciousness curving back onto itself to discover its own fundamental construction.

Insights into the subjective approach of gaining knowledge may come from other cultures and traditions. A key example is the Vedic tradition centered in India, representing the oldest known records of human knowledge and experience. The Vedic literature contains a great variety of philosophical and experiential wisdom, together with practical advice for daily living and applied methodologies for understanding the deeper mysteries of life. These records, as subjectively known or intuited by certain individuals, are thought by their proponents to be a direct rendering of all the laws of nature residing in the unified field: the actual blueprint of creation. If such a body of knowledge and techniques were accurate and could be subjected to scientific investigation and thereby elevated to the status of a subjective scientific methodology (as noted by various interdisciplinary researchers, e.g., Chandler, 1987, and Alexander et al., 1987), doors might be unlocked into the deeper understanding of human intelligence and potential. The ground state of human consciousness, as expressed by the Vedic system, is a unifed field of pure unbounded consciousness, pure intelligence, of primary ontological status. This underlying substance of life manifests itself through a series of self-referral transformations into all the subjective and objective modalities, providing an interesting commentary on some of the latest developments in physics. The pure field of consciousness can also be experienced through various subjective, de-excitation technologies to produce an unwavering window into the subtler aspects of human consciousness. Some people, such as Sibelius, Einstein, and Wordsworth, seem to have been born with the ability to experience this state of pure consciousness. Others need to learn specific technologies[7] to reach the same end.

The Vedic system describes intelligence as one of several qualities, or transformations, of consciousness. The physical symbol system hypothesis, shown earlier in Figs. 2-1 and 2-2, combines a variety of elements to produce simulated intelligence. A high-level Vedic-based description equivalent to Fig. 2-3 has a set of symbols, but this time they are embedded in the field of pure consciousness to produce the display of individual consciousness. The key difference between the two figures is the integrated basis in consciousness. In Fig. 2-2 the whole, or result, is equal to the sum of the symbols, but in Fig. 2-3 the whole, i.e., the whole of consciousness, is greater than the sum of the parts. The interacting expressions of consciousness giving rise to intelligence are senses (hearing, touch, sight, taste, and smell), mind, intellect, and ego. Emotions, the feeling level of experience, are documented as the finest level of the intellect. Memory and thinking are both aspects of the mind. The intellect is responsible for that aspect of thinking that discriminates, i.e., intellect is the subtlest level of the mind. Individual ego is closest to the field of pure consciousness (also denoted as the field of pure creative intelligence), and the senses are closest to the external manifest world. Each of these key features remains coordinated with all other features

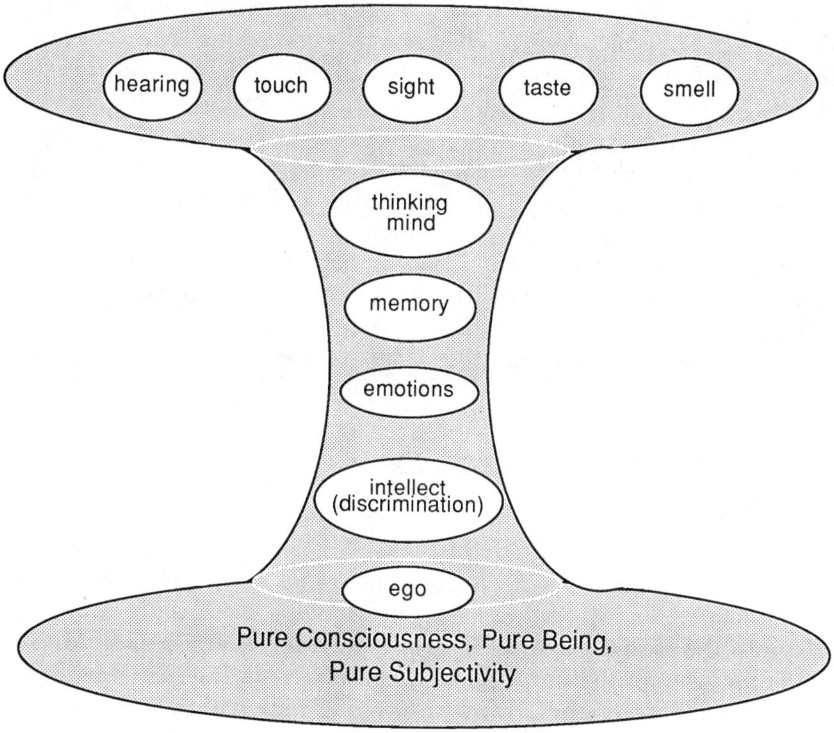


Fig. 2-3. The components of intelligence embedded in human consciousness.

through the common source, the field of consciousness. Each element is the result of specific, self interacting transformations, of the field of pure consciousness. Vedic Science promotes investigation through such a joint subjective (experiential) and objective (intellectual) approach, generating simultaneous analysis (reductionism) and synthesis (holism). The parts are never separated from the whole.

Although AI has been successful in simulating certain aspects of man's capabilities, such as memory and senses, the binding aspect of subjectivity is likely to be the key to creating real intelligence. Investigation into subjective means of gaining knowledge are likely to be instrumental in unlocking the secrets of intelligence in humans.

The demand for intelligence in AI is one of several indicators that our scientific investigative paradigm has reached a level of maturity where it is growing to encompass both subjective and objective means of gaining knowledge. The problem for many researchers in the past was that subjective experience had appeared to be too varying to produce reliable knowledge. Newer "mental technologies," such as those suggested by the

Vedic system outlined above, provide natural techniques for de-exciting the subjective thinking or intelligence process, taking it to its state of least excitation. Access to the stable ground state of awareness, invariant in both time and space, would allow researchers to arrive at valid, repeatable subjective knowledge. The Unified Field theories of physics appear to acknowledge a similar and perhaps identical unified field as the source of all the laws of nature creating and governing the physical universe. Leading physicists are talking of direct links between human awareness or consciousness and the interactions deep within the quantum fields. Some of today's top theoretical physicists (e.g., Hagelin, 1987) go so far as to equate the unified field with the field of pure consciousness, the source of the primitive elements of man's consciousness.

## 2-4. THE ESSENCE OF INTELLIGENCE IS SUBJECTIVITY

Now that the points of the preceding sections have been established, it is possible to draw one of the major conclusions of this chapter. In AI, discussions of whether subjectivity has ontological status are commonly cast into the man-as-machine versus man-as-spirit arguments. Man-as-machine assumes that mind is nothing more than the sum total of the neural switching operations in the brain. Man-as-spirit (or consciousness) asserts that mind has an existence separate from the brain and is the primal causal element in the mind/brain relationship. Most AI researchers implicitly support the first philosophy. The topic of consciousness, because of the current lack of scientific knowledge concerning its real substance and nature, is usually not even discussed. The physical symbol hypothesis, applied to man's brain, implies that if the brain could be reconstructed and properly programmed, all the intelligence inherent in man's consciousness would automatically dwell therein. The second philosophy is more in accord with the concept of pure intelligence or pure consciousness as an independent substrate of life. If the second premise is true, AI machines will never display the full integrated state of intelligence associated with living entities, until they gain a subjective interface with the field of pure consciousness. In regard to simulating intelligence, AI will remain a discipline without a basis until the elements governing the functioning of consciousness at its ground state, the state of pure consciousness, are discovered and available for engineering use.

It is the element of the "I," the element of pure subjectivity, which humans experience at the core of their consciousness and that gives rise to intelligence. The reader will recall from Chapter 1 that the type of knowledge available in expert systems is something quite different from human knowledge. Human knowledge is a living experiential phenomenon intimately related to subjectivity and intelligence, but machine knowledge lacks these self-referral and flexible qualities. In the Vedic literature, knowledge is said to be intimately related to human consciousness or, in other words, *knowledge is structured in consciousness* (Rig Veda 1.164.39).

ऋचो अक्षरे परमे व्योमन् यस्मिन् देवा अधि विश्वे निषेदुः ।
यस्तन्न वेद किमृचा करिष्यति य इत्तद्विदुस्त इमे समासते ॥

**Richo akshare parame vyoman Yasmin deva adhi vishve nisheduh**
**Yastanna veda kimricha karishyati Ya ittadvidusta ime samasate**
**Rig Veda, I.164.39**

Richa is situated in Akshara: knoweledge is structured in consciousness, the nonchanging transcendental basis of all relative existence, in which reside the impulses of creative intelligence responsible for the whole manifest universe.

He whose awareness is not open to this level of reality, what can these eternal expressions of knowledge accomplish for him? He whose awareness is open to it—the field of pure consciousness, the home of all knowledge—is profoundly established in it.

In AI, the intelligence of the machine is said to come from the machine's knowledge. Compared with human knowledge, according to this Vedic statement, there is a fundamental problem in AI, in that the basis of the knowledge, the consciousness, is nonexistent in the machine. Knowledge is like ripples in the fabric of consciousness and cannot really be separated from it. Knowledge is seen as the subjective appreciation or awareness of the fundamental impulses of the laws of nature, which are described in the Vedas as the impulses of consciousness. The interesting feature of the second part of the quotation is one has to go to that level of awareness directly to validate this quintessential merger of subjective and objective reality, i.e., that this knowledge is self-validating.[8]

The concept of human knowledge is further elaborated by the Vedas into three components: the *knower,* the *known,* and the *processing of*

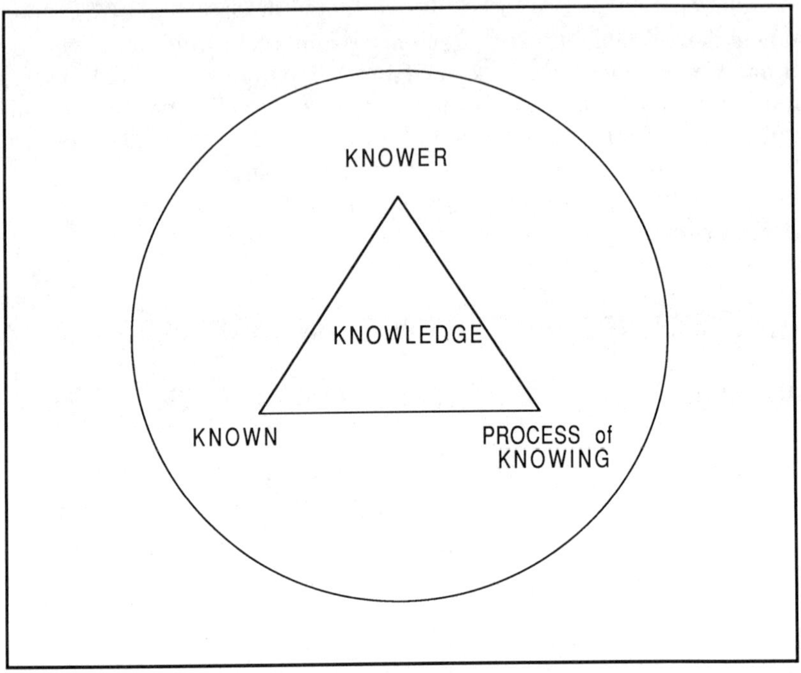


Fig. 2-4. The three elements of human knowledge experience from the Vedic viewpoint.

*knowing,* (Fig. 2-4). The knower is the subjective element in this triangle, and without the knower there is no knowledge as we experience it. It is the liveliness of the knower that can draw on all types of knowing, such as experiment, experience, inference, judgment, intuition, qualitative simulation, and reasoning, to enliven the flat lifeless elements of the known. AI knowledge-representation schemes, coupled with inference engines, represent only the poles of the known and some aspect of the processing of knowing. Without the knower, unfortunately, there is no applied and active intelligent agent, and therefore there is no knowledge. Knowledge can be seen as the center of the triangle, or togetherness of knower, known, and process of knowing. Knowledge, intelligence, and consciousness are intimately interrelated.

It is conceivable that the time will come when cognitive science disciplines, including AI, will understand the laws of nature composing and governing a set of ground state fundamentals giving rise to the phenomena of human consciousness and intelligence. At that time AI will perhaps become capable of fulfilling its highest aspirations.

## 2-5. THE INTELLIGENCE OF THE EXPERT SYSTEM IS IN THE EXPERT, NOT THE MACHINE

Returning to a less philosophical realm, the simulated intelligence found in expert systems is commonly understood to be based on the knowledge representation and inference schemes used in the system. The degree of intelligence displayed by the expert system is often viewed as a function of the fit between the domain problem and the expert system mode of problem solving. Far more important, however, is the skill of the knowledge engineer in producing an appropriate corpus of logically specified knowledge from the domain expert. Above all, the real credit must go to the intelligence of the domain expert who was capable of consciously or unconsciously collecting and formulating the necessary knowledge into a coherent functional system. Without the intelligence and the holistic functioning of the expert's consciousness, expertise would not exist. The intelligence starts with and stays in the expert. A small degree of simulated intelligent behavior has been implanted in the machine.

A tape recording provides a good analogy. When a scientist or politician gives a brilliant speech, the audience infers on the basis of the words it hears that the speaker is highly intelligent. If the same audience, later, hears a tape recording of the same speech, it still infers that it was the original speaker who was intelligent; it does not impute wisdom to the tape recorder. The intelligence of the taping and playback mechanism lies in the ability to faithfully reproduce, i.e., through rote memory, the symbolic structure (language) associated with intelligent humans. Expert systems are much like the tape recorder. Some conditional branches may have been inserted into the script, but the foundation technology is the same recording of smart phrases on magnetic or electronic media. The early RCA phonograph advertisements showed a dog confusing a machine recording with his master's voice. Expert system developers and users should be wiser.

Generally human expertise is taken to be a form of learned knowledge. It is here that expert systems experience problems. Hubert and Stewart Dreyfus, two of AI's critics, have identified five stages of human skill learning, which they call the *novice, advanced beginner, competence, proficiency,* and *expertise* levels.[9] Their novice performs a task using a set of context-free rules operating on idealized symbols. The novice is personally detached from the problem-solving situation as he analytically makes decisions by "following the rules." The advanced beginner, however, is able to incorporate situational, context-sensitive elements into his performance as well, but decision making remains rote and analytical. At the third level, competence, the individual incorporates goals, priorities, and planning in managing his skills. He continues to be detached in his understanding and deciding, but he tends to be more involved in the outcome. A person at the proficient skill level uses intuitive organizing and understanding, but still makes decisions analytically. He uses holistic pattern matching in approaching the problem, is involved in the understanding process, but is detached in deciding. The last skill level, that of the expert, involves intuitive decision making and total, involved commitment throughout the process. Decision making at this level is more of a process of spontaneously knowing what to do rather than analytically deciding what to do.

Current AI expert systems technology stops somewhere short of the competent level in the Dreyfus' scheme. Although some AI proponents may argue that intuition is nothing more than as yet undiscovered rules, intuitive faculties are still beyond the scope of expert systems technology. The final level of true expertise, according to this model, remains in the awareness of the expert and cannot yet be placed in the machine.

## 2-6. AI: THE ADVANCING FRONTIER OF OBJECTIVE COMPUTER SCIENCE

The point of this rather long and circuitous discourse on the nature of intelligence and consciousness is to bring the perspectives on the current foundations of AI, and thus expert systems technology capabilities, present and future, into proper focus. This discussion on natural and machine intelligence can be summarized in the following five points:

- Machine-simulated intelligence is an entirely different phenomenon from that natural intelligence found in biological systems. Simulated intelligence is a behavioral description applied to the activity of machines.
- Simulated intelligence depends on a set of ground state primitives. The physical symbol system hypothesis assumes that such a set of primitives can be stated in terms of symbols, symbol structures, and interactions among the structures.
- The primitives for deep intelligence simulation are not known to AI. It is not known if a set of fundamental, isolatable primitives of human intelligence exists, for this natural intelligence is an expression of the holistic, self-interacting field of consciousness.
- If such a set of ground state primitives does exist, it is not known whether physical symbol systems are sufficient to simulate deep knowledge.
- Simulated intelligence lacks subjectivity, which is at the core of natural intelligence.

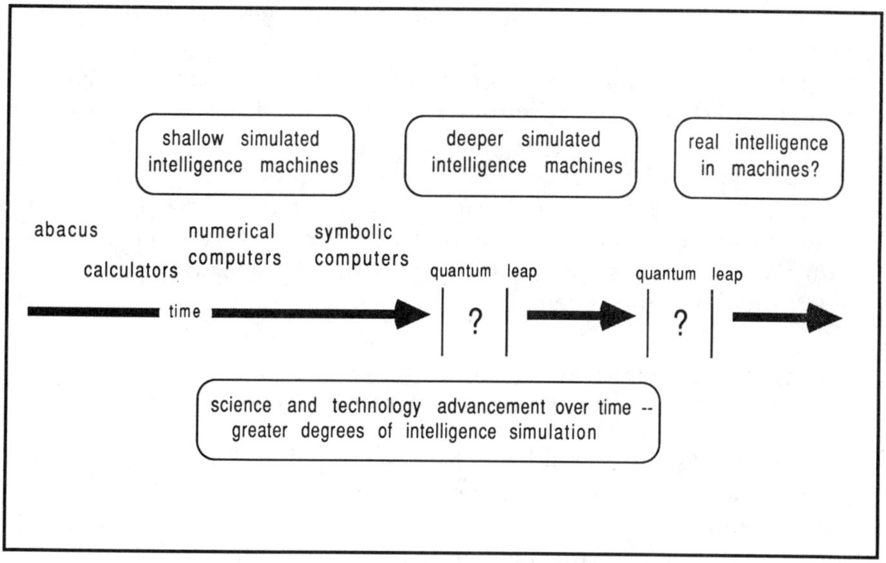


Fig. 2-5. The continuum hypothesis for simulated intelligence.

Taken as a whole, the lack of subjectivity, real intelligence, and the critical elements of consciousness in AI systems remove the systems from the realm of the mysterious or inexplicable and put them squarely back into the world of traditional computer science. AI at this time, as indicated in Fig. 1-11, represents just the leading edge of computer science moving in the direction of increasingly capable information-processing systems. In fact many of the more complex MIS systems which have over a decade of evolution behind them (e.g., some airline reservation systems) are a good deal smarter than a lot of AI research systems.

Although the continuum of continued developments in AI, as shown in Fig. 2-5, will move the discipline in the direction of increasingly convincing displays of simulated intelligent behavior, there is no reason to believe that AI systems will suddenly receive the qualities of true intelligence or subjectivity at some point in this continuum of development. Sophisticated self-referral mechanisms, such as self-monitoring, self-adjusting, and learning subsystems, should increase the quality of the simulation, but the comparison is still one of making the leap from the finite to the infinite, as in taking a limit in calculus. Faster machinery, complicated multiprocessor network configurations, and complex parallel algorithms will also increase the quality of the simulation. None of these developments, however, is expected to imbue the machine with the fullness of common-sense knowledge and intuition expressed in real intelligence.

The expert systems technology of today, therefore, can be treated like numerous other classes of software products available in today's commercial markets. The expert system technology can benefit a sophisticated range of application areas and can be quite useful within those areas, but there is no internal magic in such systems. The magic, if any, is found in the ability of the expert and the knowledge engineer to codify the primary tenets of the expert decision-making process and insert them into the system.

## 2-7. COMPARISONS WITH DATABASES, SPREADSHEETS, AND WORD PROCESSORS

Having established a set of key philosophical points, it is now possible to review the status of expert systems technology comparing it, on one hand, to human consciousness, and, on the other hand, with traditional software programs. Returning now to the practical theme of implementing expert systems with their current capabilities for problem solving, the primary implication of this chapter is that expert systems software technology is not so radically different from other conventional software technologies. The discussions of the previous sections, which may be reviewed by reading the main points at the end of this chapter, show that expert systems are far from synthesizing true intelligence. As a consequence, the properties of expert systems technology and human intelligence are distinct and separate. From the pragmatic implementer's point of view, the properties of expert systems technology, as will be elaborated in the following chapters, place it firmly in the realm of traditional computer science. These new expert tools have many similarities—and some differences—compared with other classes of software tools. It can be argued that Newell's physical symbol system hypothesis, instead of being a formula for simulated intelligence, is better appreciated as a formula for productive software tools. There has been a clear trend in software products commonly in use in business and industry toward generic symbol-manipulating tools. Word processors, spreadsheet calculators, database managers, and expert systems, for example, are all based on two elements: a set of symbols and a set of rules. The rules define the interactions among the symbols, together with the operations that can be performed on the symbols or composite symbol structures. Although the symbol/rule set structure of the expert system technology has not been discussed in detail, it is worth spending a little time establishing a comparison perspective for traditional symbol/rule set tools before moving onto the details of knowledge engineering. The following paragraphs discuss the high-level similarities between expert systems shells, word processors, spreadsheet calculators, and database managers.

The lowest level primitives in word-processing software are essentially the characters available on the ASCII keyboard. *Symbols* can be defined as items with two properties, *name* and *form*, that map one descriptive construct (name) onto a larger, less directly manageable entity (form). ASCII characters are classic symbols as they map the set of sounds (forms) onto a visable, recordable, and more tangible set of line shapes (names).

Characters are combined by various rules to form words. Rules at this level include "i before e, except after c," and that every word should have at least one vowel. At the next level words come together to form sentences, then sentences to form paragraphs, and paragraphs form documents. The word is taken to be the smallest unit of meaningful information; hence the word is the primary symbol in word processing. Standard word processing functions include insertion, deletion, replacement, and copying of characters, words, groups of words, sentences, and so on. Additional rules center, justify, or condense text; set headings and footings; create standard letter forms; and access multitalented printing routines. True, many of the rules of English language manipulation are not codified in introductory word processors, but advances toward comprehensive word processing are being made. Spelling checkers verify that the combination of characters is in fact a true member of the set of words. The UNIX tools to be found in the Writer's Workbench include "Style" and "Diction," bringing additional rules to the writer's service. The more rules embodied in the code (assuming they are designed to be easily used), the easier it is to produce good results with the system.

The same type of operand (symbol)/operation (rule) combination exists in spreadsheet calculators. The cell is the basic symbol of the system, be it filled with character, numeric, calculated, date, or monetary information. Formulas linking cells are the basic rules driving the tool. A greater degree of surface structure is apparent in the spreadsheet than the word processing system, in terms of its row/column orientation needed to fulfill its functions. English is actually considerably more structured than the average spreadsheet, but word processors leave much of this sophistication to the user. Typical rules structuring a spreadsheet include copying the value of cells, directing that a change in one cell update the values of other cell, causing columns or rows to be added or deleted, and generating special print formats for horizontal or vertical printing. Of the many functions available within a spreadsheet calculator, the set of cell-linking formulas makes it such a powerful construct. The symbolic nature of cells is clear once the spreadsheet has been set up for a specific purpose. A cell may be named "return on investment," "total square footage," or "required MIPS rate," but in every case it refers to some larger form outside the spreadsheet. By working at the symbolic level, the user is able to manipulate real-world entities far more easily than by addressing the constructs directly. Electronic engineering design aids, for example, follow this same symbolic pattern by removing the need to build a physical prototype to establish the behavior of a proposed circuit.

Database products provide symbol/rule capabilities similar to spreadsheets, but with greater flexibility for entire record management. The typical database rule functions—add, delete, duplicate, and reorder—can apply to fields or records. Higher level rule operations allow mass maintanence of physical and logical records across multiple files. Databases, especially relational databases, have the flexibility to model almost any set of real-world entities. Of course, the models are composed of discrete, time-instant snapshots of some larger entity, but they still fit into the general theme of general-purpose, symbol-manipulating software tools.

In an expert system the basic symbols are the domain facts (declarative knowledge), and the generic rules (procedural knowledge). The rules may be either domain heuristics or the domain-independent metarule set of the inference engine. For the popular rule-based system, reasoning will typically occur from a set of given facts to a conclusion based on those facts, or from a particular end goal to possible causes for that goal. The overall operation of inference engine rules is to traverse the inference net formed by the set of domain facts and heuristics. The domain heuristic rules, in this software tool example, represent atomic relationships between domain facts and single-step inferences based on those facts.

What can be said to be the key difference between the three software symbol/rule tool sets mentioned above and an expert system technology? The primary distinction is that the expert system tends to manage symbol/rule sets of a higher level of abstraction than the other three. The knowledge items of facts and heuristics often require a subtler mode of designer and user thinking than with more traditional programs. This need for subtler thinking can be translated into three divisions.

The first concerns the use of rules of logic, in the way that humans use logic, at the center of the expert system framework. The end user of the expert system interacts with the system through user-friendly interfaces, but the knowledge engineer (systems analyst) and programmers must think in terms of knowledge representations based on virtually any kind of symbol and inexact logics based on uncertainty and probabilities.

Second, the knowledge engineer must also be able to extract this knowledge from a human expert through a series of protracted interviews. Human interactions are of vital importance. Consistency and refinement of the knowledge are ongoing concerns. The final expert system can be only as good as the refined state of the expert's knowledge. Some domains lend themselves well to knowledge engineering, others do not. If the knowledge has not already been codified in some form, it may be difficult to assess completely the potential success of the project without a substantial prototyping investment.

Third, the knowledge engineer must be adept in dealing with the concepts of knowledge as they are used in knowledge engineering. There is a much wider range of choices that need to be made, compared with the other symbol/rule systems, and these decisions can affect the programs behavior in unpredictable ways if not managed properly. The great power attributed to the expert system technology and the complexity of problems it is capable of dealing with, even in its limited capacity in comparison with human capabilities, can lead supporters of the system development astray with unachievable expectations. It is up to the knowledge engineers to have a realistic view of problems that can be solved and the exact implementation techniques that may work. Expert system development is not a cut-and-dried process; it is more like an intelligently managed trial-and-error process. There are a great number of pitfalls that could thwart a development if not managed properly.

In addition to these three differences there are a wealth of subtle similarities and variations from traditional computer programs. Some large, well-established, production DP programs are actually considerably smarter and more sophisticated than many entry-level expert systems. The overall point is that the domain of knowledge engineering itself can be very complex and require skills and modalities of thinking that not all computer professionals are familiar with. Once the expert system building technology itself is understood, however, it can be seen as not so different from other, more familiar, software technologies.

The purpose of this chapter was to clarify what expert systems are not capable of: possessing true intelligence. But this is not to belittle the great potential of the technology for creating highly profitable production systems. The subsequent chapters of this book expand upon the similarities and differences between expert systems and traditional software technologies, indicating what is new and what is not so new about knowledge engineering when contrasted with employing traditional programs or languages for traditional numeric or symbolic jobs.

These issues will be discussed in detail, starting with recognizing the knowledge needed for an expert system application in Chapter 3.

## 2-8. MAIN POINTS: WHY AI EXPERT SYSTEMS DO NOT HAVE INTELLIGENCE

• The foundation for understanding the power and limitations of expert system technology rests on understanding the concepts and differences between artificial intelligence and natural intelligence.

• *Simulated intelligence* may be a better descriptor for much of the work in artificial intelligence.

• A mainstream belief in traditional AI circles is that the totality of intelligence can be reduced to an appropriate set of symbol-level components and operations.

• If AI does not know what natural intelligence is or its building blocks, then how can it synthesize intelligence?

• If AI does not know the ground state of intelligence, intelligence in its pure form, then how can it understand the so called excited states of intelligence, notably behavior?

• A principle reason for the lack of a holistic understanding in AI is that Western science has removed subjectivity from its field of investigation for most of its 400-year history.

• Western science is now shifting from a solely objective stance to a view that science can be best described as a means of systematic investigation, encompassing both subjective and objective approaches.

• New insights into the nature of intelligence and consciousness may be gained by looking at other bodies of knowledge (notably the Veda) that are more experience- and subjectivity-based.

• These bodies of knowledge may well become subjective or "mind" sciences, combining the best aspects of the subjective and objective approaches to gaining knowledge.

• Intelligence is intimatly associated with human consciousness, and in particular the element of human subjectivity or the experience of the "I."

• Knowledge can be said to arise from the togetherness of three elements—knower, known, and process of knowing—and is directly related to the structure of consciousness.

• In regard to simulating intelligence, AI will remain a discipline without a basis until the elements governing the functioning of consciousness at its ground state are discovered and made available for engineering use.

• AI represents the vanguard of objective computer science developments, but, without the elements of consciousness and subjectivity, it cannot have true intelligence.

- A symbol maps a descriptive construct (name) onto a larger, less directly manageable entity (form).
- Expert systems are thus like other software systems and can consequently be handled with traditional software-engineering approaches.
- There are many subtle differences between different classes of software tools. The subsequent chapters delineate the particularities and generalities of system developments using expert system tools.

## NOTES

[1] Charniak and McDermott, 1985, *Introduction to Artificial Intelligence*, p. 11.
[2] Newell and Simon's original work on heuristic programs at the Rand Corporation was called *Cognitive Simulation*, a quite appropriate descriptive title.
[3] Alan Turing, 1963, "Computing Machinery and Intelligence," in *Computers and Thought*, E. Feigenbaum and J. Feldman (eds.), pp. 1–35.
[4] A. Newell and H. Simon, 1976, "Computer Science as Empiricalazzz Inquiry: Symbols and Search," Communications of the ACM, vol. 19, no. 3.
[5] This statement is attributed to H. Simon in "The Shape of Automation for Men and Management," 1965, as quoted in Dreyfus and Dreyfus (1986).
[6] Alan Newell, 1982, "The Knowledge Level," in *Artificial Intelligence*, vol. 18, pp. 87–127.
[7] Refer to Maharishi Mahesh Yogi's "Bhagavad-Gita. A New Translation and Commentation Chapters 1–6" (Yogi, 1967) Appendix I for a description of the technique of Transcendental Meditation.
[8] A distilled essence of the Vedic philosophy, put into a framework accessible to the Western reader, can be found in *The Science of Being and the Art of Living* by Maharishi Mahesh Yogi (1966), Livingston Manor, NY: MIU Press.
[9] H. Dreyfus and S. Dreyfus, *Mind Over Machine: The Power of Human Intuition and Expertise in the Era of the Computer*, New York: The Free Press, 1986.

## FOR FURTHER READING

Baron, R. J. (1987). *The Cerebral Computer*. Hillsdale, NJ: Lawrence Earlbaum.

Dennett, D. C. (1981). *Brainstorms: Philosophical Essays on Mind and Psychology*. Scituate, MA: Bradford Co. (MIT Press).

Dreyfus, H., S. Dreyfus (1986). *Mind Over Machine: The Power of Human Intuition and Expertise in the Era of the Computer*. New York: The Free Press.

Haugeland, J. (ed.) (1981). *Mind Design: Philosophy, Psychology, and Artificial Intelligence*. Scituate, MA: Bradford Co. (MIT Press).

Minsky, M. (1986). *A Society of Mind*. New York: Simon & Schuster.

Searle, J. (1984). *Minds; Brains and Science*. Cambridge, MA: Harvard University Press.

Simon, H. A. (1981). *The Sciences of the Artificial*. Cambridge, MA: MIT Press.

Winograd, T., Flores F. (1986). *Understanding Computers and Cognition*. Norwood, NJ: Ablex.

Yogi, M. M. (1966). *The Science of Being and the Art of Living*. Livingston Manor, NY: MIU Press.

Yogi, M. M. (1967). *Bhagavad-Gita. A New Translation and Commentary. Chapters 1–6*. Baltimore, MD: Penguin Books.

# Chapter 3
# Recognizing Knowledge in Order to Select an Application

## SECTION HEADINGS



## OVERVIEW

The ability to recognize knowledge is the primary skill required of a knowledge engineer. Perceiving and understanding an expert's knowledge in terms of laws of nature create a useful perspective for formalizing knowledge. The next step is codifying the knowledge in a form appropriate for representation in the expert system. Knowledge chunk rules, or schemas, can be formulated in different ways, and general guidelines and strategies are provided to match formulations to specific applications. Central among the reasons certain categories of knowledge should or should not be implemented in an expert system is the benefit of an appropriate expert systems application. The issues of development time and cost are discussed, resulting in a summary of features to look for in candidate expert system applications.

## 3-1. SELECTING THE EXPERT SYSTEM APPLICATION

Selecting a suitable application problem is the first stage in the expert systems development life cycle. Although it is tempting to purchase an expert systems building tool and then look for problems the tool can manage, it is sound advice to scout out applications first. Any given application may require several tools to be used at various stages of its development from feasibility prototype to production system.

The process of choosing an application area is similar to a mini-prototyping of the expert system. In this process, the manager or knowledge engineer examines

- the feasibility of extracting knowledge from an expert or an existing set of rules
- potential encodings of this knowledge into one of the knowledge-representation schemes, e.g., rules, frames, objects
- the payoff from developing the system: capture of expertise and savings of costs and time
- the potential for integrating this new expert system with existing hardware and software

Much of the knowledge-engineering process is not fundamentally different from conventional systems analysis. The distinction is the domain of investigation, which, in expert systems development, is a corpus of human knowledge. Specifically, expert systems engineers deal with a domain of human cognitive/logical knowledge that can be represented in a specific, physical-symbol system of knowledge-representation structures and inference mechanisms. Choosing an appropriate application area is essentially a systems analysis approach applied to knowledge engineering. The programming techniques used to implement the expert system are similar to those used in other software-engineering projects involving complex data structures (particularly list-oriented ones) and sophisticated logic control structures.

A number of criteria should be used in sizing up a potential expert systems application. Is the application area primarily cognitive/logical? Does a set of rules or formulas for solving the problem already exist? Are there experts who routinely solve the problem? How long does it take the expert to solve the problem? What is the degree of uncertainty in the problem? Is management commited to capturing expertise for problem solving, maintaining corporate knowledge, and training novices? Is the development cost-effective? These and other application-selection issues are examined in this chapter. The reader is invited to

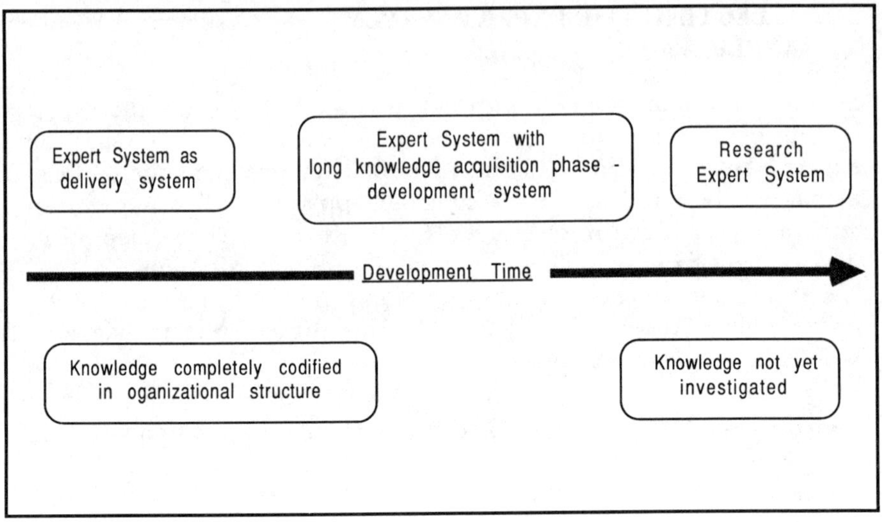


Fig. 3-1. Knowledge readiness and time of expert system development.

step into the first stage of the development cycle and consider potential applications.

A key consideration is the current completeness of the knowledge to be encoded in the expert system. If, for example, a manual for managing oil spills in an oil refinery exists, but is not widely used because the knowledge is not easily accessible, then an expert system could provide an immediate *delivery vehicle* for the application. If the application area has had little or no formalization of knowledge, however, then a skilled knowledge engineer will have to begin this work from scratch. This engineer may be required to spend anywhere from 6 months to 2 years or longer systematically debriefing the experts, building prototype systems, and refining the body of domain facts and heuristics. Such an extended knowledge-acquisition phase may make the project infeasible. Figure 3-1 indicates the positioning spectrum for potential applications in terms of their ripeness for implementation. At one end of the spectrum are the delivery vehicle developments, and at the other are the high-cost, long-duration developments, which are more appropriately described as research projects.

In the remainder of this book, the generic term *rule* will be used to indicate an abstract representation-independent quantum of knowledge. The term *IF/THEN rules* will refer to the knowledge structures found in the specific rule-based representations. Most of the commercially available expert system building shells reviewed in Chapter 5 are *rule-based* development tools using IF/THEN-type condition/action rule statements for knowledge representation. Expert systems programming languages, such as LISP and its derivatives, use a general rule-like structure in relating object/attribute pairs in their list-oriented data structures. PROLOG is even more rule-oriented. *Frame-based* or *associative network-based* development tools also represent general rule types in the form of relationships (e.g., "IS A") that structure frame or network hierarchies, possibly with procedural attachment and associated inheritance properties. Because all these different knowledge forms can be called *rules*, this generic term will be used to include the class of all knowledge-structuring relationships (see Fig. 3-2), including, but not limited to, condition/action IF/THEN rules.

The principle activity of the knowledge engineer is recognizing the generic rules, or chunks of knowledge, in the problem domain. The expert's thought and action constitute much of the area of study. Analyzing the knowledge structure of potential application areas may result in one of three outcomes.

| Representation Strategy | Description |
|---|---|
| Condition/Action Pairs | chains of IF/THEN rules form inferencing sequences |
| Frames | organized structured knowledge chunks linked into hierarchies or heterarchies |
| Associative or Semantic Networks | elementary symbolic knowledge chunks linked by relationship arcs into graph-like structure |
| Procedural Programming | standard nested subroutine programming strategies |
| Logic Programming | programming schemes based on first-order predicate logic |
| Object-Oriented Programming | self-contained "object" knowledge structures communicating via message passing |
| Access-Oriented Methods | "demons" or "triggers" automatically fired as a set of conditions become true |
| Blackboard Strategies | independent "knowledge sources" asynchronously contribute and extract data from a multipartition blackboard |

Fig. 3-2. Expert systems representations for generic knowledge rules.

- The domain is unsuitable for expert system development,
- The domain is too complicated for economical and timely development with current expert system technology, or
- Feasibility prototyping of the system should proceed.

In the last case ("leap now rather than wait"), the expert system building tools and support environment tools appropriate for the application can be selected, and at least pilot development can proceed.

## 3-2. CAPTURING KNOWLEDGE BY IDENTIFYING LAWS OF NATURE

The next three sections outline some general strategies for finding and capturing knowledge. First, the knowledge engineer must be able to identify and express succinctly the problem domain expertise for the expert system. To do this, the knowledge engineer must know what to look for and how to look for it. This can be viewed fundamentally as a process of identifying the laws of nature governing the domain area. Although we do not usually think in this way, the problem-solving rules of the expert's cognitive/logical/rational thought process can be appreciated as laws of nature functioning within a mental stratum of man's awareness. The human thought patterns and mental capacities used in acquiring, organizing, and accessing knowledge are not commonly described as laws of nature, but these laws are concrete structures within man's consciousness and intelligence. The knowledge engineer must look for these logical rules or laws of nature expressed in the expert's thought, as well as the laws representing the players and actions in the domain field. As noted in Chapter 1, these laws are most clearly identified in the mature physical sciences, such as biology and chemistry. Rather vague rules evolve to become more like laws as the knowledge in the area matures. The more complex and abstract laws of nature governing the activity of softer sciences, such as the social and psychological sciences, can and have to be identified as well. The perspective of distilled rules and heuristics as concrete laws helps to set the stage for rule hunting.

Although knowledge engineers may tend to perceive these laws as residing in the expert's subjective realm, the laws tend also to have corresponding objective external status. This was noted in the previous chapter in terms of the intuitive insights geniuses have, scientist and nonscientist, that are experimentally verified later. Large-molecule chemistry illustrates the point of soft rules evolving into hard laws. DENDRAL at Stanford University addresses the interpretation of mass spectroscopic and nuclear magnetic resonance results for identifying large molecules. The diagnosis of small molecules is an established hard science, for which the governing exact laws of nature are well understood. Diagnosing large molecules, however, commonly proceeds with inexact rules of thumb that tend to be expert-specific. There is a boundary dividing the exact sciences from the inexact sciences that moves forward each year. Items that used to be covered by inexact rules of thumb have repeatedly been refined and are now addressed by exact laws of nature. Although the heuristic approach is commonly considered a subjective process dependent on the expert, the job of the knowledge engineer is to externalize this process and move it into the realm of an objective set of rules.

A common misunderstanding is that systematic knowledge is the sole property of modern science. To clarify the process of establishing knowledge, it is useful to see how cultural traditions based on a set of principles have been handed down from generation to generation. The guilds of medieval Europe maintained and refined the knowledge relevant to such exacting skills as carpentry and stone masonry through the master/apprentice relationship. Rules governing an area of life are often layered, sometimes nearer the surface and more obvious, and sometimes at deeper levels requiring more investigation to find. Much of traditional folklore surrounding food and eating hygiene in the home is based on sound principles for maintaining life and health. Many cultures recommend a variety of prescriptions to heal diseases, such as herbal or other treatments, that are just now receiving scientific attention. If a group of experts can agree on a body of knowledge, then that body can probably be characterized as a set of rules or laws. The laws governing societal customs may not be as simple in nature as the laws of physics, but as more and more of the conditional clauses are identified and refined, the laws can become accurate in their own right.

The point is that laws of nature govern the activity of all areas of life. The range of natural law is from the smallest subatomic particles to the largest clusters of supergalaxies, from the activities of a single cell to the activities of the earth's family of nations. Each discipline chooses a particular stratum of life and investigates the laws of nature functioning within it. Each problem a human expert solves is in itself a miniature discipline governed by a specific set of rules or laws. Each society throughout the world has a broad range of technical and nontechnical knowledge that can be formalized as laws. The more advanced societies tend to own larger bodies of precisely structured knowledge, but the value of traditional folklore should not be underestimated. This viewpoint of the ubiquity of the laws of nature should be adopted by the industrial manager or knowledge engineer when sizing up prospective application areas and deriving the rules of expertise.

When searching for the laws of nature that represent accurately an area of knowledge, the knowledge engineer must look for the underlying principles and not be sidetracked by the individual facts. For instance, it is possible to describe the behavior of the stone thrown in the air in the opening illustration of this chapter by detailing the position and velocity of the stone at every single instant of flight. Not only does one path have many points, but also any given stone could follow many possible paths. A better technique is to condense the infinite number of paths and points into a generalized law of nature (e.g., $\underline{s} = \underline{u}t + 1/2\ \underline{a}t^2$) that represents the stone/air/thrower system. Mathematical equations have proven themselves over the centuries to be an ideal way of documenting laws of nature. What is important is to select the right kind of mathematics for the problem area. The knowledge expressed in the equation for the stone gives the position of the stone at any moment in time, and subtle transformations (differentiation) on the equation yield the object's velocity and acceleration as well. The relevant knowledge of the stone's trajectory, assuming no other external forces, such as air resistance, are active, is found in this classical physics space/time equation.

In the process of analysis necessary for evaluating potential expert systems applications, the knowledge engineer must be careful not to get lost in the myriad facts and details of the domain knowledge. Analysis should proceed by looking for the unifying principles that provide connections between the component parts or facts of the system. An example of the confusing nature of "facts" is found in a large oil refinery, where each category of petroleum distillate from bitumen to liquid petroleum gas is handled by a different organizational department. At first sight each petroleum compound appears to be different, having its own procedures and guidelines, and therefore its own unique and exclusive set of knowledge. Further research, however, shows that molecular weight is a key variable that determines many of the procedures for handling the compound. Once the concept of *recipes* is added to remove the ambiguity from mixed molecular weights, as found in blended fuels, the myriad facts can be condensed to a considerably smaller set of universal rules. An example of a universal rule that is the same for all molecular weights is the principle of conservation of mass; it is common to all transformations in the oil refinery. Volume by itself, however, is not conserved throughout the refinery, as it is a function of temperature and pressure (students of physics will remember $PV = RT$). Different departments may refer to the same rule by different names, but in reality, as Shakespeare noted, "a rose by any other name would smell as sweet."

The distinction between this kind of knowledge evaluation and traditional systems analysis is the object of investigation. For the expert system, the object is the set of rules that characterize the expert's logical thinking process. In more traditional areas of systems analysis, progress can usually be made without considering the subjective realm. In contrast, a viewpoint and framework for expert systems knowledge must be identified before the application area can be analyzed and represented. If the expert relies too heavily on hunches, intuition, or common sense, which cannot be easily laid out in a set of rules and relationships, even using uncertainty, then the application may not be suitable for expert system development.

## 3-3. EXPRESSING LAWS OF NATURE AS IF (. . . = . . .) THEN (. . . = . . .) RULES

Systems analysts are familiar with defining component modules and their interactions to describe a computer application. In conventional programming, these interactions are usually structured in the form of a module hierarchy activated by procedure calls. Such top-down or bottom-up procedure-oriented design techniques may also work for some expert systems applications, but others require symbolic structuring forms more closely aligned with the rules of logic used in human thought.

Experts often express their knowledge informally as "Well, since *A*, *B*, and *C* have occurred, so then I do *E* and F," "While *X* or *Y* is present, we proceed with *Z*," or "If *A* and *B* or element *C* is present, then this indicates that the fault is probably in *D*." These sets of conditions and actions can be captured in the form of IF/THEN rule statements. This is the most widely used modality for representing knowledge in current expert systems technologies. For instance, consider the following example of an expert's knowledge represented in a chlorine vaporizer expert system[1]

IF the steam mass flow is less than the steam-to-chlorine ratio times the chlorine vapor mass flow,
AND the output of the level controller is greater than 80%,
AND the level flow deviation alarm is not on,
AND the level is not increasing,
AND the chlorine feed mass flow is greater than the chlorine vapor mass flow,
AND the standard deviation of the vapor mass flow is less than 5%,

THEN send this message: CHLORINE LEVEL SIGNAL IS PROBABLY ERRONEOUS. CLOSE CHLORINE FEED VALUE IMMEDIATELY.

This specific rule of thumb, as a localized knowledge chunk or law of nature, indicates an action-oriented relationship between the steam mass flow, steam-to-chlorine ratio, the chlorine level, level controller, level flow deviation alarm, the chlorine feed mass flow, and the vapor mass flow. The action based on these relationships suggests that the chlorine level signal is probably wrong and the chlorine valve should be closed.

Three other examples of human logical/expertise expressed in the form of IF/THEN rules are given below. The first is from MYCIN, an expert system that diagnoses blood infections.[2] The second rule is from SACON, a system for determining structural analysis strategies for structural analysis engineering.[3] The last rule gives advice on drill sticking for oil rig drilling in the DRILLING ADVISOR expert system.[4]

**MYCIN RULE**

IF (1) The stain of the organism is grampos, and
(2) The morphology of the organism is coccus, and
(3) The growth conformation of the organism is chains
THEN There is suggestive evidence (0.7) that the identity of the organism is streptococcus.

**SACON RULE**

IF The material composing the substructure is one of metal,
The analysis error (in %) that is tolerable is between 5 and 30,
The nondimensional stress of the substructure is greater than 0.9, and
The number of cycles the loading is to be applied is between 1000 and 10,000,
THEN It is definite that fatigue is one of the stress behavior phenomena in the substructure.

**DRILLING ADVISOR RULE**

[This rule applies to episodes and is tried to find out whether there is a conical hole in the well.]

IF (1) The action being done just prior to the occurrence of the problem is drilling,
(2) The formation at the bottom of the hole is a hard formation,
(3) The type of bit used when the problem occurred is one of: jet-roller-bit cvl-roller-bit
THEN There is suggestive evidence (.5) that there is a conical hole in the well.

If rules of expertise can be formally expressed (mathematically or logically) as laws of nature, then missing information can be noted and perhaps deduced by the relationships expressed in the law. The classical physics rule $\underline{F} = m\underline{a}$ presents the possibility of determining either the force ($F$), mass ($m$), or acceleration ($a$) of a body when the other two values are known. This one law of nature could be written as three rule forms

IF ($F$ is known) AND ($m$ is known) THEN ($a = F/m$) or
IF ($F$ is known) AND ($a$ is known) THEN ($m = F/a$) or
IF ($a$ is known) AND ($m$ is known) THEN ($F = ma$).

When laws are broken into their smallest possible parts, the inference engine is free to combine them as necessary to produce the desired results. For example, $\underline{F} = m\underline{a}$ could have been inserted into $\underline{s} = \underline{u}t + 1/2\underline{a}t^2$ to give $\underline{s} = \underline{u}t + 1/2\underline{F}t^2/m$, but such a formulation would have made the system less flexible and have made deduction harder for the inference engine. In the DRILLING ADVISOR rule above, if the type of bit used in the drilling is not known, the system can either ask for the information or possibly deduce the information based on other facts in the knowledge base. In this way, the expert's rules can provide a template for the expected knowledge. Frame representations in particular, to be discussed in Chapter 4, are specifically designed to structure the incomplete knowledge of expertise.

Systems analysts and programmers are quite familiar with writing high-level code using IF/THEN/ELSE statements. Looking for expert knowledge is not necessarily a foreign task when one is familiar with high-level language coding. In fact, some early expert systems were criticized as nothing more than a large list of conventional IF/THEN statements managed by a rule interpreter. There are, however, important differences. Both the MYCIN and DRILLING ADVISOR rules above have a certainty factor associated with the result. Also, the condition elements in the premise part of the rule (IF) may have certainty factors as well. This type of uncertainty, characteristic of the real world and easily managed by the human expert's qualitative reasoning, is very difficult to deal with in traditional programming languages. Most expert system shells have built-in non-Boolean models for dealing with these kinds of uncertainties, which continue to be functional even if the expert's knowledge requires 1000 rules. It is very likely (confidence factor 0.95) that the profitable expert systems applications the reader is considering will involve uncertainty to capture the expert's knowledge.

Although the IF/THEN-rule-based representation format has been choosen for this discussion, the principles discussed also apply to other representation schemes, such as frames (schemas) and objects. Frames may be required when the packets of knowledge in the domain come in larger chunks and include a number of smaller, localized pieces of knowledge. IF/THEN-type rules, or procedures, are often attached to or included in frames to capture the actions. The same can be said for object-oriented systems where individual knowledge-chunk objects have clearly defined message-passing interfaces to express the actions between the knowledge-chunk objects. The examples in Chapter 4 and Chapter 6 will make these points clearer.

## 3-4. HUMAN KNOWLEDGE VERSUS MACHINE KNOWLEDGE

When selecting the most appropriate representational method for an application's knowledge it is worth remembering the points made in Chapter 2, regarding the way knowledge is structured in human consciousness. From a practical viewpoint the engineer can select from two main knowledge representations, namely, rules or schemas. Within the category of schemas, or frames, a variety of alternative forms cover a range from attached rules to self-acting objects. The knowledge the knowledge engineer is structuring in the machine is only an approximation of the human expert's patterns. The word *approximation* is key here, because it explains why those searching for perfection become frustrated with their inability to map human structures onto machine structures. Often there is a feeling that 10% more work will make the model function as desired, but the key point is that, if the application is too ambitious, no amount of work will reach the goal. Knowledge engineers have to learn to make compromises.

Recall from the discussion in Chapter 2 that human knowledge is essentially a subjective experience. Knowledge is not simply a set of facts neatly tucked away in one corner of the mind or brain, but is an experiential phenomenon arising from the holistic functioning of consciousness. Consciousness is the medium upon or within which the expert spreads out his constructs and reasons with them. An expert's knowledge is structured in his consciousness. The consciousness in which expertise abides is a multidimensional, time-varying, superfluid-like field phenomenon. Consciousness cannot be viewed as a single, flat invariant sheet. It is much more like a rubber sheet that can stretch or be compressed, except that it contains a multidimensional space. The topological transformations of consciousness differ from those mathematics transformations used in rubber sheet geometry, in that they are continually restructuring and reorganizing the contained multiple dimensions of knowledge to increase the access and utilization power from within. As discussed in the previous chapter, the expert's knowledge has a self-referral quality that allows it to produce new and more powerful structures of knowledge from within itself. Awareness of this phemonenon has recently spread to educational theory: an assimilation period of a month or more is given after a set of classes to allow the student's awareness to structure the new knowledge into a more meaningful whole before an examination.

To a very small degree, this field phenomenon may be modeled as an associative network of distributed information. Many AI researchers have assumed that they can model consciousness with a flat, two-dimensional, invariant sheet. Obviously two dimensions are not enough, so the questions arises as to how many time-varying dimensions would be needed in a data structure or knowledge representation scheme to capture the knowledge imbedded in this most flexible medium of consciousness? Even the three-dimensional structure of the neuronal brain, if it could be replicated, is at least one level of indirection removed from the real field of knowledge, the field of consciousness. Only future research will reveal how complex the data structures will need to be to begin to handle deep knowledge. This complex difference between human and machine knowledge does not simplify the problem of searching out and encoding knowledge.

Even though the expert's knowledge is organized and structured in his consciousness, this pattern of organization and structuring may not be a part of the expert's conscious awareness. When searching for a suitable expert systems application, the knowledge engineer must look beyond what the expert says he does to a way to formalize that knowledge in a set of rules. IF/THEN rules, schemas, or objects, are primarily methods for representing shallow knowledge. If the system needs to represent deep knowledge to be functional, it may not be suitable for expert systems development.

## 3-5. KNOWLEDGE COMES IN LAYERS

As discussed in Chapter 2, knowledge depend on the knower, known, and process of knowing. Thus, as the object of knowledge or system under investigation changes, so does the knowledge involved. Similarly, the knowledge depends to a great degree on the perceiver of that knowledge. The domain expert may see his expertise quite differently than the knowledge engineer would.

Consider first the concept of different levels of the object or system. Perception of an object, such as a table, changes depending on whether it is viewed at a mechanical, chemical, atomic, or nuclear level. Different laws of nature operate on each of these levels, and, from a pragmatic perspective, each of these levels of the "table system" can be viewed as totally different sets of rules. In fact, if all the nuclear properties are known, then the atomic properties can be inferred. Similarly each grosser level is a function of the subtler level beneath it. Another property of these layers from physics is that deeper levels are more powerful and more universal than surface layers. This applies to layering of other types of knowledge as well, as noted in Chapter 1, in the discussion on layering of software. The important point for the expert systems developer is to investigate the level of the object or system most appropriate for the application in hand. If the consideration is too superficial, the rules may not yield the necessary power. If it is too deep, the rules may likewise be too primitive to be applied.

To illustrate layered objects, consider an expert system to advise on the procedures for an oil refinery catalytic cracker ("cat cracker") turnaround. When a turnaround occurs the plant is renovated, improved, and reassembled for another 3 to 5 years of duty. The turnaround is usually a stressful time for everyone involved because every day the plant is down the refinery loses production. To model the cat, most of its workings are of a mechanical or physical chemical nature, but some of the areas, such as the chemical transformations controlled by the catalyst, fall under chemical engineering. Of the different disciplines mentioned here, chemical engineering is the deepest level, then physical chemistry is more toward the surface, and then mechanical engineering. What the knowledge engineer has to do is to make as many rules as possible operate at the mechanical level, followed by fewer physical chemical rules, and then by even fewer chemical transformation rules. If everything was modeled with chemical understandings at the level of the behavior of individual molecules, the expert system could be far more complex than necessary.

A second consideration of levels of knowledge concerns the human subjective side. The human information-processing system, as discussed in Chapter 2, has layers of perceiving and processing information through the senses, mind, intellect, ego, and so on. The flavor of the knowledge characterization is different depending on which of these modalities are dominating in the expert or knowledge engineer's awareness. Clarity of wakefulness also affects the state and quality of the knowledge. If people are wide-awake, then the system has a chance to be seen as it really is, but if they are sleepy, perception of the system can be radically altered. Knowledge is different in different states of consciousness. Sensory knowledge can also contradict mental knowledge. People in a train may perceive the landscape to be moving and themselves to be sitting still. Once the mental or conceptual thinking level is applied to the perceptions of riding in the train, or the movement of the sun in the sky the observers' deeper levels can see that really they are moving and the landscape is fixed. Moving on to the intellectual level of the observer, a whole new set of conclusions may be reached concerning the movement of the earth around the sun. The conclusion the expert systems developer should understand is that all these layers and perspectives on knowledge are true to some degree for one purpose or another.

If the project is to build an expert system for designing solar homes, one needs to precisely know the sun's path for all times of the year to maximize energy intake. For this system, it is simpler to use rules or laws of nature based on the premise of an earth-centered, rather than heliocentric, solar system, even though the latter provides a deeper understanding of the actual reality. Sensory-level knowledge of the sun's movement is more appropriate than intellectual-level knowledge for the specific solar home design problem. The rules or equations of knowledge encapsulated in the expert system do not have to be the final word in ultimate knowledge for the discipline as a whole. What is needed is a practical engineering orientation to evaluate the appropriate level of investigation needed for the application.

Some applications may require several layers of knowledge organized in a hierarchy. The MOLGEN expert system for designing or planning gene-cloning experiments has three planning spaces arranged in a hierarchy, as shown in Fig. 3-3.[5] In the *laboratory space,* lab steps are carried out on *genes, bacteria, enzymes,* or *antibiotics,* using the functions of *sort, screen, merge,* and *transform.* The *design space* plans by forming and executing lab steps according to such criteria as propagating constraints or proposing goals. The *strategy space* does *metaplanning* (it plans the plans) by selecting and executing design steps according to heuristics, such as *focus* the design or *guess* a design step. The knowledge engineer should be on the lookout for such vertical, as well as the more common horizontal, knowledge structures.

Another important result pertaining to layering of rules is that permutations and combinations of basic rules create new rules for the expert systems designer. Returning to a physics example, all electromagnetic theory can be condensed into just Maxwell's four equations. From these four, such things as electromagnetic waves can be deduced, leading to much of the broad fields of optics, radio astronomy, X-ray technology, and so forth. To expect an expert system to routinely deduce optics from Maxwell is asking too much. A better approach is for the human expert to spell out the permutations and combinations in detail and formulate them as new additional rules in the base system. The number of rules of thumb that need to be specifically encoded into the expert system for designing electric motors may rise into the thousands, even though they all spring from one basic set of four

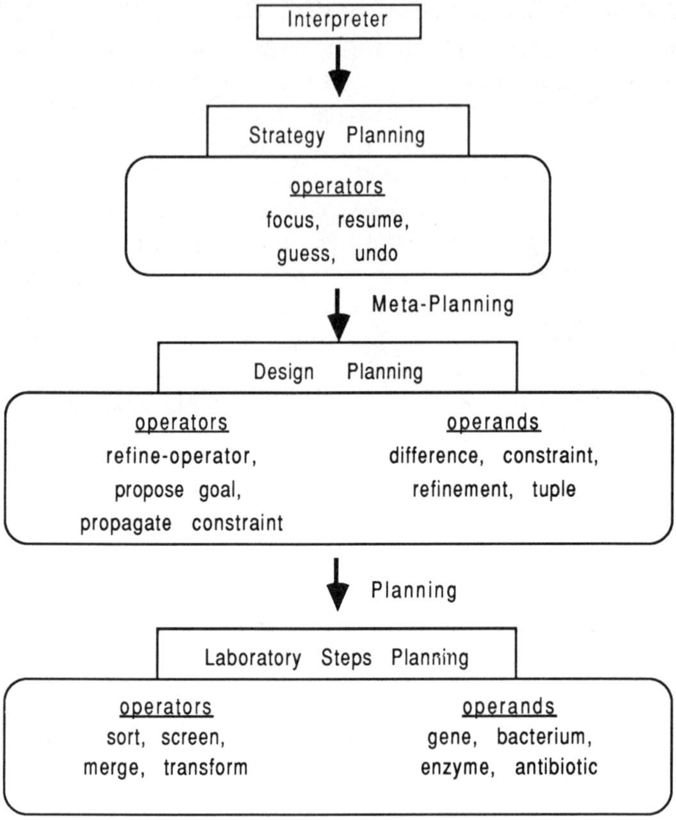


Fig. 3-3. The planning hierarchy in MOLGEN (adapted from Stefik, 1981a).

equations. This example from the field of electric motors can be seen as one level in the tree of electromagnetic theory. The tree has the base of its trunk at Maxwell's level, but its branches are many and varied. This discussion leads again to one of the major conclusions of this chapter: for an expert system to work, it has to be based on a very narrow field—the exact level of the experts' domain knowledge, the formulation of the domain task, and the perception of the problem by the experts must be specified in advance and adhered to while the system is developed.

## 3-6. CAPTURING, MAINTAINING, AND CONTINUING EXPERTISE

Now that some of the more general features of knowledge suitable for expert systems implementation and strategies for finding this knowledge have been pointed out, what are some specific heuristics to use in looking for an application area? The following points indicate some of the possible directions.

Human knowledge and expertise are among the main resources of any industry. Unfortunately, these resources can slip away due to resignation, transfer, firing, or death, allowing much of the company's wealth of knowledge to degrade over time. Application areas where this loss of expertise may happen are prime targets for expert systems development.

The Aldo in a Box expert system developed by Campbell Soup Company and Texas Instruments illustrates this point. Aldo Cimino, a 44-year veteran hydrostatic and rotary sterilizer debugging expert, was nearing retirement. The 150 rules in Aldo in a Box encapsulated Cimino's knowledge and allowed it to be maintained by the corporation after his retirement. This type of knowledge capture is particularly important in industries where product development life cycles are very long, such as the 20-year cycle often found in the aerospace industry. Boeing Computer Services, for example, has made a major investment in expert systems, primarily due to the long aircraft product life cycles. Expert systems such as Aldo in a Box allow a company to condense and formalize its knowledge assets compactly. Such formalized systems can also be used as intelligent assistants to experts or as training devices for novices.

The desire for duplicating expertise can bring up other areas for expert systems development. An insurance company may have offices in 20 cities, but only one expert to handle exceptional disability claims. An expert system could multiply this expert and make his knowledge simultaneously available in 20 cities at once. Such systems can be designed to function either as a "full expert" or as an "assistant." The latter approach is often more viable, because then the most complicated claims requiring human attention can be automatically sent to the expert himself.

Other applications areas may be found by examining expertlike functions that must be performed in hazardous or remote environments. The primary applications for industrial robot arms are the "3H" (heavy, hot, hazardous) and "3D" (dull, dirty, dangerous) environments. Robots are being placed in an increasingly wider range of work environments not well suited to humans, ranging from sewer systems inspection, to nuclear waste cleanup, to extraterrestrial exploration. The Rover 1 and Rover 2 robots developed at Carnegie-Mellon University visited the radioactive basement at the Three Mile Island nuclear power plant and reported on the damage. Expert systems are needed to provide simulated intelligence in these types of advanced robotic applications. As an example from another area, PC-based paramedic expert systems could be developed and shipped to underdeveloped nations or remote isolated areas, such as the polar regions. The possibilities for expert systems development in these types of domains are just beginning to be realized.

Project areas where company policies are not formalized provide other opportunities for expert systems development. The customer-service department of a large department store may have a variety of return/refund policies for different products. These policies often change, and new products may be added or others removed. An expert system used as both a troubleshooter for special customer-service claims and as a training aid for customer-sevice employees can help formalize the history of the institution's policies beyond the span of current management.

Existing systems analysis tools can provide good techniques for discovering potential application fields. A system designer may incorporate one or more expert systems into a larger information system (IS) to handle some of the more complicated processing tasks. Consider the following example. IBM's Business System Planning (BSP) methodology, sometimes referred to as the *iron cross,* allows areas of complex data structures to be identified and bounded. The approach of BSP is to analyze and bound a broad candidate IS by proceeding in four steps to identify

1. the departments or people involved (users)
2. the activities or tasks performed by each user (activities)
3. the data needed to perform these activities (data types)
4. the current information systems that provide these data types (information systems)

A data type is defined as the user's view of a data element or set of data elements. The current information systems list usually covers a very wide range of tools, including such things as paper forms, blackboards with chalk, telephones, adding machines, messengers on bicycles, personal computers, and so on. The four lists are then organized on a single chart in the form of a cross (Fig. 3-4). The resultant four quarters, which are laid out on large sheets of squared paper, allow the interactions to be identified and documented.

- The upper right quadrant shows which IS provides which data types.
- The lower right quadrant details which activities need which data types before they can start.

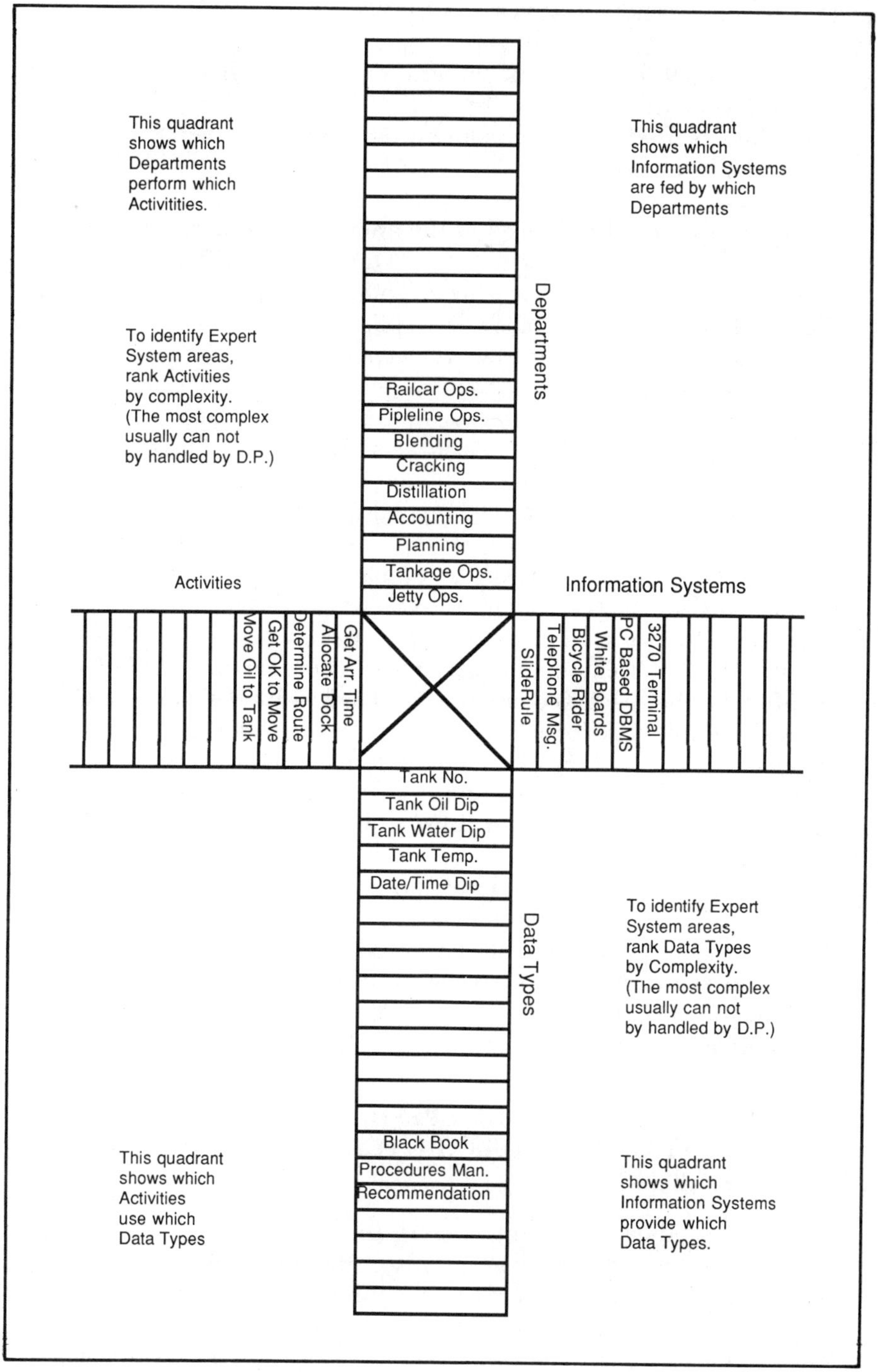


Fig. 3-4. Locating potential applications through system reorganization—IBM's business system planning.

- The upper left quadrant relates ownership, or driving, of information systems by department.
- The lower left quadrant shows which departments perform which activities.

Checkmarks should be placed in the appropriate squares to document the relationships among the four lists. One way to verify the accuracy of the resultant cross chart is to use Tom DeMarco's (DeMarco, 1979) Bubble Diagram methodology to duplicate the documentation of the flow of activities with their interconnecting data types.

Once the completed cross chart has been drawn up, the next step is to redraw it with just three axes, so that all or nearly all of the existing systems are replaced by one new information system. The phrase *nearly all* is the key to identifying candidate expert system applications. The best place to start is with the data types list. Certain data types are simple data elements with a single unique value in context. Other data types are complex assemblies of facts and rules that have been treated historically as one entity by the majority of users. A simple data element may be the identifier of a truck, whereas a complex data type may be a black book of procedures to follow in the case of toxic chemical spillage after a truck accident on the road. Keeping track of trucks with their unique IDs is a relativly simple task for information systems technology, but handling complex data structures has to be left to more appropriate technology. In addition to sorting the data types by degree of complexity, the other three axes may also be sorted using a similar criterion. As a result the application zones requiring advanced or complex technologies may be singled out. Many of the IS developments of the 1970s and early 1980s left these complexities unimplemented, allowing them to remain with. the same set of manual handling procedures that they always had. Now that expert systems technologies are available, many of these old "rejected advances" should be reanalyzed to see if significant returns on investment can now be obtained.

## 3-7. ISSUES OF ACCURACY, SPEED, REPEATABILITY, RELIABILITY, AND FLEXIBILITY

There are other motivating factors for expert system development beyond knowledge capture and transfer that may influence application selection. For instance, a police patrol car dispatcher expert system may provide faster and more accurate analysis of standard assistance requests than a human dispatcher. An expert system for business law could provide more consistently repeatable and reliable analysis of statutes than lawyers, not to mention saving the lawyer from monotonous noncreative work. XCON, the well-known expert system for configuring DEC computer systems, developed by Carnegie-Mellon University and Digital Equipment Corporation (Maynard, Massachusetts), performs at the level of a technical editor who examines and completes customer orders. Although a human editor may take more that 20 minutes to complete an order, XCON typically completes orders in less than 1 minute.

Speed, accuracy, and repeatability—the standard virtues of modern computer technology—can be put to good use in expert systems. But if an application area requires extensive exception handling then the area may not be a good candidate, due to the limited band of knowledge available in the expert system. The patrol car dispatching system may lack the flexibility to deal with infrequent natural disasters, such as an earthquake, for such events are out of its domain. The system, used as an assistant, can be instructed to immediately alert the human operator on duty to handle the 5% of emergencies beyond its knowledge. Human performance is far superior to machine performance in problem solving requiring the flexibility of generalized intelligence and a broad base of common-sense knowledge and reasoning. In these situations the human expert is faster and more accurate than the machine.

Application areas where reliability of knowledge is important should also be considered for implementation. Many factors affect the human expert's thinking process, including health, diet, family, superiors, and so on. Every corporation would like to have its top experts functioning at peak performance at least 8 hours a day, 5 days a week. Humans, however, have up-and-down cycles. They get sick and miss work. Computers, especially fault-tolerant computers, have demonstrated their ability to be on the job at full performance most of the time. The human expert may not always be thinking at peak efficienty; he may provide inconsistent performance based on factors beyond his control affecting his thought process, such as allergies, hay fever, or the common cold. Expert systems, though, can provide a means for making the experts' knowledge more consistent and reliable. Hiring many human experts might be thought to be an approach to provide backup. If an integrated circuit manufacturer, however, relies on the expert knowledge of four VLSI chip designers in making key decisions, there may be four different, and possibly inconsistent, views expressed. A single expert system could combine the knowledge of all four designers, resulting in reliable, consistent advice.

Machines generally produce more accurate, repeatable, and faster outputs in appropriate task areas than humans. Expert systems, like most experts, are not always 100% accurate. Users of any expert system application should be content with an accuracy around 95% depending on the sophistication of the rule set. If the application demands higher accuracy, say for a complex human-life-critical domain, it may not be suitable for expert systems development. Designers may be tempted to trust difficult and complex tasks, such as nuclear power station control or cruise missile dispatching, to expert systems, but there is a catch here. If the job is too critical to tolerate human errors, then it is likely to be exactly the wrong job to trust to an expert system. As mentioned earlier, expert systems may be allowed to act as independent agents in very limited domains where the liability is well bounded, but these dangerous tasks are not exactly limited domains with bounded liability.

Although the expert system speed criterion is adequate in the police car dispatcher system, an expert system guidance and missile firing system for fighter pilots or a process-control system in a volatile industrial setting may not have adequate speed. Interpretive LISP-based systems have a reputation for being slow. The pilot's system might need to be reduced to a hardware chip to increase its speed to acceptable levels. The process-control system may work in one expert system development but not another, due to speed differences. Obviously, potential applications for real-time expert systems must be analyzed very carefully.

New commercial tools are becoming available for dealing with complex real-time applications. For instance, the PICON (Process Intelligent Control System) developed by Lisp Machines, Inc. [1](Andover, Massachusetts), can augment and amplify existing distributed process-control systems containing up to 20,000 measurements and alarms.[6] The software runs on a specialized parallel-processing LISP machine produced by the manufacturer with both AI processing and conventional processors for interfacing with the process-control system. Measurements and alarms can be ordered and prioritized in the expert system, supporting the functions of process control and faulty sensor diagnosis and detection. Process control has become a focus of attention for candidate expert systems applications, but in spite of the new tools and interest, the designer should still bear in mind the limitations and drawbacks identified in this book.

## 3-8. ISSUES OF COST AND DEVELOPMENT TIME

Expert systems are not inexpensive to develop, and in many cases the bottom line in choosing an application is the payoff. Does the cost-benefit ratio or the return on investment justify the expense of developing and maintaining an expert system?

---

* Lisp Machines, Inc. went out of business in the latter part of 1987, due in part to the shift of expert systems applications to conventional hosts.

Managing oil loss in a refinery or scheduling hospital operating room use are two examples where high yields on investment are based on relative operating expenses and income factors. Developing an expert system for diagnosing leaks in a golf course's underground sprinkler system, however, may not be at all cost-effective. An expert system used for inventory analysis once a year in a small department store may not justify the time and energy needed for development. Then again, a daily production system used minute by minute to drive the corporation would be a strong candidate for development. The theme of this book, developing production expert systems, emphasizes selecting applications within the mainstream of a corporation's activity that have significant payback opportunities.

The PROSPECTOR expert system, which aids geologists in exploring for rare minerals, and the DRILLING ADVISOR, which assists the oil-rig driller in determing the causes of sticking drill bits, have both been highly cost-effective. These high-yield areas made them good candidates for implementation. A nonproducing oil rig, for example, may cost its company up to $1 million per day, and a shut down nuclear power plant costs about $500,000 per day.

Substantial time and cost resources are necessary to develop any significant expert system. Most production systems require anywhere from 2 man-years work on up, with a estimated 2 to 6 man-years of effort for small to medium-sized applications. These estimates may be reduced somewhat if there ia a precise match between the application and an existing expert system building shell tool. XCON is an example of another good yield choice. DEC's AI Technology Group claims the system saves the company roughly $18–20 million per year in manufacturing costs.[7] This savings has not come without cost; DEC has invested over 20 man-years in the project since its beginnings in 1979.

Experts tend to be very busy. Their time commands the highest rate within the company, yet a great deal of their time, and patience, is required to develop a system. If the expert is not available and willing to devote the required time, the application area should be avoided. Management must be willing to justify the risk involved in expert systems development, as well as the commitment to accept time and cost overruns if the project is not completed on schedule. Because expert systems technology is new, time and cost overruns are common and must be expected and accepted by management.

One of the most obvious means for controlling the time and cost outlay for development is by picking application areas where the knowledge is already partially or fully encoded. When a set of rules already exists, such as a procedural or training manual, the development can be contained as a delivery vehicle application. This approach can greatly reduce or eliminate the time needed for debriefing an expert and codifying the laws of nature governing the area. Another savings approach is to choose applications requiring only the shallowest knowledge. Those requiring more knowledge engineering to generate deeper knowledge structures can be developed later, possibly with the aid of more advance technologies (smarter tools). Managers should avoid taking on a long-term research expert system venture as the first project unless the corporation's resources and timeframe allow.

One ballpark approach to sizing up the cost and development time for a project is to start with Boehm's classic book, *Software Engineering Economics,* and then add between 1 man-hour and 1 man-week for the knowledge engineer to identify each rule. Usually the expert has to work with the knowledge engineer 25% of the time to maintain productivity. Level Five Research has encoded Boehm's *consolidated cost model* into the commercially available COCOMO1 expert system. Of course, 1 man-hour to 1 man-week per rule is a very rough figure. XCON's 3000 rules in 20 man-years is roughly equal to three rules per man-week. Complex medical expert systems tend to be nearer to one rule per man-week. Aldo in a Box, however, took closer to 1 hour per rule for a simple, bounded under-200 rule set. These estimates relate to the issues of the complexity of the application's knowledge structures—how close it is to being a hard science, and so on. Central to all estimation techniques is the need to quantize a field's knowledge, so that the raw facts for cost inferencing are available.

## 3-9. QUANTIZING A FIELD'S KNOWLEDGE

How do you determine the amount of knowledge necessary to capture the expertise of a field? Expert systems in the field have a range of anywhere from 25 to 10,000 rules, or knowledge chunks, in the knowledge base. Both the depth and the breadth of the knowledge influence the number of rules necessary.

IBM's System/38 planner has 120 rules (Stroebel et al., 1986), Aldo in a Box has 151 rules, SACON has 170 rules with 140 consultation parameters, and DIPMETER ADVISOR, a system for inferring subsurface geological structure from dipmeter drilling logs, has 90 rules with 30 predicates. MYCIN, the blood infection diagnosis system, has hundreds of medical domain facts plus about 500 rules. PROSPECTOR's knowledge base contains about 35 models with hundreds of nodes and about 100 rules arranged in an associative network. The Schlumberger PIES expert system for bipolar semiconductor fault analysis contains 342 failure types, represented as frames, together with about 600 associational links between the failure cases (Pan and Tenenbaum, 1986). Westinghouse's Process Diagnostic System (PDS) for diagnosing

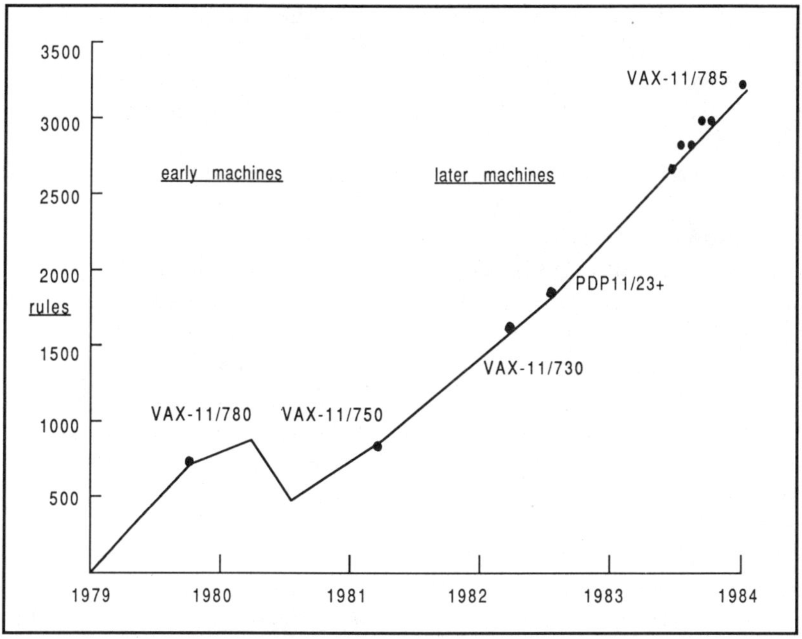


Fig. 3.5. Growth of the XCON Expert System (adapted from Bachant and McDermott, 1984).

gas turbine faults started as a 25-rule prototype in 1982 and has since grown to identify approximately 350 conditions using over 8,500 rules (Osborne, 1986)

XCON required something under 500 rules in 1980 to configure VAX-11/780 computer systems, as shown in Fig. 3-5. The hump in the graph where the number of rules dropped from about 1000 to 500 was a result of rewriting the system from the OPS4 language to OPS5. After four more years of work, at a rate of about 4 person-years per year, the system contained about 3000 rules and could configure 10 different DEC products. (Bachant and McDermott, 1984).

It may be difficult to tell how large a knowledge base is needed to represent the domain expertise. The above examples have been given so that some estimates may be possible by comparison. One approach to sizing a candidate application is to read the literature on a variety of similar systems. Another approach is to attempt to draw out a rough tree on paper at the outset. Even if the whole tree is not delineated, it is possible to extrapolate the number of rules by sizing a segment of the whole. Commonly, such a tree will have multiway branches in addition to some more standard two-way branches. The two-way splits can be coded as single IF/THEN/ELSE statements, but the multiple splits will need compound rules. Depending on the tool in hand, the application complexity may be proportional to the number of nodes, or it may be more closely coupled to the total number of two-way splits obtained from a decomposition of the nodes.

The boundaries of the task must be clearly defined at the outset of the project, but many systems such as XCON have continued to grow. If the application is not strictly bounded, then time and cost overruns become inevitable. Lack of bounding can also result in the noncompletion of any part of the project. Applications with a few hundred rules, in the range of, say, 200 to 700, are the most appropriate size for success. Success here means two things; completion within a managable time/cost expenditure, coupled with enough sophistication to provide a good return on investment. Very large systems (over 1000 rules) may experience unacceptable performance degradation and development overruns if the knowledge base cannot be sufficiently partitioned. Upgrading the system's hardware can alleviate this problem.

Another perspective on domain size can be gained by looking at the expert's response time in a problem-solving session. If the expert requires less than 10 minutes to solve the problem, the problem might be easily solved using less risky conventional programming techniques. At the other extreme, if the expert requires more than a few hours to solve domain problems, then the knowledge may be too complex for current expert systems development. Around 30 minutes to 1 hour for solution by a human expert seems to be a good middle ground to map onto a few hundred (e.g., around 500) rules. Even though restrictive guidelines have been given here, a clear trend throughout the industry is that the size of knowledge bases is increasing.

## 3-10. TIME AND COST ESTIMATES FOR EXPERT SYSTEMS DEVELOPMENT

This section will probably be one of the first turned to by project managers considering expert systems development and looking for hard-and-fast time and cost estimates. Unfortunately, there are no specific schedules available due to the short history of knowledge engineering. Although time and cost estimates have been available for years for standard DP software engineering, in such texts as *Software Engineering Economics* by Boehm, no such rules exist for the newer knowledge engineering. Very rough rules of thumb are about the best that can be offered.

As noted above, a small to medium-sized expert system can be expected to require some 2 to 6 man-years of effort. To fully integrate into a production environment will take longer. The following guidelines have been suggested for the different phases of the expert system development life cycle, as addressed in the main sequence of chapters in this book. Assessing a potential application may take anywhere from a few days to a few weeks of a project manager's time, including potential interviews with the field expert. Qualifying an application is well-handled by consultants limited to 10 days at the low end and rising to 30 or more days for sophisticated domains. If multiple domains are to be qualified, then a separate study should be allocated to each one.

Prototyping a system typically involves 1 to 2 man-years of the knowledge engineers and programmer's time, plus 0.5 man-year's work from the domain expert. If the domain knowledge is well documented and the goal of prototyping is to demonstrate feasibility of the tool set, rather than feasibility of the expert systems appraoch, then the allocated time can be cut dramatically. The minimum allocation for a prototype is about 1 month of senior systems analyst's attention, coupled with 2 months of a skilled programmer's time. Much of the protoyping phase is spent assembling the tool set items, such as compilers, graphics managers, disks, and so on, so any delivery delays will naturally delay the completion date.

Complete system building from the prototype to finished product can be expected to require anywhere from 2 to 5 man-years of effort. Robust production applications may require more time, due to the later phases where the finished system is brought into daily production. If the application is of a small delivery vehicle nature, then it may be possible to bring the effort level down to around 3 man-years, but, again, when time and cost overruns are included, the figure can easily climb back into the 6-man-year range. Putting the system into production after its full development is a complex matter to estimate, as only at this stage are many misconceptions identified. Only when every aspect of the system is working smoothly can the project really be said to be finished. Feedback loops, resulting in the repetition of early stages, can be inevitable if even one of the many guidelines addressed in this book is not adhered to. These time guidelines are presented as rough indicators only. Of course, there is always the possibility that robust applications may be completed in less time.

One simple rule of thumb is to anticipate between about 1 man-hour and man-week of time to develop each chunk of knowledge, or rule. Only in a very *shallow* protoype knowledge base or in a delivery vehicle environment can advances be made at the rate of a rule per hour. At the other end of the spectrum, if the problem is ill-defined and large, then a man-week per rule can be expected. If progress is slower than even this, it may be more appropriate to dramatically narrow the scope of the problem so that just a single phase is addressed in the first implementation.

The complexity of the knowledge base must be seen as a function of the complexity of the expert's domain knowledge. Early expert systems researchers (Stefik, 1981; Aikins et al., 1983) have outlined a series of incremental increases in knowledge-development difficulty. These incremental steps require increasingly complex and sophisticated knowledge-engineering techniques, most of which are beyond the range of currently available commercial tools (unless one programs entirely from scratch). The simplest problems require small solution spaces, the data are fixed and reliable, and the knowledge and heuristics are reliable. The increasing degrees of complexity are indicated by the following list of knowledge base needs

- Unreliable data or knowledge
- Time-varying data
- Large but factorable solution space
- No evaluators for partial problem solutions
- No fixed sequence of subproblems
- The subproblems interact
- Efficient means of guessing is needed
- A single line of reasoning is too weak
- A single knowledge source is too weak
- Representation methods are too inefficient to represent the knowledge, so entirely new representations must be generated.

Many of the expert systems developed under a number of these conditions are considered research systems and should be avoided, unless that is the aim of the application work.

The last step of estimating expert systems development is to translate the time figures into cost figures. As groundwork all the time figures should be organized on a project-planning tool, such as Apple's MacProject. All the tasks for each worker should be delineated to give a total number of person-days for each worker. Using a spreadsheet calculator, such as Microsoft's Excel, in conjunction with the project planner simplifies many of the arithmetic steps. The full dollars-per-day rate for each staff member, for consultants, and for other workers is then entered into the spreadsheet and multiplied by the person-days to give labor-dollars. Overhead factors, such as utilities, office rent, and payroll taxes, should not be forgotten as part of the full labor rates. Prices for equipment must also be included to give total costs. As is addressed in the following chapters, an expert system shell could cost anywhere between $100 and $60,000, and hardware could typically run between

$3,000 for an entry level IBM/PC or PS/2 and $500,000 for a configured VAX 8650 or IBM 4381. Other factors should be represented in the total cost: support environments for development tools, debuggers, interfaces with humans and other systems, sensor systems, signal processors, transducers, specialized hardware, and many other items, depending upon the application. Of course there are many rules of thumb for selecting and sizing computer configurations, but these are left to the discussions in subsequent chapters and with computer vendors. Even though computer software and hardware cost is nontrivial, it is still likely to be the largest and the most unavoidable expenditure.

## 3-11. APPLICATION CATEGORIES SUITABLE FOR EXPERT SYSTEM DEVELOPMENT

Several different types of examples of expert systems applications have been suggested in this chapter. In this section the suggestions for potential application areas and criteria for evaluating candidate applications are summarized.

Waterman (1986) provides a summary of potential application categories, as shown in Fig. 3-6. Any particular expert system may incorporate features from one or more of these categories in its problem solving. These types of problem categories may be found in such areas as agriculture, chemistry, computer systems, electronics, engineering, geology, information management, law, manufacturing, mathematics, medicine, meteorology, military science, physics, process control, or space technology areas.[8]

The following list of potential tasks based on the work of Dym (1984) illustrates some specific application areas of concern in aeronautical, civil, and mechanical engineering[9]

**Diagnosing, interpreting, and monitoring problems**

- assessing fatigue and wear in structures
- monitoring and diagnosing rotating machinery
- monitoring physical degradation of such infrastructure elements as piping networks and roads
- assessing failure for structures and soils
- choosing among modeling and analysis tools
- evaluating designs

**Planning and design tasks**

- Environmental assessment for proposed designs of structures, roads, and other infrastructure elements,

| Category | Problem Addressed |
|---|---|
| Interpretation | Inferring situation descriptions from sensor data |
| Prediction | Inferring likely consequences of given situations |
| Diagnosis | Inferring system malfunctions from observables |
| Design | Configuring objects under constraints |
| Planning | Designing plans of actions |
| Monitoring | Comparing observations to anticipated outcomes |
| Debugging | Prescribing remedies for malfunctions |
| Repair | Executing a plan to administer a prescribed remedy |
| Instruction | Diagnosing and rectifying student performance |
| Control | Controlling overall system behaviors |

Fig. 3-6. Generic categories of expert systems applications (adapted from Hayes-Roth et al., 1983).

- Selecting structural configuration for preliminary design,
- Planning for maintenance and rehabilitation of machinery, infrastructure, and other objects that wear and degrade over time,
- Configuring interactive devices in constrained spaces, such as the layout of all the parts in a coping machine or the distribution of equipment and materials around a construction site,
- Task is cognitive/logical—no common sense required,
- Desirable capture of knowledge for
- Maintaining expertise or corporate policy
- Duplicating expertise
- Transferring expertise
- Training novices
- Experts are better than novices at solving the problem,
- High yield supports time and cost commitments,
- Incremental development is desirable, allowing prototyping of a small subset of the knowledge,
- System can be carefully phased into use,
- Project is not in the critical path for other developments,
- Base of rules may already be available,

- The product will be accepted as creditable and authoritative,
- Some percentage of incorrect or nonoptimal solutions is allowed,
- Introduction of the system should not conflict with existing company policies or strategies.

**Specific domain and knowledge characteristics**

- Vocabulary of domain facts and heuristics has on the order of a few hundred concepts,
- Books, manuals, or other sources of information already encapsulate some or all of the knowledge,
- Experts are in general agreement about the knowledge,
- If more than one expert is involved, one has the primary role
- Problem takes the expert approximately 0.5–4 hours to solve,
- Data and test cases are available.

**Human commitment factors**

- Expert is enthusiastic and committed,
- Management is enthusiastic and committed,
- End users are enthuiastic about the product,
- End users understand the product's potential,
- Experts and knowledge engineers are available for the required time,
- Experts can effectively communicate the knowledge.

Applications that do not meet the specifications outlined in this chapter are probably not suitable for expert systems implementation. The earlier discussion on the limitations of expert systems, in Section 1–5, provides additional material on areas which are not yet viable application domains. A number of features not currently practical to implement may soon become so, notably, time-varying data, multiple lines of reasoning, and real-time systems. Instead of rejecting these more advanced applications outright, there is value in estimating when the appropriate intelligent tools will be available and then waiting for that time.

## 3-12. MAIN POINTS: RECOGNIZING KNOWLEDGE IN ORDER TO SELECT AN APPLICATION

- One of the easiest expert systems applications to implement is a delivery vehicle, where the knowledge has already been structured in an existing manual or book.

- The more diffuse the current structure of a domain of knowledge, the more time is needed to extract knowledge from the expert and place it in machine form.
- Once analyzed, domain problems may fall into one of three areas
  —The domain is unsuitable for expert system development,
  —The domain should be appropriate for future expert tools,
  —Feasibility prototyping of the system should proceed.
- A common misunderstanding is that systematic knowledge is the sole property of modern science. In fact many traditional sets of knowledge exist, such as what food is edible and what is poisonous.
- All areas of the universe's functioning are governed by laws of nature.
- Research has shown that, with different degrees of accuracy and success, the expert systems' knowledge representations are able to model laws of nature.
- Expert systems rules are somewhat like IF/THEN statements in programming languages, but they are nonprocedural and generally have an uncertainty factor to cater to inaccuracies.
- As a human expert's knowledge is structured in his multidimensional, fluid consciousness, knowledge engineers should expect two-dimensional, static machine representations to be only approximations.
- It is necessary to pick the appropriate level of the object and the subject to locate the best rules for a particular application.
- Various traditional systems analysis methodologies may be employed to locate areas of a corporation with highly complex data structures, areas that may be suited to expert systems implementations.
- Expert systems can be faster and more accurate and can provide more repeatable results than human experts.
- Human experts, in contrast, are better at handling exceptional cases and situations requiring flexibility, common sense, or reasoning from first principles.
- Well-chosen expert applications tend to have good returns on investment, as such domain areas have generally not yet been "mined" by traditional computer technologies.
- The number of rules for a production application can range from 50 to 5,000 or more. The most appropriate size for managable success is a few hundred rules, say 200 to 700.
- Estimating an expert system development is similar to traditional software projects, but extra time must be added to extract knowledge from the expert.
- Extraction can proceed as fast as one rule per hour, but one rule per day is a more realistic figure for nontrivial projects.
- In selecting an application, the primary consideration is not the

actual domain (e.g., should it be medicine or tool diagnosis, etc.), but whether the qualities of the application are implementable with current technology.

## NOTES

[1] Rich Merritt, 1986, "Artificial Intelligence Tackles Industrial Tasks, *The Industrial and Process Control Magazine,* January, p. 42.
[2] E. H. Shortliffe, 1976, *Computer-Based Medical Consultation: MYCIN.*
[3] C. Rich and B. Buchanan, 1985, Expert Systems Tutorial No. 9—Expert Systems, Part 2, Conference Tutorial Program, Ninth International Joint Conference on Artificial Intelligence, p. 15.
[4] C. Rich and B. Buchanan, 1985, Expert Systems Tutorial No. 9—Expert Systems, Part 1, Conference Tutorial Program, Ninth International Joint Conference on Artificial Intelligence, p. 10.
[5] M. Stefik, 1981, "Planning with Constraints (MOLGEN: Part 1)," "Planning and Meta-planning (MOLGEN: Part 2)," *Artificial Intelligence,* vol. 16, pp. 111–140, 141–170.
[6] Rich Merritt, 1986, "Artificial Intelligence Tackles Industrial Tasks," *The Industrial and Process Control Magazine,* January.
[7] Dwight Davis, 1986, "Artificial Intelligence Enters the Mainstream," *High Technology,* vol. 6, no. 7, July, p. 16.
[8] Waterman, 1986, *A Guide To Expert Systems,* Reading, MA: Addison-Wesley, p. 40.
[9] C. L. Dym, 1984, "Expert Systems: New Approaches to Computer Aided Engineering," Intelligent Systems Laboratory Series ISL-84-2, Xerox Palo Alto Research Center, Palo Alto, CA, p. 28.

## FOR FURTHER READING

Hayes-Roth, F., Waterman, D. A., Lenat, D. B. (eds.) (1983). *Building Expert Systems.* Reading, MA: Addison-Wesley.
Waterman, D. A. (1986). *A Guide to Expert Systems.* Reading, MA: Addison-Wesley.
Hewett, J., Sasson, R. (1986). *Expert Systems 1986: USA and Canada.* Ovum, Inc., Princeton, N.Y.

# Chapter 4
# Strategies for Selecting Expert Systems Tools: Features and Other Requirements

## SECTION HEADINGS



## OVERVIEW

Having established the ground work for understanding expert systems technology and the concepts relevant to selecting an appropriate application, the next stage of the expert system development life cycle is to select appropriate tools for the job. Different tools may be needed for different phases of a project—from prototyping to development to production. For most projects, expert system development tools and user aids on the market can be employed (as opposed to high-level languages) to speed development time, lower costs, and raise the quality of the finished product. Even with expert system shells there will be some programming, but the emphasis of this book is on the many considerations that need to be thought through for a successful implementation, rather than on the details of programming syntax. In this chapter, general product features and strategies are discussed in preparation for the comparison of leading and emergent expert systems shell products in the next chapter. For this phase, the knowledge engineer has to analyze the selected application in terms of its tool feature requirements as a prerequisite to researching available tools.

## 4-1. SELECTING THE RIGHT TOOLS FOR THE PROBLEM

The previous chapter outlined tips for selecting suitable expert systems applications. Knowledge engineering was also introduced by describing the process of knowledge investigation and capture in potential application areas. Now that readers have had the opportunity to consider potential applications in their areas of interest, the discussion now proceeds to the second stage of the expert systems development life cycle. This process begins with identifying potential tool set features as a preamble to actual tool selection appropriate to the application for each subsequent stage of development. The first aspect of this phase is to consider general guidelines for identifying and evaluating features available in expert systems building tools and aids. The designer then is to view these possible features from the perspective of the selected application. Because the range of potential applications is very great, the discussion will focus on possible tool features and their benefits, rather than detailed examples for specific jobs. Readers will observe that most of the applications discussed are large production systems. It should not be forgotten however, that certain applications can comfortably fit on a machine the size of an IBM PC or PS/2. It is the tendency in the other direction, thinking that all applications can fit on PCs, that is dangerous. Two sample "case study" production applications with matching tool configurations are discussed at the end of Chapter 6.

Although expert systems building shell tools are being emphasized to expedite development, it is important to remember that a shell is not the only key tool needed in the development. The system development and use environments usually require broad and complete tool sets containing such things as user interfaces; interfaces with databases, spreadsheets, or graphics software; compilers; debugging aids; editors; knowledge-acquisition and entry aids; and so forth. Commercially available tools sets vary considerably in the type and quantity of support environment provided. The project manager should be careful to structure an appropriate, functional, and complete development environment for maximum efficiency in systems development and use.

Expert system builders must plan for the completed production system environment as well. An expert system, although completed in knowledge development, debugging, testing, and user interfaces, is not complete until it has become a part of the production environment itself. For this move to occur, various system interfaces must be designed and created. For example, the expert system usually has to be integrated with existing software and hardware. Manuals for using the system and forms for appropriate fact capture and entry must be developed. Training sessions must be organized, and educational materials prepared and tested.

Each completed production system will have its own unique characteristics and requirements. For instance, an auto accident insurance adjustment system may need to send adjusted claims reports to the insured, other parties in the accident (including their insurance companies and agents), state and local law enforcement agencies, and the company's own agents. Although paper handling on the prototype and early production models may not seem a problem, moving the system into full production can create a quantum leap in the requirements for paper-handling tools and procedures. Production use of the system could require new printing, folding, inserting, and mailing machinery, together with software to drive the system and maintain quality. Knowledge engineers may not be familiar with the world of finishing equipment, but if their application is successful they may become well-versed in the mail equipment offerings of Pitney Bowes (Stamford, Connecticut) and Bell & Howell (Evanston, Illinois). The vision of the expert system manager must encompass the totality of the development as well as the totality of the production environment. Key considerations include complete project analysis, implementation strategies, growth planning, and consideration of all the tool features needed at each stage in the development.

Project managers should resist the tendency to buy a particular expert system building product and develop any and all applications with that single generic product. A corporation that requires user software to be standardized to dBase III for database, Multimate for word-processing, and Lotus 1-2-3 for spreadsheet work will be tempted to choose one expert system building tool for all applications. This strategy should be avoided for expert systems work. Though database, word-processing, and spreadsheet operations may be fairly uniform throughout the company's departments, an extremely broad range of application-dependent requirements exist for expert systems, which influence the choice of the most appropriate tools. The cost and time outlays and the complexity of expert systems development demand that the chances for success be maximized and the risk be minimized. The central point here is to maximize the chances for the project's success by choosing appropriate tools. The way to do that is by fine-tuning the match between the tools and the application requirements in all stages of development and production. This is not to imply that a single, very flexible tool set may not work for many different applications, but to caution against a blanket use policy that might appear to save time and costs but could actually lead to greater costs, or jeopardize the project's success. More specifically, the price range for inferencing tools on essentially the same hardware ranges from $65,000, which can consume budget capital, to under $100. The $100 tool could save funds but is likely to lack the power and sophistication needed to produce successful applications.

Choosing an appropriate tool set is further complicated, because different tools may be needed at different stages in the development. A prototype system based on a small subset of the domain problem is usually necessary to assess the viability of the application area as well as the particular tools in use. If the development tools are not adequate or appropriate, others must be selected, and the prototyping repeated. Expansion to other more sophisticated tools may also be necessary as the knowledge base grows, as in the case of rewriting XCON from OPS4 to OPS5. Growth in the number of users is another key factor that can change the tool choice.

There are a number of other common-sense considerations as well. The actual development tools—hardware and software—should usually be kept separate from other production systems, e.g., mainframes, in use, due to the CPU and main memory-intensive requirements of symbolic processing. If such systems are mixed and the machine is overloaded, data integrity and reliability of production-use systems can be jeopardized. If previously purchased resources, such as a database machine, are used by the expert systems project without careful capacity planning, then problems can arise. Developing expert systems, especially real-time or embedded ones, in a mixed development and operations environment can frequently crash the production machine.

Another important consideration in tool selection is the issue of *porting*. If several environments are to be used for different phases of the project then software will have to be ported from one environment to another if rewrites are to be avoided. Porting can be particularly complex in the final life cycle stage when taking the application developed on, say, a fast symbolic-processing machine and compiling it to run on a standard production machine. Integration with other existing software also occurs at this time. Specialized AI LISP machines may provide the ideal development environment, but anything from PC/AT-type machines to mainframes may be the vehicle of choice for delivery of the production system. Tools for all three stages of the process—

prototyping, development, and the production environment—must be encompassed within the project manager's design.

Managers should also be on the alert for those problems that could result from the *success* of the newly developed expert system. Consider the following scenario. Suppose the delivery system is to be a single-user PC/AT operating under MS-DOS. When the system moves into production, it immediately receives good reviews, and management decides to expand to have three unconnected PCs running in parallel. Suppose that each PC is connected via modem and phone line to remote terminals, and users engage in the consultation service by calling in questions. The program asks questions of the user during consultation to generate its medical advice. During this dialogue, the program needs to know if the patient has, for example, some of the more obscure symptoms associated with a hernia. The nurse does not know this answer and must hang up to check with the doctor or examine the patient. To handle this pending problem, which is a key problem for many applications, the system must be able to store the current state of the consultation and then return to the same state when the nurse calls in again. The nurse may not get the same PC as before. Suddenly, there is a need for a multiuser, database system, operating under something like the UNIX operating system, to resolve the pending problem.

A truly successful expert system will probably not stop with only 3 users. An initial 3-user PC/AT XENIX configuration may grow to become 3 complete XENIX configurations, for a total of 9 users, which again reintroduces the pending problem. The next expansion may be to a series of MicroVAX IIs, each supporting 8 users. The next stage could require a 40-user 8650 VAX, and finally on to large Sierra IBM 3090s, so the entire medical staff, internal and external, has access to the system. In this scenario, the original expert system designed to run on MS-DOS has expanded to a large number of users via UNIX to MVS/XA or IX/370. The original design specifications in this example were completely unrealistic for the final large-scale delivery environment. Managers should be forewarned of such success problems.

This example illustrates the potential scope of the production expert systems development process. Managers must look far beyond the specific tool features discussed in the remaining sections of this chapter to the development and production system requirements as a whole to consider all the key questions. Which knowledge representation schemes are most closely aligned with the problem's architecture? Are database interfaces needed? What explanation facilities are required? Does the expert system need to be able to learn? Are management summary reports necessary for an analysis of the expert systems' conclusions? Is graphics the best way to represent the knowledge structures to the user?

Is an interface to accounting needed for billing? These feature questions must be supplemented by traditional systems analysis questions. Is the system going to be for single or multiple users? Must the system perform in real time? What response time is needed?

Some help in answering such inquiries is available from the expert systems vendors through either promotional materials or sales representatives. Managers should exercise their options to obtain all the information needed before purchasing tools. Vendors will often release proprietary information to well-established enterprises (e.g., Fortune 1000 companies) with large-scale buying power, upon receiving formal requests for information (RFI) and appropriate signed nondisclosure agreements. This type of technical information is often necessary to analyze potential interfaces with the company's current software packages. A formal request for proposal (RFP) may net the potential user a 30- to 60-day trial period with the product before acceptance and billing. This option should be exercised whenever appropriate.

Product managers should be aware that so-called *vaporware* (vaporware, though akin to hardware or software, is something that is promoted, but is not yet available for purchase) is no less prevalent in expert systems tools than in any other commercially available hardware or software area. A vendor's product-release date is not an ironclad guarantee of availability. Vendor's development schedules are not immutable. *Caveat emptor.* If an exciting, new product just coming on the market promises to be 20% faster or offers a new "improved" natural-language, knowledge-acquisition interface, the system designer or manager should seriously consider whether the new features are actually needed for the application at hand. Is the extra power really needed? Is the potential risk of buying a new product justified by the increased power it affords? Do the more advanced features need a more skilled project team that is currently available? In most cases, the well-tested and fielded products are probably the best choice.

A variety of tools exist on the market today. In the final analysis, no expert systems building shell tool will be best for all applications. Similarly, no tool will be a worst possible choice for all applications. At the more elaborate end of the spectrum, one expert systems building shell may offer two or three kinds of knowledge-representation schemes with three different models for managing uncertainty. In contrast, a simple rule-based shell with no uncertainty schemes may suit some applications perfectly and be much easier to learn. In addition, a simpler shell may support some feature, such as learning by example, which could be used to advantage in a specific domain problem, though the larger, more sophisticated shell/tool environment may not. The simpler shell is also probably available at a fraction of the cost. The basic heuristic is to carefully match the tools to the application. Keep in mind that a tool that is mediocre for 10 applications may be perfect for the 11th.

## 4-2. KNOWLEDGE-REPRESENTATION STRUCTURES AND INFERENCE MECHANISMS

*Knowledge-representation schemes* and *inference mechanisms* represent the two key internal features of an expert systems building shell knowledge base, as indicated in Fig. 4-1. Domain-dependent and domain-independent knowledge are encapsulated in the knowledge-representation data structures used to store the expert's knowledge and techniques for deduction based on that knowledge. Traditionally these structures have been based on a symbolic list processing language, such as LISP (and its derivatives) or PROLOG. Although expert systems can be developed in any language, including FORTRAN, C, PASCAL, Assembler, or Ada, LISP-based tools have dominated the market in the past. There is a trend, however, of vendors rewriting LISP-based products in C or a similar compiling high-level language to speed up execution times on conventional machines.

The knowledge-representation schemes currently used in commercially available expert systems shell tools can be divided into three primary categories: *rule-based* representations; *frame-based* representations, which include *semantic* or *associate networks;* and *object-oriented* representations. These tools are in addition to the regular procedural (or functional) orientation of LISP-like programming languages. The

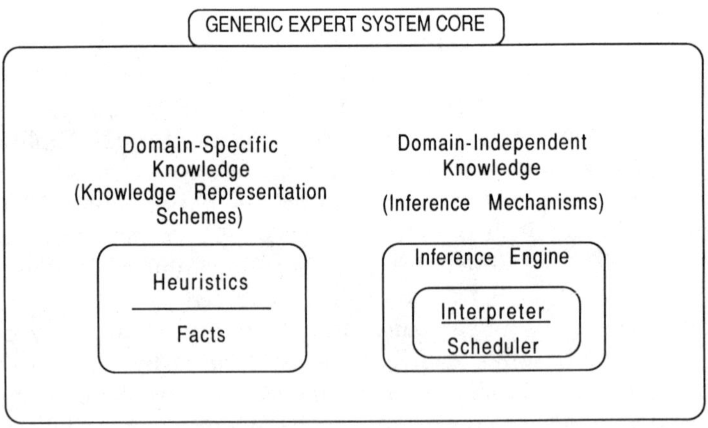


Fig. 4-1. The Generic Expert System Core.

other major *logic-based* programming, as exemplified by PROLOG, is also gaining in popularity due to its simple logical inference mode of operation.[1] Future expert systems building shell tools may evolve to incorporate *access-oriented* or *constraint-oriented* techniques. Although the first commercial tools were mostly rule-based, it is expected that the other varieties of knowledge-representation methods will become more predominant with time. The candidate knowledge-representation and inference mechanisms will now be considered.

## Rule-based representations and chaining

The rule-based approach, traditionally established by *production rule languages* like OPS5, is by far the mostly widely used representation scheme. Several rule examples have been presented in Chapters 1 and 3. The rules take the form of IF/THEN or IF/THEN/ELSE statements and combine factual and heuristic domain knowledge. Features such as multiway branch rule structure similar to the SWITCH or CASE statements in modern high-level languages will be appearing more often in the future. Individual IF/THEN rules are linked together to form *rule chains,* which can then be used to deduce information about the domain.

To illustrate the knowledge representation and inference features available in rule-based systems, a simple example for an automated teller machine (ATM) will be presented. ATMs represent a prime example of an existing machine that could benefit from the guidance of an expert system to enhance its flexibility. Many larger banks have found that the cost per transaction is significantly reduced by employing ATMs as an alternative to human tellers. The problem with increasing the number of ATMs, to further lower banking costs, is that these machines are not smart enough to handle anything other than the simplest of transactions. The issue is all the more poignant as banks desire to move into the areas of ATM bill payment and other advanced electronic services. The local computational aspect of these machines is often highly underutilized, for most ATM manufacturers are safe-building companies with no track record in harnessing the power of dedicated minicomputers. Computer Automation's (Irvine, California) Naked Mini Division furnishes the computers for many ATMs. The other reason for overpowering these computerized safes is "design for change." This spare computational capacity could be employed fo expert systems processing. Figure 4-2 presents a set of rules for the operation of extracting money from a checking or saving account at an ATM. Only a small illustrative subset of the rules guiding the machine's performance is presented. This rule set does not allow for user errors, resulting in multiple trials or repeated functions (users would find this unforgiving expert system quite unsatisfactory). The rules in this case present a simple algorithm for extracting cash from an account.

The rule chains for the rule set shown in Fig. 4-2, appear in Fig. 4-3, using the identifier letters assocaited with each of the premises and conclusions found in the rules.

The inference engine mechanisms used with this type of condition/action rules are called either *forward-chaining* or *backward-chaining*. Forward-chaining infers conclusions from facts in the database, typically starting with an initial set of input facts from the user. Using this method of inference, conditions of rules (the IF part) are examined, and if a rule's conditions are satisfied, the action (the THEN part) is performed. Backward-chaining attempts to find probable causes for a conclusion or goal sometimes supplied by the user; other times taken from a small catalog. If a rule conclusion (action) is known to be true, then conditions

**Rule 1**

IF (A) the card has been entered, AND<br>
(B) the account is current, AND<br>
(C) the access code is valid,<br>
THEN (D) the user is validated.

**Rule 2**

IF (A), and<br>
(E) the account is not valid,<br>
THEN (F) return card and print receipt.

**Rule 3**

IF (A), AND<br>
(G) the access code is invalid,<br>
THEN (F).

**Rule 4**

IF (D), AND<br>
(H) the user has entered the requested amount, AND<br>
(I) the requested amount is ≤ the account balance, AND<br>
(J) the requested amount is ≤ $200.00,<br>
THEN (K) release the cash.

**Rule 5**

IF (K), AND<br>
(L) the card has been removed,<br>
THEN (F).

Fig. 4-2. A sample set of rules for ATM cash extraction.

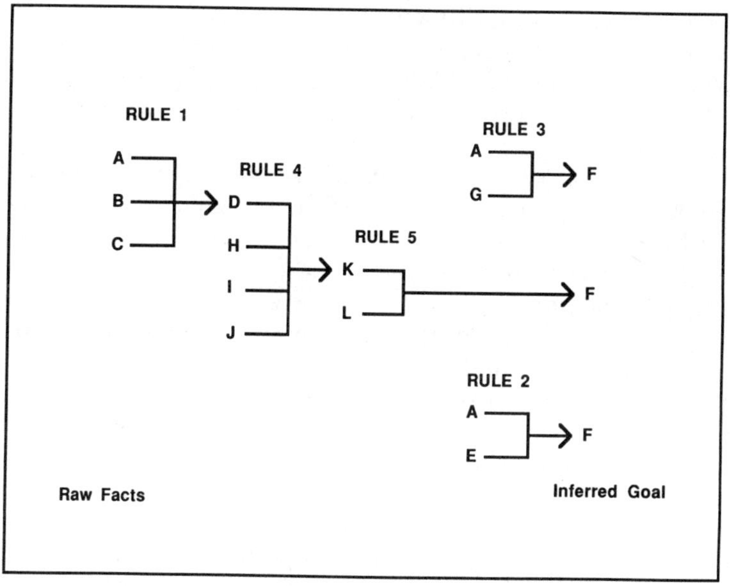


Fig. 4-3. The rule chain for the example of Fig. 4-2.

that could have given rise to the rule conclusion (or action) become subgoals, and the inference mechanism tries to establish the validity of these subgoals recursively. Forward-chaining advances from input data to conclusions, and backward-chaining moves from a conclusion, or goal, backward through the rules to try to determine the probable causes for that goal. The power of backward chainers can be enhanced by letting the computer ask for facts as and when they are needed.

The rule-based expert system's inference engine has two parts: the *rule interpreter* and the *scheduler*. The role of the rule interpreter in the inference engine is to continually evaluate all rules in the system to locate those whose conditions are satisfied. The scheduler then orders the *firing* of all such rules. Many schedulers employ *metarules* to provide the principles that determine what sequence rules should be fired in.

In the ATM example, forward-chaining proceeds as follows. The rule interpreter continually cycles through all five rules, looking for rules that have their conditions satisfied. (For this simple example, assume the scheduler is not needed.) The conditions of the rules are facts in the database. Rules 1–3 cover some of the possible cases for card entry and validation. When the card has been entered, fact (A) becomes true in the database. The account is checked, and the result is either that fact (B) (the account is valid and active) or fact (E) (the account is invalid) is added to the base. If the interpreter finds facts (A) and (B) in the knowledge base, nothing happens. If the interpreter finds both (A) and (E) as facts in the database, then rule 2 is fired, fact (F) is added to the database, and the simple ATM system quits, because (F) is a *goal state.*

If (A) and (B) are knowledge-base facts, then the addition of fact (C) from a software subsystem checking access codes will cause rule 1 to fire and add fact (D) to the base. If conditions (H), (I), and (J) also become facts in the database, then the cash is released [(K)]. If and when the cash is taken by the user, then rule 5 adds the goal state (F) to the facts already known, and the cycle is completed.

Backward-chaining works in the reverse direction, from the goal state to find probable causes leading to the goal state. Suppose that the user's card gets jammed at the end of the cycle [(F)], and the diagnostic component of the expert system wants to determine the actions leading to this goal state. One solution is just to keep a transaction log of all fired rules and reverse the steps, but this is not foolproof enough for real life. Assume that this log was never created or was accidently erased when the machine jammed, but that the facts remain in the database.

In this diagnostic cycle, the rule interpreter finds all the rules that have the goal state [(F)] as the THEN part. This includes rules 2, 3, and 5. For each rule, the conditions now become subgoals, and the system seeks to prove the validity of each of these conditions. For instance, if (A) and (E) are known facts, then it can be inferred that the only rule fired was rule 2, because (A) and (E) are not the action parts of any other rules. Similarly if (A) and (G) are true, then it can be inferred that rule 3 was invoked. If, however, (K) and (L) are facts in the database, then the interpreter will try to ascertain the validity of conditions (D), (H), (I), and (J), for (K) is the action part of rule 4. The rule chain of 5, 4, 1 is then followed in this reverse order, and the transaction sequence reestablished.

This ATM example presents only two of many possible alternative ways of using either forward- or backward-chaining. In many applications, the expert system will ask questions of the user to fill in information (knowledge-base facts) as well. The classic model for the forward- and backward-chaining found in many products is taken from the MYCIN blood infection diagnosis system and its skeletal framework EMYCIN. EMYCIN stands for "Empty MYCIN," as it is an empty general-purpose shell with no domain facts. MYCIN uses forward-chaining to reason from laboratory test information to the probable identity of a disease organism along a path of accumulating evidence. MYCIN also reasons backward (backward-chaining) to determine what tests should be run given the probable identity of an invading organism. PROSPECTOR, another standard model, also has capabilities for reasoning both forward and backward on rules. PROSPECTOR has an advanced feature of being able to accept any fact input at any time, whereas MYCIN can take facts only when it asks for them. On the whole, backward-chaining is a more efficient means of inference if it can be used, for only those rules that are relevant to the goal are activated.

In general, the rule-based representation scheme is often the best approach for an application when the domain knowledge has been derived from the expert's experiences in problem solving over a number of years. Forward- and backward-chaining on rules are two primary features to look for in expert systems building shells that employ rule representations. Some tools offer only one of these inference mechanisms, and other support both. Most variables in rules are "single-valued," i.e. only one value can be stored at a time. Some more advanced rule forms offer "multi-valued" variables, and a current fact can match any one of a variables values. The majority of the shells on the market support the rule-based representation scheme. The question of managing uncertainty with rules is covered in a later section.

### Frame-based representations and inference

The second major knowledge representation scheme is called the *frame-based,* or *schema,* representation originally discussed in the literature by Marvin Minsky.[2] This representation data structure is similar to a PL/1 structure or a PASCAL record. A frame basically represents a stereotyped characterization for a situation where the frame's *slots* can be organized and filled with such elements as data, procedures, rules, or references to other frames.

Figure 4-4 shows a frame hierarchy for an oil pump example that includes five types of frames: main, general pump maintenance, drive,

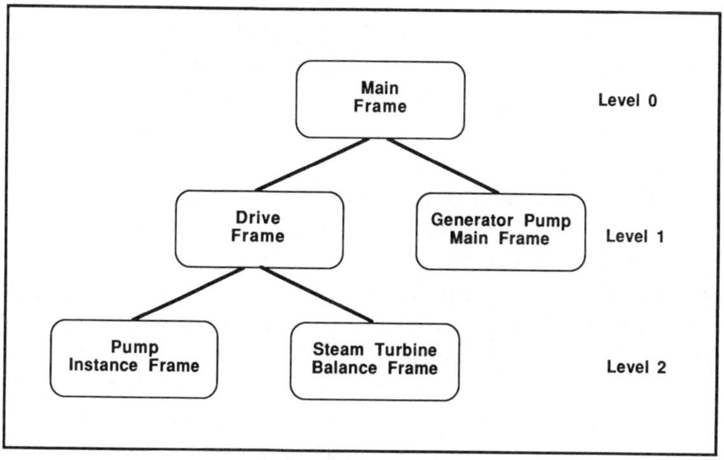


Fig. 4-4. Frame hierarchy for the oil pump example.

pump instance, and steam turbine balancing. Figure 4-5 presents the details of the different frame types. The mainframe contains the general characteristics of the oil pump, including its function, parts, and the factors affecting the pump's function. Each type of drive has its own drive frame, which indicates the type of drive, any special parts, the capacity, particular instances, and special maintenance characteristics. "Crude feed pressurizer" is a special instance of the steam drive frame and is represented in a pump instance frame along with relevant data. The steam turbine balancing frame provides another area of specialized knowledge.

*Procedural attachment* (also called *methods*) is one of the approaches for attaching action-oriented knowledge to slots in the frame. Usually these procedures will be activated if a change occurs in a slot, that is, if new information is added or old information deleted. Because each slot in a frame can be used as an expected value, missing information can cause a procedure activation that might be used to prompt the user for the information, estimate it from historic data, or request the sampling of sensor data.

Inference in frame-based representations is usually accomplished via a set of IF/THEN-like rules, procedures, or frame-linking slots, which structure a frame hierarchy or heterarchy. These frame networks can be conceived of as graphs, and inference as a type of graph traversal. The network consists of frame *nodes* representing complex bodies of knowledge interconnected by the *frame-link* slots. The totality of the network forms an *inference network* through which properties and characteristics of objects (structures) can be inferred. Each frame collects appropriate data items and procedural knowledge, so by association all such items are available. The frame hierarchy supports inference from general characteristics of an object (represented only once) to multiple specific instances, and properties can also be inherited according to the hierarchy links. For instance, Crude Feed Pressurizer, as a steam driven pump, is also an oil pump and has bearings, shafts, and turbines.

Topologically, associative or semantic networks are essentially equivalent to frame networks. Due to the current prevalance of "frame" tools on the market, associative nets are being included in the frame discussion. It would be equally valid to include frames in a discussion of associate network structure in expert systems work. Traditionally, the semantic network arose from neural and cognitive modeling research.[3] The network consists of nodes representing simple symbol structures interconnected by *labeled arcs*. As with the frame representation, a graph-like traversal of the inference network allows properties and characteristics to be inferred. Associative networks are good representations for domain problems requiring a substantial degree of highly

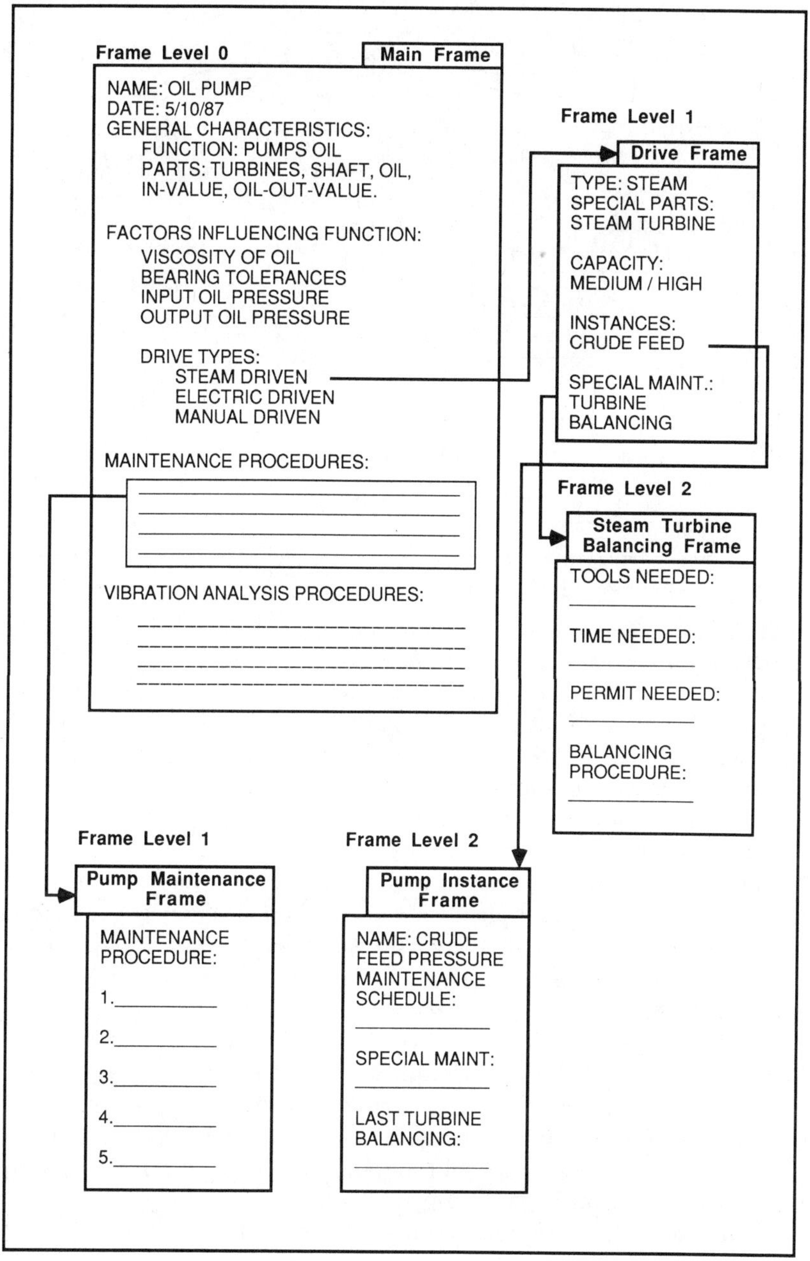


Fig. 4-5. Frame structure for the oil pump example.

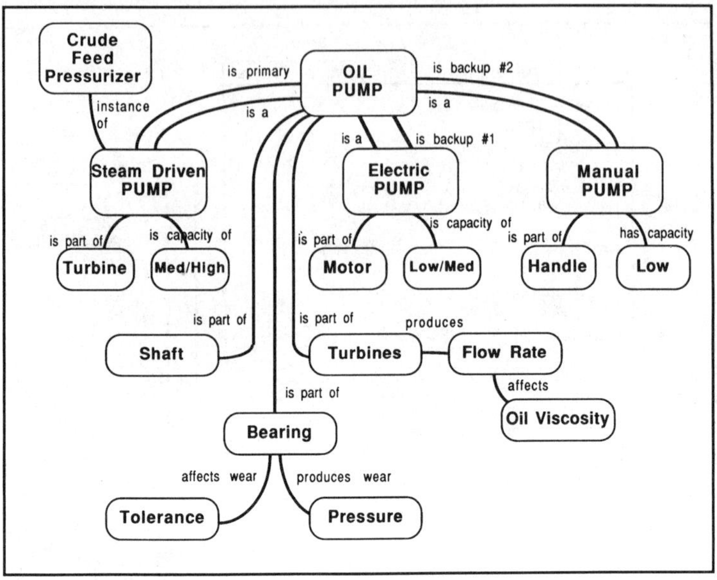


Fig. 4-6. Associative network for an oil pump.

specialized associative linking of small primitive items. From the perspective taken here, the primary difference between frame networks and association networks is in the size and complexity of the node, the frame representing an aggregate of complex information and the association node a simpler feature. The association nodes typically have little meaning outside the context of the network, whereas a frame is a relatively complete package in itself.

Figure 4-6 illustrates a simplified association network for the oil refinery oil pump example. The various database items are represented as nodes in the net, and relationships between the nodes are expressed by the arc descriptors. For instance, a steam driven pump is an oil pump according to the "IS A" link. The steam turbine is a part ("IS PART") of the steam driven pump, and the pump has a capacity ("IS CAPACITY OF" in reverse) medium- to high-volume. Crude Feed Pressurizer is a particular instance of a steam driven pump. Multiple relationships between nodes of the knowledge network can be generated, as when the electric driven pump is an oil pump and also the first backup pump for the primary steam driven pump.

Various inference queries can be addressed by traversing arcs from node to node. Flow rates are produced by turbines, which are parts of the oil pump, and are affected by the viscosity of the oil. The flow rate and viscosity nodes in this case would be numeric or tabluar values that could be used in computing various hydrodynamic properties. Properties can easily be inherited according to the inheritance hierarchy. For instance, because Crude Feed Pressurizer is a steam-driven pump, it is also an oil pump, and because it is an oil pump, it has bearings, shafts, turbines, and associated tolerances, pressures, flow rates, and so on.

*Procedural attachment* to nodes is possible as well. Any node in the network could have one or more procedures associated with it. If a node is accessed during the inference procedure, a procedure or function may be activated, in addition to generating new facts for the knowledge base. For instance, the pressure, flow rate, and oil viscosity nodes could be real-time procedures that compute current values based on sensor data whenever the nodes are accessed.

How could the association representation and inference scheme be used? There are several possibilities. A more detailed version of this network could be used by an expert system designed to perform vibration analysis diagnostic testing on the most critical moving parts in the pump, such as the bearings. Signature analysis based on signal processing of the vibrational modes of mechanical equipment can be a powerful diagnostic tool. An expert system employing an inference network, however, would be a useful adjunct to the base signal processing unit, so that patterns could be recognized among the mass of data.

Overall, frame-type representations are a useful feature if the knowledge is organized into packages where all the data elements and procedures are known in advance. All expected slot items can be requested by the system, and default values can be provided as appropriate. Creating a new diesel engine drive type for the oil pump example requires only adding another instance of the drive frame and appropriate pump instance frames. The entire frame hierarchy could also be copied and edited for a similar application, such as for large industrial water-cooling pumps. A significant amount of the information and procedures may stay the same, greatly reducing the setup time for the new system. The use of inheritance to save development time for a family of systems is a key reason for employing frame-based representations. The need for graphical descriptions, which change as the real-world entities they are modeling change, is another key plus for the frame-based approach.

The potential for representing simple objects or structures and any type of relationship between the structures is the prime reason for choosing shells supporting this type of representation. Application areas with well-established organizational taxonomies are good candidates for this type of representation. If a shell allows attachments of IF/THEN rules or procedures to the nodes of the network, the flexibility and power of the representation scheme are greatly enhanced.

## Object-based representations

One final representation technique appearing in some of the expert systems building shells and environments is known as the *object-oriented,* or *object-based,* representation. This scheme developed out of the work on earlier languages like SIMULA, and FLAVORS. The work on SMALLTALK-80 at Xerox Palo Alto Research Center (PARC—Palo Alto, California) has been the source of most of the developments on the object-oriented approach. In this representation scheme, the objects, which may be similar to the network frame, are modeled after intelligent communicating entities. Each object has its own internal structure and established behavior patterns or routines. Thus, the object comprises both data and operations on data. Note that the mixing of process and data, which is the essence of object-oriented design, is the antithesis of database design. Objects are usually defined as *classes* with various *instances,* and inheritance of characteristics from one parent class object to a child instance is possible. These *intelligent agents,* or *actors,* as they are sometimes called, communicate via *message passing.* The objects communicate by sending messages that invoke the recipient's procedures, or *methods,* and operate on its internal data. Thus for a simple set of "integer objects," to add 2 to 3, a message of "add 3" is sent to the object "2," which causes object "2" to become "5." This approach is similar to the interactions of independent modules in languages like Concurrent PASCAL or the rendezvous of tasks in Ada. The asynchronous, concurrent activity of the objects provides a key tool for developing simulation expert systems where many unrelated tasks may be active at the same time. More will be said about object-oriented programming in Chapter 6.

Another similar high-level scheme is called the *access-based,* or *access-oriented* programming technique. Knowledge structuring in this methodology is very much like that in the object-based system, except that any changes in internal state of the object triggers internal procedures, resulting in automatic message sending. This type of representation can be very useful for graphics displays where any type of variable change should be registered on the screen. Only a very few of the commercial products support this type of scheme. Some frame products also allow such *demons* or *triggers* to be used as slots.

One final knowledge-structuring strategy is called the *blackboard model.* In this scheme, *knowledge sources* (KSs) perform specific functions much like the objects or frames (with procedures and rules) discussed above. The KSs interact with each other via a common information or knowledge *blackboard.* The functions and operations of the various KSs in a system cause them to deposit and retrieve information from specific areas of the blackboard. Each KS's functions are oriented toward the specific areas of the blackboard (i.e., types of information) it can receive from the other KSs via the blackboard. The key difference between this scheme and the object-oriented scheme is that the specific source of an information packet is not so important, only that some appropriate KS has deposited it. This scheme has been used extensively for cognitive modeling and can be examined in Nii, 1986*a,b*.

Some of the expert systems shells now offer the ability to do a type of *what if?* reasoning. This is sometimes called *hypothetical reasoning*, and it allows the user of an expert system to explore one or more alternative inference possibilities without having to rerun the system from the start. This usually involves a temporary storage or stacking of the current state of inference before moving onto another alternative. Some of the more sophisticated shell tools allow even thousands of multiple-world views to exist simultaneously, which provides an excellent medium for temporal reasoning involving many different possibilities.

A concise comparison of the various AI programming schemes and paradigms can be found on Bobrow and Stefik (1986).

## LISP and PROLOG

Sometimes the differences between representation and inferencing techniques are minimal, for in essence these techniques are just different variations on the same problem-solving themes. The different approaches have been developed independently at different university, private research, or commercial concerns, so there is significant overlap. When it comes to selecting an appropriate method for an application it may be that no high-level, commercially available shell with preprogrammed knowledge-structuring techniques is the best for a particular problem. The system developer may need greater flexibility created by generating new types of highly specialized knowledge representations and inference modalities. In these cases, there are several versions of the AI programming languages LISP and PROLOG available that can be used to expand preprogrammed shell tools or to develop knowledge acquisition aids or support tools or to develop systems from scratch.

The five types of high-level knowledge-structuring methods just outlined have traditionally been implemented in some dialect of the programming language LISP. The expert systems building shell products tend to hide language specifics from the engineer, but when working in the integrated environments, interaction with LISP or PROLOG primitives is often unavoidable. It is good at this juncture to provide a glimpse of the style of programming used in LISP and PROLOG. Chapter 6 offers more information on specific vendors' products.

The time, cost, and programming expertise required to develop an expert system in either a LISP derivative or PROLOG should be expected to be much greater than using the high-level shell. Greater flexibility can be gained, however, by creating knowledge structures completely tuned to the problem requirements.

LISP (LISt Processor) is a list-oriented, symbolic-processing language developed by John McCarthy at MIT in the early 1960s. Many dialects of the language are available at this time. The LISP programming environments are often very well developed with appropriate features, for LISP has been the main workhorse of the American AI research community. Sophisticated editing and debugging utilities are typically available with the language. The language supports the uniform treatment of program code and data, which means a LISP program can modify its own list-oriented code as easily as program data. Automatic memory management is a standard feature, with execution-time binding of variables. Attempts have been made to standardize all the varieties of LISP by producing one Common LISP or an ANSI Standard LISP. Currently, however, many of the numerous LISP dialects are machine-dependent and are not 100% interchangeable.

Fact rules in LISP are expressed in the form of attribute, object, and value triples. In a LISP-like language, the fact that the bank card has been entered into an ATM might be represented as

```
(entered (card) (machine))
```

Rule 1 of the ATM example of Fig. 4-2 would be written in a form something like

```
Premise ($AND (entered (card) (machine))
              (valid (account) (validaccounts))
              (valid (code) (accesscodes)))
Action   (conclude (user) (valid))
```

LISP and its various dialects are procedural and functional languages based on the use of nested subroutines and recursion. Programmers can employ a powerful set of predefined functions and operations or define specialized subroutines and functions. A recursive functional definition for computing a factorial might look like

```
(DEFUN FACTORIAL (X)
(COND ((= X 0) 1)
(T (* X (FACTORIAL (- X 1))))))
```

The factorial of $X$ is being computed according to a list of potential "conditions" (COND). If $X$ is 0, then the result returned is 1. Otherwise, the $T$ for true causes the inner parentheses to be evaluated recursively. That is, $X$ is multiplied by the factorial of $X - 1$ in the standard LISP prefix operator notation. Numerous texts have been written on LISP programming, and the interested reader is directed to McCarthy (1980) Winston and Horn (1984), and other references listed at the end of the chapter.

PROLOG-like language development tools provide a *logic-based* approach to representing and using knowledge. In these increasingly popular AI languages, such as SMALLTALK and PROLOG in its various forms, the goals (the "what") are separated from the means to achieve the goals (the "how"). PROLOG uses sophisticated pattern-matching techniques, as LISP does, to form simple logical deductions based on first-order predicate logic *Horn clauses*. (A Horn clause is a restricted clausal form with only a single consequent, or result, statement as shown below.) When constructing inference engines, it is generally recognized that PROLOG is easier to use than LISP. Regarding flexibility in mathematics and graphics, however, PROLOG is usually not the language of choice. In theory, logic languages, such as PROLOG, employ exhaustive search of all Horn clause rules, but in reality implementations are better described as backward-chaining rule interpretation using *clause unification* and *backtracking*. Many implementations incorporate built-in, relational database facilities and efficient compilers.[4]

The general form of the Horn clause used in the various PROLOG dialects looks like a reversed IF/THEN statement. The IF/THEN statement has the form

IF condition 1 AND condition 2 AND . . . AND condition *n*
THEN result

The general form of the Horn clause puts the *consequent* (result) first, followed by the *antecedents* (conditions). The ":-"symbol is read as *if*.

consequent :-antecedent 1, antecedent 2, . . . , antecedent *n*

Assertive statements in the language declare facts, such as

Assert (IsPartOf (oil pump,shaft))

which says that a shaft is a part of the oil pump. Read procedurally, the Horn clause rule statement says that the consequent is the goal and the antecedent are subgoals that the system should try to prove (in the order antecedent 1, antecedent 2, . . . , antecedent *n*) to verify the goal. This deduction process is very much like backward-chaining. The attempt to prove a subgoal can result in a recursive chain of subgoal proof attempts. If the system finds it cannot verify or prove one of the subgoals, then it goes on to the next rule having the appropriate goal or consequent. A classic example showing the basic inferencing in PROLOG, as shown in Bobrow and Stefik (1986) is the following

Rules: Uncle (X,Y):-Brother (X,Z), Father (Z,Y);
Uncle (X,Y):-Brother (X,Z),Mother (Z,Y)
assert: Assert (Brother (John, Paula)); Assert (Mother (Paula, Kathy)).

As a consequence of the above statement the program deduces that John is Kathy's uncle.

The power and compactness of PROLOG code was recently demonstrated at the IEEE PROLOG Teleconference, with the encoding of the entire EMYCIN inference engine, with its propagation of uncertainty, in just one page of PROLOG. Unfortunately, PROLOG implementations do not always provide high performance, particularly for large rule bases.

The primary emphasis in this book is on the use of the expert systems building shells with LISP or PROLOG programming environments used only as adjunct support tools. The interested reader can find more information on PROLOG programming in Clocksin and Mellish (1984), Rogers (1986), and other references listed at the end of the chapter.

## 4-3. FACT UNCERTAINTY AND UNRELIABILITY OF RULES

One of the key features available in most expert systems development technologies is the ability to represent and reason with the *fact uncertainty* characteristic of the real world. The rules illustrated in the operation of the ATM shown in Fig. 4.2 are examples of the most concrete form of rules, in that they contain no uncertainty attached to the conditions of the premise or action. Each rule is presumably asserted with complete confidence in its truth. Such is so with standard IF/THEN/ELSE rules of traditional programming languages as well. Unfortunately, it is often true that the types of data facts to be represented in expert systems are not known with such certainty.

The well-established hard sciences, such as biology, physics, and chemistry have matured to where they have a great degree of certainty in the laws of nature expressed in these disciplines. The knowledge in an expert system for inorganic chemistry, for instance, may require almost no uncertainties in the knowledge facts. The less-developed soft sciences of sociology and psychology, however, must resort to a range of sophisticated probabilistic models based on uncertainty to cope with areas where less is known about the laws of nature governing the problem's activity.

Expert systems applications fall somewhere on a continuum ranging from completely accurate, accepted-as-true fact data, to data items about which little (if anything) is known. In the latter case, the system may try to infer something about the little-known or unknown data. Hence, an important feature of an expert systems building shell or language is its techniques for managing uncertainty in fact knowledge.

The equivalent feature to fact uncertainty relating to the integrity of a knowledge-base rule is called *rule reliability*. Given the certainty and reliability of the facts in a rule and all the knowledge represented in the rule as a whole, how reliable is the rule? Rules may be somewhat unreliable even if all the facts of the rule conditions are expressed with 100% certainty. Consider this rule: if the sun is shining and the relative humidity is less than 100%, then it is not raining. This rule may be true most of the time, but in certain cases it is not true. The ability to rate the reliability of rules is an important feature for many expert systems applications. This reliability rating may be attached to the rule (e.g., then it is not raining (0.6)), may be a user-supplied item, or it may be generated implicitly by the inference engine. In the latter case, the scheduler could, for instance, determine the reliability of a rule based on the number of conditions used in the IF part of the rule. Rules with more conditions are generally considered more reliable.

The most complete knowledge-representation organization would allow for both fact uncertainty and rule uncertainty, although systems without one can create the effect of both. A rule of the form

```
    IF  A (0.4) and
        B (.08) and
        C (0.2)
  THEN  D (0.7)      (60,0.001)
```

might be interpreted in a specific product as saying that fact certainties of at least 0.4, 0.8, and 0.2 for facts *A*, *B*, and *C*, respectively, will be good enough to imply the conclusion (*D*) with a certainty factor of 0.7. The last factors, 60 and 0.0001, might represent some measure of how encouraging it is to find the evidence of the conditions available or how discouraging it is to have the evidence of the three conditions not present in the scheme of the inference path as a whole. Various nomenclatures exist among different expert systems shell products. Another classification of goal states is to give two numbers for appropriateness and agreement. If multiple experts are involved an agreement score is invaluable. A further inference step is then used to give go/no go decisions.

Often probability is coordinated with metaknowledge to form a sequencing guide for rule firing. Rules of the above degree of complexity are not needed in all expert systems, but certain types of systems (e.g., PROSPECTOR) have employed rules with all these dimensions. If developers think they can develop a PROSPECTOR look-alike system on a standard PC-based shell, however, they will usually be in for an unpleasant surprise.

An expert systems application may begin as a system employing uncertainty, but as system development continues, the uncertainty factors are removed. For instance, concerning an insurance company's policy for managing accident claims, the actuaries may work with fact and/or rule uncertainty in the development stages of an expert system. When the completed system is put into production, however, it must produce repeatable, i.e., deterministic or algorithmic, results in all the company's branch offices. In this situation, the knowledge engineers in liaison with the actuaries may gradually remove the uncertainties by refining or adding rules until the uncertainties can be eliminated. The power of the system may be ultimately limited by this process, but the price may be acceptable in trade for achieving the repeatability goal. In other applications, such as meteorology, unreliabilities may be gradually worked into the system as the development and evolution continues. In such complex applications, refinement of the uncertainty factors to obtain accurate forecasts can be a major aspect of the system development work.

In summary, features to look for in expert systems building products include the ability to represent fact uncertainty and rule reliability. In addition the product should be able to easily modify the knowledge structure representations and possibly their inference engines to change these probabilities as necessary during the development cycle.

## 4-4. LOGIC AND MATHEMATICS

There are two aspects to the logic and mathematical facilities of a shell, namely those directly accessible to the knowledge engineer and those employed by the system. Although these are separate functional facilities, the engineer can frequently have significant indirect access to the system-managed mathematics. As both are really under user control, most vendors have focused first on the inclusion of the system-managed logics and mathematics, but greater abilities for custom developer-defined facilities are now being provided by vendors.

The measures of fact uncertainty and rule unreliability presented in the previous section pose an interesting problem. How does the expert system reason with these types of uncertainties? How are the uncertainties combined? Conventional programming environments typically support only the *Boolean logic* operations, i.e., the familiar conjuctive/disjunctive (and/or) functions operating on *true* or *false* premises.

Expert systems shells offer various models for performing logical operations with uncertain or inexact information. This is typically called *inexact reasoning*. *Probabilistic models* based on Bayes' conditional probability theorem of combining evidence is one technique available in many tools. Bayes' theorem is stated as

$$P(H_i|E) = \frac{P(E|H_i) * P(H_i)}{\text{sum } n = 1 \text{ to } k\ P(E|H_n) * P(H_n)}$$

where

$P(H_i|E)$ = the probability that hypothesis $H_i$ is true given evidence $E$,
$P(E|H_i)$ = the probability that evidence $E$ is true or observed given the truth of the hypothesis $i$,
$P(H_i)$ = the a priori probability that hypothesis $i$ is true in the absence of any specific evidence, and
$k$ = the number of possible hypotheses.[5]

The hypothesis, in our terminology, is condition-associated with the premise or conclusion of a rule. If the uncertainty factors associated with premise conditions are actual probabilities, then Bayes' theorem can be used to combine the collective evidence. The mineral prospecting expert system PROSPECTOR used this approach.

Other applications may require custom-designed, application-specific methods for relating and combining certainty factors and reliability measures. Custom-built MYCIN used probability-like measures of certainty and reliability, but also a specialized inexact reasoning mechanism for inference on these measures. Extremely sophisticated inexact reasoning abilities are still research items, but commercial products should be expected to continue to advance in these areas in the years to come. Many of the first-generation shells provide access to only one uncertainty propagation methodology, but other more sophisticated tools are now starting to support both standard system-defined techniques and options for developer-designed "logics."

A third type of logic available is called *fuzzy logic*. This mechanism can represent inexact facts, as well as qualitative measures, such as *large, small, near,* and *far*. Although a few shell tools support elementary fuzzy logics, these systems are still very much in the experimental stage and should not be relied on too heavily. A cut-down version of fuzzy logic is sometimes found in the handling of fact uncertainty, where, instead of using specific probabilities, the system employs such terms as *always, almost always, sometimes, infrequently,* and *never*. These limited implementations tend to map specific probability ranges onto the textual terms.

Besides logic, one other feature can be found at the heart of most business and industrial applications: the use of mathematics. Does an expert systems building shell support the use of extensive variables, mathematical expressions, and functions to perform real-time calculations on knowledge-base data? The ability to use standard business or scientific calculations can be crucial to applications. Can these data items be drawn from other databases or screen inputs as well? There are three main approaches to the provision of mathematical functions. The first is access to high-level languages and their mathematical library functions, and the second is access to the specific language the shell tool has been built in. The third involves a custom language specified by the vendor as part of the developer interface to the shell. The degree of flexibility for each approach varies from tool to tool. The mathematics, even in financial planning, can rapidly become involved using such features as depreciation, amortization, compound interest, and commission structures. Predicting the behavior of commodity prices, to judge the best times to buy and sell, can become even more mathematically intricate. The advantage of vendor-supplied mathematical primitives is that inferencing and deduction can continue within the shell without the need to write external code calls. The extra code to transfer control and variables to a high-level language routine can take time to develop and also slow down execution time.

## 4-5. EFFECTS OF RULE SEQUENCING AND USE OF METARULES

Recall that the inference engine for a rule-based system contains both a rule interpreter and a scheduler. For the standard *rule-interpretation cycle* operating in a forward-chaining mode, the interpreter will check the conditions (premises) for *all* the rules in the knowledge base, unless the knowledge base has been partitioned. During one cycle, several rules may have their conditions satisfied by facts currently existing in the knowledge base. All the rules cannot be *fired* simultaneously in a serial computer, so the scheduler must make some decisions about how to prioritize the rules for firing. These priorities could simply be an ordering of the rules in the sequence they were found, or it could be based on more complicated information, such as rule reliability or the rule's author. Some systems just fire the rules in the sequence they are stored in the knowledge base, others according to probability priorities, and others may pick any rule for firing at random. The order in which rules are fired can effect the way the inference chain develops, quite possibly resulting in completely different conclusions being reached.

The techniques used by the scheduler to order rules that are ready to be fired is an important feature to look for in a rule-based representation scheme. The knowledge engineer needs to know the scheduler's mode of operation to develop rule sets that reach the desired conclusions. Additionally, expert systems building shells differ in the way they remove or modify knowledge-base rules. In some cases, rule removal, modification, or addition is managed in the same way as record removal, modification, or addition in a typical database program. Actual records may only be marked for deletion, for instance, not actually deleted until "garbage collection" occurs. In a rule-based expert systems shell, marking rules for delete but not removing them may affect the way the scheduler checks rule premises and therefore orders rule firings. The conclusions reached could vary depending on the strategies employed. Vendor literature does not always address these points, but in almost all applications the knowledge engineer must understand how the inference engine is working. Using paper and pencil to bench test the engine's performance is often a good approach.

Some shells are now providing the knowledge engineer with the capability of adding their own *metarules*, rules that represent strategies for managing rules. Metarules, in short, are rules about rules. An example of such a rule might be

| | |
|---|---|
| IF | more than one rule has its premises satisfied in one rule recognition/execution cycle |
| THEN | fire the rules in the order of their priorities |

These priorities may be assigned by the knowledge engineer at the time of entry, or they could be determined by the scheduler itself according to a rule such as

| | |
|---|---|
| IF | the priority information is needed for rules with their premises satisfied |
| THEN | prioritize the rules on the basis of the number of conditions in the rules' premises |

This means that a rule with five conditions in its premise will be fired before a rule with three conditions, using the heuristic that the former is more complete, due to the amount of data satisfied in its premise.

Another example might be to use the rule-incorporating data supplied by the user rather than using data inferred by the program, based on the assumption that the supplied data will more likely be accurate than the inferred data.

Metarules are one technique for representing *metaknowledge*, or knowledge about knowledge, in expert systems. Metaknowledge capabilities may give future expert systems a degree of self-knowledge. Such *self-referral* behavior could allow the programs to monitor some aspects of their own behavior and make dynamic adjustments as appropriate, provide explanations reasoned from first principles, and induce new knowledge from existing facts. The capabilities of metarules in current expert systems shells are quite limited in this respect, but they do offer some flexibility in controlling the strategies used in the system. Thus the ability to structure metalevels of knowledge in the expert system is an added advantage for most expert systems applications and is perhaps an essential feature for complex domains.

## 4-6. USER INTERFACES FOR KNOWLEDGE-BASE DISPLAY

Various approaches are available for displaying either knowledge-base facts or heuristics. The three main classes of approach can be described as graphics, natural language, and, more traditional, key-word-based computer interfaces. Some of the earliest work on expert systems assumed, either explicitly or implicitly, that a natural-language-man-machine interface was a prerequisite for progress. The more recent view is that various kinds of graphical constructs can provide a superior way of communicating knowledge structures, especially complex ones, to users. The key problem with natural language is that it has a highly limited bandwidth, in terms of bits per second communicated between man and machine, which can slow consultations to a snail's pace.

The usual natural-language approach is to use a *phrase-oriented* interaction to understand and display English-like sentences geared to the human language mode of expression. Consultation expert systems have traditionally been developed around this modality, with the system continually prompting the user for data in the early knowledge-acquisition phase and then returning a conclusion in terms of a sentence or paragraph. Natural language has its advantages for domains with a highly specific vocabulary, such as certain aspects as medical diagnosis. If the expert system is consulted via a telephone conversation, then natural language also lends itself to being read out and dictated over the phone.

The movement toward graphical displays for knowledge is clearly at hand, so it is worth examining some of the reasons for using graphics in expert systems. The first point to note is the shift from batch printouts to business graphics. Large printouts, especially for numerical analyses, are not the most helpful tool for senior managers and executives. The information becomes overwhelming. The executive strains to focus attention on the most crucial elements of massive documents. Even executive summaries are of limited help, primarily because the human mind desires to comprehend in terms of holistic patterns. The executive summary presented in graphical form, however, gives the viewer the gestalt experience of seeing the entirety of the information as an integrated whole, rather than as isolated facts and figures. The spatial, holistic right hemisphere of the brain is able to comprehend the whole of the results of the production reports at one glance and hold this total picture while the analytical left brain searches out and pinpoints key features for further analysis. This gestalt phenomenon is, of course, not limited to the business world. An astrophysicist who has been laboring over the analysis of magnetic interference data from a space probe may see the entire analysis with striking new insight if carefully prepared visual summary materials are provided. Computer-aided design (CAD) has moved to the same graphical style of interaction to provide a visual symbolic framework that resonates with the natural cognitive mechanisms used by humans.

The style of the user interfaces adopted for the system should be greatly influenced by the type of input/output interactions required. Simple inferences and conclusions can be effectively communicated by English phrase interfaces, but more complex and sophisticated information is better presented by graphical chart or contour systems. Beyond the element of complexity is the sheer volume of output. Many expert systems applications may begin with only a small or medium volume of printed results, but comprehending the output can become suddenly unwieldy as usage of the system continues to grow and printed output increases. For example, an investment management expert system may start with just a few clients and moderate printing requirements easily managed by the originally selected equipment. After expansive growth, however, such a system can easily grow to generate 30 boxes of quarterly statements that require over a week to print. A graphical print representation of the majority of these data could result in a 90% reduction of printed material and enhance comprehension.

Another justification for increased use of graphical displays comes from response time. Even if an executive could comprehend the masses of information presented in nongraphical form, what is the cost of the executive's time spent in working out the patterns in the data? More time-critical applications, such as process control, do not have the flexibility to allow the operator to spend hours leafing through printouts before reaching each conclusion. The operator of a highly volatile chemical process must be able to analyze imbalances in the process and take corrective action in a matter of minutes or seconds. An expert system could supply the critical exception data in seconds but if the operator requires a few minutes to sort through the visual dialogue to determine the proper action to take, the time advantage of the expert system will be lost. A graphics display can give the operator an instantaneous view, resulting in quick decision making. An even more extreme example would be display information supplied to fighter pilots. Heads-up displays, based on half-silvered mirrors, allow the pilots to look straight ahead to view the landscape below and at the same time see the plane's gauges projected and reflected on the mirror. Millisecond analysis and reaction time determine life and death in such professions, so computerized equipment outputs must permit quick assimilation by the user. Graphical or symbolic displays provide the only realistic means for almost instantaneously communicating the results of such embedded expert systems.

Two dominant subsets of graphics that have become popular are (1) the icon/pop-up/pull-down-menu/windows and (2) bar/pie/histogram charting. The use of icons for graphical display has been found to be a powerful approach where the entities to be reasoned with can be represented on the screen. These kinds of icons are susceptible to the object-oriented paradigm, where each object inside the computer is represented as a visible object on the screen, and where all changes to the internal state of the computer's objects are made visible to the user. Such an approach can take much of the mystery out of what the expert system is doing while it is inferencing. In addition, the inference conclusions in such domains as factory layout planning and user interface design can be ideally displayed in the form of icons.

In the final analysis, the capabilities provided by a shell tool or other external tools for developing the end user interface are extremely important for the success of human-machine interaction.

## 4-7. GRAPHICS, DATABASE, AND PROGRAMMING INTERFACES

Although the facilities within the expert shell are important, equally significant are ways to get out of the shell environment to access other facilities. The three main types of external interfaces are for graphics, database, and programming. These facilities can also be provided within the shell, but if any deficiencies arise it is always helpful to have the option to extend the shell or access external routines. One approach is to treat all three interfaces as separate entities, with an individual exit route for each one, while the contrasting approach is to adopt a single exit via just a programming or file-transfer interface.

Data required in the expert system may be supplied by means other than menu, command, or natural-language interfaces. Similarly conclusions may have to be routed to other places, in different formats, than the screen or printer. Some expert systems building tools offer interfaces to graphics software displays or graphics tablets to input data.

A number of the more expensive expert systems shells already include internal graphical facilities, but if for various reasons these high-end tools are not appropriate, then external, third-party graphics packages may be integratable with the expert systems shell. The types of graphics tools that might be connected with an expert system vary from the simplest form of visual data representations to complex data analysis and display software packages. In MIS environments, the first potential level of data compression and display is found in the simple business graphics tools of the histogram, bar chart, and pie graph. Popular business graphics software, such as Lotus 1-2-3 or Microsoft Chart, can be used for such simple displays. Integration with an expert system here is relatively straightforward via standard file-transfer mechanisms. Once the inferences are moved over, a single button is often sufficient to alter the form of the chart from bar to histogram to pie form. No specialized programming is needed to construct or alter the form of the chart, for the charting capabilities are limited to only a simple summary of the data. Even this simple form of graphical summary, however, may be sufficient to trigger the insight required by the astrophysicist.

Many expert systems applications, however, have more dimensions in their data structures, which, in turn, demand more sophisticated statistical analysis and display techniques. Graphics packages, such as SAS/Graph from SAS Institute, Inc. (Cary, North Carolina), and the range of graphics tools from Integrated Software Systems Corporation (ISSCO, San Diego, California) and Precision Visuals, Inc. (Boulder, Colorado), offer a variety of features not available in most simple business graphics software. In these more science-oriented products, 30 or 40 parameters can be provided to define elaborate graphs or displays. Scatter charts, cluster analysis, and statistical refinement tools may be used to transform raw data into understandable structures. The raw ASCII character graphics of the simplest systems, where letters are arranged to construct columns or graphs, are replaced by sophisticated pixel graphics, often displayed in three dimensions and in color.

The data-transformation and image-processing capabilities of the advanced graphics programs are enormous, but there is a price to be paid. For the most part, these processing capabilities and displays must be programmed from the ground up. The interfaces between the expert system and the graphics package have increased dramatically in complexity from the simpler "one-button" business graphics packages. The system manager must be prepared to deal with this interface of increased complexity to get the desired results. The common-sense heuristic suggests choosing the simplest graphics package that will satisfy the application and end user requirements and avoid the additionally complex interfaces if possible. If this is not possible, then adequate resources must be allotted for the development of more complex interfaces.

*Database* and *spreadsheet* capabilities are options available with some expert tools through interfaces to other software packages. A few shells even contain databases or spreadsheets within their core structures. The degree of coupling possible between the knowledge base and the spreadsheet or database should be carefully investigated. The lowest level of interaction is file transfer, which in the worst case may be only a one-way mechanism. File-transfer destinations often include the leading third-party MIS products; however, more generic formats are always valuable. Higher level couplings may allow variables used in the knowledge representations to be bound to particular database items, so that whenever one end of the link is updated, the other end is automatically kept in line. The automatic connection may be only a one-way link, however, allowing only inference expression calculations to be performed based on database or spreadsheet numerical data.

An example of using a database interface would be an expert system-based front end for a personnel-administration database. The goal of this expert system may be to choose the best current employee to move into a new or potential position based on analyzing the records of the personnel database. In addition to finding perfect matches, the system will find many near-matches, which in turn can be translated into training schedules to improve the appropriateness of a candidate for a given job. In such a system the expert shell would have to read records from the database to make its deductions. Training schedules would also have to be written back to the personnel database once conclusions had been reached. As a consequence a two-way link would be needed. File-transfer could do the job, but if the database were volatile, it would be desirable to have access to the most uptodate data at all times via on-line access link.

The final, and usually most important, interface is one of programming languages. The expert system almost always has to be integrated with other software and hardware systems to become fully a part of the production environment. Database, graphics, or spreadsheet interfaces may not be enough to integrate the old and new software. Even if the high-level language used in the shell, such as LISP or PROLOG, is accessible, it may not interface with other traditional software tools. Therefore, a key application-dependent feature to look for in an expert systems building tool is the type of traditional programming interfaces supported. The languages that expert systems are built for and interface to include both traditional high-level and symbolic languages. If the base language is a symbolic language, programming interfaces have to bridge a wide conceptual gap. Moving from the constructs of a symbolic language to COBOL or FORTRAN is not always easy, so even if an interface exists, it may not always behave as expected. Usually the programming interfaces bridge into scientific languages, notably FORTRAN and Assembler. There is a trend in interface destination toward C and PASCAL, following the pattern noted for the base languages of expert shells. Some high-level tools allow the knowledge engineer or programmer to have direct access to the underlying AI programming language. From LISP or PROLOG, more application-specific bridges can be built to selected destinations. The other key advantage of having access to a base symbolic language is that custom-made knowledge structures can be generated to supplement the supplied rule, frame, network, or object-oriented representation schemes.

## 4-8. "HOW" AND "WHY" EXPLANATIONS AND "HELP" FACILITIES

One crucial, but often underemphasized, feature for both the knowledge engineer and the end user of an expert system is the inference-path explanation facilities provided. While reasoning from first principles during a run of the expert system is still primarily a research issue, rudimentary explanation facilities are available in most expert systems building shells. The most common approach is to keep a log of the inference chain and then print the chain in reverse order as the justification of "how" a result was reached. Unfortunately, the rules as expressed in the system may bear little resemblance to the actual reasoning process used by an expert. To resolve this problem, some tools allow additional attached information to be associated with each rule, node, or frame, perhaps as a special slot, which is used for the explanation mode.

The logically related question asks not only how did the system arrive at the result, but "why?" This requires a more sophisticated reasoning mechanism to infer and present in an English-like form the details of the inference chain beyond and above just printing the contents of rules. Because the "why" analysis may require a different mode of analysis and explanation, a completely different explanation model may be necessary to capture the required explanatory knowledge in a different form. Most of the current implementations of "why" on the market lack these deep mechanisms. Limited "whys" to justify why a specific question was asked are often accomplished by attaching one text string to each question, which is triggered simply by the "why" command. *Shallow-explanation models* that merely reconstruct the inference path from memory are the most common. *Deep-explanation models*, which are often completely separate from the set of used rules or allow the program to reason from first principles, are quite rare. Future market developments are expected to unfold products with these more advanced explanation capabilities.

As with any high-level software system (e.g., database, spreadsheet, graphics tools, word processors), on-line "help" facilities are significant for user traning, comfort, and efficiency. Knowledge engineers can take advantage of on-line access to help facilities when designing the knowledge representations or inference strategies. Developers should also have the ability to create context-sensitive and general help routines for the end user that may be invoked at key points in the program's execution. The help facilities provided by the vendor may be context-sensitive, or they may require the user to navigate through pages of textual information. A valuable compromise between context-sensitive and free-form help is accomplished with navigation services that show what information, of what depth, is available for topics selected by the user. Help facilities may also come in the form of aids for knowledge acquisition that prompt the knowledge engineer or end user (depending on the stage of development) when information is missing, inconsistent, or unclear.

Another name used for these help services is *explanation facilities*. The more standard theme of "how" and "why" explanations may also be supplemented by "what" explanations, which provide definitions and details for terms and rules. Due to the lack of an industrywide standard vocabulary, purchasers must ensure that their understanding of the facilities offered matches the vendor's.

## 4-9. KNOWLEDGE ACQUISITION, MAINTENANCE, AND LEARNING

Finding an expert system building shell tool with the right type of representation and inference mechanism is just one of the features necessary for a successful development project. Support software used to install and maintain knowledge facts and heuristics can be equally or more important. It is this type of user interaction with the internal expert systems structure that is generally critical for the system's success.

There are four key features in this area: (1) the input processes used by the knowledge engineer to enter knowledge-base facts and heuristics into the system during development, (2) the input processes used by the end user in supplying information, or data, while employing the system, (3) the techniques available to the knowledge engineer for updating the knowledge structures or their contents, and (4) the capabilities of the expert system to "learn" on its own, either from tutorial examples or from normal cases.

Expert systems building tools provide a variety of knowledge-entry methods. These methods are often related directly to the type of representation used. During development, for instance, on the surface level, rule-based systems should prompt the knowledge engineer for both premises and actions of the rules as well as any associated certainty factors. Frame-based systems can prompt the knowledge engineer at each stage of the development of a frame hierarchy and then request the information to systematically generate the slot types of each frame. The potential buyer of a product should ask several questions. What input/output facilities come with the shell? What are the recommended support environment tools? Does a knowledge-acquisition tool support iconic or symbolic entry of knowledge? Natural language phrase entry? Graphical entry? Is there a knowledge-acquisition program that allows the expert to input some of the domain knowledge directly, without the aid of the knowledge engineer? Obviously, the ease of modifying the existing knowledge structures is of key importance to the knowledge engineer and is a primary feature for choosing a tool.

The same questions should be asked concerning tool capabilities for the end-user interface developed by the knowledge engineer. In addition, other relevant questions should also be considered. What high-level facilities can be employed to make the knowledge input and output processes swift, easy, and nontaxing on the end user?

The knowledge engineer's job goes far beyond the simple entry of the knowledge structure's forms and content. What facilities does a shell tool provide for editing existing knowledge structures? If compilers are necessary, how easily are they invoked? How much faster is the execution speed of the compiler over the interpreter? Do the compiler and interpreter always produce the same results? What types of debuggers are available, and how efficient are they? One of the key features of expert systems building shells is the separation of domain-dependent and domain-independent knowledge (e.g., search strategies) in the system. What facilities are provided for modifying the domain-independent knowledge? How can the explanation facilities be used to refine the knowledge of the rule sets? Adding, updating, or deleting rules can cause inconsistencies in the knowledge-base rule set. Do the tools provide aids for automatically checking fact or rule consistency in the knowledge base (this is sometimes called *truth maintenance*)? These are all questions concerning features of interest to both the knowledge engineer and the project manager, for they impact on both the time and cost constraints of the project.

A final feature is *machine learning*. Although machine learning, even in research AI systems, is still in its infancy some very basic tools are available for rudamentary learning in the current batch of expert systems building tools. The two alternatives currently available are *learning from examples* and *learning by induction*. In some places in the literature these two are merged under *induction*. When learning from examples, software subsystems provide a method for inputing examples or test cases. The chain of reasoning employed in the example is used to establish rules for the expert system. In the second case, learning by induction, the knowledge (facts and rules) in the knowledge base are used to infer the presence of other data or to generate new rules for the system. Some systems combine learning from tutorial examples with induction to speed knowledge acquisition. Michie at the University of Edinburgh in Scotland has been a leader in this field, and some of his key ideas are implemented in commercial products.

## 4-10. MACHINE REQUIREMENTS, RAM, DISK, MIPS, ALU, AND PERIPHERALS

Most expert systems building tools are machine-dependent. To provide the necessary performance, developers have often opted to bypass the operating system to talk to the hardware directly. As the development of an expert system proceeds through the stages of prototype, development, initial delivery, and maturation, different hardware systems are usually required. In particular there is frequently a strong contrast between the development and the delivery environment. In addition, the different software development products may necessitate different supporting hardware systems. For instance, an expert systems building shell built upon LISP may run efficiently only on LISP hardware machines and may not be available to run on VAX UNIX FranzLisp. A key feature to analyze, therefore, is the hardware configuration requirements for a particular tool.

This problem may be further compounded by the expert system "success syndrome" mentioned earlier. An expert system designed to run on a single microcomputer may be forced to migrate to different machines and operating systems as demand for use increases, even to the level of a large mainframe. The engineer should study what capabilities an expert system shell has for migration up a machine line. What is the final expected delivery system? Will the system written in one shell have to be rewritten in another shell if migration from a smaller to a larger more powerful machine environment becomes necessary? Are any facilities available that can be employed to avoid a rewrite.

Expert systems generally use large amounts of main and auxiliary memory and are CPU-intensive. In this sense they are far more akin to CPU-bound scientific programs than to I/O-intensive commercial ones. Thus as an expert system expands it tends to run out of CPU capacity before I/O bandwidth becomes the constraint. In some cases, even before the CPU capacity is filled, the tool itself can impose arbritrary maximums due to certain internal table capacities. The system manager should be asking many questions here. What are the minimum RAM, disk, and CPU MIPS (millions of instructions per second) requirements for various sizes of expert systems developed with a specific tool? How many logical inferences per second (LIPS) are needed to meet user response-time requirements, and how many LIPS will the candidate configurations provide? How much swap space is needed on disk to support the virtual storage overhead of the tool? At what point is machine saturation reached? Can the loading for the expected usage be measured? What are the ramifications for existing software packages, if the expert system is to reside on hardware currently in use? Are there further hidden hardware requirements for integrating the system with the enterprise's other systems? Will the system require other specialized hardware peripherals, such as plotters, printers, and graphics input or output devices? Are specialized floating-point accelerators or array processors needed to handle any intensive arithmetical or graphical operations? In a large proportion of applications, a floating-point accelerator is a highly cost-effective investment, due to the large amount of arithmetic needed to propagate probabilities through inference trees.

High-resolution graphics, windows, and color displays based on bit mappings require extensive CPU cycles and RAM. If the tools under consideration support these user-friendly display modes, what is the effect on machine loading and response time? Does the current application actually require graphics and/or color, or is the faster response time offered by other tools without frills more important for the application?

To answer these questions for large applications, sizing calculations are needed to determine the potential loading on the machine. A spreadsheet calculator is one of the best ways to approach machine sizing. It would be helpful if there were one standard template for all expert systems sizings, but, unfortunately, configurations vary so much that each template is almost always dedicated to one application. Analysts must become skilled at composing sizing formulas at the screen while they investigate the many parameters and boundaries that surround any implementation project. While considering requirements for machine hardware, the system designer or manager must also keep the goal of the expert system implementation clearly in perspective. For instance, if the expert system application reduces the time for a job from 20 minutes of the human expert's time to under 2 minutes by the computer, the result time is impressive. If the success of the system attracts more and more users, however, response could again creep upward toward the 20-minute mark, frustrating the users and thwarting the system's time-saving purpose. Designers of the database expert systems operating in a multi-user environment should be particularly aware of the way sizing boundaries change as users are added. A sensible approach is to create a metaspreadsheet with constraints along its *Y* axis and number of users along the *X* axis. The term *meta* is used here, because several background spreadsheets may be required to supply these high-level conclusions. The points where demand exceeds supply, for each system constraint, can then be identified as the system grows. Such an approach can allow the dates for new hardware purchases and software migrations to be identified in advance. Even if the dates are not accurate, the analysis can still identify the trigger points and approriate actions as the system grows.

In summary, a number of important hardware-related issues must be addressed for the development and delivery of an expert system. Most of the questions asked above are not unique to expert systems development. The questions are representative of standard queries investigated by a software/hardware systems analyst in developing a new computerized system. The issues are brought up here to point out the need for a careful analysis before committing to either one or another software products or one or another supporting hardware systems.

## 4-11. RULE CAPACITY, VOLATILITY, AND RESPONSE TIME

Some of the earliest expert systems building shells (most of them rule-based) had fixed limits on the number of allowed rules. Such strict limits were one of the major drawbacks to implementing production applications on an off-the-shelf shell. Rule capacities have expanded greatly since these early shells. Any system will have a fixed upper limit, due to such things as addressing ranges, but the boundaries are not as limiting as they were in the earliest systems. Most of the shells discussed in the next chapter do not impose such restrictive software limits as to make them unusable for production. Then again, careful capacity planning and monitoring is essential, even if the vendor claims that its package has no limits, to ensure that the application does not grow out of the shell limits whatever they may be. For development of a limited application an inexpensive shell with an upper limit of 500 rules may be the ideal. Decreased rule capacity is often the key limitation of earlier versions of shell products, so care should be taken not to choose a tool with a fixed rule limit for applications that are expected to grow over time.

The early products often kept all their rules in RAM for fast response time. When inference engines are not optimized or are running in an interpretive language, then RAM-based rules are essential. Expanding the rule base onto disk is the common approach to increasing capacity. Disk-based expansions can be implemented in several ways. Probably the best way is to use the operating system services to provide virtual storage (VS). Paged *virtual storage,* or *virtual memory,* as it is sometimes called, makes the rule set appear to be all in RAM. Infrequently accessed pieces can be paged out to disk without degrading the entire response time. On operating systems without VS, it is often up to the user program to provide a VS mechanism. MS-DOS and Macintosh, for example, do not provide VS, so shell implementations often provide their own paging facilities. UNIX almost always provides VS and tends to create a smoother, more transparent paging environment than the custom MS-DOS-based tools. Shell vendors creating their own VS-type extensions often do it with varying degrees of grace. Some implementations place groups of rules in a small collection of disk files, which are opened and closed as needed.

A common term for expanding the rule base is to *link* various models, using a specific feature of the shell. If the application falls neatly into a series of modules with highly limited interactions between them, it may be possible to implement it with linked models. If, however, the tree cross-refers to itself in a number of places, creating a more complex web of rules, then linked models are difficult to implement. Virtual storage algorithms on sophisticated operating systems, such as MVS/XA or VMS, frequently provide a more optimum set of pages in real storage than simple custom algorithms. The power of the large operating system VS algorithms, which have evolved over a decade or longer, should not be underestimated. Most linking algorithms are new, but developments are likely to occur to increase their efficiency.

To make a comparison with spreadsheet calculators, the early versions, such as Visicalc, had strict limitations on the number of available rows and columns. The 64KB CP/M machines created strict boundaries, which needed the arrival of the 640KB MS-DOS units to be transcended. Lotus 1-2-3 replaced Visicalc's lead primarily because of its ability to provide more cells. Other products, such as Microsoft's Multiplan and Chang Lab's Microplan, offered linked sheets as a route to expansion. Although the linking approach was a technically feasible style of operating large sheets, the user reaction was that it was difficult to manage and slow in response time. It is likely that linked expert shells will suffer the same fate as linked spreadsheets.

Another issue is the *volatility* of the rule set. A grouping of rules may provide adequate response times when it is first implemented, but its performance could degrade in the face of change. Adding rules, deleting some, and changing the contents of others can have a major impact on certain inference engine implementations. If the tool employs numerous points to link related rules in the rule base, then updates will affect all affected pointers. At one level the situation is akin to simple disk-based access methods. An indexed sequential access method (ISAM) file will usually have a fast response time for both sequential and random access when first created. Additions to ISAM files, however, can degrade performance at a rapid rate. Doubling a file size can often result in snail's pace accesses. IBM's Virtual Storage Access Method (VSAM) is an alternative to ISAM that uses a more sophisticated algorithm to maintain response times in the face of volatility. Even with a VSAM-type access method, reorganization of the file and its indexes will be needed after a large amount of update activity. Knowledge-base designers have to consider all the constraints and matters usually addressed by database designers, plus others specific to knowledge engineering. If rules are updated frequently, then time will have to be allocated for regular reorganizations. In between reorganizations, which can be lengthy, response times can be expected to degrade.

One final feature to analyze is the system's response time. The objective of improving the response time for an application may be a primary motivation for developing the expert system. For example, if the current handling of a situation is with manual paper facilities, then a benefit of computerization should be increased speed of processing transactions. Increased handling speed is often also vital to hold competitors at bay. Thus, the overall time needed to take one case through the expert system is usually crucial. The manual system may have taken 20 minutes, and for the computerized expert to be cost-effective, it may have to come in at under 5 minutes per case. These end-to-end requirements bear back on the shell's ability to process a given number of rules in a certain amount of time.

Different software products have radically different speeds in terms of "rules per second" processed. Interpretive products generally run slower than compiled ones. Inductive tools, which tend to compile, often have a considerable edge on inferencing ones, which are frequently interpretive. If an interpretive inferencing system is delivered on specialized hardware, then it can often regain its lost speed.

The efficiency of the tool is often based on the quality and the complexity of its implementation. Tuning, over 2 or 3 years of produce life, has improved the quality and speeded up many of the maturer offerings. Enhancements to overflow the rule base from RAM onto disk, be it using VS, modularization, or linking, may, however, consume the response time improvements gained from tuning. Another factor, as found with traditional programming languages, is that a greater degree of abstraction or indirection can incur a time penalty due to the need for more layers of software translation. Employing more layers of mapping is an accepted knowledge-engineering trend for the provision of more powerful constructs, but caution is needed here when it comes to meeting response-time constraints. Compilation and a traditional DP language are usually the key features to employ if response time must be optimized. Large amounts of RAM, fast disk-seek times, multiple spindles and a high MIPS rate are also crucial. In any situation all these factors should be carefully analyzed, but especially careful attention should be paid to time-critical, transaction-processing applications.

## 4-12. PRICING AND AVAILABILITY

The cost of expert systems development tools varies considerably. This variation is due in part to the range and assortment of functions available in different tools and in part to the type of business entity that developed the tool. In general, however, there is only a weak correlation between cost and function, primarily because the field is still in its infancy. Cartels and pricing agreements among vendors tend to arise only in markets with established products.

In most markets, the stability and recognized value of products tend to be established only over a period of several years. During this time product costs tend to normalize as consumer choice becomes the ultimate measure of a tool's commercial success. Expert systems building and support tools are still in their very first few years of exposure to this marketplace normalization cycle. Pricing structures are still experimental, with many vendors offering trial schedules or discounts to see how they affect sales.

The environment in which a tool was developed and its purpose may also affect its price. For example, tools developed in a university setting, perhaps with the aid of federal grant money, may be available to the public at a much lower cost than tools developed by a private enterprise, which has had to bear the entire cost of development, marketing, and promotion. After the universities, the entrepreneurial start-up vendors tend to be the ones offering the lowest prices, although even this is not a firm rule. Some startups have tried to charge large sums in an attempt to recoup development costs while keeping the promotional budget to a minimum.

A broad guideline for pricing expert systems tools, as with all software products, is that price is proportional to machine size. Usually mainframe products cost more than minibased products, and PC-based tools are the least expensive. In some markets, such as the relational database field, the price of software is roughly 25% of the naked hardware cost. In this expert systems market, however, software price can far exceed hardware price, especially at the low end. It is possible to pay $3,000 for PC hardware and over three times that for the software. Most buyers of PC systems, who are used to paying 30 to 50% of the hardware value for their total software purchase are in for a surprise with expert systems technology.

Depending on the size and sophistication of the tool, various other factors affect product pricing and should be reviewed to obtain a complete system price. Does the price pay for an individual product, such as a shell or a language, or are other items (e.g., compilers, LISP interpreters, training, or support functions) in the package? In contrast are additional purchases compulsory to make the base product work? Are other hidden costs, such as maintenance, or accessories needed for the application? Start-up costs can generally be expected to be higher for expert systems tools than for other classes of software, due to the needs for consulting, systems design services, training classes, and so on. Instead of looking just at the price of the individual package, one must look at the total project cost. The checklist for a full configuration in Chapter 6 lists more aspects that have to be considered to obtain full costs for the project. In general, the buyer can expect to find the total costs to be highly individualistic, specific to the current application. As a general rule, when all software, hardware, consulting, training, and knowledge-engineering costs are taken into account, a large-scale production expert systems budget can easily exceed $1 million.

Concerning product availability, the newness of the expert systems field and the rate at which new products are emerging are confusing to the potential buyer. Common sense suggests a cautious approach to products making their first appearance on the market. It is not unheard of in the software industry that a stand-alone expert system PC shell demonstrated at a trade show is in reality a PC emulating a terminal linked via modem to a mainframe running a prototype. This development code may be written in a fourth-generation language and be far from portable to the candidate delivery platform. Buyers must, above all else, be careful not to purchase such *vaporware*. There are three things seen at trade exhibitions: hardware, software, and vaporware. In the expert systems shell field, experience shows that products that exist only in the marketing literature or still have one foot in the laboratory do not qualify as either software or hardware. Frequently not until a product is ordered does the question of its availability arise. Some vendors have even been known to accept orders, not telling frustrated purchasers that the product does not really exist until some nine months later. A strong purchasing team that knows how to expedite orders and to spot a problem early-on can be invaluable when acquiring the elements of a knowledge-engineering tool set.

Vaporware is only one aspect of the purchasing problem. The pressures of a hot, new market for expert systems tools can cause products to be released before they have been fully debugged and tested. Buyers should beware unless, knowingly or unknowingly, they are willing to serve as alpha or beta test sites for the product. These caveats apply, of course, to all new fields of software product development, but they are especially pertinent in an expanding and competitive market. Market positioning is a key concept here, for almost all available products have some value if their correct position can be established. The vendor literature may or may not exaggerate the robustness and stature of the tool. Careful detective work is needed to evaluate the real status of new tools and match them to applications.

## 4-13. VENDOR STABILITY AND GROWTH

The last area for consideration in analyzing an expert systems building tool is the company supplying the tool. Expert systems building tools and support products on the market come primarily from three sources: (1) universities or research organizations, (2) large commercial concerns, or (3) small start-up companies. These three categories of enterprises represent vastly different product backgrounds and developer interests and tend to influence the type of continued research and development (R&D) and support for marketed products.

Universities and private research groups were primarily responsible for the development of most of the first-generation, custom-built expert systems. The primary goal of these institutions is often basic research; applied research is secondary. Universities generate fundamental knowledge, rather than create production applications. Although the historical perspective has been limiting, current trends show increasing collaboration between universities and private industry in joint basic/applied research ventures. For this reason, liaison between end users and research universities may be fruitful. Users must be careful to assure that collaboration does further their application goals and does not merely fund university research.

Large commercial corporations, like research organizations, also tend to have extensive R&D departments, but they usually transfer experimental technology to commercial applications. As successful marketing is usually critical to continued existence, the thrust of making experimental code into robust products tends to be more established. The size, stability, and age of such enterprises usually say a great deal about their ability to translate ideas and knowledge into working, salable products. Even though size is often a sign of success, it does have its disadvantages and can lead to inertia and stagnation. New ideas in American business tend to come from small companies, and almost nowhere is this more apparent than in expert systems technology.

Start-up companies have provided a significant part of expert systems development. Many were founded by former employees of university, research, or large commercial organizations who felt they had better ideas or approaches to products. Some of these startups have now grown to respectable sizes and lead the market in product quality, service, and sales. Service is frequently deemed a reason for using a larger vendor, but a number of the small companies have surprisingly good support available.

Many product vendors offer extensive consulting and development services. The products these vendors eventually market are often the evolutionary result of a number of successful consulting installations. A central kernel, or set of tools, successively refined over repeated applications provides the basis for a tool with an extensive history of development, field testing, and refinement before it reaches the general market. In such a situation the software product may really be a vehicle for selling consulting services; although this mix of product and consulting is usually vital to the user for success.

A key point to consider in selecting a vendor is follow up services. Both large and small commercial vendors have a real-life commitment to helping your application succeed. Their livelihood and reputation depend on it. Universities and small research organizations may not have the same commitment to successful fielded or production systems. Even large corporations often conduct their development in an ivory tower research environment (e.g., Xerox Palo Alto Research Center (PARC) (Palo Alto, California), IBM's Thomas J. Watson Research Center (Yorktown Heights, New York)). In these kinds of situations the sales force is far removed from the developers, and that insulation may prevent purchasers from getting the deep explanatory support they need.

What practical indicators of a company's stability and growth are pertinent in evaluating a potential expert systems product vendor? The year founded, number of employees, total gross income, total R&D expenditure, gross income from expert systems products, number of products sold by version, and gross expert systems R&D expenditure represent one set of general financial indicators of the company's stability.

Similar questions can be asked of a particular product. How much time was spent developing the product? What was the end-to-end person-year involvement? What was the total budget for the product development? When was the product officially released? How many versions have been released? How many installations have been made? All of these are important questions for determining the stage of development and use of a product. For example, a product that is in its fourth version since its release 5 years ago and has 300 installations has probably received extensive refinement. A newly released product with outstanding potential, but having fewer than 20 installations, can still be considered to be in beta testing.

Also important in vendor analysis are the educational services provided by the vendor. In most cases, the degree and quality of these services is a strong indicator of the character of the company as a whole, and particularly of its commitment to satisfying the customer and providing the technical support to ensure a successful installation. Typically four different kinds of user support or learning modalities are available: (1) vendor-site or client-site training sessions; (2) training and user manuals or videos; (3) hot-line telephone consultation support; and (4) the experimental approach, which suggests that the user of the product figure the product out by himself. If a vendor recommends option 4, it may be best to look for a different product and supplier. Options 2 and 3 may be sufficient for products that are not unduly complicated, but the best of all possible situations includes 1–3. Production applications, especially those using new shells, will tend to require a lot of telephone consultation. Potential purchasers of a product should ask to examine copies of the educational training materials and the user, reference, and tutorial manuals. Some of the questions to address are: Are the materials well-written, well-organized, comprehensive, and appropriate for the product users? Are the vendor's product development and extension goals consistent with the buyer's own long- and short-term goals?

A sound method for evaluating both a product and its supplier is to request a list of successful applications, customers, and installation sites. A few minutes on the phone with these product users will usually bring to light the strengths and weaknesses of both the product and the vendor. In particular, weaknesses may be identified that would be otherwise impossible to find without weeks of hands-on labor. Customer service capabilities and service response time may also be quickly gauged by such brief but insightful interviews with end users of the product.

In conclusion, estimating the total project development cost is not easy. Also evaluating the real stability and quality of potential tool suppliers for different stages of the project is not straightforward. Management must commit itself to sufficiently deep analysis of systems and vendors and must then stand by its decisions.

## 4-14. MAIN POINTS: STRATEGIES FOR SELECTING EXPERT SYSTEM TOOLS — FEATURES AND OTHER REQUIREMENTS

• Tools should be carefully selected to match the different phases of the application to

—increase the chances of success
—speed development
—improve the quality of the finished product and
—save money.

• Tool selection should always come after, and not before, application selection.

• Tool selection is a multidimensional task that should compare some 30 different features of the candidate tools.

• Well-implemented expert applications tend to grow, so expandability paths should be central to almost all selections.

• The best researched and proven inferencing mechanism is the rule-based representation.

• The inference engine deduces by chaining rules together in either or both the forward (from facts to goals) or backward (goals to facts) directions.

• Frame-based representations, also known as schemas, are inferenced by the traversal of their networks.

• Frames are connected to form networks by frame-linking slots. Other slots may be filled with attached procedures.

• Various other knowledge-representation approaches exist.

• Almost by definition, expert systems shells have to be able to handle inexact reasoning based on rule unreliability and fact uncertainty.

• Shells can be sensitive to the sequencing of rules, but this sensitivity may be controlled with metarules, which are rules about rules.

• Graphical user interfaces are able to communicate complex knowledge structures, making them suitable for many advanced applications.

• Natural-language user interfaces, although good for specialized vocabularies, tend to have a narrow bandwidth, making them rather slow.

- A high-level language programming interface is almost a necessity for any nontrivial development.
- Database interfaces, either accessed directly or via a programming language, also turn out to be vital for many classes of application.
- Explanation facilities, including "why a question is being asked" and "how a result was inferred," are excellent for training end users to operate new expert systems.
- Various tools exist to aid knowledge acquisition, including learning from examples and learning by induction.
- Expert systems tools tend to be machine-dependent, consuming large quantities of RAM and CPU MIPS.
- The earlier shell products tended to impose strict software limits on the size of the knowledge base, but newer products tend to be only hardware-constrained. It is important to know the limits, however large they may be.
- Product functionality is not at all well-related to product price, and tool prices for essentially the same hardware range from under $100 to over $65,000, so good selections may save considerable money.

## NOTES

[1] PROLOG's popularity has been enhanced by its selection as the "language of choice" for Japan's fifth-generation computer development project. Feigenbaum and McCorduck (1984) and Bramer and Bramer (1984) provide more information on this project.
[2] Marvin Minsky, "A Framework for Representing Knowledge," in *The Psychology of Computer Vision*, P. H. Winston (ed.), McGraw-Hill, New York, 1975.
[3] An early example of this type of work can be found in *Explorations in Cognition*, edited by Norman and Rumelhart, Freeman and Co., 1975.
[4] See the paper by R. A. Kowalski for one of the first introductions to logic programming: "Algorithm = Logic + Control," *Communications of ACM*, vol. 22, pp. 424–436, 1979.
[5] Elaine Rich, 1983, *Artificial Intelligence*, p. 186.

## FOR FURTHER READING

Anderson, J. R., Corbett, A. T. (1986). *Essential LISP*. Reading, MA: Addison-Wesley.

Bobrow, D. G., Stefik, M. J. (1986). "Perspectives on Artificial Intelligence Programming." *Science*, February 28, 1986, pp. 951–957.

Charniak, E., Riesbeck, C., McDermott, D. (1987). *Artificial Intelligence Programming*, 2d ed. Hillsdale, NJ: Lawrence Earlbaum.

Clocksin, W. F., Mellish, C. S. (1984). *Programming in Prolog*, 2d ed. New York: Springer-Verlag.

Cox, B. (1986). *Object-Oriented Programming: An Evolutionary Approach*. Reading, MA: Addison-Wesley.

Goldberg, A., Robson, R. (1983). *Smalltalk-80: The Language and its Implementation*. Reading, MA: Addison-Wesley

Goldberg, A. (1984). *Smalltalk-80: The Interactive Programming Environment*. Reading, MA: Addison-Wesley.

McCarthy, J., Abrahams, P. W., Edwards, D. J., Hart, T. P., Levin, M. I. (1980). *LISP 1.5 Programmer's Manual.* Cambridge, MA: MIT Press.

Rogers, J. B. (1986). *A Prolog Primer.* Reading, MA: Addison-Wesley.

Stefik, M., Bobrow, D. G. (1986). "Object-Oriented Programming: Themes and Variations." *The AI Magazine*, vol. 6, no. 4.

Stefik, M., Aikins, J., Balzer, R., Benoit, J., Birnbaum, L., Hayes-Roth, F., Sacerdoti, E. (1983). "The Architecture of Expert Systems." In *Building Expert Systems.* Hayes-Roth, F., Waterman, D. A., Lenat, D. B. (eds.), Reading, MA: Addison-Wesley.

Sterling, L., E. Shapiro (1986). *The Art of Prolog: Advanced Programming Techniques.* Cambridge, MA: MIT Press.

Wilensky, R. (1984). *LISPCraft.* New York: Norton.

Wilensky, R. (1986). *Common LISPCraft.* New York: Norton.

Winston, P., Horn, B. (1984). *LISP* 2d ed. Reading, MA: Addison-Wesley.

# Chapter 5
# Expert System Shell Tools—Product Analysis by Feature

## SECTION HEADINGS



## OVERVIEW

This chapter presents a perspective on the features found in expert system shells currently on the market. The product comparison matrix indicates the key features offered by a sampling of some 30 different tools. Many products are discussed in the chapter, and selected leading and emergent tools are detailed in the comparison matrix. The same pattern of feature analysis outlined in Chapter 4 is continued here. This material is not meant to be a buyer's guide to expert system shells, but rather a tool-analysis strategy guide. The reader may take the overview information as an introduction to many of the products and a starting point for more in-depth research and analysis to select the best matching expert system building tools for a specific application. Expert systems programming languages and environments will be discussed in the next chapter.

## 5-1. PRODUCT COMPARISON MATRIX

In this chapter the features of a number of the expert system building products on the market will be reviewed briefly. The goal is not to provide an exhaustive analysis of all tools and their features (which would be quickly outdated), but rather to further elaborate the feature-analysis theme developed in Chapter 4 through concrete examples. The product comparison matrix on the following pages (Fig. 5-1) takes the set of features discussed in Chapter 4 and reviews a sampling of different commercial products with respect to these features. The matrix can be read either horizontally, to gain a view of a particular product, or vertically, to see how a certain feature is covered by different products. Because many new products are expected in the market in the next months and years, any analysis like this cannot cover all products. In addition vendors are constantly upgrading there products, so, al-

| Product | Manufacturer or Distributor | Phone | Primary Knowledge Representation/Inference |
|---|---|---|---|
| ACORN | Gold Hill Computers<br>163 Harvard St.<br>Cambridge, MA 02139 | (617) 492-2071 | lattice of frames (inheritance) |
| Advisor Design Software/ Advisor Expert Controller | Ultimate Media, Inc. (UMECORP)<br>275 Magnolia Avenue<br>Larkspur, CA 94939 | (800) 445-3967 | IF/THEN rules (forward and backward chaining) - up to 7 premises per rule |
| Aion Development System/PC (ADS/PC) | Aion Corporation<br>101 University Avenue<br>Palo Alto, CA 94301 | (415) 328-9595 | IF/THEN/ELSE/ELSEIF rule objects (forward and back-ward chaining) |
| Aion Development System/MVS (or VM) (ADS/MVS or ADS/VM) | Aion Corporation<br>101 University Avenue<br>Palo Alto, CA 94301 | (415) 328-9595 | IF/THEN/ELSE/ELSEIF rule objects (forward and back-ward chaining) |
| Automated Reasoning Tool (ART) | Inference Corporation<br>5300 W. Century Blvd.<br>Los Angeles, CA 90045 | (213) 417-7997 | IF/THEN rules (forward, backward, and mixed chaining |
| ENVISAGE | Systems Designers Software, Inc.<br>444 Washington Street<br>Woburn, MA 01801 | (617) 935-8009 | IF/THEN rules (forward and backward chaining) |
| ESP ADVISOR | Expert Systems International<br>1700 Walnut Avenue<br>Philadelphia, PA 19103 | (215) 735-8510 | IF/THEN-like rules (Prolog backward chaining) |

ACORN has been renamed GoldWorks by Gold Hill Computers.

Fig. 5-1. Product comparison matrix.

| Product | Manufacturer or Distributor | Phone | Primary Knowledge Representation/Inference |
|---|---|---|---|
| ESP Frame-Engine | Expert Systems International<br>1700 Walnut Avenue<br>Philadelphia, PA 19103 | (215) 735-8510 | frames (inheritance) |
| Expert-Ease | Jeffrey Perrone & Associates, Inc.<br>3685 17th Street<br>San Francisco, CA 94114 | (415) 431-9562 | rules induced from examples |
| Expert Edge | Jeffrey Perrone & Associates, Inc.<br>3685 17th Street<br>San Francisco, CA 94114 | (415) 431-9562 | IF/THEN rules (backward and limited forward chaining) |
| Expert System Developing/ Consulting Environment (ESDE/ESCE) - VM or MVS | IBM<br>P.O. Box 10<br>Princeton, NJ 08543 | (609) 734-8759 | IF/THEN rules (forward and backward chaining) |
| 1st-Class | Programs in Motion, Inc.<br>10 Sycamore Road<br>Wayland, MA 01778 | (617) 653-5093 | rules entered or induced from examples (forward and backward chaining) |
| GURU | Micro Data Base Systems, Inc.<br>PO Box 248<br>Lafayette, IN 47902 | (800) 344-5832<br>(317) 463-2581 | IF/THEN rules (forward, backward, and mixed chaining) |
| INSIGHT2+ | Level Five Research<br>503 Fifth Avenue<br>Indialantic, FL 32903 | (305) 729-9046 | IF/THEN/ELSE production rules (forward and backward chaining) |
| Integrated Knowledge Environment (IKE) | LISP Machine, Inc.<br>175 Cabot Street<br>Lowell, MA 01854 | (617) 458-9100 | IF/THEN rules (forward and backward chaining) |

Fig. 5-1. continued.

though it is possible to say that product *X* has feature *Y*, it is not so easy to state categorically that product *Z* does not have the competitive feature *Y*. As soon as such a statement is made in the trade press it prompts vendor *Z* to add feature *Y*, and even before it is implemented the feature is promised in the sales literature. For this reason the ~ symbol is used to denote current absence instead of a blanket no. The ~ symbol is also used to indicate areas where the vendor was unwilling or unable to specify details. Company statistics are often not released by private start-ups. The reason may be that they have not been compiled yet or that they do not enhance the vendor's image, or that the vendor believes that the release could give the competition some undesired advantage.

We noted previously that the commercial expert systems building tool industry is still in its infancy. The earliest tools appeared in the marketplace about 1982. The rapid development of the industry has not yet reached that point of stability and maturity where all the key vendors for the next few years can be singled out. Attempting to identify all

| Product | Manufacturer or Distributor | Phone | Primary Knowledge Representation/Inference |
|---|---|---|---|
| Knowledge Craft | Carnegie Group Inc.<br>650 Commerce Court, Union Square<br>Pittsburgh, PA 15219 | (412) 642-6900 | frames (inheritance semantics) |
| Knowledge Engineering Environment (KEE) | Intellicorp<br>1975 El Camino Real West<br>Mountain View, CA 94040 | (415) 965-5500 | frames (inheritance and hierarchies) |
| Knowledge Engineering System (KES) | Software Architecture and Engineering<br>1600 Wilson Blvd., Suite 500<br>Arlington, VA 22209 | (703) 276-7910 | productions rules (IF/THEN) (backward chaining with object classes) |
| Knowledge WorkBench (KWB) | Silogic, Inc.<br>9841 Airport Blvd. Suite 600<br>Los Angeles, CA 90045 | (213) 337-7477 | IF/THEN/ELSE rules in the form of special Prolog clauses (backward Prolog chaining) |
| LOOPS | Xerox AI Systems<br>2400 Hanover St., Bldg. 32<br>Palo Alto, CA 94304 | (415) 494-5800 | Objects (like Smalltalk) - (message passing) |
| M.1 | Teknowledge Inc.<br>1850 Embarcadero Road.<br>Palo Alto, CA 94303 | (415) 424-0500 | IF/THEN rules (forward and backward chaining) |
| Personal Consultant Easy | Texas Instruments Incorporated<br>P.O. Box 80963<br>Dallas, TX 75380 | (800) 527-3500 | IF/THEN rules (forward and backward chaining) |
| Personal Consultant Plus | Texas Instruments Incorporated<br>P.O. Box 80963<br>Dallas, TX 75380 | (800) 527-3500 | IF/THEN rules (forward and backward chaining) |

Fig. 5-1. continued.

current and projected features for all available tools is not only taking aim at a moving target, but seeking to hit a target without clearly defined boundaries. The strategy employed in this chapter, therefore, will be to highlight through example the style of analysis project managers should use in deciding which tools to select. This chapter does not attempt to provide in-depth profiles of each company and its products, as such matters are constantly changing. Substantial introductory-level insight into particular products will be gained, however, as a by-product of the survey.

Fortunately, there are signs of increasing stability and acceptance of the relatively new expert systems technologies. Teknowledge, Inc. (Palo Alto, California), one of the leading expert systems vendors, received the first patents for expert systems software in computer-integrated manufacturing (CIM) in the fall of 1986. The first patent protects the feature in the company's S.1 product that allows a user to organize knowledge types for large-scale expert system applications. The second patent covers an S.1 feature extending the capabilities of traditional

| Product | Manufacturer or Distributor | Phone | Primary Knowledge Representation/Inference |
|---|---|---|---|
| Process Intelligent Control (PICON) | LISP Machine, Inc. 175 Cabot Street Lowell, MA 01854 | (617) 458-9100 | IF/THEN rules (forward and backward chaining) |
| RuleMaster | Radian Corporation 8501 MoPac Blvd., PO Box 9948 Austin, TX 78766 | (512) 454-4797 | IF/THEN or induced rules (forward and backward chaining) |
| SAGE | Systems Designers Software, Inc. 444 Washington Street Woburn, MA 01801 | (617) 935-8009 | IF/THEN rules (backward chaining) |
| S.1 | Teknowledge Inc. 1850 Embarcadero Road Palo Alto, CA 94303 | (415) 424-0500 | relational frames (class hierarchy and inheritance) |
| TIMM | General Research Corporation 7655 Old Springhouse Road McLean, VA 22102 | (703) 893-5900 | IF/THEN rule format, auto generated from user data (emulated forward and backward chaining) |
| TIMM-PC | General Research Corporation 7655 Old Springhouse Road McLean, VA 22102 | (703) 893-5900 | IF/THEN rule format, auto generated from user data (emulated forward and backward chaining) |
| XSYS/EXSYS | California Intelligence 912 Powell St. San Francisco, CA 94108 | (415) 391-4846 | IF/THEN /ELSE rules (forward and backward chaining) |

Fig. 5-1. continued.

programming languages in the small-scale, expert systems shell. Other large and small expert systems products vendors are seeking such formal recognition for software products, and signs of maturation are beginning to appear as the technology continues to gain official technological approval.

The range of market products available is broad, from very simple software tools priced at under $100 to extremely sophisticated tool sets in the $50,000–$70,000 range. The vendors themselves vary from small start-up companies with a few employees, to special divisions of international corporations with thousands of employees. The larger, more sophisticated tool sets (e.g., ART, KEE, Knowledge Craft, S.1), offer a great variety of knowledge representations, interference schemes, user and software interfaces, and development utilities. Their power does not mean that these tools are always the best choice for every application, notwithstanding the price tags. All things considered, there is no one best tool or tool set that will suit or cover every application. A cost-benefit analysis must be performed for a specific application without being overly influenced by projected needs for the future. As noted before,

*(text continued on p. 154)*

| Product | Other Knowledge Representations | Other Inference Mechanisms | Fact Representation Strategies | Fact Uncertainty | Rule Unreliability | Mathematics |
|---|---|---|---|---|---|---|
| ACORN | IF/THEN, WHEN/DO, IF/DO rules, object-oriented progrmg | forward, backward, goal-directed forward chaining | dependency networks, multi-valued slots, sets, defaults, "when-modified" demons | yes | yes | LISP mathematics Rete algorithm |
| Advisor | ~ | ~ | facts and conditions are called "logical conditions" - 127 allowed - compiled in k. base | ~ | ~ | math through external progs. in dedicated env./ AND, OR, NOT |
| Aion PC | state object for decomposition during developmt. | ~ | parameter objects - standard Pascal data structures, or user defined complex structures | yes | yes | Pascal library math support functions |
| Aion VM/ MVS | state object for decomposition during developmt. | ~ | parameter objects - standard Pascal data structures, or user defined complex structures | yes | yes | Pascal library math support functions |
| ART | frames, viewpoints, logic and object-oriented progrming, blackboards | inheritance, logical dependencies, truth maintanence, temporal and hypothetical | relational data base, objects of various types | Bayesian, fuzzy, user defined | Bayesian, fuzzy, user defined | extended Rete algorithm "for all", "there exists", "not in db" and standard operators |
| ENVISAGE | ~ | fuzzy logic, Bayesian inference, demons | string, record, arrays, integer, object, assertions - strong typing | yes - scales, ranges, probabilities | yes | arithmetic capabilities |
| ESP ADVISOR | knowledge base sections - partitions | pseudo-forward chaining through sections | numerical values, phrases, categories, boolean facts | ~ | ~ | arithmetic and tran-scendental via PROLOG and 8087 coprocessor |

Fig. 5-1. continued.

| Product | Other Knowledge Representations | Other Inference Mechanisms | Fact Representation Strategies | Fact Uncertainty | Rule Unreliability | Mathematics |
|---|---|---|---|---|---|---|
| ESP Frame-Engine | IF/THEN rules demons | forward and backward chaining on rules | objects, slots, sets | ~ | ~ | arithmetic and tran-scendental via PROLOG and 8087 coprocessor |
| Expert-Ease | ~ | ~ | logical and integer attributes (up to 255 values/attribute, 31 attributes per problem | ~ | ~ | ~ |
| Expert Edge | ~ | auto truth maintan-ence of knowledge base, Bayesian stats. | object, attribute, values | yes | yes | numeric variables, calculations and equations in rules |
| IBM (ESDE/ESCE) | problem decomposition modules | scaled uncertainty propagation | boolean, numeric, string, multi-valued capability (Pascal based) | yes | yes | arithmetic and boolean operations |
| 1st-Class | ~ | nine statistical calcs., ID3 induction, "what if" capabilities | numerical or logical factors | yes | yes | arithmetic and boolean operations |
| GURU | ~ | fuzzy logic | db records, spreadsheet cells, variables | yes | yes | standard numeric functions plus log, exponential, trig, and statistical functions |
| INSIGHT2+ | ~ | "what if" reporting | numeric, string, facts, object-attribute states, facts shared between modules | yes (can customize) | yes (can customize) | full arithmetic, log, trig, etc. - AND, OR, and NOT operators |
| IKE | frame objects, icons | inheritance | objects, attributes, values and icons | yes | yes | standard arithmetic expressions - ZetaLISP functions |

Fig. 5-1. continued.

| Product | Other Knowledge Representations | Other Inference Mechanisms | Fact Representation Strategies | Fact Uncertainty | Rule Unreliability | Mathematics |
|---|---|---|---|---|---|---|
| Knowledge Craft | IF/THEN rules, logic and object-oriented programng, agendas, methods | forward and backward chaining, demons, procedural attachment, "what if", time sim. | slots in schemas, of any LISP values, including bags, lists, sets, etc. | yes | yes | assess to either LISP or Prolog functions |
| KEE | IF/THEN rules, procedures (methods), object programming | forward and backward chaining, "what if", simulation, truth maint. | objects(units), values, attributes classes, variables in rules, multiple values per slot | easy customization | easy customization | LISP functions and libraries, set logics for classes |
| KES | "hypothesize and "test" (frame-like), statistical models, demons | frame network with abduction reasoning, Bayesian statistics, inheritance | numeric, symbolic, string, etc., user-defined, variables in rules | yes - quantitative or symbolic factors | yes | libraries of functions - complex numerical functions |
| Knowledge Workbench | entity relationship model | 3 types of reasoning plus user-defined, top-down search | predicates and arguments - object-attribute-values, double precision floating point | yes | yes | Prolog functions - true, false, and unknown responses |
| LOOPS | access, rule programming, LISP procedures | ~ | objects can be extended with annotated data structures | user defined | user defined | Prolog or LISP arithmetic and functions |
| M.1 | ~ | ~ | integers, reals, variables, constants, atoms, strings, structures | yes | yes | arithmetic operators and functions (plus calls for C functions) |
| Personal Consultant Easy | ~ | ~ | object-attribute-value triplets, default and limited methods | yes | yes | full mathematics/float point expressions, AND, OR, NOT operators |
| Personal Consultant Plus | frames, LISP functions, access-oriented functions | inheritance, problem decomposition procedures | object-attribute-value triplets, default and limited methods | yes | yes | full mathematics/float point, LISP expressions, boolean ops., user-define |

Fig. 5-1. continued.

| Product | Other Knowledge Representations | Other Inference Mechanisms | Fact Representation Strategies | Fact Uncertainty | Rule Unreliability | Mathematics |
|---|---|---|---|---|---|---|
| PICON | frame objects, icon hierarchy, other rule types | inheritance, simulation chaining, simulation | icon attributees, slot attributes, virtually anything from complex numbers to user-defined | yes | yes | variety of ZetaLISP functions, including complex arithmetic |
| RuleMaster | hierarchical design of modules | network transitions | scoped variables, abstract data types, user defined operations | yes | yes | yes |
| SAGE | ~ | fuzzy logic, bayesian inference | constants, objects, assertions | yes - use of scales | yes | arithmetic functions/ AND, OR, NOT, EXCLOR |
| S.1 | IF/THEN rules, rule categories, procedural attachment | forward and backward chaining, demons | object-attribute-value triplets, default values, strongly typed language with primarily static variable binding | yes | yes | arithmetic operators and functions, "for-each", "exists", etc. (+ C funs.) |
| TIMM | frame-based system | analogical partial match inferencing, demons, procedural attachment | factors and factor values - integers, phrases, with ordering (none, linear, circular, etc). | yes | yes | through external, linked subroutines (FORTRAN) |
| TIMM-PC | frame-based system | analogical partial match inferencing demons, procedural attachment | factors and factor values - integers, phrase, with ordering (none, linear, circular, etc.) | yes | yes | through external, linked subroutines (FORTRAN) |
| XSYS/ EXSYS | ~ | ~ | attribute, value, object triplets, tables - numeric and string variables, operators | yes | yes | full arithmetic operations |

Fig. 5-1. continued.

| Product | Meta-Strategies | Written In What Language (Compilers Needed) | End-User Interface | High Level Language Interfaces | Graphics Interface |
|---|---|---|---|---|---|
| ACORN | goal-directed forward chaining | LISP - compiler included (interpretor also included) | icons, pop-up, mouse-driven | C (includes interface building facilities) | integrated module |
| Advisor | ~ | assembler | menus, English-like text, colored logical values - "yes", "no", "don't know" resp. | assembler in dedi-cated applications | ~ |
| Aion PC | procedural control | Pascal - no special compiler needed | menus, English-like text, pop-ups, windows, color, custom screens, save and rerun later | Pascal, FORTRAN, C, or Assembler - DOS commands | integrated pie, bar, and line chart - also Pascal-callable routines |
| Aion VM/ MVS | procedural control | Pascal - no special compiler needed | menus, English-like text, pop-ups, windows, color, custom screens save and rerun later | Pascal, FORTRAN, C, or Assembler | integrated pie, bar, and line chart - also Pascal-callable routines |
| ART | user controlled prioritized goals and subgoals | LISP and C | English-like language, icons, menus, windows, (generated with Artist tool) | standard operating system-specific call-in and call-out | integrated graphics with scaling, rotation and zoom |
| ENVISAGE | yes- actions and demons | Pascal, no special compiler needed | English-like language, menus | Pascal, FORTRAN, Ada | through language interfaces |
| ESP ADVISOR | sections - and with PROLOG-2 interface | PROLOG-2 (PC - $145-$1495) or PROLOG-1 for VAX ( $1895 -$3275) needed | window-based text - displays paragraphs of advisory text | to PROLOG-2, thence to C and FORTRAN | via PROLOG-2 |

Fig. 5-1. continued.

| Product | Meta-Strategies | Written In What Language (Compilers Needed) | End-User Interface | High Level Language Interfaces | Graphics Interface |
|---|---|---|---|---|---|
| ESP Frame-Engine | demons | PROLOG-2 (PC -$145-$1495) | window-based frame display | to PROLOG-2, thence C and FORTRAN | via PROLOG-2 |
| Expert-Ease | ~ | UCSD p-System - included | example viewing, English, graphic decision tracing | ~ | ~ |
| Expert Edge | ~ | C - no special compiler needed | menus, windows, color capability | ASCII interfacing | ASCII interfacing |
| IBM (ESDE/ ESCE) | control blocks | Pascal - no special compiler needed | menu-driven, "redo" and "undo" options for saving session | Pascal, PL/1, COBOL, FORTRAN, assembler, etc. | ~ |
| 1st-Class | blackboard, chaining of k bases | Pascal and Assembler - no special compiler needed | menu selection, pend and resume session | import/export ASCII files - any DOS executable language | high level language interfaces |
| GURU | rule-firing order, degree of search for unknowns | C and Assembler - no special compilers needed | natural language, menus, command language, color display and graphics | C and SQL-like query language DOS commands | sophisticated inte-grated business package |
| INSIGHT2+ | goal selection metaphor | Pascal - no special compilers needed | menus,pop-ups,windows funciton keys, color, save and restart session | all external program execution - standard ASCII parameters | through high level languages |
| IKE | rule priorities | ZetaLISP PLUS and CommonLISP | menu-based English-like language or graphical display | ZetaLisp or CommonLisp as appropriate | through language interface |

Fig. 5-1. continued.

| Product | Meta-Strategies | Written In What Language (Compilers Needed) | End-User Interface | High Level Language Interfaces | Graphics Interface |
|---|---|---|---|---|---|
| Knowledge Craft | yes - restrictions, truth-maint., documentation | CommonLisp | multi-windows, pop-up menus, commnads, icons | CommonLisp (machine dependent calls to FORTRAN, etc.) | 2D integrated graphics with scaling, rotation and zoom included -- else via CommonLisp |
| KEE | classes, hier-archies, agendas, rule ordering | CommonLisp | menus, multiple windows graphical and icon displays, commands | CommonLisp (machine dependent functions) | integrated graphical toolkit - zoom, mag-nify, multiple views |
| KES | classes | C - no special compiler needed | menus, commands, or third party packages | C, C-callable languages (e.g., FORTRAN, etc) fully embeddable | through C |
| Knowledge Workbench | yes | Prolog and C | natural language with windows - menu based | C - UNIX calls | through C |
| LOOPS | hierarchy of class objects | LISP (compiler along with Xerox AI package included) | menus, windows, icons, graphical displays | LISP, also closely coupled with Quintus Prolog | built-in gauges, dials, buttons -- interface through Prolog |
| M.1 | meta-proposition and meta-facts | C - no special compiler needed | windows, pull-down menus, color, help, value checking, etc. | C or assembler | file transfers, or through C calls, also "Windows for C" |
| Pers. Cons'l Easy | static rule prioritization | PC Scheme (a modern LISP) - no special compilers needed | pop-up menus, lang. phrases, icons, retrace and change values | MS-DOS commands | system for using third party icons |
| Personal Consultant Plus | dynamic or static rule prioritization | PC Scheme (a modern LISP) - no special compilers needed | pop-up menus, lang. phrases, icons, retrace and change values | complete LISP envirn-ment, object prgrm, C and MS-DOS | system for using third party icons |

Fig. 5-1. continued.

| Product | Meta-Strategies | Written In What Language (Compilers Needed) | End-User Interface | High Level Language Interfaces | Graphics Interface |
|---|---|---|---|---|---|
| PICON | user-defined capabilities | ZetaLisp PLUS and CommonLISP | menus, icons, graphical | ZetaLisp or Common-Lisp as appropriate, or any data stream | any data stream (including real-time data) |
| RuleMaster | hierarchy of modules | C - no special compiler needed | English-like language - user defined | C, FORTRAN, or any language callable from C or FORTRAN | through language interfaces |
| SAGE | ~ | Pascal - no special compiler needed | textual - scrolling line-by-line | Pascal, FORTRAN, Ada | through language interfaces |
| S.1 | block structure control, rule groups, etc. | C - no special compiler needced | default is graphical on UNIX machines, otherwise textual unless custom designed | C | through C<br>"DV-Draw" |
| TIMM | link multiple systems into network or hierarchy | FORTRAN-77 compiler | menu-driven - English - like languge dialog | VAX- all languages, others - FORTRAN or Assembler | high level language calls |
| TIMM-PC | link multiple systems into network or heirarchy | FORTRAN-77 - Ryan-McFarland version 1.0 (or higher) compiler | menu-driven -English - like languge dialog | IBM Prof. FORTRAN, PASCAL, or Assembler | high level language calls |
| XSYS/ EXSYS | knowledge base hierarchies | LISP (requires IQLISP from Integral Quality, Seattle - not included) and C | English-like text | any lang. passing/ receiving parameters and values | call external graphics packages |

Fig. 5-1. continued.

| Product | Database Interface | Explanation Facilities | Context Sensitive Help | Developer Tools | Induction/Learning by Example |
|---|---|---|---|---|---|
| ACORN | Dbase (II/III), Lotus 1-2-3, or C callable routines | yes | yes | GMACS editor and browse function | ~ |
| Advisor | ~ | inquiry justification | ~ | interactive rule and fact editor - text form - compiled before inference | ~ |
| Aion PC | external language routines, Lotus 1-2-3, dBASE III, R:base 500 | why, how, and what | yes | customizable object and text editors,windows, run-time debugger , syntax and semantics checking | ~ |
| Aion VM/ MVS | external language routines | why, how, and what | yes | customizable object and text editors,windows, run-time debugger, syntax and semantic checking | ~ |
| ART | SQL-like interface | how and why | yes - command oriented | Studio - structure or text (PROSE) entry for objects, browsing, tracing, break-pointing, and graphical | modified ID3 utility - Art by Example |
| ENVISAGE | through language interfaces | yes | yes | screen editors for rules, objects - tracing facilities | ~ |
| ESP ADVISOR | via PROLOG-2 | how and why | explain facility | text paragraphs editor - standard text editor - tracing | ~ |

Fig. 5-1. continued.

prototyping with a relatively less expensive tool is often one of the best strategies for gauging the need for more sophisticated tool sets. Expert system consultants, as discussed in Chapter 9, can be one of the best resources for effectively analyzing and comparing potential tools for a project.

The tools on the market, as illustrated by the sample tools presented in the comparison matrix, can be roughly divided into four categories. The first category, *specialized tools*, includes Advisor Design Software (Ultimate Media, Inc., Larkspur, California), PICON (LISP Machines, Inc. (LMI), Andover, Massachusetts), and such more specific products as Palladian Financial Advisor from Palladian Software, Inc. (Cambridge, Massachusetts). Ultimate Media's Advisor is the only tool listed that runs on Apple II, Commodore, and other computers with an 8-bit 6502 processor as well as MS-DOS machines. A special feature of this tool is that expert systems produced with the system can be instantiated in firmware and used as an embedded system for various kinds of control processes. PICON, however, is a combined software/hardware product that runs on the powerful LMI LISP machines. The system contains two

| Product | Database Interface | Explanation Facilities | Context Sensitive Help | Developer Tools | Induction/Learning by Example |
|---|---|---|---|---|---|
| ESP Frame-Engine | via PROLOG-2 | how and why | explain facility | word processor and development editor | ~ |
| Expert-Ease | ~ | decision tree trace | ~ | induction from example, rule text editor - consistency checks | induction from examples |
| Expert Edge | dBaseIII, Lotus 1-2-3 Multiplan, VisiCalc | yes | yes | natural language (text) interface - automatic conflict checking | ~ |
| IBM (ESDE/ESCE) | SQL, DB2, VSAM | how, why, what | help-not context-sensitive | smart editors, syntax and semantic check, screen gen., incremental compile | ~ |
| 1st-Class | high level language interfaces | yes | yes | text, spreadsheet, tree editors - or ext. editors. | induction by examples ( 3 modes) |
| GURU | sophisticated integrated relational db - also dBase III files | yes- attached to rules | yes | rule set manager and text editor | ~ |
| INSIGHT2+ | dBASE II,III - VAX, Datatreive and RS-1 file formats | yes | yes | natural language kb editor, tree reporter, auto or custom screens | ~ |
| IKE | through language inbterface | yes | menus only | graphical monitoring and editing of inference tree | ~ |

Fig. 5-1. continued.

32-bit processors, one for LISP processing and a Motorola 68010-based CPU for monitoring and controlling up to 20,000 different process parameters. PICON is promoted as the state of the art in process control equipment and can also be used in other highly complex applications, such as weather forecasting, satellite monitoring, and financial market monitoring. These specialized tools are not the standard fare for commercial expert system development, but represent one of the rapidly expanding frontiers of real-time expert systems control processing.

The remaining three tool categories contain standard expert system development shells and are differentiated primarily by capabilities and cost of the tools. The least expensive, or *smaller tool* category includes ESP ADVISOR and ESP Frame-Engine (Expert Systems International, Philadelphia, Pennsylvania), Expert-Ease and Expert Edge (distributed by Jeffery Perrone & Associates, Inc., San Francisco, California), 1st-Class (Programs in Motion, Inc., Wayland, Massachusetts), INSIGHT2+ (Level Five Research, Indialantic, Florida), MICE (Machine Intelligence Corp, Bohemia, New York), Personal Consultant Easy (Texas Instru-

| Product | Database Interface | Explanation Facilities | Context Sensitive Help | Developer Tools | Induction/Learning by Example |
|---|---|---|---|---|---|
| Knowledge Craft | multi-user integrated db on VAX, also RMS access -- others through CommonLisp | user defined | yes | rep. schema editors, error handling schema, screen gen., icon managers, debuggers | ~ |
| KEE | KEEconnection for SQL bases, Intelliscope to query db's from KEE | yes | yes | specialized editors, graph rule trees, icons, tools kit browsers, debuggers | ~ |
| KES | through C | why, justifiy | yes | text editor entry (e.g., VI, Wordstar), logic debuggers, rule firing traces | Bayesian induction from statistical examples |
| Knowledge Workbench | Universal Data Base Interface to most relational data bases | yes | yes | UNIX Emacs and VI editors and Prolog tools (trac, debuggers, etc.) | possible through meta-strategies |
| LOOPS | through language interfaces | user defined | user defined | graphical object editors, extensive LISP tools | ~ |
| M.1 | file transfers, C calls- can build relational db internally | yes | yes | ASCII text editor input, windows, traces, debugger menus, browser, etc. | ~ |
| Personal Consultant Easy | external DOS files or dBase II, III, III+ | why, how, review and change answ. | yes | rule editors, validation, trace and debugging aids, screen dev. tools | ~ |
| Personal Consultant Plus | external DOS files or dBase II, III, III+ | why, how, review and change answ. | yes | rule editors, validation, trace and debugging aids, screen dev. tools | ~ |

Fig. 5-1. continued.

ments Inc., Dallas, Texas), RuleMaster (Radian Corporation, Austin, Texas), SAGE (System Designers Software, Inc., Woburn, Massachusetts), TIMM-PC (General Research Corporation, McLean, Virginia), and XSYS/EXSYS (California Intelligence, San Francisco, California). In general these tools employ a single representation scheme and are targeted to a microcomputer for a price under $2000. More specifically, many are IBM PC-based tools for under $500. Several of the products in this category, notably ESP ADVISOR, INSIGHT2+, RuleMaster, and EXSYS, are also available in non-PC, multiuser versions. Such expansion paths can make a low-cost development feasible without blocking future options for larger delivery platforms.

The *middle-range tools* include ACORN (Gold Hill Computers, Cambridge, Massachusetts), Aion Development System/PC (Aion Corporation, Palo Alto, California), ENVISAGE (Systems Designers Software, Inc., Woburn, Massachusetts), Expert System Environment (IBM, Princeton, New Jersey), GURU (Micro Data Base Systems, Inc., Lafayette, Indiana), IKE (LISP Machines, Inc., Andover, Massachusetts), KES

| Product | Database Interface | Explanation Facilities | Context Sensitive Help | Developer Tools | Induction/Learning by Example |
|---|---|---|---|---|---|
| PICON | any data stream (including real-time data) | yes | yes | graphical monitoring and editing of inference tree, icon editor, mouse | monitor and adjust its own rules |
| RuleMaster | through langauge interfaces | yes | yes | pop-ups, knowledge base editor | rule generation through examples |
| SAGE | through language interfaces | yes | yes | text editor for objects and rules, tracing facility | ~ |
| S.1 | through C | yes | yes | graphical display, multiple developers, save test case debuggers, syntax check | ~ |
| TIMM | high level language calls | yes | yes | induction, knowledge base editors | generalization of rules |
| TIMM-PC | high level language calls | yes | yes | induction, knowledge base editors | generalization of rules |
| XSYS/ EXSYS | call DB II/III and other DBMS | yes | yes | text, data batch file, and instruments monitoring rule editors | ~ |

Fig. 5-1. continued.

& KES II (Software Architecture and Engineering, Arlington, Virginia), Knowledge WorkBench (Silogic, Inc., Los Angeles), M.1 (Teknowledge, Inc.), Personal Consultant Plus (Texas Instruments,) and TIMM (General Research Corporation). Product prices for this group run from $2000 up to around $25,000. IBM's product is one of the exceptions at $60,000, but its single knowledge representation and lack of graphics firmly exclude it from the sophisticated level. Vendors are constantly adding features so that some of the middle-range tools have freshly arrived from the low end, while others are on their way to entering the sophisticated class.

The final group contains the most expensive, *sophisticated tool sets* usually employing multiple knowledge-representation schemes coupled with graphical display mechanisms. Pricing in this group (up to approximately $70,000) generally includes extensive training and development support from the vendor. The products included are ART (Inference Corporation, Los Angeles, California), Knowledge Craft (Carnegie Group Inc., Pittsburgh, Pennsylvania), KEE (Intellicorp, Mountain View California), and S.1 (Teknowledge, Inc.).

| Product | Report Generators | Runs on What Hardware/ Operating System | RAM / Disk Needs | Other Needs or Other Products This Product Works With |
|---|---|---|---|---|
| ACORN | history of user queries | IBM PC/AT (MS-DOS) 80386 machine | 5M bytes (est.)/ 1 floppy drive - hard drive recommended | mouse recommended |
| Advisor | recursion stack printing (backward chaining) | Apple II+, IIe, IIc, Commodore 64/128, Atari 800 (+XL & XE), and 6502 architectures - or IBM PC/AT for Controller developmt | ~ | other products - KNOWLEDGE ENGINE or EXPERT CONTROLLER for mechanical control |
| Aion PC | report generation language | IBM PC , XT, AT and compatibles (PC-DOS, 2.0 or higher) | dev.- 512-640 Kbyte/ hard disk or qd floppy exec. - 448-640 Kbyte/ hard disk, qd, or 2 dd | ~ |
| Aion VM/ MVS | report generation language | IBM S/370 (MVS/TSO, VM/CMS, CICS execution capability) | 2 Mbyte region/ 10 cylinders of type 3350 storage (or DASD equivalent | IBM Graphical Data Display Manager (GDDM) and PGF needed for graphics |
| ART | Studio tool set | Symbolics, TI Explorer, LMI, Sun 3, Apollo, VAX (VMS, UNIX) IBM RT/PC | 4 Mbytes/ 140 Mbytes | high resolution bit mapped screen (1K x 1K), mouse |
| ENVISAGE | log of terminal interactions - report facility | DEC VAX or MicroVAX (VMS) | 2.5 Mbytes | ~ |
| ESP ADVISOR | print consultation sequence | IBM PC, XT, AT and compatibles DEC VAX (VMS), mircoVAX II (VMS) | PC - 384 Kbytes/ 2 floppy drives - hard disk recommended | optional -- PROLOG-2 interface for extensions and customization - ($395 for PC) |

Fig. 5-1. continued.

These four categories roughly classify the various types of tool available. Less so than for most software products, price is not a direct measure of the functional capabilities of the tool. To further complicate the price arrangements, some vendors include such extras as on-site maintenance, bug fixes on demand, training classes, software updates, and extensive development assistance in the purchase price, but other suppliers do not.

It is not reasonable to try to provide an exhaustive feature-by-feature analysis of all products on today's market. The rapid rate of growth and development in the commercial expert system tool market will quickly render any such detailed presentation obsolete. A prime example is the porting of products to an ever-widening circle of hardware/software configurations. Another example is the continual upgrading of products' features by modification and addition. The key purpose of this chapter is to alert the expert system purchaser and developer to the various types of features available across all tools, not to analyze all tools for a particular set of application parameters. When it comes to addressing application-specific issues, the approach in this book is to ask questions that can be answered only by someone who has analyzed the

| Product | Report Generators | Runs on What Hardware/ Operating System | RAM / Disk Needs | Other Needs or Other Products This Product Works With |
|---|---|---|---|---|
| ESP Frame-Engine | print consultation sequence | IBM PC, XT, AT and compatibles | 512 Kbytes/ 2 floppy drives - hard disk recommended | optional -- PROLOG-2 interface for extensions and customization - ($395 for PC) |
| Expert-Ease | ~ | IBM PC, XT and some compatibles | 128 Kbytes/1 floppy, 2 floppy drives or hard disk recommended | ~ |
| Expert Edge | session trace | IBM PC, XT, and AT or compatables (DOS 2.0 or higher) | 256 Kbytes, 512 K rec. recommonded/ 2 floppy disk drives | ~ |
| IBM (ESDE/ ESCE) | rule tree on display | IBM 370, 4300, 30xx (VM or MVS versions) | ~ | Graphical Display Data Managment., Document Composition needed |
| 1st-Class | report generator of query sessions | IBM PC or compatibles/ PC DOS 2.0 or higher | 256 Kbytes, 512 K recommended/ 1 floppy, hard disk optional | supports all displays and printers |
| GURU | yes - reports also in form of business graphics | IBM PC, XT, AT, RT and compatibles (PC-DOS, MS-DOS, UNTRIX-32) and VAX (VMS) | PC - 640 Kbytes/ hard disk recommended | other products - full access to MDBS III data base |
| INSIGHT2+ | line of reasoning, tree reporter, generated facts, rule steps, etc. | IBM PC, XT, AT or compatibles (PC-DOS or MS-DOS) - DEC VAX (VMS) | PC -512 Kbytes/2 floppy or hard disk drive - VAX - 8 pages | ~ |
| IKE | decisions and conslusions | LISP - LMI Lambda and TI Explorer (ZetaLISP PLUS); CommonLISP supporting workstatns | 4 Mbytes | ~ |

Fig. 5-1. continued.

context of that specific application. As the market is constantly changing, any application-specific answers will also change, so analytical studies can not be avoided.

The approach used here will be to discuss product features, in the vertical columns in the comparison matrix. This reductionistic presentation does not foster a complete view of any single product, but the reader can achieve this goal by surveying the entire product row in the matrix and then supplementing that information by referring to corporate product literature and sales personnel. Other available publications (e.g., Walker and Miller's *Expert Systems 1986: An Assessment of Technology and Applications*) attempt to provide more in-depth coverage of specific products at a given sampling time.

One final note concerns feature description terminology. Expert system tools have typically developed in either university/research environments or private industry. Although a reasonably standardized jargon does exist in the field, there is no universally established set of definitions for all aspects of expert systems tools. In general, those AI/expert system corporations formed by former university or research

| Product | Report Generators | Runs on What Hardware/ Operating System | RAM / Disk Needs | Other Needs or Other Products This Product Works With |
|---|---|---|---|---|
| Knowledge Craft | screen or trace prints | Symbolics 3600, TI Explorer, VAX and MicroVAX (VMS), Sun 3 (UNIX) | 16 Mbytes suggested | 3- button mouse preferrable / other product -Language Craft by manufacturer (natural language interface developer) |
| KEE | print screens to files | Symbolics 3600, TI Explorer, Xerox 1100, Sun, Apollo, IBM RT PC, HP 9000, VAXstation | Symbolics 4Mbytes, TI 8 Mbytes, Sun 12 Mbytes, Xerox 3.7 Mbytes | PC-Host Delivery system using PC's and VAX |
| KES | directed output to file | VAX and MicroVAX (UNIX,VMS), IBM, Gould, Apollo, Tektronix, HP 9000, IBM PC's and RT and compatibles (MS-DOS, UNIX) | PC - 640 Kbytes/ hard disk | combination products - KES + UNIFY = VERIFY, KES + IDMS in VAR relationship |
| Knowledge Workbench | report generator of Unify | Sun, Masscomp, NCR, Plexus (UNIX, Sys 5, and 68000-based UNIX M/CS) | 2 MBytes (4 Mbytes virtual) RAM | ~ |
| LOOPS | includes desk-top publishing tools | Xerox 1108/1109/1185/1186 AI LISP Workstations | 1.7 Mbytes/ 10 Mbytes disk minimum | 1186 workstation supports MS-DOS commands and application calls |
| M.1 | execution trace storage | IBM 370 (VM), PC, XT, AT, for full compatibles (MS-DOS) | 348 Kbytes min, 512K recommended on PC's | color board and monitor recommended |
| Personal Consultant Easy | screen print, trace or kb to file or printer, case history library | TI Professional or Business-Pro, IBM PC, XT, AT or compatible, (PC or MS-DOS) | 512 Kbytes, 640 K rec./ 2 floppy disks, hard disk recommended | ~ |
| Personal Consultant Plus | screen print, trace or kb to file or printer, case history library | TI Business-Pro, Explorer, IBM PC/AT or comp. - delivery only: PC, XT, TI Professional (DOS) | PC - 640 Kb - 2Mbytes/ floppy disk and hard disk for development | ~ |

Fig. 5-1. continued.

institute professionals tend to use more research-oriented terminology. Corporations that have traditional software engineering backgrounds tend to use a hybrid terminology based on both traditional AI jargon plus conventional software terminology. The potential user must be careful to identify exactly what the vendor personnel are referring to in a description, even when talking to technical support groups one would expect to speak the same language. There is a need for even greater caution when reading product literature (most often prepared by marketing, rather than technical people) and talking to sales personnel, who probably lack the technical breadth and experience to relate product features and capabilities outside their own vocabulary.

## 5-2. KNOWLEDGE-REPRESENTATION STRUCTURES AND INFERENCE MECHANISMS

The knowledge-representation structures and associated inference mechanisms outlined in Chapter 4 were based on a few primary

| Product | Report Generators | Runs on What Hardware/ Operating System | RAM / Disk Needs | Other Needs or Other Products This Product Works With |
|---|---|---|---|---|
| PICON | continual monitoring and reporting | LISP - LMI Lambda and TI Explorer (ZetaLISP PLUS); CommonLISP supporting workstatns | 4 Mbytes | MAP compatible |
| RuleMaster | ~ | PC XT/AT compatibles (MS-DOS) VAX (UNIX,VMS), UNIX workstations, HP, Vectra, Integral PC | PC - 500 Kbytes / 10 Mbytes minimum | ~ |
| SAGE | log of terminal interactions | IBM PC, XT, AT or compatible (PC-DOS, MS-DOS) PDP-11 (RSX11-M) | 256 Kbytes/ 1 floppy disk - 2 disks recommended | ~ |
| S.1 | report formatter | IBM 370 (VM), VAX and MicroVAX(VMS,Ultrix), HP 9000 Tandem, AT&T, NCR, Sun,Apollo IBM RT PC, IBM AT (delivery) | 348 Kbytes | ~ |
| TIMM | yes | IBM, Amdahl, VAX, Prime, Zenith 100 (any OS which supports FORTRAN 77) | 640 Kbytes | ~ |
| TIMM-PC | yes | IBM PC-XT/AT or compatible (MS-DOS 2.1 or higher) | 640 Kbytes | math coprocessor chip needed |
| XSYS/ EXSYS | standard or custom reporting | IBM PC, XT, AT (PC-DOS 2.0 or higher) and VAX (VMS) | PC- 256 Kbytes min., 640K rec./ 1 floppy drive, hard disk optional | 8087 coprocessor needed for PC uncertainty / other prod. - TABLET for tables and FRAME for frames by same vendor |

Fig. 5-1. continued.

schemes: IF/THEN production rules, frames (including associative networks), objects, and access triggers or demons.

The rule-based expert system building tools, based on earlier IF/THEN production rule models, were the first to proliferate on the market. SAGE was one of the first tools, as was Expert-Ease. Expert-Ease had the special feature of allowing rules to be induced through the entry of examples according to a scheme developed by Michie; rules, however, could not be entered manually by premise and conclusion. Some tools, such as the Aion Development System, INSIGHT2+, Knowledge Work-Bench, and XSYS/EXSYS, have extended rule forms with ELSE or ELSEIF actions as well. Another important feature is whether the rules can include temporary variables in either the conditions or the conclusion to be evaluated when the rule is fired. Almost all the rule-based products now support intermediate variables, but some of the earlier products did not.

The majority of the products in the matrix show that the rule-knowledge representation scheme is the primary or only representation scheme. The simplest tools follow the EMYCIN-like, backward-

| Product | Response Time (rules/second) | Knowledge Chunk Limit | Released | Price | Other Data -- Copies Sold<br>Corp: Income/Employees/Founded |
|---|---|---|---|---|---|
| ACORN | ~ | memory limit (applications up to 24 Mb.) | 3/87 | $4995 | ~<br>$2,000,000 / 50+ / 1982 |
| Advisor | 250 | 255 rules/ 127 facts | 1985 (10/86 for controller version) | $99.50 ($5000 for controller version) | 100 (7 for controller version)<br>~ / 40 / 1984 |
| Aion PC | ~ | ~ 2000 objects | 10/85 | $7000 - run time version $750 | ~<br>~ / 25 / 1984 |
| Aion VM/ MVS | ~ | memory limit | MVS-8/86<br>VM- 12/86 | $60,000 (CICS add $15,000 - run time version $25,000 | ~<br>~ / 25 / 1984 |
| ART | 100 - 300 | none | 2/85 | $65,000 (first copy) | 400+<br>~ / 130 / 1979 |
| ENVISAGE | ~ | memory limit | 8/85 | $15,000 and up | 10<br>$82,000,000 / 1600 / 1969 |
| ESP ADVISOR | 13K LIPS on PC/AT | ~3000 | 6/84 | PC - $895<br>VAX - $2950-4800 (PROLOG extra) | 1000+<br>~ / 28 / 1981 |

Fig. 5-1. continued.

chaining, goal-directed behavior pattern with uncertainty. For instance, Personal Consultant Easy and SAGE are both low-cost, introductory tutorial systems for learning about expert systems strategies. Generally rules are presented to the systems through a rule editor, which allows premises and actions to be entered by the applications designer. ESP Advisor and Knowledge WorkBench create PROLOG-based rules, and goal-directed, backward-chaining is then implemented as standard deduction in PROLOG. Other products, such as Expert-Ease, 1st-Class, RuleMaster and TIMM/TIMM-PC, have implicit rule structures formed by induction from examples. 1st-Class and RuleMaster have the advantage of supporting regular IF/THEN-type rule entry as well. A number of different concepts of "rules" exist in commercial products, and the buyer should be aware that each vendor may have its own definition. One vendor's "rule" can very well be another vendor's "object."

Goal-directed backward-chaining is the simplest form of IF/THEN rule representation/inference mechanism (e.g., M.1, and SAGE). The next level of inferencing capabilities includes forward rule chaining, in addition to backward-chaining (e.g., Advisor, Aion, IBM ESE, S.1, and

| Product | Response Time (rules/second) | Knowledge Chunk Limit | Released | Price | Other Data -- Copies Sold Corp: Income/Employees/Founded |
|---|---|---|---|---|---|
| ESP Frame-Engine | 13K LIPS on PC/AT | ~ | 8/86 | $895 (PROLOG-2 inter-face $395) | ~ <br> ~ / 28 / 1981 |
| Expert-Ease | ~ | 2-300 examples/ problem - multi-ple problem links | 1983 | $695 | ~2000 <br> ~ / 6 / 1983 |
| Expert Edge | ~ | memory limit | 9/85 | $1500 (run time versions available) | ~ <br> ~/ 6 / 1983 |
| IBM (ESDE/ ESCE) | ~ | | VM - 8/85 <br> MVS - 7/86 | $60,000 (for both dev. and consultation mods.) | ~ <br> $50.1 Billion / 400,000 / 1914 |
| 1st-Class | ~ | 240 ex./module - mult. modules to disk limit | 7/85 | $495 (unlimited run-time copying) | 600 <br> ~ / 6 / 1985 |
| GURU | 20 actually fired, more may be considered by inference engine | memory only | 12/85 | $6500 run time versions ~$400 | 100+ <br> ~ / 300 / 1979 |
| INSIGHT2+ | ~ | 2000 rules/rule set | PC - 5/86 <br> VAX - 12/86 | PC - $485/$95 run-time -- VAX $4800-$14,400 | 3500 <br> ~ / 10 / 1984 |
| IKE | ~ | none | 1986 | $15,000 | < 50 <br> ~ / < 200 / 1979 |

Fig. 5-1. continued.

INSIGHT2+). Recall that forward-chaining is useful for inference from basic data to conclusions based on those data. Virtually all the medium- to upper-priced shells include both forward-and backward-chaining. The highest degree of rule integration is found in such tools as ART and GURU. These tools support a mixed mode of forward- and backward-chaining, where forward- and backward-firing rules can be interleaved at the rule level during traversal of the inference net. Most other systems support only inference according to one method at a time during an inference, or perhaps the use of linked rule sets that support one method or the other. Developers are advised to keep this consideration in mind as they analyze tools and the knowledge structure best suited to the application.

Although it is not detailed in the table, products also vary according to the number of premise conditions or actions allowed for each rule. These limits are sometimes noted in the product literature, but more often the buyer must procure technical manuals or telephone the vendor's technical support staff to gain this information.

| Product | Response Time (rules/second) | Knowledge Chunk Limit | Released | Price | Other Data -- Copies Sold Corp: Income/Employees/Founded |
|---|---|---|---|---|---|
| Knowledge Craft | ~ | none | 9/85 | $50,000 (includes 2 weeks training for 2) | 170<br>~ / 140+ / 1984 |
| KEE | ~ | none | 1983 | $55,000 (includes 9 da. training + 2 da. consulting + site fee) | 1200<br>$18,500,000 / 200 / 1980 |
| KES | ~ | no software limit | 10/83 | PC - $4,000<br>workstations- $7000<br>VAX&Gould-$25,000<br>IBM(MVS) - $60,000 | 200<br>~ / 60 / 1978 |
| Knowledge Workbench | 15 K Lips | disk space only | 5/86 | $24,150 or $8,100/ year - separate modules avail. | 15<br>~ / 25 / 1983 |
| LOOPS | 52 KLIPS on Xerox 1109 | several thousand objects and rules | 8/86 | $4,500 | 200+<br>$8.7 Billion / 100,000 / 1961<br>(1974 started in AI) |
| M.1 | ~ | ~1000 facts and rules | 6/84 | $5,000, execution copies $500, training 1 week @ $2,500 | M.1 + S.1 > 1250<br>$15,000,000 / 175 / 1981 |
| Personal Consultant Easy | ~ | ~400 rules with 640K DOS limit | 1984 (8/86 latest version) | $495 ($95 run-time copies) | 1000's<br>$6 Billion / 80,000 / 1930 |
| Personal Consultant Plus | ~ | ~1000 rules with extended or expanded memory | 1984 (8/86 latest version) | $2,950 ($95 run-time copies) | 1000's<br>$6 Billion / 80,000 / 1930 |

Fig. 5-1. continued.

For many applications, rule-based systems are the most appropriate tools for capturing expertise derived from experience. In contrast, certain other applications need a more formal, systematic, *structuring* of knowledge. The frame-based products provide this kind of structure and are the second most popular of representation form. Other terms used to refer to constructs similar to frames are schemas, icon hierarchies, and partitions. Invariably, inheritance of properties from frame to frame in these hierarchies is the main mode of inference tied to the frame representation. ART, KES, IKE, Personal Consultant Plus, PICON, TIMM, TIMM-PC, XSYS/EXSYS (through an extra module) all support frame representations, as well as rule representations. These tools have been given a primary-rule status and secondary-frame status in the comparison matrix. ACORN, ESP Frame-Engine, and Knowledge Craft, however, have been designed as primarily frame-based systems. In each case, IF/THEN-type rules are also supported, usually as a special type of slot in the frame prototype. Because the support of more than one inferencing technique has become so widespread, it shows up the

| Product | Response Time (rules/second) | Knowledge Chunk Limit | Released | Price | Other Data -- Copies Sold<br>Corp: Income/Employees/Founded |
|---|---|---|---|---|---|
| PICON | up to 1000 | memory only | 1984 | $60,000 | < 50<br>~ / < 200 / 1979 |
| RuleMaster | ~ | 1000 rules on PC | 12/84 | DOS -$995 - others<br>1-user - $5,000<br>mult-usr- $17,500 | 200+<br>$65,000,000 / 1100+ / 1969 |
| SAGE | ~ | memory limit | 4/82 | $499 | 85+<br>$82,000,000 / 1600 / 1969 |
| S.1 | ~ | none | 7/84 | single user $25,000<br>multi-user $45,000<br>execution $9,500<br>2-wk. train $5000 | S.1 + M.1 > 1250<br>$15,000,000 / 175 / 1981 |
| TIMM | ~ | 5000+ per network | 1981 | $19,000<br>unlimited run-time copying within organization | <50<br>$62,000,000 / 775/ 1961 |
| TIMM-PC | ~ | 500+ per network | 1981 | $1900<br>unlimited run-time copying within organization | <50<br>$62,000,000 / 775/ 1961 |
| XSYS/ EXSYS | 100 in forward mode, 100+ in backward mode | 5000 on PC (640K), more on VAX | 5/83 | PC-$995 umlimited runtime (rt) copies<br>VAX-$5-10,000, depend on rt copies | 62<br>$100,000+ / 4 / 1983 |

Fig. 5-1. continued.

tools that are limited to rules only, such as IBM's ESE and Teknowledge's M.1. Frames, as argued by Software A&E are especially good for diagnostic, selection, and classification problems.

Quite often the distinction between frames, networks, and objects is blurred. From the most general viewpoint, both frames and rules can be seen as special cases of object programming. ACORN, ART, and Knowledge Craft support object-oriented programming styles, and IKE and PICON illustrate the object or frame structures in the form of icon hierarchies. Logic programming, which is more akin to writing in the basic symbolic programming language, is supported by ART, LOOPS, and Knowledge Craft. The rather infrequent technique of access triggers, or demons, is employed in ENVISAGE, the ESP Frame-Engine, Personal Consultant Plus, and the TIMM products. The term *demons* is often associated with the UNIX world, where it is used to describe concurrent processes, such as printer drivers, that are always active. A wider use of the term demons, as described for Knowledge Craft, covers the attached procedures to be found within frames. When various conditions are met, the demon process becomes active, similar to a

SMALLTALK method, and changes the state of selected variables in the system.

The concept of an associative network representation, as outlined in Chapter 4 is not so frequent in product descriptions. MICE and MIS Expert from Machine Intelligence Corp. (Bohemia, New York) are specifically semantic network systems, although many of the system constructs are hybridized with more standard rule mechanisms. These two tools can have powerful icon constructs attached to nodes to illustrate the progress through the inference network. ACORN's frame system is described as a lattice framework containing a dependency network. KES also has a frame network. RuleMaster performs inference by network transitions through knowledge-base modules, and the TIMM systems use an analogical pattern-matching scheme to navigate through the search space (network) induced from examples. Because most of the inference implementations are subtly or distinctly different from each other, no watertight compartmentalization of methods should be attempted for these various tools.

Modular development and access are important features for knowledge bases. This splitting up the knowledge representation into modules may be denoted as *rule sets, knowledge modules, sections* (e.g., ESP Advisor), or *state objects* (e.g., Aion). For frame-based systems, of course such knowledge partitioning is implied in the concept of the frame. The modular frames are then linked into a frame hierarchy or heterarchy (network). In other tools, such as Expert-Ease or 1st-Class, limited, smaller knowledge chunk clusters are created and must be combined to form larger knowledge bases. These capabilities allow the developer to partition the knowledge base into appropriate functional groupings with carefully specified linkages. Such modularization aids in decomposition for development, effectively prunes the search tree according to initial inputs, and speeds execution times.

Procedural attachment for frames is noted for Knowledge Craft and the TIMM procucts. Other frame-based systems tend to denote procedural attachment functions as simply *rules*. Rules of sufficient depth and complexity and the ability to perform several rule functions in sequence can be equivalent to a procedure activation. Once procedural attachments become the major way of changing internal system states, then the frame approach moves in the direction of object-oriented programming. The ability to perform such operations is a key example of matters that should be discussed with a vendor's technical support staff.

A number of tools support various degrees of what if or hypothetical analysis. 1st-Class, INSIGHT2+, and IKE are three such tools. Generally this means that part or all of an inference chain session can be "put on hold" while another branch of the chain is pursued. In 1st-Class, a what if question causes the entire program to be rerun, so that user query sessions can be pended and resumed. In IKE a truth-maintenance system for exploring hypothetical what if situations allows the user to change his mind during the consultation. This change causes the inference process to backtrack and correct the inference chain back to the point where the user was firm.

The most extensive tool sets offer even more than these elementary capacities through elaborate hypothetical and simulation capabilities. For instance, ART has a "hypothetical viewpoints" system (like what if) for constructing, comparing, and automatically evaluating hundreds or thousands of different alternatives. KEE's "KEEworlds" module also allows the creation and comparison of world models representing different hypothetical situations. The logical consistency of each such world is kept in line by an "assumption-based truth maintenance system." Knowledge Craft also has "event management" capabilities to introduce the element of time-driven developments into complex simulations.

The final matrix column related to the area of knowledge representation notes some of the particular fact-representation strategies used by vendors. In most cases, the data-structuring capabilities are a direct expression of those provided by the language the system was written in. For example, a system written in PASCAL will generally pass on its strong typing for variables even up to the user interface. Fact objects range from such simple data types as integers, floating-point numbers, and text phrases to more complex user-defined structures, including frames and objects. The most standard facts representation for rule based tools is the *attribute-value-object* triplets. One object, such as an oil tank, can have many attributes, such as height of oil, oil temperature, capacity, and number of inlets. Each attribute can have only one value at a time, so to store values they are held as a triplet along with pointers to the relevant object and attribute. The term *object* used here is the primitive element, different from the objects used in object-oriented programming.

The entries in the matrix are not meant to be an exhaustive evaluation or comparison of all the techniques employed by different vendors. As noted before, these items have been expressed in the terminology of each vendor, and some descriptions are aimed at fundamental data types, while others are described in more abstract terms. The bottom line is that it is up to the buyer to verify that the short-list products do support the features required for the application. A concrete example is that a product does in fact support the use of real floating-point numbers and operations if these features are central to the application at hand.

## 5-3. FACT UNCERTAINTY AND UNRELIABILITY OF RULES

The majority of the systems included in the comparison matrix support some form of both fact uncertainty and rule unreliability. The apparent exceptions are Advisor Design Software, ESP ADVISOR, ESP Frame-Engine, and Expert-Ease. These nonprobabilistic systems have been categorized by some observers as *decision-tree managers,* rather than expert systems shells. Without any need for probabilities, certain applications may be better handled with a traditional COBOL-style decision-tree product. A number of the report-generating aspects of fourth-generation languages provide IF/THEN structures without uncertainty measures. The primary function of the expert system shell is that it offers dialogue-style consultations between man and machine. In Advisor, this characteristic comes from the way the inference engine runs continually and reports new conclusions as the input facts change. Although the use of uncertainty is desirable and in some applications required, other applications may not require this facility.

The usual approaches for handling fact uncertainty and rule unreliability are of the form of confidence factors, scales, and ranges applied to specific facts or rules. Fuzzy logics are included in a few products (e.g., ART, ENVISAGE, GURU, and SAGE). Most products supply one or more techniques for propagating uncertainties during inference, although Bayesian statistical inference is the dominant approach. Knowledge WorkBench is an example of a product that includes three different propagation methods. Other tools (e.g., ART, INSIGHT2+) allow the developers to define their own strategies for managing uncertainty. TIMM's "partial-match analogical reasoning" uses matching on a subset of the clauses of an individual rule to handle probabilities. This inference method emphasizes the management of incomplete knowledge. Inexact knowledge is also handled by similarity as well as by exact matching on clauses.

Some of the features under "other inference mechanisms" are also techniques for managing fact uncertainty or rule unreliability. The whole approach of exploratory what if analysis is one style of investigating inferenced uncertainties and working to minimize them. These what if evaluations are primarily through the use of fuzzy logic and Bayesian statistics, although some tools, such as ART, Knowledge WorkBench, and INSIGHT2+, support user-defined inference mechanisms for managing uncertainty as well.

Uncertainty management can also be tied to metastrategies where systems are guided to minimize the uncertainty in their conclusions. If other heuristics are used to sequence the execution of rules, then the uncertainty of the conclusions can grow to be unmanageable. By now it should be clear that many of the shell features cannot be isolated and evaluated: they must be appreciated in the context of the related features. Feature tradeoff decisions have to be made by the designer for the specific application under investigation.

## 5-4. LOGIC AND MATHEMATICS

The mathematical and logical operations that can be performed during an expert system run may be vendor-created functions, items based on the language the shell tool has been written in, or straight access to a high-level or symbolic language. The specialized logics needed to manage uncertainty were discussed in the previous section. The standard logical operators AND, OR, and NOT are found, for example, such simpler products as INSIGHT2+ and Advisor Design Software. In such products as SAGE, the logical operators have been extended with EXCLOR (EXCLusive OR). Almost all products provide these logical operators within the rule structure, so that conditional and compound rules can be built up.

The provision of arithmetic facilities through user-defined functions is one of the key additions supplied by Texas Instruments in the Personal Consultant Series in upgrading the Easy product to the Plus middle-range product. GURU is another medium-category product that maintains its own mathematical and logical environment separate from the underlying base language, GURU is actually written in C and assembler for fast execution speed, but it still supplies a rich set of logarithmic, trigonometric, exponential, and statistical facilities supplementing its standard numeric functions. RuleMaster is typical of many of the shells in that it provides limited arithmetic functions and fuzzy logic within the shell, but if anything more complicated is needed, the developer must go outside the shell to find it.

The full LISP programming environments are extremely rich in mathematical and logical functions, particularly when the different dialect extensions and field-developed facilities are added. There are several ways to access its mathematical and logical functions without complete system development in LISP. The Intellicorp product KEE, for example, was originally written in the rich LISP extension of a preliminary version of LOOPS from Xerox. LOOPS, which stands for LISP Object-Oriented Programming System, brings the full SMALLTALK-80 style of object-oriented programming and many other user-created functions to the LISP world. Several other shells, including ACORN, IKE, and PICON, follow this pattern of providing access to the underlying LISP mathematics. PROLOG access is provided in shells such as ESP Advisor, ESP Frame-Engine, and Knowledge WorkBench. In a number of vendor's products, LISP and PROLOG can intercommunicate, so, for example, the LOOPS user can access Quintus PROLOG when running on Xerox D Series machines.

In some expert system tools, such as TIMM and TIMM-PC, specialized external subroutines can be developed in the underlying language (FORTRAN for the TIMM products) and linked to the shell to be called at run time. Rulemaster and KES are two of the many products that link into high-level languages, frequently C, to provide many kinds of mathematical and logical functions. Aion, following the pattern of its base PASCAL, provides access to the PASCAL library of mathematical functions. This approach works well in the Aion environment, as its fact representation follows the standard PASCAL data structures. Aion's user-defined complex number structures do extend the PASCAL data types, so more care has to be taken with them when accessing mathematical functions.

A key ability in rule-based systems is the ability to use both variables and operators in either the IF or the THEN part of the rule. In some tools, such as XSYS/EXSYS, these operators can be either system- or user-defined. ART extends the paradigm to provide some of the most sophisticated pattern-matching capabilities in rules. In ART, variables can be pattern-matched against literals or sequences of literals, logical operations include "for all" and "there exists," and it has the ability to determine what is not in the database. These abilities can be further augmented by arbitrary user-written code. As with all these different expert system functions, it can be seen that a large range of provisions exist in the tools. It is up to the buyer to see what level of sophistication the application demands and then purchase accordingly.

## 5-5. EFFECTS OF RULE SEQUENCING AND USE OF METARULES

The sampling of products in the comparison matrix display the wide range of sensitivity to rule-sequencing options available on the market. At one extreme are simple products like ESP ADVISOR, in which, if the conditions of more than one rule is satisfied, the first one sequentially in the knowledge base is fired. In ESP ADVISOR, the text to be displayed with rules is stored sequentially in the knowledge base, without indirection, so sequence is all-important. PROLOG-based tools, such as knowledge WorkBench, tend to be highly procedural, too. Though most manufacturers do not refer to their rule-control capabilities as *meta rules*, a good number offer some means for determining rule firing order or prioritization (e.g., ART, 1st-Class, GURU). Knowledge-base partitioning, as in ENVISAGE, RuleMaster, and SAGE, can also assist in rule ordering. Often the sequence of rule modules can be user-controlled even if the strategies for sequencing the firing of rules within a module cannot. With some products, such as XSYS/EXSYS and RuleMaster, utilities or compilers automatically rearrange the rule orderings for the fastest execution time.

The user should understand the effects of rule sequencing on product performance. Otherwise, rearranging the sequence during an edit session can cause unwanted side effects, such as modifying the conclusions for queries that were previously thought to be debugged. In some products, like Aion, the physical sequence of the rules in the knowledge base has no effect on the shells' conclusions. Others, such as INSIGHT, M.1, PICON, and IKE, can have sequence effects that may not be anticipated in advance. Yet others, such as 1st Class, Personal Consultant, and GURU, allow the knowledge engineer to set priorities and define the sequence of control.

The larger tool sets generally provided the greatest opportunities for metalevel functions. Knowledge Craft, for instance, has a separate metaknowledge scheme that allows such diverse functions as chronicling of knowledge-base development, maintenance of dependency relationships to provide local-area knowledge-base specialization, or the tailoring of relations on a schema (frame) by schema basis. ART allows the user to prioritize goals and subgoals, which is especially valuable in certain forward-chaining applications. IKE allows priorities to be associated with different rules, which permits a variety of metastrategies to be formulated. GURU offers one of the crispest sets of meta options, creating flexibility while not making the system too complex for nonexpert users. The engineer who has control over the 100 developer-set controls for the GURU operating environment, ranging from printer settings to the use of colors, is able to select from a small set of firing sequences, including random sequence, probability sequence, or storage sequence. Another piece of metaknowledge in GURU allows the developer to establish the degree to which the system should attempt to infer an unknown value. The ability to create user-defined error routines, as in Knowledge Craft, is another valuable metacapability that can be expected to appear in more systems in the near future.

## 5-6. USER INTERFACES FOR KNOWLEDGE DISPLAY

The most popular end user interface modality among expert system shell products is the English-like text phrase dialogue. It would not be correct to use the term *natural language* to describe the vast majority of

English like interfaces. Some progress in natural language has been made, and, if this is important for the application, then GURU. Knowledge Craft, KES, and Knowledge WorkBench should be investigated. Usually the English-like "canned" phrase dialogue is supported by menus or window facilities. Popups are available in ACORN, the Aion products, and INSIGHT2+. Although Aion may not have the most sophisticated knowledge structures and inferencing mechanisms, its user interface is impressive. If a development aim is to impress executives who have little knowledge or engineering experience, then employing a professional-looking color/window/popups tool can be beneficial. In contrast, a tool like RuleMaster, even though excelling in learning by example and induction, may be judged by the same executives as lacking in visual impact.

Although the majority of systems are oriented toward the traditional text string-type user interfaces, change is happening at a fast pace. When it comes to full functional bit-mapped graphics with all the support tools to develop visual applications, three tools stand out: ART, KEE, and Knowledge Craft. These three may be among the most expensive tools available, but for the highest quality built-in bit-mapped graphics they are the tools. At a lower level of sophistication, icons can be designed by system developers and employed in ACORN, IKE, MICE, and PICON. Color screen displays are available in Advisor System Design, the Aion products, and INSIGHT2+. If color is not available directly, then certain operating systems, such as Santa Cruz Operation's Xenix on a PC/AT, allow the programmer to select screen text colors dynamically. The expert system shell must have a high-level language interface to access the color selection controls, but if this is available, as in RuleMaster or KES, then the color capabilities of Advisor and INSIGHT can be emulated.

ESP ADVISOR has the special feature of being able to display large amounts of text. Each block of text is stored at development time and has rules associated with it. This facility makes the tool valuable for storing entire manuals on-line and can even eliminate the need for condensing existing stores of knowledge to elementary rule form. Of course, the ESP text strings are not parsed by the inference engine, but they are still triggerable on demand by system conditions.

Utilities are included in many products that aid the developer in designing user interfaces, such as with INSIGHT2+ where both automatic screen generation and custom screen design are supported. The advanced tools, again, offer more sophisticated facilities for interface design. For instance, ART supports rule-based interface animation, and KEE has "KEEpictures," a device-independent, object-oriented graphics package that can be used to construct dynamic composite images from primitives. SimKit, a package available from Intellicorp which works with KEE, allows expert systems to have libraries of graphically displayed simulation objects that are useful for what if reasoning. These KEE facilities are extensions of the LOOPS "gauge concept." Gauges allow system variables to be displayed on the screen and updated in real time, similar to the dials on an automobile's dash board. When gauges are combined with screen-based pushbuttons, then almost any style of electromechanical person-machine interface can be emulated. Xerox, for example, has used LOOPS-based expert systems to assist in the design of photocopier user controls. S.1, like Knowledge Craft and LOOPS, provides graphic development services to trace rule trees allowing the line of reasoning to be observed. In S.1, for example, the knowledge engineer can zoom in or out to see the overview or details of the inference path. Although development graphics obviously help the developer, other tools are needed to bring graphics to the production environment. Teknowledge is rapidly extending M.1 and S.1 in this graphic direction to maintain S.1's position in the sophisticated category of tool sets.

Without a high-resolution, bit-mapped display, many of the more graphical styles of shell interface are impractical. The IBM PC resolution permits only the most rudimentary graphics to be displayed, but as developed in the next chapter, machines such as the Sun, Apollo, Symbolics, Tektronix 4400 Series, Xerox D Series, and TI Explorer offer far more possibilities. Graphical expert systems interfaces, as opposed to natural language, appear to be the industry trend for the future.

## 5-7. GRAPHICS, DATABASE, AND PROGRAMMING INTERFACES

Virtually all the products support accesses to other programming facilities. In contrast to the earlier closed expert system shell tools, most vendors are now marketing products with so-called open architectures. The open architecture allows products to be interfaced with other software modules and systems in a commercial production environment (this area is discussed in more detail in Chapter 8).

The "high-level language interfaces" column in the matrix shows the range of possibilities for the various products. The simplest interfaces are not actually "high-level language" interfaces at all. For instance, the 6502-based Advisor Design Software supports interfaces in assembler language in dedicated embedded applications. Expert Edge, 1st-Class, INSIGHT2+, and XSYS/EXSYS allow interfacing through standardized ASCII data or parameter file transfers. The file-transfer mechanism is not as fast or as flexible as a direct high-level-language subroutine interface, but it is certainly better than nothing. Language interfaces almost always allow the expert system to call other modules, but a few, such as KES, allow other modules to call the expert system. Certain PC-based products, such as Personal Consultant Easy, GURU, and Aion/PC, are able to invoke various MS-DOS commands from the expert system shell, and products running on UNIX can frequently access UNIX commands, as with Knowledge WorkBench or RuleMaster. The UNIX shell facilities of pipes and I/O indirection, when coupled with an appropriate UNIX-based expert system and the C programming language, can provide a very flexible environment with almost no constraints.

Most products provide support for the high level languages they were written in, as well as for other related languages. For example, the Aion products, written in PASCAL, offer interfaces through PASCAL, FORTRAN, C, or assembler. Similarly, ENVISAGE and SAGE (written in PASCAL) interface through PASCAL, FORTRAN, and Ada. The FORTRAN-based TIMM shells support FORTRAN and Ada calls on all applicable machines and all standard languages on VAX machines. A number of vendors support a family of interlinkable compilers, so once access has been obtained to, say, C, then access can be gained to FORTRAN, PASCAL, Ada, etc. automatically. The ZetaLISP Plus or CommonLISP base for the PICON and IKE tools allow only calls to those languages. Through Expert Systems International's extended PROLOG language, PROLOG-2, used to write ESP ADVISOR and ESP Frame-Engine, C and FORTRAN can be accessed. The key feature for the buyer to investigate is not just the language available, but also the support facilities provided within the tool for building these interfaces. Fig. 5-2. summarizes the frequency of base languages and interface languages for the product matrix samples.

When it comes to database interfaces that mimic the high-level language access, ART has an SQL-like database interface, and the built-in relational database in GURU allows interfaces based on SQL-like query languages as well as C. ACORN, which its vendor describes as a "fifth-generation tool", has a three-tier data heirarchy. At the top level a high-level expert system shell allows easy object description and expression of rules and relationships. The middle level gives the developer access to the knowledge-representation language. At the lowest level, the developer can access the Common LISP base directly. The LOOPS system has been extended by Patel Labs to access relational databases on a separate host, via a natural language interface.

Graphics, database, and spreadsheet interfaces come in three main forms: as an integral part of the main packages, "hooks" to external

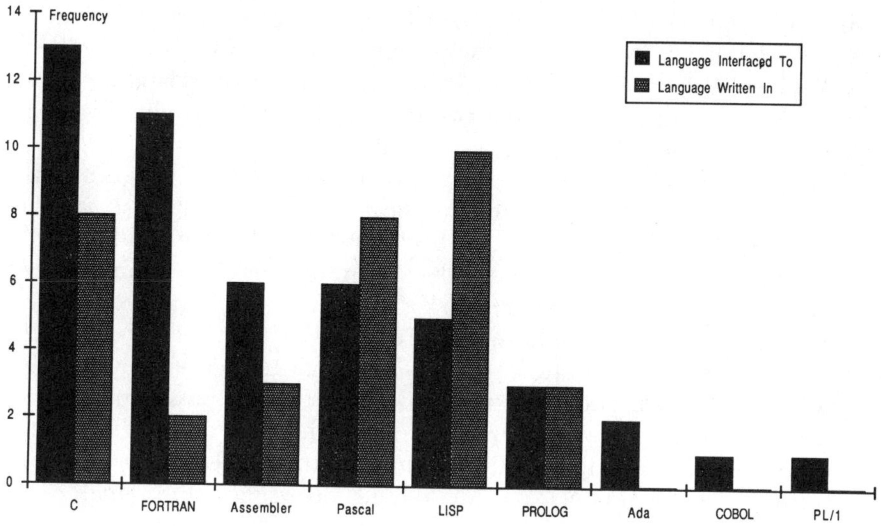


Fig. 5-2. Languages written in and interfaced to.

packages, and the ability to write interfaces via the high-level language interfaces just discussed. Integrated graphics-display capabilities of various degrees of sophistication are provided by ACORN, the Aion products, KEE, ART, GURU, and Knowledge Craft. Business graphics, providing bar, pie, and line graphs are included in the Aion and GURU products. The high-end packages ART and Knowledge Craft support scaling, rotation, and zoom as part of the general handling of bit-mapped images. GURU offers some of the most sophisticated business graphics, including color, points, line types, fill patterns, symbols, and logos. Due to the lack of popular standardized graphics packages, the remaining tools support graphics only through their language interfaces (e.g., DV-Draw and DV-tools for KES). At the low end of graphics capabilities is the ability to place a fixed bit-mapped image on the screen as a consequence of a specific rule action. The photographs included in this book show the Personal Consultant's portrayal of a robot and a snail to clarify the nature of questions asked by the system. ART, like many of the object-oriented systems has an artist tool for editing bit-mapped images.

The popularity of database and spreadsheet programs on PCs has resulted in a number of specific product interfaces, such as to dBase II/III (ACORN, Expert Edge, GURU, INSIGHT2+, Personal Consultant Easy, XSYS) and Lotus 1-2-3 (ACORN, ADS/PC, Expert Edge). The non-PC products generally allow high-level language interfaces to almost all database products. INSIGHT2+ explicitly supports DataTrieve and RS-1 formats in its VAX version. The Knowledge WorkBench uses a "Universal Database Interface" for accessing most relational data bases. RuleMaster has a similar access module, but it has specifically been implemented for Unify. Integrated databases are found only in ART, GURU, and Knowledge Craft. As has been discussed elsewhere in this book, most serious expert system applications require database access, so, unless work is spent creating a bridge to a third-party product, the shell choices are limited. Nonetheless, quite a few of the third-party RDBM's, such as Oracle (Menlo Park, California) and Informix (Menlo Park, California), are significantly more powerful than those contained within an expert system shell, so there can be advantages to developing a bridge. KEE connection software allows KEE users to pass information between databases, particularly IBM's DB2, and expert systems developed in KEE. Intelliscope, also by the manufacturer of KEE, provides an integrated environment for querying, browsing, and analyzing databases.

The open architecture found in many shells allows for clean interfacing between expert system modules and modules written in other languages. For instance, in the Aion products, the ability to call or be called by other modules in other languages allows the developer to replace the security, user interface, report generator, and graphics components of the products with those written in other languages. One reason for replacing certain Aion portions would be to bind existing third-party products into the expert application. In a product like GURU, many of the candidate software tools that could be integrated are already internal. For instance, GURU can recall or store results from the expert system in the spreadsheet or database, or the spreadsheet can consult the expert system for needed information. One other unusual feature of GURU is the built-in automatic communication capabilities, which allows automatic dialup of the expert system for consultation by a remote computer or user terminal. An alternative use of the communication link is to auto dialup a second computer for a specific information request (e.g., remote database of stock prices) to gain facts during a consultation.

## 5-8. "HOW" AND "WHY" EXPLANATIONS AND "HELP" FACILITIES

Essentially all the products provide facilities for explanations. In the simplest form, as noted in Chapter 4, this may be a tracing of the rule chain produced by the inference path, which lists the rules triggered. This approach represents the "how" end of the spectrum. A more sophisticated approach allows the developer to attach text to each rule to be displayed to the end user, rather than the possibly more obscure rule format. This text style is generally more helpful for justifying "why" the inference path was taken. Explanations can, of course, be attached to frame slots as easily as to rules.

At the simplest end of the spectrum are products like Advisor Design System and Expert-Ease, which simply respond to explanation queries with a tracing of rules. More advanced systems, such as RuleMaster, can provide explanations to both specific questions from the user during consultation and automatically to explain inference conclusions as they are reached.

In addition to "how" and "why" explanations, the Aion products include a "what" option to provide additional information for such purposes as defining terms. Another advanced explanation option is the provision of a visual tree of the rules as they have been triggered. LOOPS and Knowledge Craft provide "graphical rule trees." Some applications based on LOOPS have even set portions of the tree to blink to show the current strategies the inference engine is working on as it queries the user.

Some form of "help" facility is provided with almost all the products. IBM promotes its extensive on-line help facilities, available in both the consultation and development environments, as key to introducing this advanced technology to novice users. If the help is not context-based it may be provided in the form of menus, as with IKE. Some help services are not fully context-sensitive, in the fashion of just hitting one key (such as "?") to get appropriate advice, but they do allow users to specify which command they want help with. ART and LOOPS follow this command-oriented scheme for providing assistance.

Help facilities may be geared to either the developer of the expert system or the end user. The use of menus, windows, or popups in many of the products lends itself to providing context-sensitive help. A window can temporarily override a portion of the screen to provide helpful information. Most of the more sophisticated products allow the developer to custom-design the screen menus used by the end user and to include context-sensitive help and explanatory messages as needed.

## 5-9. KNOWLEDGE ACQUISITION, MAINTENANCE, AND LEARNING

Knowledge acquisition is the process of installing the knowledge base in the expert system. It could be argued that facts supplied by the user during a run of the expert system might be called knowledge acquisition, along with data or knowledge inferred during the expert system run.

The "knowledge acquisition and maintenance" column in the matrix emphasizes the tools used to install and maintain the initial knowledge base, rather than techniques for acquiring data or acknowledging the state of consultation during the inference process.

Generally, the knowledge-acquisition editors are matched to the specific type of knowledge representation in use. The current trend is for those tool sets with multiple representation schemes to have a corresponding editing screen for each representation type. The earlier expert system building shell tools did not have such hand-tailored editors, and users often relied on standard text editors, such as Wordstar, for rule and fact entry. Most of the INSIGHT family of expert system shell tools have used Wordstar for rule entry. The Knowledge WorkBench is another example that relies upon the UNIX editors, such as VI and EMACS.

Knowledge-tracking features to be looked for include the ability to trace a session for debugging purposes and automatic type checking, or validation, as objects, rules, or facts are entered. The ability to graphically display the inference tree, as in quite a few tools, is a highly effective technique for debugging the knowledge-base rules. *Break pointing* also stops the inference flow at specified points for analysis. With frame-based systems, such as Knowledge Craft, the editor usually takes the form of a *schema editor*, capable of guiding the user through the generation and modification of frames, slot by slot. Automatic rule consistency checks that occur as new rules are added to the knowledge base is another valuable debugging aid supported by many tools. Expert Edge and INSIGHT 2+, for example, provide consistency and conflict checks.

The process of learning in the expert system building tools is essentially limited to the process of learning rules through examples. Example induction is a process of taking declarative knowledge and changing it into procedural knowledge. One exception is PICON's ability to modify its own functioning after some time in use in a particular control environment. This ability represents the cutting edge of metalearning capabilities. In the knowledge acquisition column in the comparison matrix, it is tacitly assumed that the knowledge is "acquired" when the developer enters it. Entry is usually in predetermined knowledge chunks through the stated means, typically an English-like editor, unless the ability to induce knowledge chunks through examples is indicated. The AI research topics of automatic programming and machine learning are still rather far removed from these current generation systems.

The tools incorporating induction, or learning from examples in one form or another, are ART, Expert-Ease, 1st Class, Knowledge WorkBench, RuleMaster, TIMM, and TIMM/PC. Expert-Ease claimed to be the first induction-based tool on the market. It employs a technique developed by Michie for creating rules from sets of examples presented to the system. Radian Corporation, with the aid of Michie, further refined this example induction system in the RuleMaster tool. Whereas induction is the only means for knowledge-base generation in Expert-Ease, RuleMaster supports developer-provided IF/THEN production rules as well. Some users of RuleMaster prefer to work directly with the IF/THEN rules, as working through the induction module can be a rather indirect way to achieving specific results. 1st-Class allows standard developer-rule entry together with three modes for automatic rule generation from examples. ART uses a modified form of the "iterative dichotomizer" (ID3) algorithm in its "Art by Example" module, which is one of the many in the tool set. The TIMM products incorporate a dual knowledge-acquisition model based on either conventional rule entry or induction from examples. TIMM also provides a facility for metalearning generalization of rules. Most induction systems will do some generalization, which should be under developer control, because it would not be desirable for all applications.

The analysis of reporting facilities parallels closely the product capabilities for explanation. The inexpensive products usually offer the simplest facilities, such as printing the session log or the tracing of events that transpired on the screen. The next level of reporting is complete knowledge-tree printouts showing all possible paths, goals, and conclusions. The more sophisticated tools (medium- and high-range) contain greater facilities for report generation, much like report generators associated with databases or fourth-generation language software. A valuable feature found in the Aion products is cross-reference lists between the different knowledge-base objects

- the parameter object that holds data
- the rule object that relates information between parameters
- other object types that contain information about gathering, structuring, and displaying knowledge base information
- the state object that relates the objects to each other and provides a way to decompose the problem for development.

Support software for knowledge-base validation is virtually essential for large applications. Run-time monitor debuggers, as found in the Aion products, are extremely useful. Another key feature, found in XSYS/EXSYS, and Knowledge WorkBench, and LOOPS, for instance, is incremental compilation of the knowledge base, which allows rules to be tested as they are written. Facilities for multiple, password-protected, knowledge-base versions are available in some tools. These facilities, in such tools as Knowledge Craft and the Aion products, are powerful aids for the knowledge-base administrator (Knowledge Craft on the VAX includes a multiuser database-management system).

## 5-10. MACHINE REQUIREMENTS, RAM, DISK, MIPS, ALU, AND PERIPHERALS

The vendor products presented in the comparison matrix span the full range of machine sizes, from 64KB RAM 6502 microcomputers to the largest mainframes. Only about a half-dozen of the products have been written specifically for LISP or PROLOG machines, and of these, nearly all are now supported on conventional machines as well. Most of the porting from LISP machines to conventional machines has taken place since 1985 and exemplifies the trend of expert systems technology moving into the traditional industrial and corporate environments. The porting of products to an ever-widening variety of machines can be expected to continue into the forseeable future. Any writeup that claims to have a complete list of hardware environments supported by these tools is likely to be outdated by the time it is printed.

A significant number of the low- and mid-range products have been designed for IBM PCs, XTs, ATs, and full-compatibles. Over a dozen products have their roots in standard IBM PC technology, including M.1, Aion/PC, the ESP family, INSIGHT, and Personal Consultant. The 80286-based AT-class and PS/2 models are for now the most promising development and delivery tools due to both their speed and memory capacity. Although minimum RAM and disk requirements vary from one PC product to another, the maximum 640K RAM with 20MB hard disk configuration is usually recommended for best performance. The Digital Equipment Corporation's VAX minis, running either VMS or ULTRIX, ranging from the MicroVAX II on up, are the second most popular vehicles for expert systems after the PC. VAX tools are targeted at one or both of DEC's operating systems, ULTRIX and VMS. KES, RuleMaster, ART, and GURU will run in both DEC environments; KES, RuleMaster, and GURU can also run on the PC, so there are several options for growing from PCs to VAXs. The Aion and IBM products have been engineered specifically for the IBM environment. Aion's code is portable from the PC up to the System/370 mainframes. Aion also has the advantage over IBM's tools of running under CICS, in addition to ESE's VM and MVS. Although there are many choices on the smaller hardware environments, when it comes to selecting a shell that will support hundreds of mainframe users, the options become few (e.g., TIMM, Aion, M.1 delivery, S.1, IBM's ESE). The Canadian shell TWAICE from Logicware, Inc. (Mississauga, Ontario), is another new product that runs under both MVS and VM. TIMM, M.1, and Aion support porting from PC development prototypes up to System/370 mainframes. TIMM allows the additional flexibility of running on the VAX. Figure 5-3 shows a number of the porting paths supported by the surveyed tools. An increased focus on using the IBM mainframe as a delivery vehicle can be seen from the moves of Teknowledge and Aion Development Corporation in this direction. It illustrates the widespread occurrance of the "success syndrome" described earlier.

ART, KES, and S.1 span both AI workstations and traditonal VAX environments. The LISP Machines, Inc. (LMI) products, IKE and PICON, are designed to run only on LMI machines, the TI Explorer AI workstation, and other workstations that run CommonLISP. These LISP workstations will be discussed in further detail in the next chapter. LISP-based expert tools generally require 2–4 megabytes of RAM, which is considerably more than a PC can support, but is typical for the AI machines.

As noted earlier, the base language the product is written in greatly influences other features, such as high-level language interfaces, graphics interfaces, and mathematical/logical capabilities. In some cases the underlying language is a version of LISP or PROLOG (e.g., ACORN, ART, ESP Advisor, ESP Frame-Engine, IKE, Knowledge Craft, KES, Knowledge WorkBench, and PICON), and thus these products can run well on specialized AI hardware. Even though the ESP tools are PROLOG-based tools they run only on PCs or, in the case of ESP Advisor, under VAX VMS. In other tools the languages are conventional programming languages, such as C, Pascal, FORTRAN, or native assembler. The LISP- or PROLOG-based products require an appropriate operating system to run, which generally includes the interpreter or compiler needed. Pascal- or C-based tools tend to need only the standard Pascal or C compilers.

Few of the products require any other special machine requirements. One exception is the need for a special coprocessor chip (e.g., Intel 80287) to handle some of the mathematics in PC products (e.g., KES, TIMM-PC, XSYS).

One of the more unusual configurations is that required for ACORN. This product runs on a PC/AT enhanced with Golden Hill Computer's 286 or 386 Developer hardware system, which effectively boosts RAM in the PC/AT up to 15 or 24 megabytes. Speed is increased as well, making the PC/AT a competitor for some of the lower end AI workstations at a fraction of the cost. TI's Personal Consultant Plus is an example of a more conservative RAM expansion that can be boosted up to 2 M megabytes with memory additions on the PC/AT. The Explorer workstation from TI provides a solid expansion path for the Personal

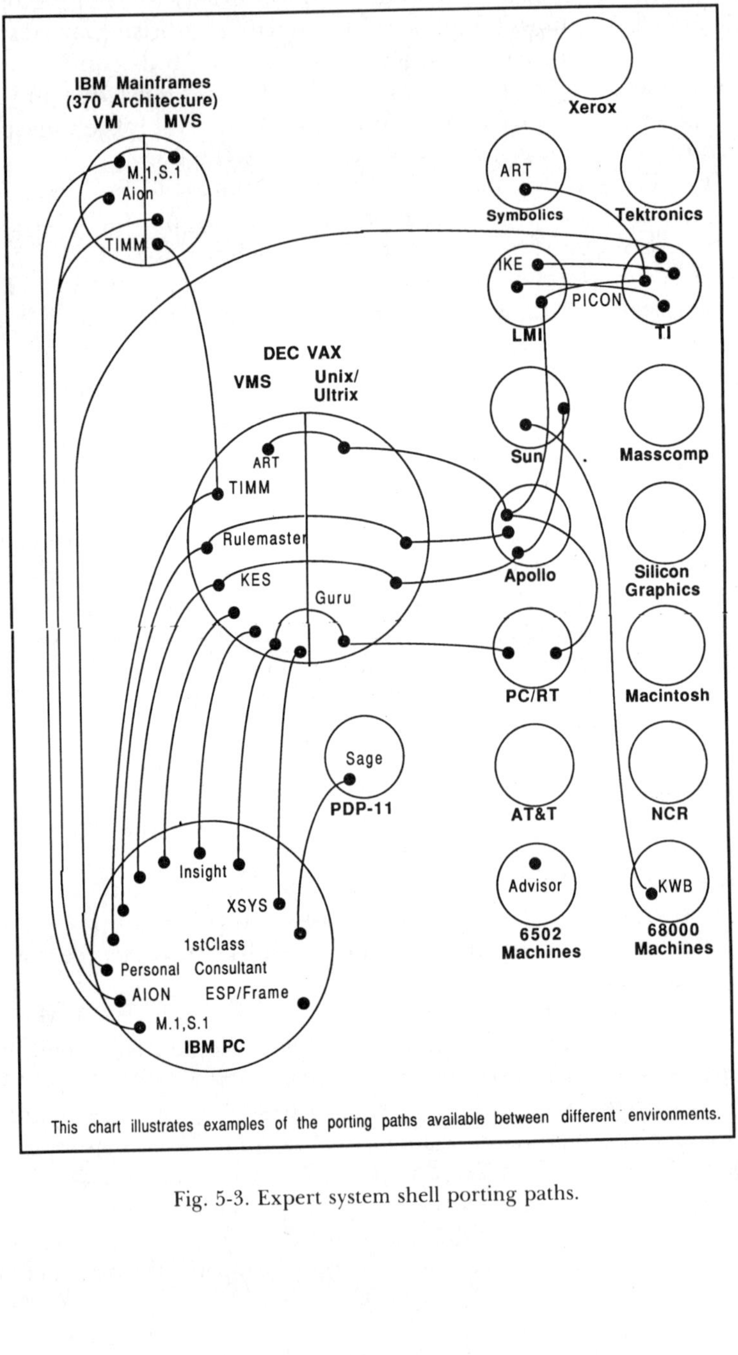


Fig. 5-3. Expert system shell porting paths.

Consultant Series, as it runs the Plus product. As more of the PC-based tools have features added to them, the boundaries of MS-DOS, at least in its version 3.0 form, are likely to become restrictive. AI workstations, such as the TI Explorer or the Sun-3, can have up to 16 megabytes RAM. Offerings from Apollo or Sun, based on the 68020 processor, can execute UNIX expert shells, such as KES, ART, KEE, RuleMaster, and the Knowledge WorkBench, at speeds in excess of 2 MIPS.

Another interesting configuration is supported by the KEE 3.0 PC-Host delivery system. The host machine runs a full implementation of Common LISP. Any of a wide range of PCs can then be linked to the host to deliver the KEE-built expert system. The application can extract, revise, and reason with data from standard PC spreadsheets and databases. This facility makes run-time KEE applications virtually machine independent. As KEE is written in LISP, and if engineers are available to port it, then delivery vehicles can include almost any LISP-executing host, such as DEC VAXs, UNIX machines, and IBM mainframes.

The development vehicle versus delivery vehicle issue is still an unsettled question in commerical expert system technology. As the matrix shows, AI expert systems are no longer tools that run only in esoteric environments. Full upward compatibility within a product line is an important feature that will be seen increasingly in the future (e.g., Aion products, TIMM). The future of specialized AI machines for commercial applications is an open question as delivery systems are appearing in a wider range of conventional hardwares. With the advent of LISP-chips for PCs, minis, and mainframes, and the increasing speed capabilities of AT-class computers with the aid of products like Gold Hill Computers' 286 and 386 Developer, LISP machines will have a run for their money in both development and delivery markets.

Some product manufacturers support integration of their tool with other tools. Usually these tools are by the same manufacturers. For instance, Advisor Software Design works with specialized products for mechanical control (KNOWLEDGE ENGINE and EXPERT CONTROLLER), which can be embedded in a chip set with Applied Knowledge hardware. ESP ADVISOR and ESP Frame-Engine can be customized (e.g., for fuzzy logic or probabilistic reasoning) by purchasing a PROLOG-2 programming interface. Knowledge Craft works with the manufacturer's own Programming WorkBench (mouse control for bit-mapped workstations, windows for knowledge-base editors, and debuggers), and XSYS/EXSYS can be interfaced to the company's frame and table search utility products (FRAME and TABLET).

## 5-11. RULE CAPACITY, VOLATILITY, AND RESPONSE TIME

Many of the early PC-based systems, such as M.1, Expert-Ease, and INSIGHT, had strict software limits on the number of knowledge chunks or rules allowed. These were generally software, not hardware, limitations. For the most part, these types of restrictions have been removed. The current trend is that the number of knowledge chunks in most systems is now limited only by the amount of RAM that can be directly addressed by the operating system. Even if a PC/AT can hold many megabytes of RAM, only the first 640KB is of any use to most of the MS-DOS-based systems. With production expert systems, the RAM or disk space available can still be a critical limitation, especially for the PC products.

The effects of editing the rule base on response time can be either significant or not important. Those systems that compile their knowledge bases optimize the object code after each editing session. Large amounts of editing, however, can have a serious adverse effect on interpretive systems due to the lack of optimization. If the application demands frequent updates to the knowledge-base, then some form of compiler is key. Such products as LOOPS employ an incremental compiler, which gives many of the run-time benefits of a compiler, while maintaining the development flexibility of interpreters.

Response time is usually measured in rules per second or logical inferences per second (LIPS). For those vendors who release such information, the range for PC products is about 100–300 rules per second. The larger, more powerful LISP machines, custom-designed for logical inferences, boast rates of about 13,000–15,000 LIPS. It should be understood that LIPS are often benchmarked on a PROLOG system, where each inference is a considerably smaller step of logal than the typical multivariabled, multiconditioned rule on a nonsymbolic system.

The PICON expert system tool was designed to handle knowledge bases of thousands of rules, or frames, very quickly, so that it can perform in a real-time process control environment. Early performance characteristics showed the ability to process over 200 rule frames per second in a 2000-rule prototype. Improvements in software and hardware are expected to produce speeds in excess of 1000 rules/second on 10,000+ rule systems.

The size of the knowledge chunk structures varies considerably from one product to another. Some vendors do provide information about the maximum likely number of rules in the system; others just note that it is memory-limited. The 6502-based Advisor Design System again represents one end of the spectrum with a maximum of 255 rules and

127 facts, obviously related to the 8-bit word. Expert-Ease, another early tool, allows 200–300 examples per problem, but multiple problems can be linked to form a larger rule set up to the memory size. Similarly, 1st-Class allows a maximum module size of 240 examples, and multiple modules can be linked. TIMM-PC allows mutliple networks with 500 rules per network. INSIGHT2+ supports a maximum of 2000 rules per rule set. With 640K RAM, the vendor claims that Aion/PC can contain about 2000 objects, ESP Advisor about 3000 rules, RuleMaster about 1000 rules, and XSYS about 5000 rules. These are likely to be rough estimates based on an average knowledge chunk (rule) size.

The limitations on PC-based products are key considerations for building the expert system. In general, expert systems with only a few hundred to roughly a thousand rules can be developed on PCs. The majority of the PC products do not support virtual memory and disk paging. An exception is Aion/PC, which allows virtual memory with paging. Performance may well be an issue with such a system. The ACORN system, however, as noted previously, has the capability of expanding RAM up to 24 megabytes, which should allow for a large system development. This type of memory expansion is likely to be seen with more and more products geared for AT level PCs.

Some of the more advanced tool sets have utilities to streamline the knowledge base. For instance, ART's "viewpoints" system reduces the time and space required to run an expert system by automatically determining relationships and symmetries in a problem. If this type of analysis were done automatically and dynamically, it would fit into the metaknowledge category.

## 5-12. PRICING AND AVAILABILITY

Product prices start at $100 and end near $70,000. The high-end vendors also provide consulting services, so it can be argued that there is no real upper limit. Compared with other classes of software, the prices are on the expensive side, but it can be argued that vendors have to recover their sizable R&D expenditures. At the beginning of this chapter, the products were divided into four different categories, three of them based on pricing. There is a rough correlation between cost and the size and complexity of the tool set, the larger sets offering the greatest variety of representation and inference schemes, as has been evidenced by the points presented in this chapter. Even so, the commercial expert systems market has not reached the stage of maturity where there is a direct correlation between the product price and the real value of the product to the expert system developer.

Most vendors offer a variety of pricing schemes. The prices listed in the matrix are for "first copy" only. Discounts for multiple copies or volume purchases are either explicitly supplied by vendors or they are negotiable. As the market is so new, most volume purchases can be expected to be negotiable. For PC products, the single-copy pricing is straightforward. The product is usually copy-protected, and a fixed fee, typically in the $700–$1500 range, is charged. Multiuser systems however, usually have various prices based on number of users, number of separate machines at the same location, and so on. Multiuser licenses tend to be considerably more expensive than ones for single-user PCs, so purchasers should not be surprised by starting prices in the $5000–$25000 range. Some products, such as Knowledge WorkBench, come in modules, which can be purchased separately. For example, the CORE contains the central base of the expert system—the knowledge base and the inference engine. If inexact reasoning is required, the IRM (Inexact Reasoning Module) is needed. If extensive natural-language processing is required, the NLP module has to be purchased. Silogic, Inc., has prices for CORE, CORE+IRM, CORE+NLP, and all three together. As shown in the matrix, Silogic also provides a yearly leasing arrangement, as well as perpetual licensing-purchasing. Similarly, the three representation modules of KES (rules, frames, Bayesian statistical reasoning) can be purchased separately or together. Another vendor program of interest is the time-sharing service offered by General Dynamics of TIMM on a remote VAX 11/780.

Another key element noted for some products in the matrix is the explicit OEM/VAR (original equipment manufacturer/value added reseller) arrangement offered by certain vendors. Those not listed prefer to negotiate these arrangements privately. The increasing large-scale development of production expert systems within corporate or industrial settings, or by software houses for resale, has created a need for pricing schemes for both development and run-time-only copies of the tools. For instance, Aion Corporation's $7000 ADS/PC product has an execution-only version (AES/PC) selling for $750, while the mainframe version execution-only sells for $25,000 compared with the $60,000 development version. There are specific development/run-time product arrangements for a number of products (e.g., GURU—$6500/$400, INSIGHT2+—$485/$95, Personal Consultant Plus—$2950/$95). California Intelligence offers an unlimited run-time copying of the XSYS PC product for the single $995 development license. Programs in Motion, Inc., has the same policy for 1st-Class at $495. The TIMM products ($19,000 for minis and mainframes, $1900 PC version) have a supplied utility called "EXONLY" for creating run-time programs. Unlimited distribution of these run-time copies is allowed within the buyer's corporation. As competition in this area increases, more beneficial arrangements for VARs and OEMs are likely to be developed.

The vendors are also moving into the specialized, packaged expert systems market, where the shell has already been filled with knowledge by the corporation. One example is the TIMM Tuner product ($5600) for tuning VAX/VMS operating systems offered by General Dynamics Corporation, the producer of TIMM. Another example is COCOMO1 ($485) by Level Five Research, Inc. (based on its product INSIGHT2+), which performs software-development estimates using Boehm's Consolidated Cost Model.

The purchase or licensing fees listed in the matrix are prices provided by the vendor. They may or may not include such items as manuals, training, development assistance, support services, software maintenance, update contracts, and so on. For example, INSIGHT2+ includes a comprehensive, indexed manual, sample knowledge bases, tutorials, external program source bindings, and telephone support for the base price. For the lower priced products, obviously such items as on-site training are not going to be included (most of these systems are designed to be "self-learning"). Teknowledge, Inc., offers a "Quick Start" program for its M.1 product ($7500), which includes 1 week of training in general knowledge-engineering techniques, and 1 week of training in M.1 use. California Intelligence has 3-day on-site training programs ($4500 for up to nine people) for its XSYS/EXSYS products. The cost of the Knowledge Craft product includes a 2-week training course. Knowledge engineering consulting (from problem selection to prototyping) is included with every purchase of ART. As pointed out in Chapter 4, the buyer is encouraged to develop comprehensive cost estimates for a product based on all the aspects of purchasing, installing, maintaining, educating, integrating, and so on.

## 5-13. VENDOR STABILITY AND GROWTH

After a buyer has addressed all the above product feature issues, in the light of the specific application, the selection process is still not over. The stability of the candidate vendors has to be analyzed to evaluate whether support and updates will be available when needed. An acknowledged feature of American business is that small corporations tend to be able to adapt more quickly than large ones, and thus a large portion of innovation comes from the smaller companies. As a generalization, most of the highly desirable, feature-rich, products tend to come from companies that are not very large. The more established vendors, as another generalization, may be responsible for the less feature-rich and less cost-effective products. The bigger establishments have larger overheads and also may have been involved in a broader range of R&D, for which expenditures have to be recovered.

What the potential buyer must do is evaluate the strength and staying power of the candidate vendors and then decide; choosing among features, price, and availability. The word *availability* is used to sum up the variety of supplier attributes that can influence its ability to continue to deliver the product to the buyer. In addition, products that have not yet reached the market have to be analyzed to allow a decision of true availability, given the buyer's schedule, budget, and product needs. If the application demands an unusual set of features, a small vendor with a product coming to market in 6 months may still be acceptable.

Judging supplier strength is not easy. The four key numbers that would help in assessing availability, notably, number of installations, company income, number of employees, and year founded, are often unavailable. To begin with, the buyer has to distinguish between expert system shell revenues and revenues from other sources. Radian Corporation, Texas Instruments, Xerox, and IBM, for example, gain only a small portion of their total incomes from expert system shells. Other vendors, such as Aion Corporation, Level Five Research, and Expert Systems International, depend on expert systems for their continued existence. Micro Data Base Systems, Inc., and Lisp Machines, Inc., occupy a middle ground where their past has not been in expert systems, but their future depends on them.

Most of the vendors are not public, so they do not have to release company incomes—and the public ones tend to be so large that expert systems do not significantly contribute to income. The number of employees is usually a better guide than income, but of course not all employees may be working on expert systems or even computer work. The year founded is often easier to find, but it should be clarified by finding out whether there was a switch from consulting to product work. Some vendors may have had significant periods of R&D before they became incorporated, and others may have spent a long time establishing a corporate structure before commencing development. The number of installations, if available, can say a lot, but even it can be misleading. The number of years the product has been sold will obviously have a bearing on the number of installations. Some of the low installation figures may be for new products only. Others with few sales may still have been very successful, say due to large government contracts that have resulted in considerable product refinement. Some vendors just do not release information, but others use these statistics in marketing. KEE, for example, has been licensed to more than 20 Fortune 100 companies. Level Five Research has granted major licenses to such firms as DuPont and Harris. Growth is also important as it can indicate success, but it can also lead to instability and cash-flow problems resulting in failure. There are several aspects to growth, including growth of company as a whole, growth of the expert system division, and growth of the product line—which may take the form of new features or may be delivered as new products.

Experience shows that the most exciting products always tend to be just around the corner, just out of reach. Attempting to place the order frequently sorts the solid products from the rest. In some cases, however, only when delivery is demanded does the absence of the product become clear. In yet other cases, the product can be delivered, and only several months into development are its inadequacies discovered and understood. Running into a long series of boundaries cannot be avoided in most developments. Having an enthusiastic and skilled staff to supply an equal series of solutions is one important factor. Having done one's homework on product and supplier strength is another.

## 5-14. MAIN POINTS: EXPERT SYSTEM SHELL TOOLS—PRODUCT ANALYSIS BY FEATURE

Although much of the early work on knowledge engineering was aimed at creating flexible tools, most of these are not to be found as established market products. LOOPS, EMYCIN, and SeRIES-PC (SRI International—Menlo Park, California) are examples of such earlier tools. KEE was originally implemented in LOOPS, but the subsequent implementations of KEE have created "industrial-strength" LOOPS with explanation and inference facilities. This trend of increasing product robustness, following such patterns as S.1 being industrial-strength EMYCIN, can be expected to continue. Of the many products discussed in this chapter, the most flexible, and at the same time stable,—KEE, S.1, ART, and Knowledge Craft—can be expected to be the ones employed for challenging production applications.

- The product comparison matrix can be read either vertically to provide an analysis of how certain features are commercially implemented or horizontally to provide details on specific products.
- A representative sampling of leading and emergent products is included in the comparison matrix. Such a survey should not claim to be complete, as new products are constantly coming on the market.
- Expert System Development Tools can be split into four main categories

—specialized tools (e.g., for process control or real-time work)
—smaller tools (one knowledge representation, no graphics, generally under $2000)
—middle-range tools (generally $2000–$25,000)
—sophisticated tool sets (multiple knowledge representations, graphical user interfaces, up to approximately $70,000)

- The earliest tools, appearing in 1982, tended to be strictly backward-chaining, rule-based ones, without probabilities or arithmetic.
- The high-end sophisticated tool sets tend to include multiple knowledge-representation schemes (notably rules and frames), have several inferencing mechanisms, and support powerful graphical development and user interfaces.
- Most low-end tools have evolved over a 4-year period to include probabilities, a high-level language interface, and internal arithmetic.
- Translations have been occurring from LISP or PROLOG into C or PASCAL for many tools, e.g., S.1, M.1, KES, Personal Consultant, to improve response times, portability, and embeddability.
- Implementers have tended to use the term *schemas*, or frames, to include semantic or associative networks. Many alternative and viable forms of the schema approach exist.
- A majority of products on the market now include some form of both fact uncertainty and rule unreliability.
- Mathematical functions needed during inferencing have been implemented in three ways

—vendor-created functions
—items based on the language the shell is written in
—access to a high-level or symbolic language

- There is no standard approach for controlling the effects of rule sequencing, although the use of explicit metarules is the industry trend. If these sequencing effects are not understood, they may create bugs in the knowledge base.
- A high-level language interface, available in almost all products, should be considered a necessity for nontrivial applications.
- Some products include database managers; others have special-purpose database interfaces; and others leave the interfacing up to the programmer through a language interface.
- Spreadsheet and graphical interfaces follow the same pattern as database interfaces.
- Essentially all products provide explanation facilities, but a minority provide a full set of "how," "why," and context-sensitive "help" functions.

- Only a handful of products have specific knowledge-acquisition aids to facilitate knowledge capture.
- The smaller tool category has been almost exclusively targeted at the IBM PC, but there is a strong trend to offer VAX UNIX and VMS support as a growth path, which is being fueled by the increasing RAM and MIPS needs of applications moving into production.
- There is also an emergent trend of tools becoming available on the IBM mainframe operating systems MVS or VM, perhaps running under CICS or TSO, with development still occurring on the PC.
- Most early tools had strict software limits on the number of rules they could handle, but newer products tend to be limited only by hardware.

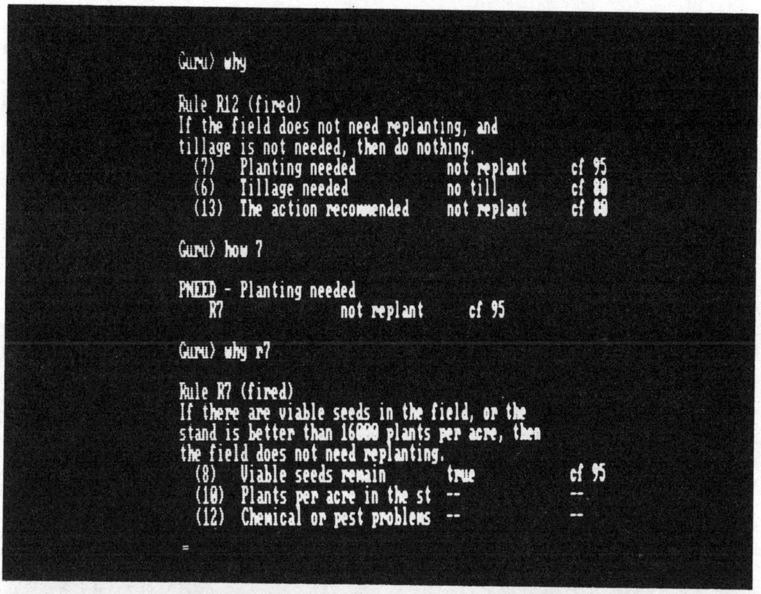


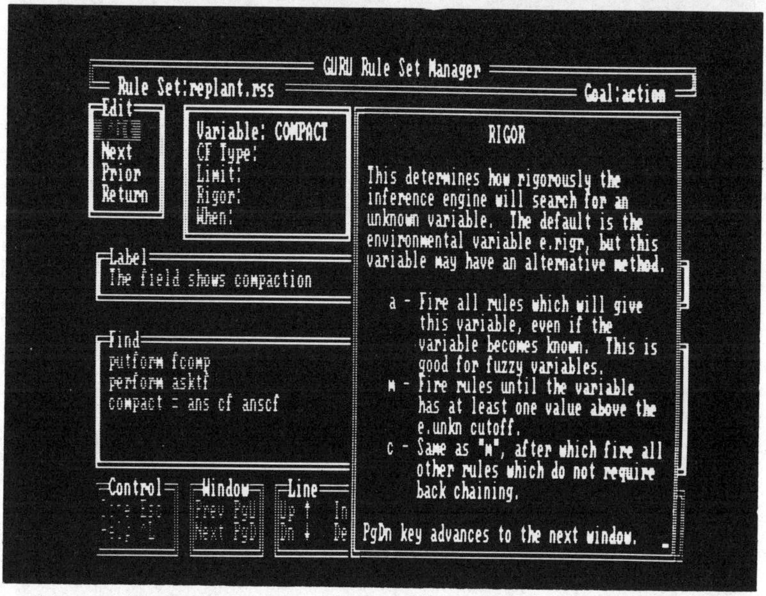


*Top*, a dialogue with the GURU expert system for an agricultural application. The user asks "why" a conclusion was reached, "how" the value of variable 7 in Rule 12 was attained, and "why" Rule 7 was fired. Confidence factors are indicated by "cf" notations *(Courtesy of Micro Data Base Systems, Inc).*

*Bottom*, GURU's "command phrase style" of developer interface. Overlapping windows are provided in this "ASC11-style" rule set editor. The editor is showing the "compaction" fact, or variable, in the agricultural expert system shown above. *(Courtesy of Micro Data Base Systems, Inc.).*

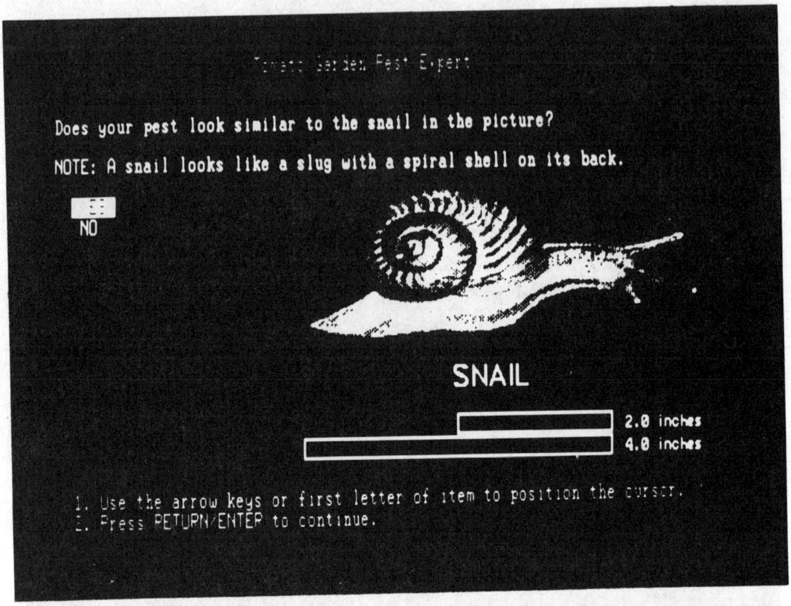


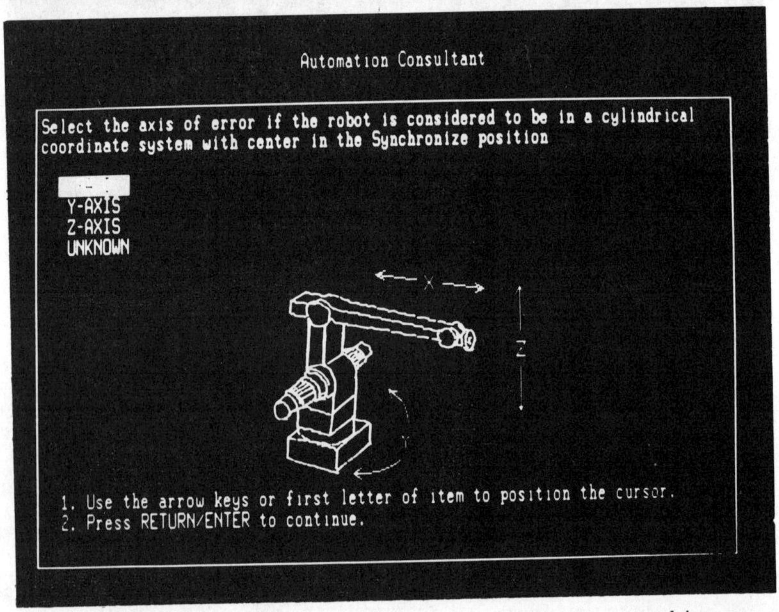


*Top*, the Personal Consultant Plus expert system shell allows bit-mapped images to be associated with dialogue questions. This is one of the simplest ways to introduce graphics into an expert system to facilitate fact or heuristic expresssion during consultation *(Courtesy of Texas Instruments, Inc.)*.

*Bottom*, A second example of bit-mapped attachment for a robot-debugging system. The activity is selecting arm coordinate schemes *(Courtesy of Texas Instruments, Inc.)*.

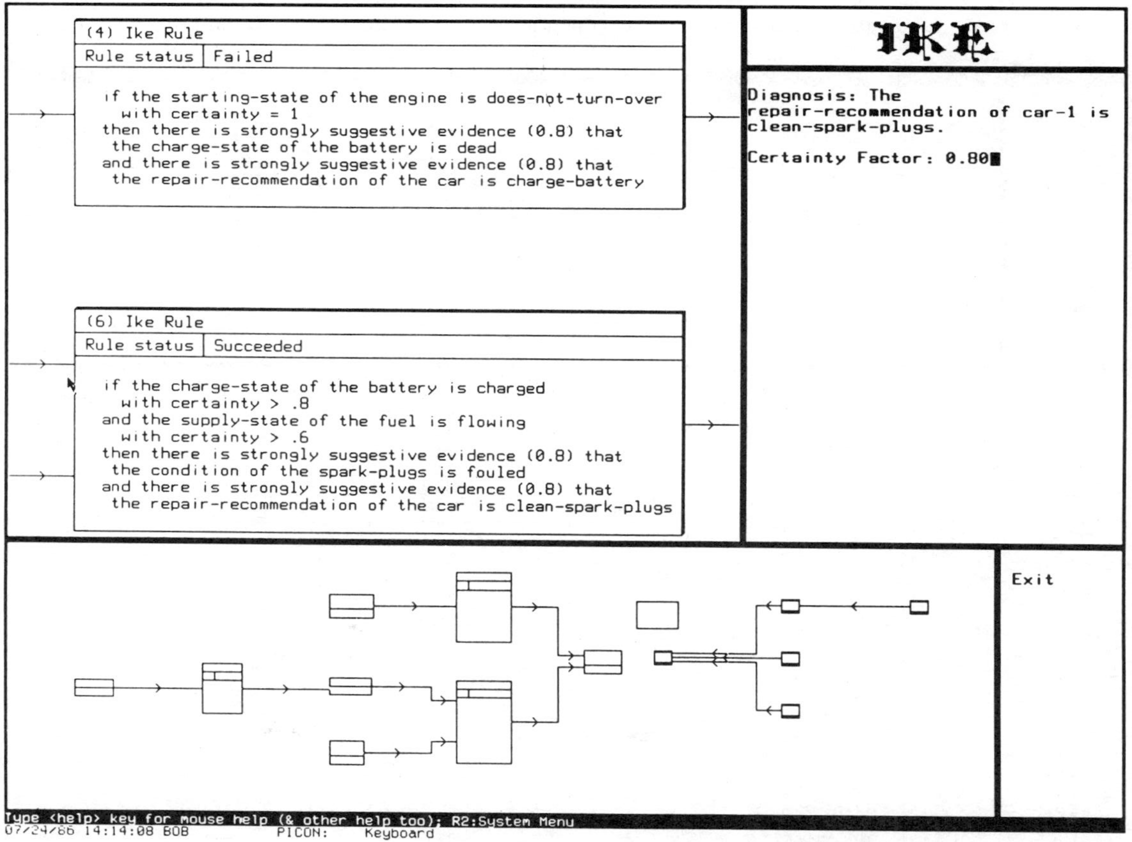


During consultation, IKE (Integrated Knowledge Environment) builds a graphical inference-history tree. The user can explore parts of this inference history to understand how the consultation results were determined. The upper left window displays a magnified portion of the inference tree; the upper right window shows the final diagnosis *(Courtesy of LISP Machines, Inc.)*.

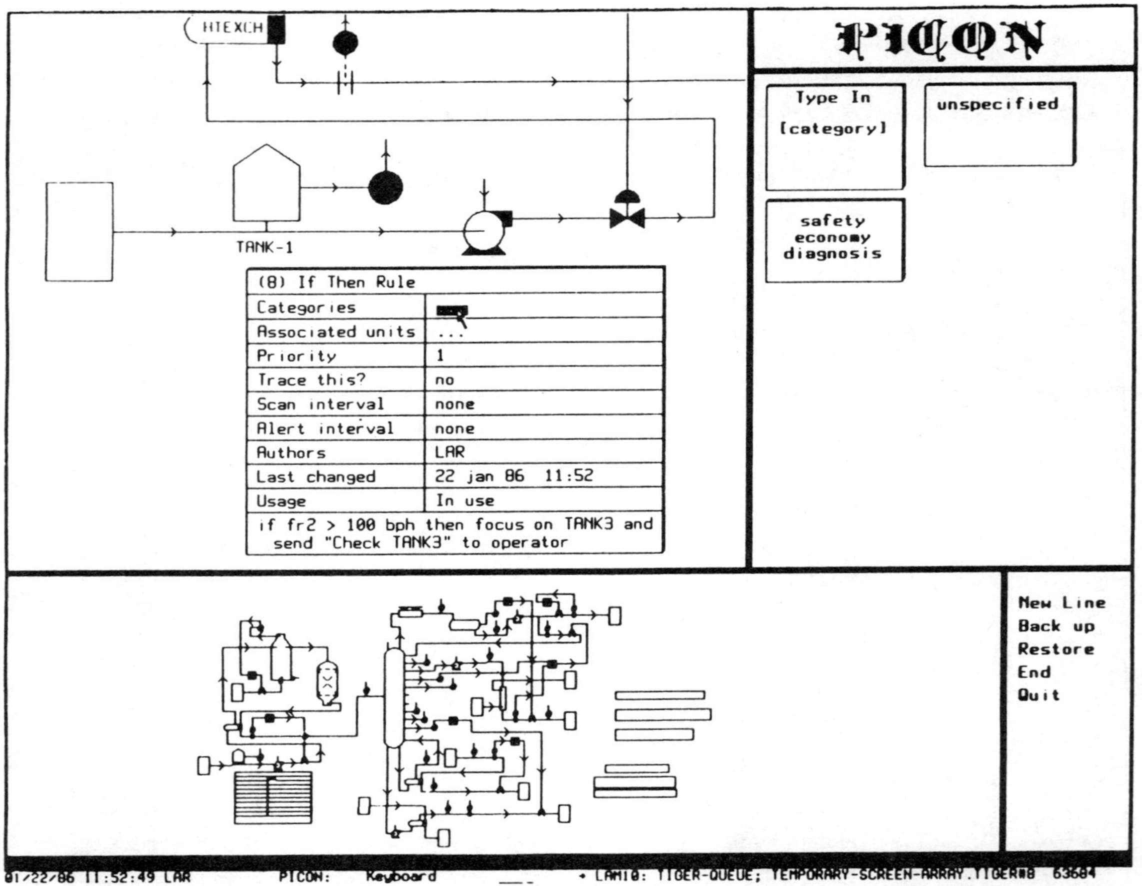


PICON is an icon-based inferencing tool for process control that combines icons and rules together in frames. Here, a chemical engineer is modeling a plant chemical processes by connecting icons and filling in a frame knowledge. An IF/THEN rule is being added, and the associated units, such as Tank-1 or Heat Exchanger, are about to be defined *(Courtesy of LISP Machines, Inc.)*.

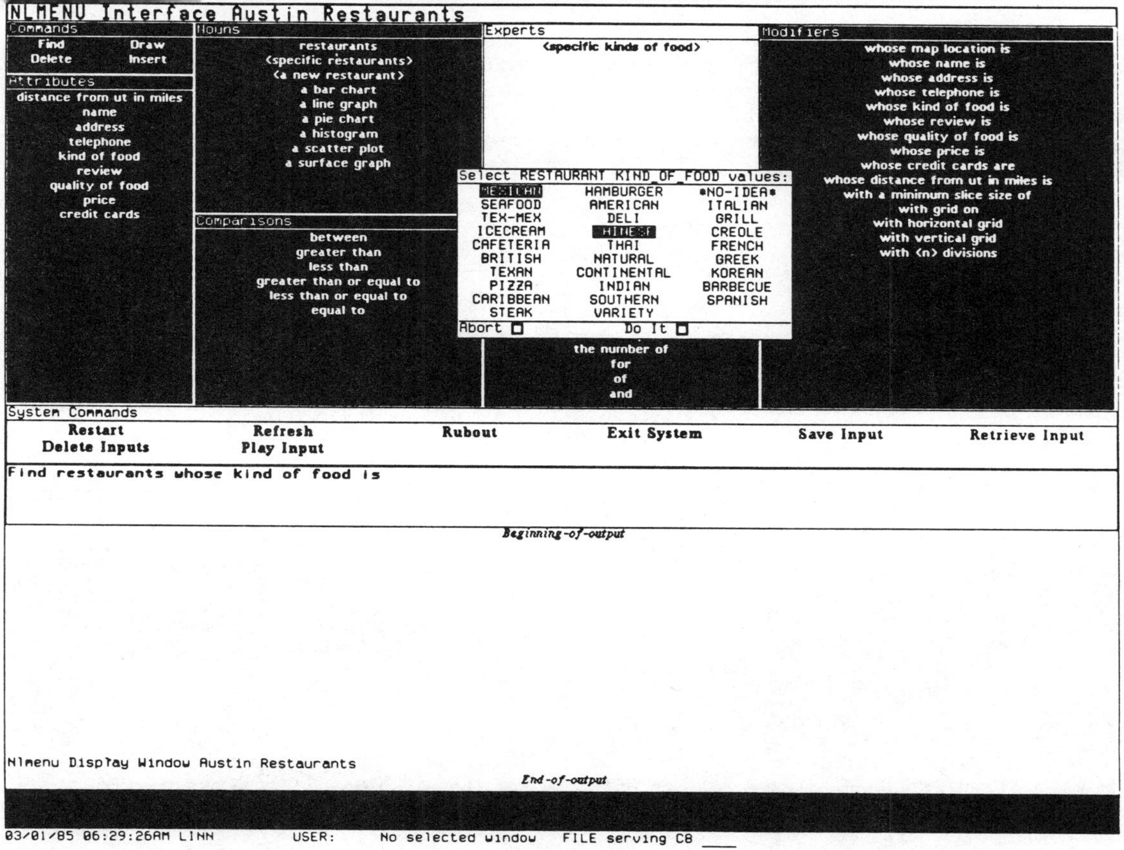


The following four photographs show an advanced user interface generated on TI's Explorer LISP workstation. Two classes of symbols, natural language and bit-mapped graphic, have been merged in one point-and-click application interface *(Courtesy of Texas Instruments, Inc.)*. Although NL MENU is not an expert system shell, it provides a valuable user interface to shells.

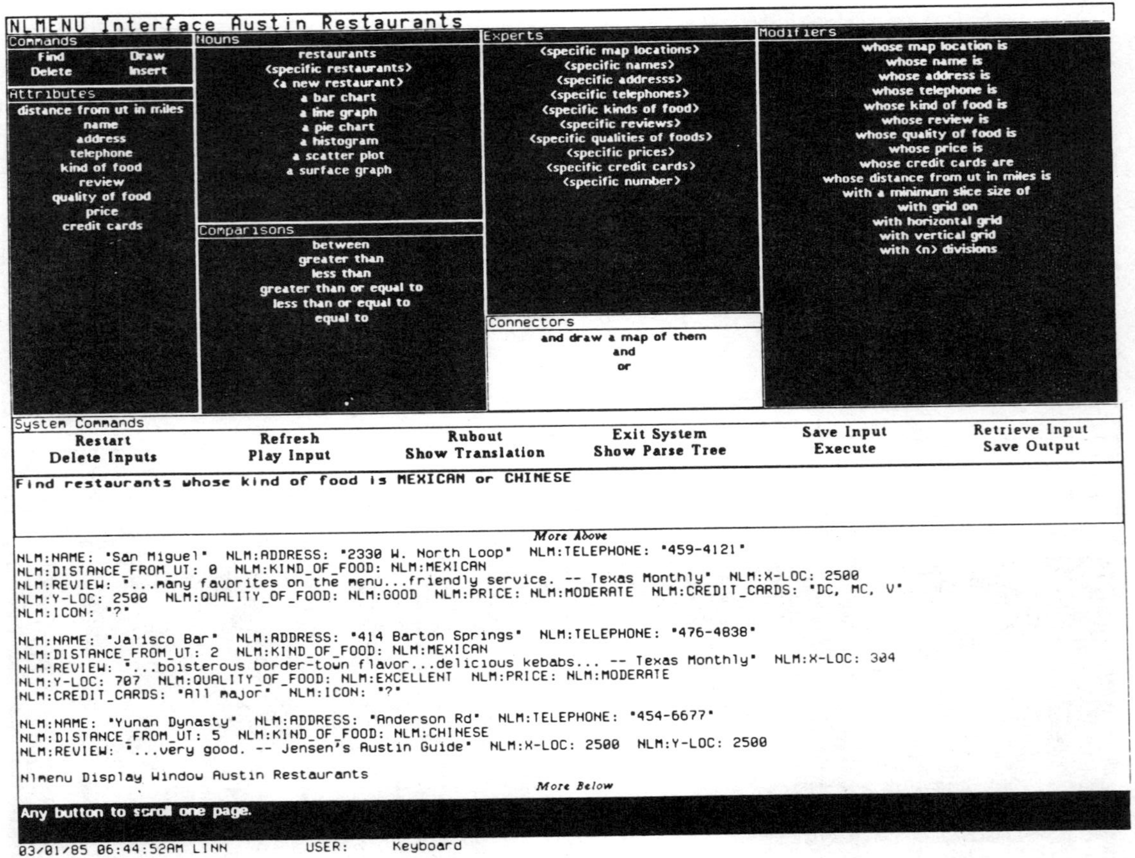


The user constructs a natural-language query sentence from given words and phrases. As the question is constructed, the system highlights the remaining valid options to choose from. In the photo, Mexican and Chinese restaurants are asked for, together with a map of their locations *(Courtesy of Texas Instruments, Inc.).*

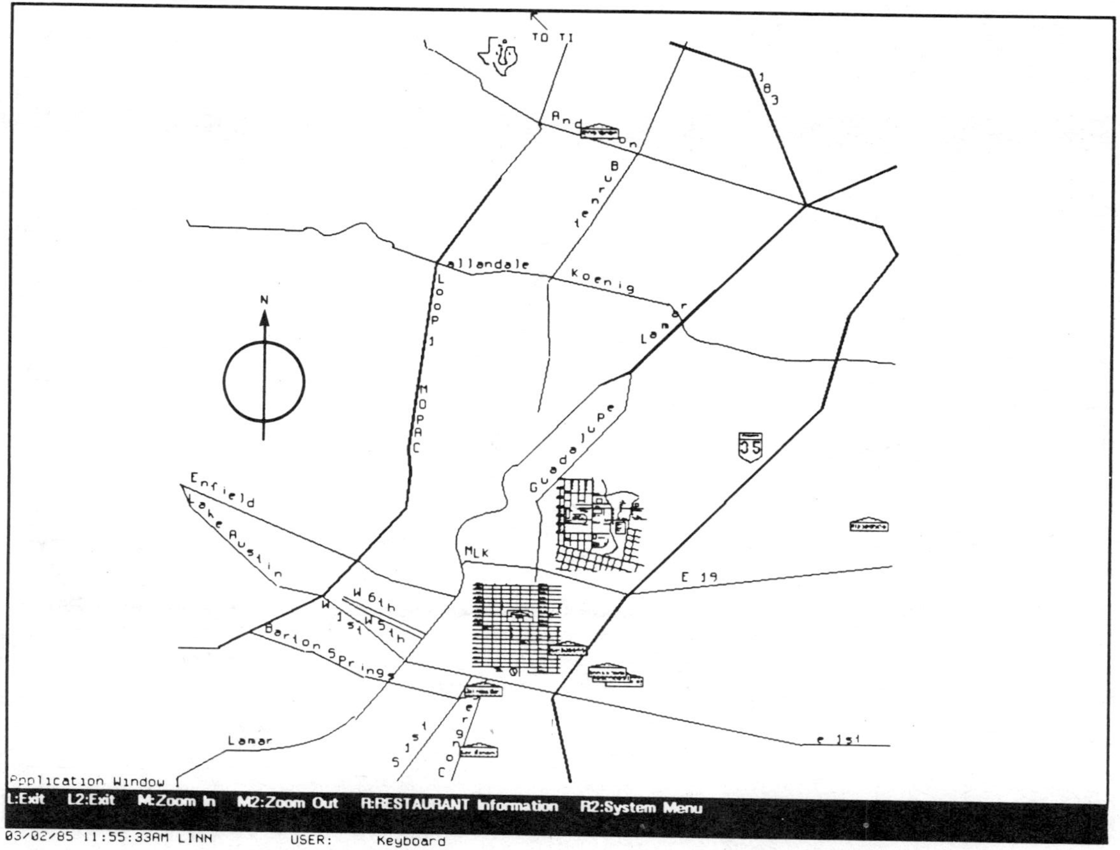


Once the query has been constructed, the LISP program draws the requested map. Restaurants are shown as house shapes, but details cannot be seen at this level of zoom. The map of the city (Austin) indicates distance and potential routes to the restaurant *(Courtesy of Texas Instruments, Inc.)*.

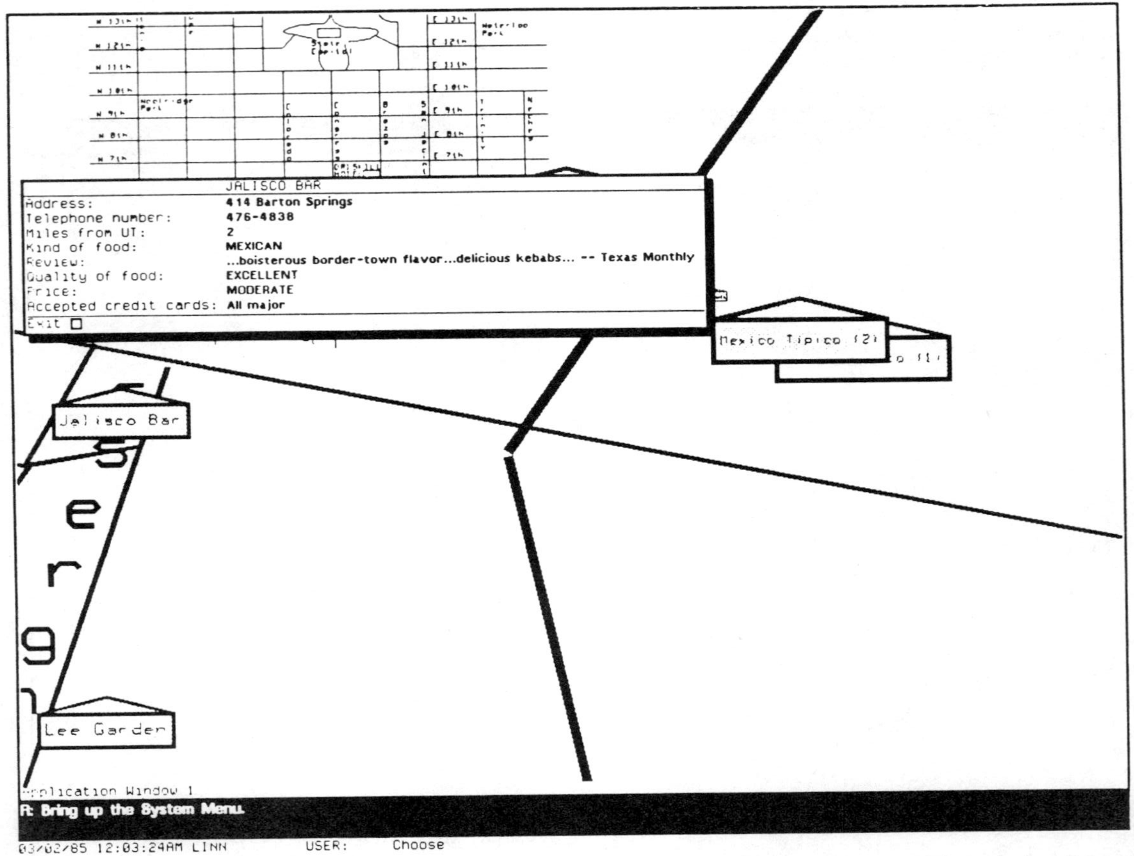


The final photograph of this series shows data-oriented text being used to annotate the graphics map. The user has zoomed in on a portion of the map and asked for specific restaurant information in Jalisco Bar *(Courtesy of Texas Instruments, Inc.)*.

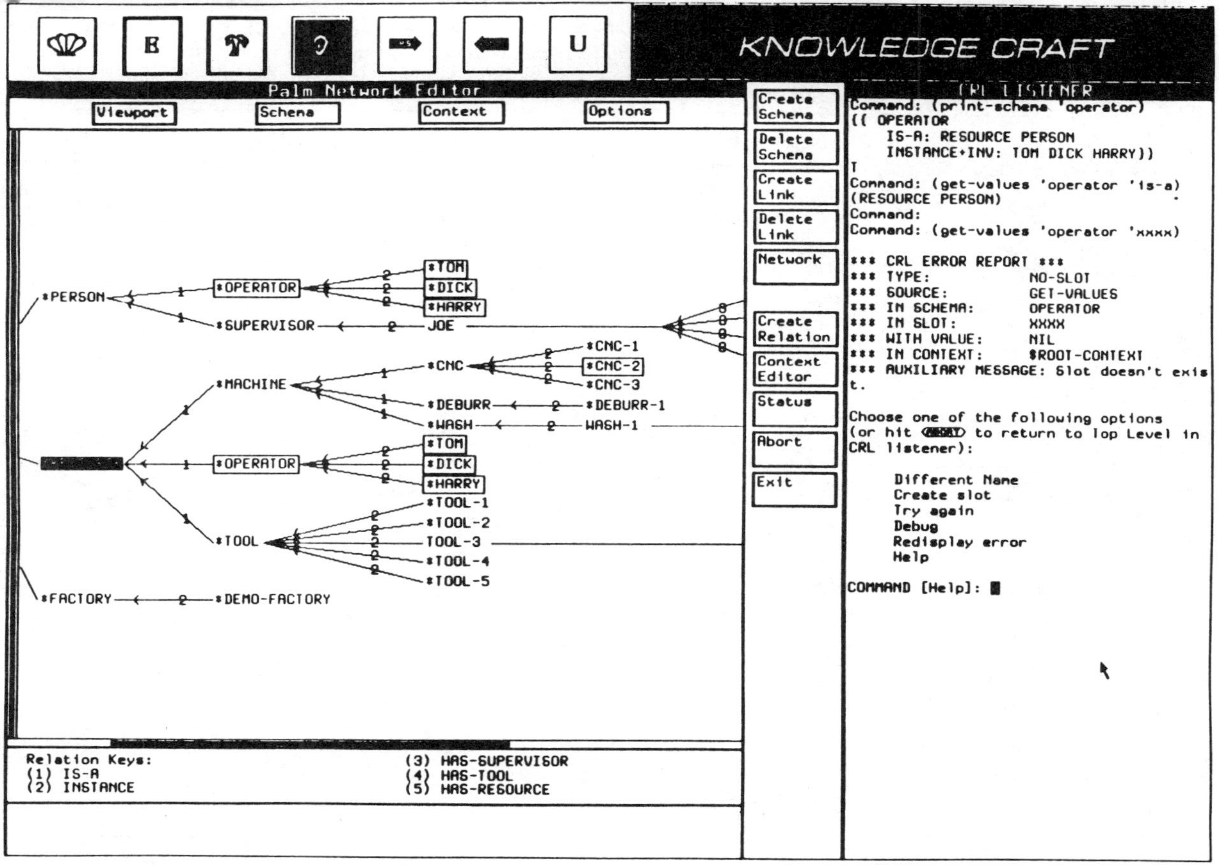


Knowledge Craft provides sophisticated graphics facilities for both development and consultation. Here an editor is being applied to the schema (frame) network. The application involves factory scheduling of various machine tools, operators, and supervisors *(Courtesy of Carnegie Group, Inc.)*.

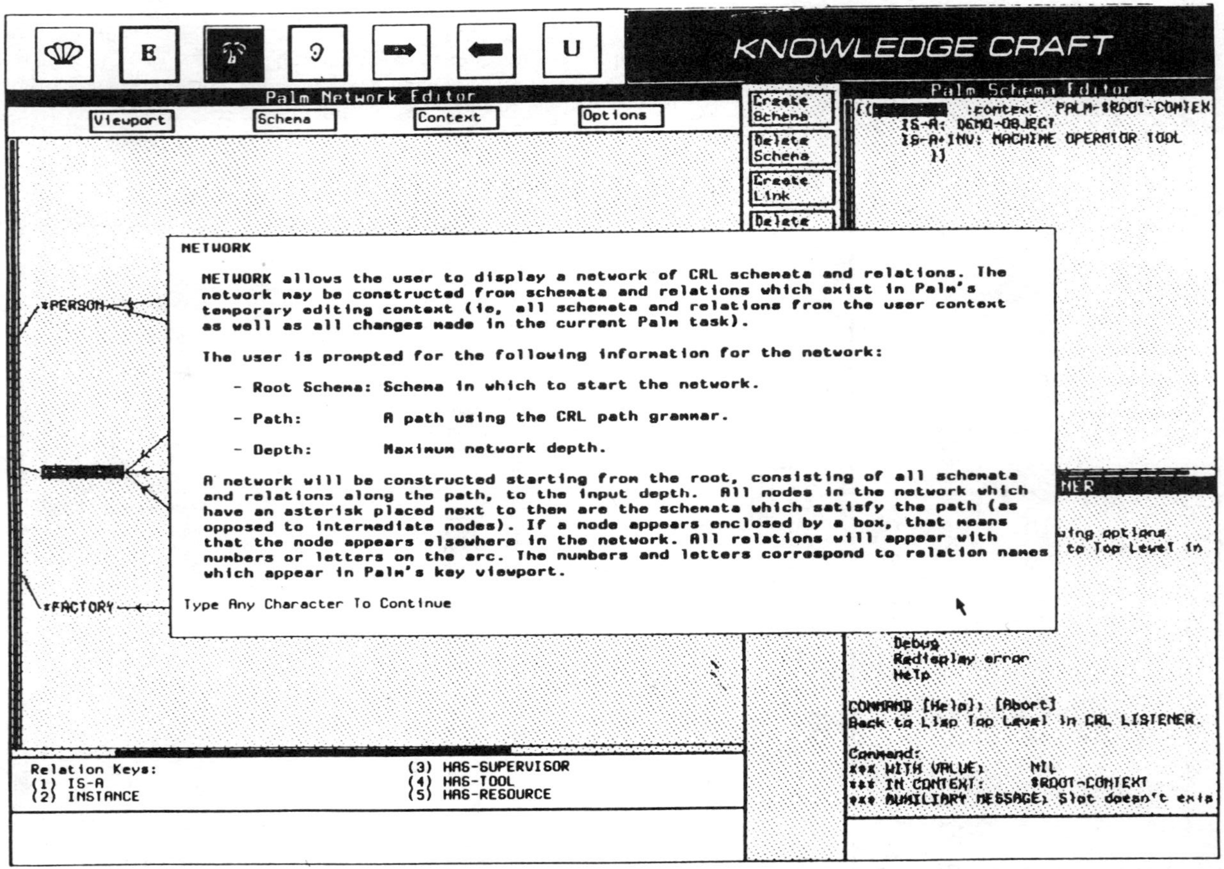


Bit-mapped windows, as opposed to ASCII-mapped ones, allow for more detailed overlapping and tilting options. A context-sensitive "help" panel has been invoked to explain how schemas and relations between schemas are arranged into a network. Function-key identified relations, such as "IS-A" or "INSTANCE," can still be seen in the lower left *(Courtesy of Carnegie Group, Inc.)*.

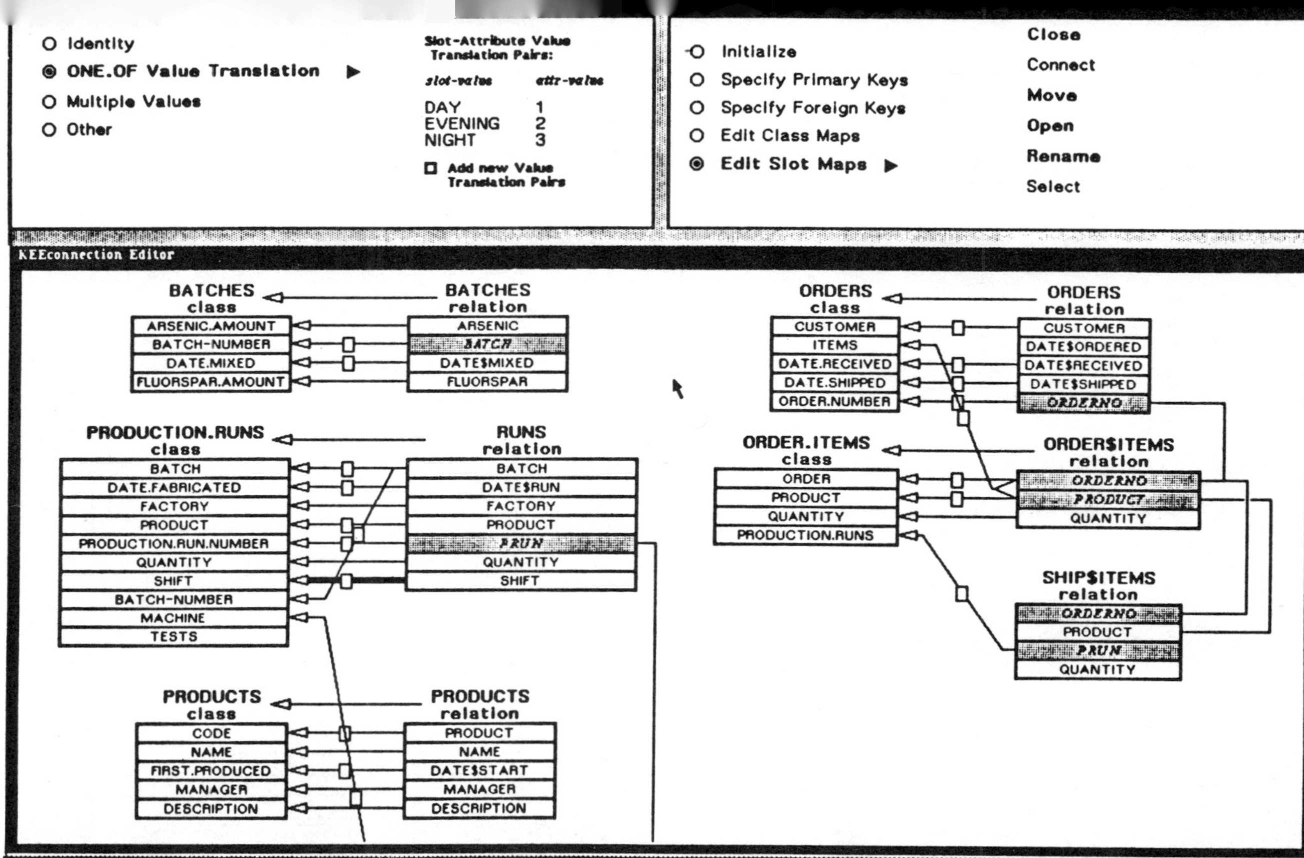


The KEEconnection schema editor in Intellicorp's Knowledge Engineering Environment (KEE) is being used here to edit mappings between KEE objects and objects in an external database. The editor is currently augmenting the connection between production shifts and manufracturing runs data *(Courtesy of Intellicorp, Inc.)*.

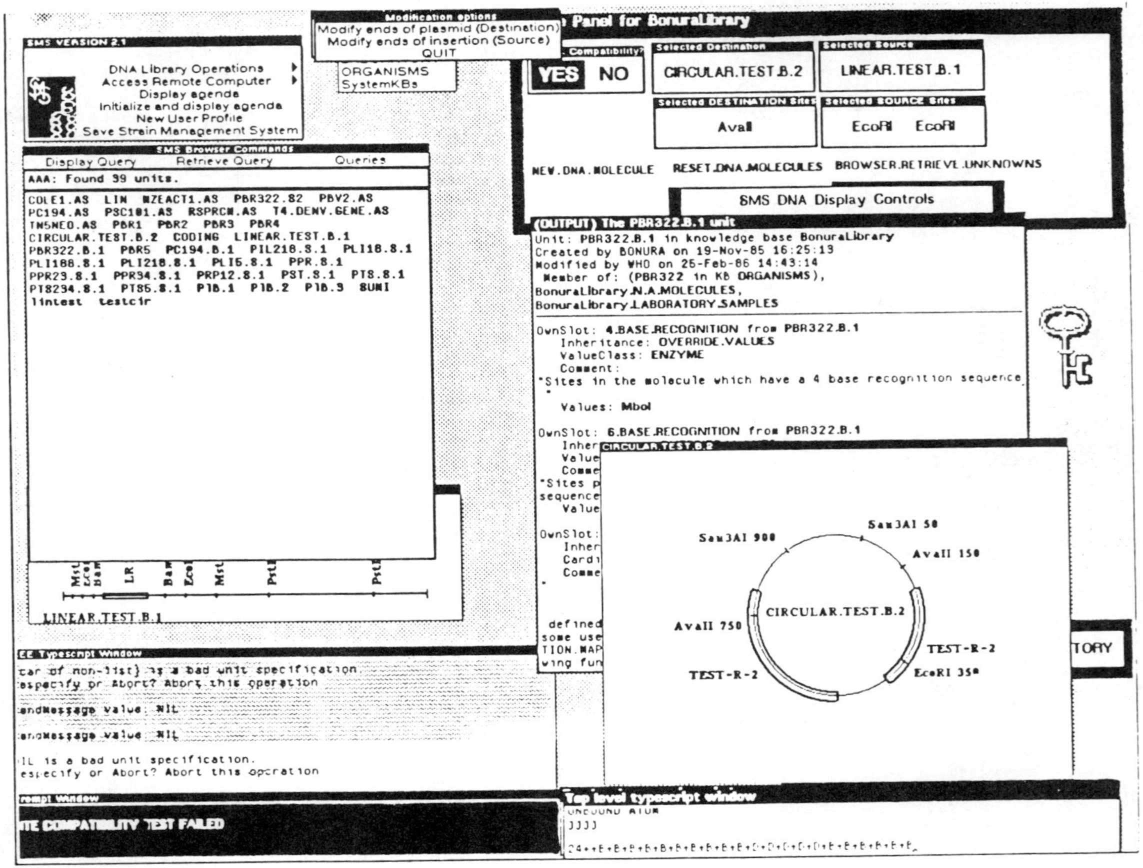


In contrast to the previous example, this photograph of a KEE-based expert system shows graphics being used in the consultation environment. The application program for Amoco/Intelligenetics Strategene is searching for compatibility between different pieces of DNA. Fifteen windows are shown on the screen *(Courtesy of Intellicorp, Inc.)*

# Chapter 6
# Specialized Hardware and Programming Environments For Expert Systems

## SECTION HEADINGS



## OVERVIEW

The introduction of expert systems building shell tools (Chapter 5) has revolutionized the development of expert systems. The impact of such advanced innovative software tools can be compared with that of the spreadsheet calculator of the database management system. Even with the power of such tools running on conventional hardware, however, complicated applications may still demand the use of more fundamental symbolic programming in the AI languages LISP, PROLOG, or others. Two key areas in the selection of a complete set of development and production tools are addressed in this chapter. The first is specialized AI hardware, especially workstations, together with symbolic programming languages. The second topic covers the addition of other elements beyond the basic tool selections to make a complete configuration.

Different tools may be needed for the different stages of development, ranging from prototyping, to field-testing, to production. Leading and emergent products in these specialized hardware and software areas are overviewed, along with other practical alternatives for expert system development. Two sample expert system tool configurations and growth paths, which start with single-user and multiuser applications, are outlined. The chapter concludes with a checklist for a full configuration.

## 6-1. TOOL SETS VERSUS LARGE-SCALE ENVIRONMENTS

The needs of real-world, production-quality expert systems raises the question of *tool sets* versus *environments* for both development and execution. The concept of simple expert system shells versus sophisticated expert system building tool sets or environments has been previously touched upon in Chapter 5. The options lie on a continuum, as there is no one clean break in the range from the simplest shells to the most advanced AI environments. This continuum of possibilities starts at the low end with single executable-module products, such as Expert-Edge or 1st Class, to tools like IBM's Expert System Development Environment with two main modules (development and consultation), and so on up the list of capabilties to include ART, KEE, S.1, and Knowledge Craft, which have multiple modules for such things as simulation, multiple viewpoints, sophisticated graphics, development aids, and natural language.

The concept of an environment as an extension of the tool set is shown in Fig. 6-1. Environments tend to provide a great range of development and execution utilities, many of which may have been developed by customers and researchers over a number of years. Within the LISP-machine domain, to be discussed shortly, environments such as ZETA-LISP-PLUS (LISP Machines, Inc., Andover, Massachusetts), InterLISP-D (Xerox Corporation, Palo Alto, California), and Genera (Symbolics, Inc., Concord, Massachusetts) provide a wide range of support utilities and capabilities. As noted earlier, some of the expert system shells have entensive if not complete access to their underlying language base. IKE and PICON, for instance, provide access to the nearly 24,000 predicates of the rich ZETALISP-PLUS programming environment on the Lambda Series LISP machines by LISP Machines, Inc.

Some of the features found in the ZETALISP-PLUS environment, for example, include utilities for easy design of custom windows and mouse-sensitive menus, a ZMACS editor with LISP-oriented aids for rapid error-free code generation, a graphical utility for examination and modification of complex structures, debugging tools, Common LISP-

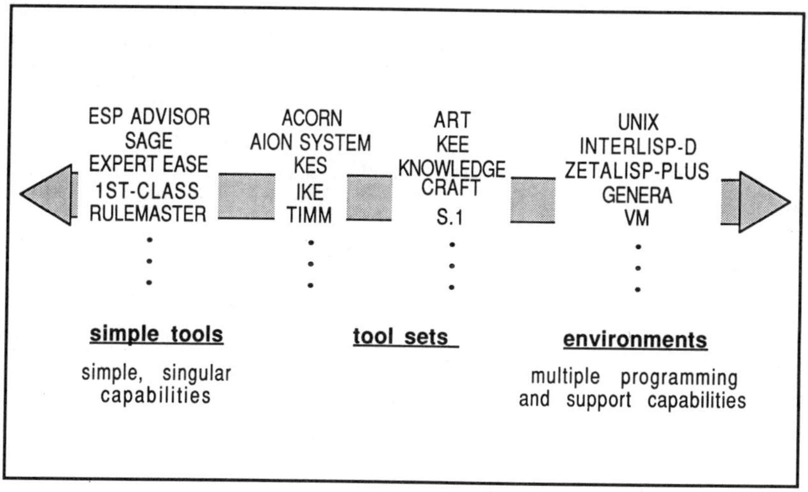


Fig. 6-1. Simple tools, tool sets, and development and delivery environments.

compatible FLAVORS, object-oriented programming language for incremental development of complex code, and an InterLisp-D portability package. Linkage editors are not needed, for code segments are incrementally compiled and dynamically linked. The Xerox InterLISP-D environment (also used for the TI Explorer) includes such features as structure-based editors for either user-defined types or system types, intelligent bookeeper and assistant utilities for error analysis and monitoring all inputs, graphical break and trace debugging tools, which show the state of the machine at many levels of detail, facilities for answering questions about programs and analyzing program behavior, and late binding or dynamic linking of variables and program modules.

Conventional environments provide another alternative to the symbolic programming environments and shells. A prime example of a sophisticated conventional environment is the UNIX time-sharing system with its wide range of tools and services. Most implementations of UNIX include multitasking services, multiuser options, a library of I/O routines, piping, I/O indirection, interprocess communication, libraries of mathematical and statistical functions, and many flexible utilities. Such tools as YACC, for creating compilers, LEX for lexical analysis, CU for terminal emulation, and UUCP for file transfer, allow powerful distributed functions to be created with only a few lines of code. Modules can be developed in the interpretive UNIX shells, such as the C or Bourne shells, by interconnecting such primitives as WC (word count), TAR (tape archive), VI (visual editor), CAT (concatenate), ECHO (resend character string), and SORT. If performance is not adequate, then selected portions of the shell script can be rewritten in C and worked into the remainder of the script. Several expert system shells run under UNIX, including ART, GURU, Knowledge Workbench, Rule-Master, and KES, allowing their basic functionalities to be extended by the user.

IBM's MVS/XA is another example of a conventional environment containing many development options. As with UNIX, when third-party products, such as relational DBMSs, graphics interfaces, statistical packages, and advanced librarians, are needed for MVS/XA, the choices are many, and the boundaries become few. At least three expert tools run on the IBM mainframe operating systems (MVS, VM), including TIMM, Aion, and IBM's ESE. To a certain extent the VAX VMS operating system can be considered an environment. Although VMS has many third-party application products, its native tool set is not nearly as rich as UNIX or ULTRIX. Other environments tend not to be nearly so rich in built-in functions. For example, even to get a comprehensive tape librarian program for Burroughs and Control Data machines is not as easy for the DP manager as it is under IBM's MVS. Software vendors have focused on certain popular operating systems to develop their products, including expert system shells. As a consequence, if the application developer has to pick something other than the leading operating systems, then third-party products are few. It is interesting to note that when researching the products in the comparison matrix, none were found that run on the IBM midrange machines (e.g., Series 1, System/34, System/38). Among the many operating systems on the market, some provide a comprehensive environment of tools, but others are more rudimentary. The central point is that a sophisticated, well-endowed development and run-time environment can save the expert system developer a great deal of work generating basic facilities, including reporting, debugging, graphics, database, statistical packages, and other specialized functions.

Along with richness of support functions and utilities, accessibility and support are other important criteria for many large-scale production environments. ULTRIX, for instance, may have a wider list of functions than VMS, but it is newer, so there are fewer customer installations. Expert system applications that perform critical functions throughout the workday must have a disaster backup recovery machine available. Such applications might be analyzing via phone the point-of-sale requirements for hundreds of an equipment manufacturer's field representatives or classifying insurance claims as an ongoing analysis of hundreds to thousands of claims received each day by the insurance carrier. For backups, these critical systems, just like traditional large-scale databases, could employ another machine on-site, exchange backup responsibilities with an associated corporation with a similar configuration, or hire a third party to perform daily backups on their machines. In certain fields of insurance and banking, government rules necessitate the provision of an off-site machine for disaster recovery. This service can be very expensive if provided by a third party, so there are strong incentives to making arrangements with a sister site running the same configuration. If the point-of-sale expert system runs on a DEC VAX 8650 under VMS, finding a similar backup site will not be difficult. The same cannot be said, however, for ULTRIX or other new hardware/operating system configurations. DEC does provide fast repair service, but many of the smaller hardware vendors are not able to be so responsive. If the user needs two sites running the same system, then each can provide the other's disaster recovery. If only one site is necessary to handle the workload, but a second machine is a legal necessity, then it may be wiser to stick with a more widespread operating system. Even if UNIX or LISP cannot be used for the production environment, that does not rule them out for development work. The evaluation of the richness of an environment must include this type of backup and recovery consideration as well.

The question of whether specialized environments, AI based or not, are needed for expert systems applications is not easy to answer. People who have engaged in large-scale, knowledge-based programming from its inception at university and private research groups often hold the opinion that any "serious" large-scale expert system development will demand a specialized LISP-machine environment. At the other extreme, small software departments specializing in PC products within large corporations argue that microcomputer products have worked well for their prototype applications. There are certainly many success stories where small-scale expert systems have been developed with the aid of only a few DOS commands beyond the facilities provided by an inexpensive PASCAL-based shell program. This small-scale initiative has been carried far into the business world by such large companies as Control Data Corporation (Minneapolis, Minnesota); its Business Advisor series of short courses on expert system development has been targeted entirely to stand-alone IBM PCs.

Should specialized environments be used in expert system development and delivery? The answer depends on the application. The project size, character, time frame, and budget available, as well as the needs for projected future projects, greatly influence the decision. The strategy for development versus delivery of the product is also central.

As the transfer of the AI expert systems technology into the mainstream of the commercial world becomes more complete, attitudes and viewpoints toward expert systems use will change. For example, the porting of a great number of expert system shells written in LISP to C has opened the door to widespread use of sosphisticated expert system shells in traditional environments. The proliferation of shell products for all different levels of problem complexity and machine/operating system requirements opens up the range of problem solving through expert systems from the simplest to the most complex. Basically simple problems should be solvable with simple shells, but complex domain problems may easily require sophisticated and specialized environments to be cost-effectively solved.

## 6-2. LISP, PROLOG, AND OTHER AI LANGUAGE OPTIONS

The products surveyed in Chapter 5 range from simple single-representation/inference tools, with limited capacity to interface with other software programs, perform reporting, and be customized, to quite sophisticated tool sets offering a variety of specialized functions. The trend toward options for customizing and interfacing with other software is well-established. The new high-level programming language interfaces, as noted in Chapter 5, are giving the expert system developer a greater degree of access to the underlying language the shell tool has been constructed in and to other languages. With these options the door is opening to the best of both development worlds: the time and effort savings of the prepackaged expert system shell coupled with the ability, if needed, to modify existing aspects of the tool or to create custom features for the application.

Although this shell-plus-programming-capabilities concept is quickly unfolding in commercial expert system building shell tools, there are limitations. There will be times when the type of representation needed for an application is not available in any prepackaged tool for the predetermined hardware. Or a prepackaged tool may be available, but it does not allow the customization or programming capabilities needed. At those times, the expert system developer will need to resort directly to the basic programming language tools necessary to build the system from scratch. Starting from first principles with a version of LISP, PROLOG, or a conventional programming language may be a more direct and effective solution than attempting to modify a vendor's shell package. Often, modifications, extensions, and integrations of shell tools can become rapidly nontrivial. If the available team does not have experience in multivendor system integration, programming the application from the ground up may be easier. At least that way a clean and simple design can be obtained.

The decision to choose a total environment or just a shell tool must depend on the total development not some isolated phase of the project. In the final analysis, it is the integration of the expert system with the remainder of the corporation's hardware and software that results in a truly production-quality expert system. A complete system requires the right RAM, disk capacity, communications ports and boards, concurrent processes for printing, multitasking operating systems, and so on, to meet the performance requirements for the finished systems. A well-built expert system with complete internal knowledge-searching capabilities is worthless if its performance is inadequate or the interfaces are too inefficient to keep up with the throughput demanded in the production environment.

The requirements for a production-quality expert system are not static over time. Specifications will change as the system moves from conception through its development phase to delivery, and the system will continue to evolve as it is used. The limiting assumptions used in the design can be outgrown on any number of hardware or software dimensions, requiring design modification, new or revised software modules, previously unknown interfaces, or more expanded hardware capabilities. Any one of the myriad changes required during the natural evolution of a successful expert system can demand great flexibility in the software tools used to design, modify, or augment the system. The success of the operation will be based on great adaptability and flexibility, which may require more than a shell product has to offer.

Flexibility is the primary justification for building the expert system directly in an AI programming language. A second justification may be performance. Too many layers of indirection in the vendor's prepackaged building tool may not present the response time necessary for critical time-dependent applications, such as jet fighter flight-control systems. For some applications, the fastest response may be obtained by programming directly in LISP on a specialized LISP machine. These machines have been custom-built with large numbers of specialized registers and vast amounts of RAM needed for very fast execution of LISP or PROLOG programs.

Although expert systems are usually constructed from expert system shell tools, or AI languages such as LISP or PROLOG, or production rule languages, such as OPS5, any language that provides a sufficiently rich set of language primitives for structuring the system's functionality could be used. Traditional programming languages—PASCAL, FORTRAN, COBOL, C, and Ada—are possibilities, although the list and symbolic-structuring capabilities usually found in AI languages would have to be developed from scratch. Other possibilities include the fourth-generation languages (4GLs), such as Mantis, Natural, Pro IV,

Informix, PROGRESS, and so on. A good introduction to these 4GL languages and their capabilities is found in Martin (1986).

In summary, the options for building an expert system are to

- Use an expert system building shell that has all the capabilities required for the project, including integrated graphics, databases, etc. (When it comes to the big picture for production applications, perfect matches are rare.)
- Use an expert system building shell that has most of the capabilities required for the project and provides high-level programming interfaces for development of the remaining facilities or interfaces—this often necessitates the ability to interleave expert system shell modules with those developed in other languages (including standardized library routines and third-party applications).
- Use programming languages, which may be symbolic, traditional, or fourth-generation, to build the system from the ground up.

Figure 6-2 is a table listing of a representative sampling of AI-oriented languages that can be used for expert system development. The table is divided into four sections. The first section lists LISP dialects, the second PROLOG dialects, the third production-rule-style AI languages (primarily OPS5 derivatives), and the last object-oriented languages, such as SMALLTALK-80, which will be discussed further in the next section. Traditionally, LISP in its various dialects has been the standard language in which much of AI has developed over the last 20 years in the United States. As noted in Chapter 4, LISP is essentially a procedural or functional programming language with extensive list-processing, symbolic-representation capabilities, and late binding of variables through dynamic linkage at run time. PROLOG, however, developed in Europe, has become the most dominant version of logic programming based on the first-order predicate calculus. PROLOG has been gaining in popularity in the United States in recent years, and the Japanese have adopted its logic-programming paradigm as the cornerstone of their fifth-generation computer initiative. Most of the first-generation custom expert systems developed in the latter 1970s and early 1980s were programmed in either LISP or OPS5-like rule languages (e.g., DENDRAL (InterLISP), XCON (OPS5), PROSPECTOR (INTERLISP), MACSYMA (LISP), INTERNIST (LISP), MYCIN (LISP)).

The sources for LISP and PROLOG languages vary considerably, as was true for the expert system shells. Some versions of LISP are native to the specialized LISP machines to be discussed in section 6-5 and are produced directly by the LISP machine manufacturers. Examples include InterLISP-D, which runs on the Xerox 1100 series workstations

| Product | Manufacturer or Distributor | Phone | Price |
|---|---|---|---|
| ExperLisp,<br>ExperCommonLisp | ExperTelligence, Inc.<br>559 San Ysidro Road<br>Santa Barbara, CA 93108 | (805) 969-7874 | LISP - $495<br>CommonLisp - $995 |
| Extended Common LISP | Franz, Inc.<br>1141 Harbor Bay Parkway, Suite 270<br>Alameda, CA 94501 | (415) 769-5656 | $2,500 - $6,000 |
| Franz LISP | Franz, Inc.<br>1141 Harbor Bay Parkway, Suite 270<br>Alameda, CA 94501 | (415) 769-5656 | $2,000 - $30,000 |
| Golden Common LISP<br>(GCLISP) | Gold Hill Computers<br>163 Harvard St.<br>Cambridge, MA 02139 | (800) 242-LISP<br>(617) 492-2071 | $495 |
| GCLISP 286 Developer,<br>386 Developer | Gold Hill Computers<br>163 Harvard St.<br>Cambridge, MA 02139 | (800) 242-LISP<br>(617) 492-2071 | 286 -$1,195<br>386 - $7,000 |
| InterLisp-D | Xerox Corporation<br>250 North Halstead Street<br>Pasadena, CA 91109 | (818) 351-2351 | bundled with<br>Xerox workstations |
| Intermetrics Common Lisp | Intermetrics, Inc.<br>733 Concord Avenue<br>Cambridge, MA 02138 | (617) 661-1840 | $10,000 com-<br>mercial -- usually<br>sold on OEM basis |
| Kyoto Common Lisp (KCL) | Ibuki<br>399 Main Street<br>Los Altos, CA 94022 | (415) 949-1126 | $700 + $700 for<br>source code |
| LISP/VM | IBM Corporation<br>P.O. Box 10<br>Princeton, NJ 08543 | (609) 734-8759 | $6,500 |
| Lucid Common Lisp | Lucid, Inc.<br>707 Laurel Street<br>Menlo Park, CA 94025 | (800) 225-1386<br>(800) 843-4204 | $3,500-$4,000 for<br>workstations, else<br>$7,500-13,500 |
| MacScheme | Semantic Microsystems<br>4470 S.W. Hall Street.<br>Beaverton, OR 97005 | (503) 643-4539 | $125 |
| muLISP-86 | Software Warehouse, Inc.<br>3615 Harding Ave., Suite 505<br>Honolulu, HA 96816 | (808) 734-5801 | $250 (interpreter)<br>+ $100 for<br>compiler |
| PC Scheme | Texas Instruments Inc.<br>P.O. Box 2909<br>Austin, TX 78769 | (800) 527-3500 | $95 |
| VAX LISP<br>(Common Lisp) | Digital Equipment Corporation<br>P.O. Box 2008<br>Nashua, NH 03061 | (800) 258-1710 | $13,100-$14,700 |
| ZETALISP-PLUS | LISP Machines, Inc.<br>175 Cabot Street<br>Lowell, MA 01854 | (603) 898-6008 | bundled with<br>LAMBDA machines |

Fig. 6-2. LISP and PROLOG product comparison matrix.

| Runs on What Hardware | RAM/Disk | Comments |
|---|---|---|
| LISP - Macintosh 512K or Plus<br>CLISP - Macintosh Plus | LISP - 800Kb<br>CLISP - 1Mb RAM | extensive Macintosh LISP environments; integrated virtual memory and graphics module |
| VAX(VMS,UNIX), Sun II-III, AT&T, Masscomp, Silicon Graphics, NCR Tower 32, Tektronix, Int. Solns. | 3 Mbytes | written in C and LISP, high level language interfaces to C, etc., EMACS-style editor, built-in Flavors object-oriented programming |
| VAX(VMS,UNIX), IBM/Amdahl(UTS), Apollo, Harris, Sun, AT&T 3B Series, Tektronix, NCR Tower | 2 Mbytes | over 5000 sold, written in C & LISP, interfaces to C, etc., graphics interfaces, built-in Flavors object-oriented programming |
| IBM PC, XT, AT or compatible (PC-DOS, MS-DOS) | 512K min, 640K sug./ hard disk rec. | over 6000 copies sold, internal interpreter, EMACS editor, interfaces to C |
| 286 -IBM PC/AT and 100% comp., 386 -IBM PC/XT, AT most comp. (MS-DOS) | 286-2Mb/hd rec; 386-6Mb/hd req. | 286 can be expanded to 15 Mb RAM, 386 to 24 Mb; 386 includes HummingBoard; complete editing & debug tools, graphic support |
| base language on Xerox 1100 series workstations | ~ | extensive development environment - see description in book text |
| IBM 370 (VM) and plug compatibles (e.g., Amdahl CMS) | 4 Mbytes | full common lisp, speed comparable to Lucid and Franz; vendor usually sells to OEM developers |
| VAX (VMS,UNIX), Sun, IBM RT PC, HP 9000, AT&T 3B, Data General, (all common microprocessors) | 1.8 Mbytes | written in C, easily customized for embedded systems, highly portable, over 2000 copies sold, compact code |
| IBM 30XX, 4300, 370 (VM/CMS) | 4 Mbytes virtual memory | extensive LISP tool set; interpreter and compiled code can be interchanged |
| VAX (VMS, UNIX), MicroVAX, Apollo, Sun, IBM RT PC, Prime 50 Series, Symbolics 3600 | 4 Mbytes minimum | wide portability across machines; EMACS-style embedded editor, windowing, debuggers, and includes Flavors object-oriented programming |
| Macintosh, HFS, and Macintosh Plus | 512 Kbytes or more/ 1 drive | conforms to 1985 Scheme standards; as fast as interpreted LISP; includes Quickdraw Graphics, trace facility, debuggers, etc. |
| MS-DOS machines | ~ | over 400 Common Lisp functions, special forms, macros, control variables, etc. - fast, not full Common Lisp, program requires ~300K RAM |
| TI Professional, Portable Profesion-al, Business Pro, IBM PC, XT, AT or compatibles (PC or MS-DOS) | 320 Kb min./ dual drives | graphics debugging, windowing, lexically scoped LISP dialect, with imperative, functional, and object-oriented programming |
| VAX (VMS or ULTRIX) or MicroVAX | .5 Mbyte / user | native-mode Common Lisp; includes compiler, interpreter, debugger, "pretty printer" for formatting output, editors; full VAX interfaces |
| native base language on LMI LAMBDA machines | ~ | full development environment -- see description in book text |

Fig. 6-2. continued.

| Product | Manufacturer or Distributor | Phone | Price |
|---|---|---|---|
| Arity/Prolog | Arity Corporation<br>30 Domino Drive<br>Concord, MA 01742 | (800) 722-7489<br>(617) 371-1243 | $350 interpreter + $795 compiler or $1,225 package |
| LM-PROLOG | LISP Machines, Inc.<br>175 Cabot Street<br>Lowell, MA 01854 | (603) 898-6008 | $12,000 |
| MicroProlog, MacProlog, SigmaProlog | Programming Logic Systems, Inc.<br>31 Crescent Dr.<br>Milford, CT 06460 | (203) 877-7988 | PC's - $89-$495, workstations and VAX $695-$2,500 |
| MPROLOG, MPROLOG P-500 | Logicware, Inc.<br>70 Walnut Street<br>Wellesley, MA 02181 | (617) 237-2254 | PC -$495<br>wrkstns - $5,650<br>VAX - $16,900<br>IBM - $.24,000 |
| POPLOG | Systems Designers Software, Inc.<br>444 Washington Street<br>Woburn, MA 01801 | (617) 935-8009 | wrkstns - $7,500<br>VAX 11 - $11,500 |
| PROLOG-1, PROLOG-2 | Expert Systems International<br>1700 Walnut Street<br>Philadelphia, PA 19103 | (215) 735-8510 | PC - $145-$1495<br>VAX $1895-$3275 |
| PROLOG/i, PROLOG/m | Chalcedony Software, Inc.<br>5580 La Jolla Blvd.<br>La Jolla, CA 92037 | (619) 483-8513 | $99 |
| Quintus Prolog | Quintus Computer Systems, Inc.<br>2345 Yale Street<br>Palo Alto, CA 94306 | (415) 494-3612 | $6,000-$17,000 |
| VM/PROLOG | IBM Corporation<br>P.O. Box 10<br>Princeton, NJ 08543 | (609) 734-8759 | $8,000 |

Fig. 6-2. continued.

(Xerox Corporation, Pasadena, California) and the TI Explorer, Symbolics Common LISP (Symbolics, Inc., Concord, Massachusetts), and ZETALISP-PLUS on the LISP Machines Inc. (Andover, Massachusetts), Lambda machines. Since the popularization of PROLOG, some of these LISP machine manufacturers also have a special version of PROLOG that runs on their specialized hardware (e.g., LM-PROLOG by LISP Machines, or Quintus Prolog for Xerox 1100 machines). Conventional hardware vendors, such as IBM and DEC, have also entered the AI market and offer either LISP, PROLOG, or both on their machines (e.g., LISP/VM, VM/PROLOG for IBM mainframes, VAX LISP, DEC Common Lisp).

Other AI vendors with longstanding LISP software offerings include Gold Hill Computers (Cambridge, Massachusetts), Franz Lisp (Alameda, California), and Lucid (Menlo Park, California). Gold Hill has specialized in LISP products for the IBM PC family, including Golden Common LISP and the GCLISP 286 and 386 Developers. Franz Lisp has been one of the prime suppliers of LISP (Franz Lisp and more recently

| Runs on What Hardware | RAM/Disk | Comments |
|---|---|---|
| IBM PC XT, AT and MS-DOS compatibles | 512Kb/hard disk (640K rec.) | interfaces to C and other languages, package includes expert system builder and SQL interface, up to 1 Gb virtual mem., free copying |
| LMI LAMBDA machines | ~ | fully integrated with the ZETALISP-PLUS environment |
| MS-DOS Pc's, CP/M, Commodore, Macintosh, VAX (UNIX,MVS), Sun, Plexus, Apollo | ~ | can add shell tool APES (Augment Prolog for Expert Systems) for an additional $350-$3,500 depending on machine |
| IBM PC or compatibles (PC,MS-DOS) VAX (VMS,UNIX), IBM (VM/CMS, OS/MVS/TSO), Tektronix, Sun, Apollo, other MC68000/UNIX | 512 Kbytes on PC | interfaces to procedural languages, portable from PC to mainframe, over 100 built-in functions, price includes extensive education or consulting on larger machines |
| VAX (VMS,UNIX), MicroVAX, Sun II, Apollo, HP 9000 | 2 Mbytes on workstations | integrated LISP, Prolog, and POP11; access to Pascal, FORTRAN, C, Ada, etc. |
| PROLOG-2 -- IBM PC, XT, AT (MS-DOS); PROLOG-1 -- VAX (VMS), MicroVAX II (VMS) | PC - 384 Kb-640 Kbytes | response time of 2500 LIPS on PC, 6000 LIPS on AT; extensive debugging tools, windowing facilities; virtual memory access up to 256 Mb |
| IBM PC, XT, AT (PC and MS-DOS) Macintosh, Mac Plus, and HFS compatible | 256 Kb - PC (320 Kb rec); 512K Mac | integrated editor and tutorial; full cross compatibility between PC and Mac versions |
| VAX (UNIX,VMS), Apollo (IX) Sun (UNIX), IBM RTPC, Xerox 1100, NCR Tower, IBM 370 (MVS, VM) | 2 MBytes minimum | written in Prolog, C, and assembler; full screen editor; interfaces to C, Pascal, FORTRAN, etc.; compatible compiled and interpreted code |
| IBM 30XX, 4300, 370 (VM/CMS) 370 (VM/CMS) | ~ | extensive tool set; several high level interfaces including LISP/VM, SQL/DS, and VM/SP |

Fig. 6-2. continued.

Extended Common Lisp) to VAX and engineering workstation users. The Franz products have been widely installed and debugged; they are portable across the entire offering line and also include interfaces to C and FORTRAN. Lucid, Inc., has been working on porting LISP to all major machine manufacturers over the last several years, although progress on such a broad front may take time.

The trend toward standardization of LISP has resulted in implementations of a "Common LISP" that is widely portable across a number of machines. In the table Common LISP implementations include the products by DEC, Franz, Inc., Gold Hill Computers, Intermetrics (Cambridge, Massachusetts), Ibuki (Los Angeles, California), Lucid, Inc., and others. This trend is likely to continue and will enhance the infusion of LISP into a variety of programming environments. Most of the PC versions that claim to run Common LISP actually include only a subset of the full language, due to the vast array of functions in the complete version.

| Product | Manufacturer or Distributor | Phone | Price |
|---|---|---|---|
| DDI-OPS | Data Directions, Inc.<br>37 Jerome Avenue<br>Bloomfield, CT 06002 | (203) 242-8551 | $995 |
| ExperOPS5 | ExperTelligence, Inc.<br>559 San Ysidro Road<br>Santa Barbara, CA 93108 | (805) 969-7874 | $325 |
| OPS83 | Production Systems Technologies, Inc<br>642 Gettysburg Street<br>Pittsburgh, PA 15206 | (412) 362-3117 | $1,950 - $20,000 |
| SAIC OPS5 | SAIC<br>PO Box 2351<br>La Jolla, CA 92038 | (619) 456-6816 | $1000<br>copying |
| TOPSI-OPS5 | Dynamic Master Systems, Inc.<br>PO Box 566456<br>Atlanta, GA 30356 | (404) 565-0771 | $125, $250, $375<br>prototyping to<br>professional grades |
| VAX OPS5 | Digital Equipment Corporation<br>P.O. Box 2008<br>Nashua, NH 03061 | (800) 258-1710 | $9,800 |
| Objective-C | Products Productions International<br>27 Glen Road<br>Sandy Hook, CT 06482 | (203) 426-1875 | PC - $500, others -<br>$2,500 up based on<br># of users |
| ObjectLISP | LISP Machines, Inc.<br>175 Cabot Street<br>Lowell, MA 01854 | (603) 898-6008 | $195 |
| Smalltalk-80 | Tektronix, Inc.<br>P.O. Box 1700<br>Beaverton, OR 97075 | (800) 547-1512<br>(800) 452-1877 | bundled with<br>vendor's<br>workstations |
| Smalltalk AT | Softsmarts, Inc.<br>4 Skyline Road<br>Woodside, CA 94062 | (415) 327-8100 | $995 |
| Smalltalk/V | Digitalk Inc.<br>5200 West Century Boulevard<br>Los Angeles, CA 90045 | (213) 645-1082 | $99 |

Fig. 6-2. continued.

Two of the products listed, MacScheme (Semantic Microsystems, Beaverton, Oregon) and PC Scheme (Texas Instruments), are versions of a LISP dialect called *Scheme*, a lexically scoped LISP originally developed for instructional purposes at MIT in 1975. The imperative, object-oriented, and functional-programming paradigms are fully integrated in Scheme, and the block structure and simple syntax makes the language easy to work with.

Versions of PROLOG are proliferating almost as fast as LISP dialects. PROLOG, as was discussed in section 4-2, is essentially a predicate-logic language implemented as a top-down, left-right search of a tree of assertions with backtracking. Many of these versions take as their base the standard advocated by Clocksin and Mellish in *Programming in Prolog*

| Runs on What Hardware | RAM/Disk | Comments |
|---|---|---|
| Xerox 1100 Series LISP Machines | 8 Mbytes of virtual memory | cost effective tool for data driven problems |
| 512 Macintosh or Plus | 512 Kb/ add-on floppy or hard disk | written in ExperLisp; requires ExperLisp by same vendor |
| VAX (VMS,UNIX), IBM PC's & DOS comp.,AT&T 3B, Tektronix 4400, HP 9000, Apollo, Sun, Conv. Tech. | 512 Kb on PC hard disk recommended | combination procedural and rule language; written in C, interfaces anything C-callable |
| Xerox 1100 Series LISP Machines | ~ | window-based debugging; mouse-driven rule editor; extensions to OPS5; interfaces to InterLisp-D; free run-time copying |
| IBM PC, XT, AT (MS-DOS) and compatibles, CP/M machines | 256 Kbytes | written in Turbo Pascal - Turbo Pascal is required to implement external procedures; source code is available |
| VAX (VMS) and MicroVAX | ~ | written in native code optimizing language BLISS-32 for compactness and performance; interfaces to any other VAX languages |
| IBM PC XT,AT (MS-DOS), VAX & MicroVAX (UNIX,VMS), Sun, Apollo, HP 9000 | ~ | object-oriented extension of C environment; addition product VICI provides interactive development environment for C and Objective-C |
| LMI LAMBDA machines and any other CommonLisp environments | ~ | runs with CommonLisp environments and is therefore portable to many machines |
| native system on Tektronics 4400 AI workstations | ~ | the original object-oriented programming environment -- see description in text of book |
| IBM PC AT (DOS) and compatibles | 640 Kb base, 512 Kb exp. mem./ hd | full implementation of the Xerox Smalltalk 80 version 2 on the PC AT |
| IBM PC, XT, AT (DOS) and compatibles | 512K bytes | integrates object-based, rule-based, and object-oriented Prolog; debuggers, graphical interface, language interfaces (including DOS) |

Fig. 6-2. continued.

(1984). Most of the major AI hardware vendors (LISP machine vendors, workstation vendors, and conventional vendors, such as DEC and IBM) market PROLOG as well as LISP versions. PROLOG environments are building up like LISP environments of the past. For instance, PROLOG-2, an extended version of PROLOG-1 by Expert Systems International (Philadelphia, Pennsylvania), has all the features of standard PROLOG plus the ability to include external code modules from other languages. It has full-screen editors, window management, modular architecture, advanced garbage collection, a tail recursion option, library routines, debuggers, error and interrupt handlers, and so on. Another interesting design is Poplog by System Designers Software, Inc. (Woburn, Massachusetts). Poplog is an integrated mixture of Prolog, LISP, and POP11.

Commands from any of the three languages can be used at any time in a program, and routines written in PASCAL, C, Ada, or FORTRAN can be linked in. Incremental compilation is also supported.

The third set of products in the chart contains primarily commercial versions of the OPS5 programming language. The *production rule* programming methodology has been discussed previously in the form of rule-based interpreter systems with chaining. One of the most interesting hybrid languages is OPS83 by Production Systems Technologies, Inc. (Pittsburgh, Pennsylvania). Many of the older OPS5 languages are written in LISP, but OPS83 is written in C. It retains the standard production rule-oriented features of OPS5, but also provides full modular-development features (e.g., separate module compilation, strong typing) associated with PASCAL and C. Compiled programs written in OPS83 are claimed to run up to 30 times faster than LISP-based OPS5 programs.

One the key performance considerations for using the LISP or PROLOG languages is whether they are interpreted or compiled. Whereas interpreted code can execute quickly on specialized LISP machines, it runs slowly on conventional computers, particularly PCs. Compiled code offers faster run time, but can tie up system resources and programmer's time during development. Another factor when selecting AI languages is whether the vendor supplies the source code with the product, which allows customization by the buyer. One final caution concerning new language implementations they will tend to contain bugs and require fixes and special support just as any new software product does. One of the advantages of languages such as Franz LISP and Golden Common LISP is that they have passed through these early release stages into maturity.

As a general strategy, those tool-purchasing corporations that are not software development houses should probably favor using the shell tools. If more flexibility is needed, specialized expert system development firms or consultants should probably be hired during the initial stages of development. Reliance on consultants should taper off as the development takes shape and comes under control of the corporation's own staff. Of course, there are many application-specific factors contributing to these decisions, and they can be addressed only in a specific context.

## 6-3. SMALLTALK AND OTHER OBJECT-ORIENTED SYSTEMS

Object-oriented programming systems are one of the newest trends in AI programming techniques. In object-oriented programming, the central entity is the *object*, which is most like a frame. The object contains descriptive data and a set of instructions defining how the object interacts with the remainder of its "object world" via various forms of *messages* that are sent between individual objects. This asynchronous operational environment is excellent for a variety of application types, including simulations and certain kinds of graphics. *Data abstraction* is a key development feature of most object-oriented systems where high-level implementation-independent descriptions of programming entities are defined in terms of the object and all possible operations that can be performed on the object. The practical advantage is that the communication protocols used by the objects during message passage are independent of the underlying implementation of the system. Objects contain internal operations and a set of external operations, or *methods*, that can be accessed by other objects. This structure operationalizes the *information-hiding* paradigm. Another important theme is the concept of object *classes*, which can be arranged in hierarchies and allow *inheritance* of properties from higher to lower classes. Individual elements of an object class come into existence through *instantiation*, creating a particular *instance* of the object out of its parent class.

The key features of object-oriented programming can be summarized in terms of the concepts of information hiding, data abstraction, inheritance, and dynamic bindings of varible and object types at run time. Object-oriented languages emphasize the "what" the programmer wants done, rather than the "how." The message passage and dynamic binding features (also known as interpretation) are sometimes claimed to be drawbacks of object-oriented languges because they tend to slow execution time. The available object-oriented tools represent a number of variations on this basic theme.

Flavors was one of the earliest of the object-oriented programming schemes in the ZETALISP environment and is now included as a special module in such languages as Franz LISP, Extended Common LISP, and LM-Prolog. The special features of Flavors include simple definition of abstract data types, generalized hierarchies, and the standard object-oriented message-passage programming paradigm. ObjectLISP is a newer, second-generation, object-oriented programming product by LISP Machines, Inc., which runs on Common Lisp machines. It is a cleaner, more elegant implementation of object-oriented programming based on experience gathered with SMALLTALK, LOOPS, and Flavors. Message passing in ObjectLISP is actually implemented as LISP function calls using standard LISP syntax, so classes and instances are not differentiated, allowing greater flexibility. The late variable-binding techniques used in ObjectLISP are a form of functional programming.

Several of the shell tools outlined in the product comparison matrix in

Chapter 5 (e.g., ACORN, ART, Knowledge Craft, LOOPS) incorporate the object-oriented knowledge-capture strategy. In all cases, the strategy is just one of several available to the user of the shell package. LOOPS is the most specifically object-oriented of the products in Chapter 5, making it difficult to distinguish whether it should be classified as a shell or an environment. An object-handling extension to LISP to make it behave like SMALLTALK-80 is at the core of LOOPS. Many other extensions, such as the CSRL inference engine, make it competitive with more expensive expert system products. When the complete LOOPS is employed, it provides several alternative programming styles, notably rule-based, access-oriented, and object-oriented. OPS5 programming can even be set up as a subset of LOOPS in the Xerox LISP machine environment.

Object-oriented programming has gained its greatest publicity and use through the promotion of Xerox's pioneering SMALLTALK-80.[1] SMALLTALK was developed during the 1970s and early 1980s as a research prototype at Xerox Palo Alto Research Center. The system ran on Xerox AI workstations (1100 series) and pioneered some of the most popular user-oriented devices, such as the mouse; high-resolution, bit-mapped screens; windows; pop-up or pull-down menus; and icons. The main advantage of SMALLTALK is its modeless ease of use, which increases programmer productivity. The naturalness of the programming style (object-oriented) encourages clean modularized code designed from a high level of abstraction. The programming methodology closely matches the style of human thinking and organization, as objects in the system are established to mirror objects in the user's mind, allowing for a more direct human-machine interface. In general, experimentation and prototyping can proceed quickly.

Various versions of SMALLTALK-like systems are available on the market, particularly in the world of personal microcomputers. Three of these products are SMALLTALK/V ($99) from Digitalk, Inc. (Los Angeles, California), which runs on MS-DOS PCs, SMALLTALK-80 (developed at Xerox PARC) from Tektronix, Inc., which runs on the Tektronix 4400 AI workstations, and SMALLTALK-80 on Xerox's 1100 machines. PC Scheme, MacScheme, and Poplog are programming languages which also have some object-related features.

SMALLTALK/V is claimed to be the highest performance PC object-oriented language that integrates object-based and rule-based programming styles with object-oriented PROLOG. Source code is included as are editors, debuggers, and a large toolkit of predefined classes and objects. Virtual memory management is available. Access to other languages (including UNIX languages with an optional communications interface—$49) and DOS commands is available.

The SMALLTALK-80/Tektronix 4404 AI workstation represents a highly streamlined AI development environment. The software is specially optimized for the 4404 machine, resulting in high execution speeds and a graphics response time fast enough to support screen animation. As noted before, design and implementation can proceed simultaneously in SMALLTALK, which gives rise to a fast, efficient, interactive development environment for complex problem solving. Objects can be progressively defined without specifying all operations for incremental development. Because small changes in the programs can be relinked in just a few seconds, prototyping is quick and efficient. Objects can be used as rules and frames. The class structure supports both multiple inheritance (network inheritance), hierarchical inheritance, and individuation of objects through the addition of special characteristics or behaviors. Over 200 predefined classes support various data and control abstractions from arithmetic operations, data aggregates such as arrays, sets, dictionaries, bags, and streams, and graphical objects. The control objects support such functions as multiple processors, iterators, procedural operations, and exception handlers. Graphical functions, such as scaling, translating, rotation, logical combination of pixels, and text-attribute modification, are supported. A range of debuggers and other support tools (e.g., to develop multiple windowing pop-up menus) are included in the package. It should be clear that the SMALLTALK-80 system provides a very rich development and run-time environment. If the execution speed issues can be addressed at the same time as solving the issue of integrating with other more traditional environments and machines, then SMALLTALK may be superior to shells for a significant number of applications.

Object-based programming goes hand in hand with icon use. Icon-based expert systems provide a dynamic approach for representing the changing state of a knowledge base. The various LOOPS tutorials and writeups on KEE, for instance, show a variety of uses for dials, gauges, scales, pushbuttons, overlapping windows, company logos, and discipline-specific symbols for clarifying the state of time-varying processes. Consultation of the knowledge base can be directly linked to icon movement and organization on the screen. Designing a factory assembly line, for example, may be accomplished with icons for lathes, machine tools, saws, presses, and other stations in the assembly line. The icons are then made to represent internal objects, so that by dragging the icons around on the screen for positioning and by defining the linkages (messages) between the tool stations, a programmer can simulate a factory. The example of the frame structure for the steam turbine presented in Chapter 4 could easily be defined in the object-oriented paradigm and used in the factory design example just mentioned.

Process control is another area where icon representations, as in PICON or Knowledge Craft, are a natural way to communicate layout and flow information to chemical engineers.

The advantage offered by the Tektronix system is low-cost development in a programming-efficient, high-level environment. Porting from the 4400 environment to other realms will tend to involve rewriting the functionality in another language, because much of it may be written in proprietary code. It can be expected that a great amount of attention will be turned to such programming systems in the next few years. Beyond the ease of programming, the graphical interface provides a means for a high-bandwidth information exchange between the developer or user and the machine. The concepts of multiple windows, icons, pop-up menus, and mouse-driven control represent the style of user interfaces most in demand from non-computer-literate professionals who have to interact with computers. In electronic engineering, for example, Tektronix has in-house tools that show two concurrent windows, one containing a schematic circuit diagram and the other the corresponding physical component layout on the printed circuit board. When the engineer points at an item on one window the system indicates its mapping on the other. The Analog Workbench, by Analog Design Tools (Santa Clara, California), although not written in SMALLTALK, illustrates the great power of using icons to behave exactly like the items they represent.

These concepts, coupled with dynamic update of all objects on the screen during development and run time, present a lively medium for knowledge development and transfer that goes far beyond the limitations of language-phase interactions. Just as engineering workstations have revolutionized the CAD/CAM industries, SMALLTALK-like systems for AI programming and expert system development should result in a much deeper penetration of the technology into various sections of society. LISP and PROLOG will probably continue to be the languages of choice in many detailed logical application areas, but the object-oriented languages are expected to become much more prominent in all types of problem areas. This trend should be particularly strong where the structural organization of knowledge (as in the case of objects or frames) is the critical element in the body of expertise, rather than a linear progression of logical steps and inferences. The concept of an asynchronously interacting society of actors or objects is central to the concept of the new blackboard-knowledge-representation models. New hardware environments are expected to increase the speed of object-oriented systems, which will enhance application capabilities as well. It is interesting to note that, although SMALLTALK itself has not been a leading commercial success, the object-oriented approach has reached the market by other channels. The object-programming extensions to LISP, other languages and various expert systems, (e.g., Franz LISP, Extended Common LISP, LM-PROLOG, Objective C (Productivity Products International), C++ (AT&T), LOOPS, Flavors, ACORN, ART, KEE, and Knowledge Craft) have collectively sold a large number of object systems.

## 6-4. DEVELOPMENT TOOLS FOR NATURAL-LANGUAGE INTERFACES

Natural-language interfaces have been the traditional standard for fully custom expert systems built in research establishments. A majority of the shell tools outlined in Chapter 5 present their user interfaces through some type of limited English-like phrase input/output. It should be understood that prerecorded English-like phrases are not usually understood as natural language. If more sophistication is required, then such shell products as GURU, Knowledge Craft, KES, and Personal Consultant Plus may help. The skilled expert system developer may want to expand on these shell tool capabilities to develop a more substantial and sophisticated interface for certain narrow applications. If the system is being developed from an AI LISP or PROLOG language, specific styles of natural language interfaces may be easier to design and implement. There are also a number of special support tools now available that specialize in this type of development.

For example, Carnegie Group Inc. (Pittsburgh, Pennsylvania), offers a natural-language-interface-developer product called Language Craft, Natural language front ends can be developed with this tool for operating systems, expert systems, databases, and other forms of conventional software applications. The Language Craft environment includes PLUME, a run-time interpreter that uses case-frame instantiation and pattern matching to parse inputs and a set of interface-building tools called the Grammar Writer's Workbench. Key features of PLUME include fast response time, robustness, ambiguity resolution, and the ability to handle fragmentary inputs. The Grammar Writer's Workbench includes a grammar editor, grammar compiler, and tracing and step-function facilities for debugging the grammar. This open-architecture product is implemented in Common LISP for widespread portability. The inclusion of natural-language facilities in GURU and Knowledge Crafts permits their vendors to promote them as AI products, rather than just expert system shells. An example of a less sophisticated, but still useful natural-language tool is contained in MicroRim's Clout interface to the R:Base relational database (Williamson, 1985).

Some specialists believe the natural-language interface is a necessity for any expert system, but, as has been noted previously, language is not always the best means for man-machine communication. Natural language would be a much more useful communication medium if machines could in fact parse and understand the subtle nuances of human speech and the written word. The inherent complexities of natural-language translation and understanding make it still one of the unresolved issues in AI research. The success and wide user acceptance of the high-bandwidth visual-iconic mode of man-machine interface, is significant when contrasted with the continued ambiguities, limited vocabularies, slow interaction rates, and inability to cope with different individuals' styles.

Natural-language interfaces may be the best means of displaying knowledge that uses a complex specialized vocabulary. The medical and legal professions are two examples where highly technical memorized terminologies are used to describe domain knowledge that does not have associated standardized visual representations. These symbolic structures may exist in the minds of the doctors and lawyers, but the dominant form of communication is still through the technical vocabulary attached to these associative networks. Medical textbooks of the past were often short on diagrams and long on technical descriptions. The medical world is begining to move into a more visual style of communication, but the legal world can not be expected to change for a while. Newer editions tend to have more illustrations. Such domains could benefit from a more symbolic layout of knowledge. Examples from molecular chemistry have shown that if a complex structure can be characterized in visual graphical form, the picture is literally worth many thousand words and can provide new insights into the organization of domain knowledge. Such a high level of direct communication is not easily achieved through language.

## 6-5. SPECIALIZED LISP MACHINES

Machines specifically tailored to LISP languages have been mentioned several times in the last two chapters. The primary LISP machines are the Symbolics 3600 series machines (Symbolics, Inc., Cambridge, Massachusetts), the Lambda series machines (LISP Machines, Inc., Andover, Massachusetts), the Xerox 1100 series (Xerox Corporation, Pasadena, California), and the Explorer (Texas Instruments Inc., Dallas, Texas). These machines are specially designed for fast execution of LISP code, whether it is interpreted or compiled. Some machines have both capabilities; others, such as the Xerox workstations, use interpretation only. Large amounts of RAM (e.g., 2–24 MB) for large knowledge sets and a vast number of registers are used to hold for quick access the various LISP primitives. Each of the four manufacturers has its own version of LISP, which is native to its machine—Lambda/ZETALISP-PLUS, Symbolics/Genera (includes Symbolics' Common LISP), and Xerox/InterLISP-D.

Even with the superior processing capabilities of these specialized machines, performance degradations do occur. These are usually in garbage collection, memory paging, and dynamic memory management (one of the repercussions of the LISP late binding-time strategy). Most LISP machines have hardware memory tags and hardware assists for run-time data checking and garbage collection. The Xerox 1185 and 1186 machines lack these specialized hardware functions and instead perform the functions by microcode at run time. For this reason, the Xerox machines are somewhat slower during benchmark tests, but overall performance is still very good due to such built-in functions as bit-mapped graphics and fast windowing. The LMI machines compile programs into microcode for fast execution. Vendors are continually upgrading their machines to further reduce these problems, and help regularly comes in the form of more advanced processor chips, such as the recently developed Intel 80386 and Motorola 68020-25MHz 32-bit microprocessors.

This greater power does not come without cost.[2] Symbolics' machines cost from $50,000 to $200,000 for full development machines in the 3600 line, Xerox costs (e.g., $20,000 for the 1186, $70,000 for the 1132) appear to be considerably lower at first glance, but the Xerox products do not have many of the standard features of other LISP machines, such as large amounts of RAM, large disk storage, integral peripherals, and array-processing boards. By the time these extras are included, the Xerox prices are within the industry standards.

One of the most recent developments in the LISP machine market has been the introduction of new lines of delivery machines, in addition to the development machines. These lower cost, scaled-down models allow large-scale corporate and industrial users to buy at quantity savings only the processing power needed to run executable applications. For example, the Symbolics 3600 AE (Application Engine) has a single board processor instead of the usual three, has been scaled down to desk-top size, and sells for $29,900 in quantities of 75 or more ($39,600 in quantities of 10) which is a considerable drop from the top-of-the-line 3670 models, which range from $100,000–$200,000. LISP Machines, Inc. (LMI), has a delivery version of its Lambda machines, the Lambda/E, priced at $39,000 versus $55,000 to $115,000 for the development LAMBDA machines. The lowest costing delivery model is offered by Xerox for the 1185 at $9,995. Texas Instruments (TI) has a $40,000 delivery version after explorer (development versions start at $47,000).

TI has also been developing a prototype compact LISP machine for delivery, which is much like a plug-in board-level version of the Explorer. This delivery product is an outgrowth of the TI Compact Lisp Machine (CLM) "LISP on a chip" developed for the Defense Advanced Research Projects Agency (DARPA). The Explorer MegaChip LISP processor is a 0.4-inch-square chip in a 2-inch-square package. TI has announced plans to port and evolve the Personal Consultant Series in the Explorer environment, which should offer an important upgrade strategy for PC users of the shells; 60% of Explorer's circuits are being encapsulated into a chip set which brings the processor down to the size of a shoe box. The anticipated delivery machine will sell for around $25,000.

Each of the vendors provides extensive hardware and software environments for LISP program development. The Xerox 1108 and 1132 AI workstations, for instance, run InterLISP-D and the LOOPS shell tool, both of which have been discussed previously, as native programs. InterLISP-D provides a full-function, integrated, program-development system, together with a supportive, efficient, run-time environment compatible with the Ethernet-based Xerox Network System (XNS). Some of the features of the 1108-1115 workstations include at least 2 MB of main memory (expandable up to 3.5 MB), 8-MB virtual memory, a 12K word-control store, floating-point hardware, one parallel I/O port, a 42-MB hard disk (with options for 80 MB or 315 MB disks), a 1.2-MB floppy disk, and a 17-inch bit-mapped, mouse-controlled, monochrome bit-mapped display with 1024 × 808 pixels. InterLISP-D provides high-performance engineering-graphics capabilities, display editor and inspector, debugging tools, text editor, direct microcode support, deep binding, transaction garbage collection, raster-scan graphics, and communications software. The Busmaster Option for the 1108 workstations gives the capability of using either IBM PC Bus or Multibus peripherals, which enhances capabilities for color monitors and printers, speech or music devices, and other peripherals. The 1132 AI workstation is the top-of-the-line model with an extended list of features, such as up to 8 MB of main memory, standard 80-MB hard disk, and so on. The 1185 and 1186 low-end development and delivery workstations have the option of adding a coprocessor to allow IBM PC software to run. This combination of LISP machine hardware with MS-DOS software support allows for flexible paths of extending PC tools with expert functions. The TCP/IP communications protocol options, such as the one offered by Golden Hill Computers, permits the 1100 and 1108 series workstations to communicate with UNIX systems.

Symbolics also has been expanding rapidly its product line to maintain its market leadership. Developments include the 3610AE applications delivery system, the entry-level 3620, the mid-range 3650, and the top-of-the-line 3670. The new CMOS/VLSI symbolic processor provides a 20–40% jump in performance while shrinking the CPU down to a desk-side-sized package. The main thrust of Symbolics' new developments seems to be easier integration with other applications and language, especially through industry-standard networking protocols. Symbolics' support of IBM's SNA and other approaches to intermachine integration will be addressed in more detail in Chapter 8.

LISP Machines, Inc., offers three machines in its Lambda line, including the LMI Lambda ($55,000, LMI Lambda 2×2, ($89,000) and the LMI Lambda 3×3 ($115,000). Each one of these models can be fitted with a conventional processor at additional cost of about $20,000, to generate the LMI Lambda/Plus line. The base model Lambda has a 32-bit LISP processor, 4 MB RAM, 474 MB of Winchester disk, a 21-slot card cage (13 for NuBus, 5 for MULTIBUS, and 3 for either), and a 19-inch high-resolution display with mouse. The base model can be field-updated to either the Lambda/PLUS, Lambda 2×2, or Lambda 2×2/PLUS. Symbolics has also followed this approach of expanding user capabilities within the same base hardware system to keep multiuser installation costs down. The LMI Lambda 2×2 has two LISP processors, two screens, and two keyboards, illustrating the use of the Lambda's bus-centered architecture to incorporate multiple processors in one frame. Similarly, the Lambda 3×3, with 8 MB RAM, has three LISP processors for three users. The PLUS versions of these three machines have an MC68010 coprocessor added to the basic configuration, allowing full use of the LISP environment plus the advantages of independent, concurrent conventional processing through UNIX System V. This type of hybrid hardware configuration underlies LMI's PICON process-control expert system shell. Some of the options for the Lambda series include up to 16 MB of RAM, a second 515-MB Winchester disk drive (for a total of 1.03 gigabytes) for very large applications, such as vision processing. Other options include medium-resolution color displays or high-resolution 3-D color graphics (1024×1024-raster image memory, 1024×768 pixels on 19-inch RGB monitor) using the IRIS system from Silicon Graphics Corporation (Mountain View, California). All Lambda machines are supplied with ZETALISP-PLUS (including a Common LISP version), one of the most powerful LISP programming environments, as has been discussed earlier. UNIX System V (resident on the optional MC68010 coprocessor) allows access to C, PASCAL, FORTRAN, and Ada programming. Other programming options include ObjectLISP, LM-Prolog, and VISTA, an object-oriented graphics tool kit for 2-D and 3-D graphics, real-time animation, simulation, and modeling. The RTIME (Real-Time Intelligent Machine Environment) module links real-time processes to expert systems using the MC68010 processor programmed in C. (RTIME is the real-time processor in the PICON system for process control.)

The features for the TI Explorer are similar to LMI's Lambda. These include a ZMACS window editor, window-oriented interactive LISP interpretor, LISP compiler, debrigging facilities, object editors, program integration facilities, performance monitoring facilities, and interface building tools. Optional software is available for text formatting, graphics development, natural language interface development, ROBMS building, network communications, PROLOG and Network representation tool kits. Hardware features include 38-bit tagged architecture for LISP, 32-bit processor for NuBus, 2-16 MB RAM, Ethernet, 140 MB disk, cartridge tape drive, and a mouse.

The processing power of these somewhat expensive, specialized LISP machines has made them the ideal choice for large-scale, LISP-based projects. Most of the manufacturers have a proprietary PROLOG version for their LISP machines as well, so these machines are often ideal from PROLOG projects as well. Many of the more sophisticated expert system shell tool kits discussed in Chapter 5 were originally supplied coded for these LISP machines, although recently the trend has been to provide conventional versions as well. Teknowledge has even moved to no longer sell its LISP version of S.1, favoring the traditional environment version instead.

One other area of interest concerns altering the IBM PC microcomputer to act as a hybrid "specialized" LISP machines. Interpreted LISP code running on an MS-DOS system is bound to be relatively slow, particularly for large applications. Compilation improves performance, but still leaves much to be desired. LISP coprocessor systems, such as Gold Hill Computer's GCLISP 286 and 386 Developer tools, however, are changing that perception by expanding the capacity of the PC/XT or AT. The GCLISP (Golden Common LISP) 286 Developer allows expansion of direct-address main memory on the AT of up to 16 MB. The GCLISP 386 Developer adds the Gold Hill 386 HummingBoard, based on the Intel 83086 chip running at 16MHz, specifically designed to run LISP applications quickly. The 386 Developer with HummingBoard on an AT performs at up to five times the speed of the 286 Developer, greatly reducing the edit-compile-debug cycle time. The base, directly addressable, on-board RAM associated with the 386 Developer is 6 MB, and can be upgraded to 24 MB. The board includes a 2K cache, parallel coprocessor for I/O support, an interface for shared memory with the base PC processor, and optional support of the Intel 80287 or 80387 floating-point processor. This type of increased memory and processing power is bringing the PC to a level of LISP-processing capabilities that by some measures may begin to rival the capabilities of the LISP machines for a fraction of the cost. The price for the 386 Developer, including Common LISP and HummingBoard, is $7000.

Numerous packaging agreements have been arranged between the LISP machine vendors and other software/hardware vendors. For example, Knowledge Craft by Carnegie Group can be purchased loaded on the LMI Lambda machines directly from LMI. Xerox offers a Quintus Prolog version for its 1100 series AI workstations. LMI sells IKE or PICON for the TI Explorer LISP machines. Tektronix sells Xerox SMALLTALK-80.

The future of the specialized LISP machine market is uncertain just now. At the time of this writing, how the development and delivery markets will fare in the competition between specialized and conventional machines remains to be seen. Certainly the development of relatively inexpensive LISP chips (e.g., CML through the DARPA funded TI project, and a similar effort under way at Xerox) that can be incorporated as a board into conventional computers is interesting. These chips should change the price-performance balance between conventional machine use and specialized hardware use in AI and expert systems work in both development and delivery. Likely prospects for the TI chip will be the Sun and Apollo workstations, for TI has already signed marketing agreements with these two companies to link the Explorer into their networks. Once in a Domain or Ethernet network, the Explorer will function as a *knowledge server* and symbolic-development tool for the entire network.

Symbolics has had the lion's share of the LISP machine market over the past few years. Thirty-nine percent of the $510 million AI hardware market for 1986 was taken by computers with specialized LISP-processing hardware, and this percentage is subdivided according to Symbolics-58%, LMI-13%, TI-12%, Xerox-9%, and 8% by others (source D. M. Data, Inc., Scottsdale, Arizona). The other 61% went to PCs, workstations (led by Apollo and Sun) and general-purpose hardware (dominated by the DEC VAX). With the development of LISP chips to embed in traditional hosts, and the increased porting of shell tools to traditional programs like C, this 39% could shrink even further. Competition will increase between hybrid machines supporting both LISP processors and conventional processors, e.g., the Lambda machines, GCLISP 386 Developer, and a new line of Hewlett-Packard Spectrum machines with large RAM, large number of registers for LISP primitives, and support for different types of coprocessors. Dataquest, Inc. (San Jose, California) projects a world market for AI hardware of $2.7 billion in 1990, compared with $335 million in 1985. The company further projects that most of this market will be oriented to large systems.

## 6-6. AI WORKSTATIONS

Engineering workstations have also become a popular means of developing AI applications, including expert systems. These machines have been converted to AI development mainly through specialized support software, but also through the addition of LISP-processing chips. Mechanical computer-aided design (M-CAD) is the leading application for engineering workstations. Electronic computer-aided design (E-CAD) is the second most popular usage, followed by desk-top publishing, software engineering, and AI. Although AI accounts for only some 5% of workstation applications, some vendors, such as Sun Microsystems, Inc. (Mountain View, California), report 15% of their sales going to AI applications. It is expected that the AI portion of usage will increase over the next few years as the number of expert system applications undergoes a burst of growth.

These dedicated workstations have high-quality graphics interfaces and a variety of software-development support features, although their LISP environments are not as advanced as the LMI and Symbolics special-purpose machines. The cost, generally in the $20,000–$50,000 range, makes the workstations an attractive alternative to the more expensive LISP machines. The machines are usually based on the MC680×0, Intel 80×86, National Semiconductor Corporation NS32032 32-bit microprocessors, or proprietary RISC chips. The primary manufacturers of AI workstations are Apollo Computer, Inc. (Chelmsford, Massachusetts), Sun Microsystems, Inc. (Mountain View, California), Digital Equipment Corporation (Northboro, Massachusetts), and IBM (Armonk, New York). Generally the AI workstations run Common LISP, Franz LISP, and PROLOG, except for the Tektronix machines, which also operate in the SMALLTALK-80 environment. Apollo has its own Common LISP, and Sun has Franz LISP and PROLOG. The VAXstation II/GPX from Digital offers one of the most flexible combinations for AI work, as it runs DEC's LISP, PROLOG, and OPS5. Most of the UNIX-based workstations, including the IBM RT, Silicon Graphics, Masscomp (Westford, Massachusetts), Access Systems Corp. (Pittsburgh, Pennsylvania), Data General (Westboro, Massachusetts), Hewlett-Packard (North Hollywood, California), Ridge Computers (Santa Clara, California), Daisy Systems Corporation (Mountain View, California), and Intergraph Corporation (Huntsville, Alabama) models, can be made to execute the UNIX version of Franz LISP. The Apollo workstations run several expert system shells, including KES, RuleMaster, and ART.

Of all the workstation models on the market, the DN3000 from Apollo has become the best selling unit of all time. Sales for the Sun-3 and Sun-4 workstations are increasing at a rapid rate, helped in part by Sun's support of such shells as ART, Knowledge Workbench, and KES.

Originally the workstations were slow at running LISP, because they were not microcoded for the language. New microprocessors and fast compilers, such as those developed by Lucid, Inc., however, have brought the performance of the Sun-3 and Apollo Domain into the same arena as Symbolics on benchmark tests. On the Sun machines, for instance, the LISP run-time checking can be turned off when the development phase is over to enhance execution time. The comments made previously about the lack of specialized hardware support on the Xerox machines apply here also. The run-time type checking tends to slow the Xerox machines, and there is a need to write very crisp, clean code to maximize processing. This programming constraint is not so important on the LMI, TI, Tektronix, and Symbolics machines.

RISC machines, such as the IBM PC/RT, Intergraph Interpro, Ridge 32S and HP Spectrum, present the possibility of low-cost, delivery vehicles for non-LISP applications. RISC machines can be characterized by a small instruction set (under 150 members), one clock cycle per instruction, few addressing modes, and many internal registers. The expert shells GURU and ART, are two examples of AI tools being ported to the RT. As LISP development machines, RISC machines have some of the same performance problems noted above. Performance is likely to improve as new RISC chips for LISP, large amounts of memory, and improved compilers become available.

The Tektronix 4400 series illustrates the type of AI capabilities associated with these different workstations. The low-end 4404 is a SMALLTALK-80, Franz LISP, and MPROLOG machine, and the 4400 provides a full Common LISP programming environment. The 4405 AI system is a single-user, desk-top model that can be used for both developing and delivering AI programs. It has an MC68020 32-bit CPU with a 68881 floating-point coprocessor. SMALLTALK-80 is the base environment, with options for Tektronix Common LISP, MPROLOG, or Franz LISP. One of the features of SMALLTALK-80 is that it does not run under an operating system; rather it includes the features normally associated with an OS within itself. The 13-inch monochrome display (bit-mapped graphics with mouse or joy stick) presents a 640× 480 pixel (video resolution) window into a 1024×1024-bit map memory. Standard RAM is 1 MB, with an additional 2 or 4 MB available. Mass storage is a 45-MB hard disk drive, which can be replaced by a 90-MB disk, and a 320-KB floppy disk drive. The 32-MB, virtual memory, UNIX-like operating system supports multitasking. Many utility programs are available, together with access to an assembler, a C compiler, and a standard I/O library. The workstation can serve as a VT100 terminal emulator and may participate in TCP/IP protocol Ethernet local area networks (LANs). The top-of-the-line 4406 AI workstation has similar characteristics, with a 2-MB RAM, the 90-MB hard disk, and a 19-inch 1280×1024-bit mapped display. Tektronics machines run approximately $12,000, $15,000, and $24,000 for the 4404, 4405, and 4406 models respectively.

Another example of a leading AI workstation that is not LISP-hardware-specific, is the VAXstation II by Digital Equipment. The VAXstation II/GPX is essentially a MicroVAX II machine, with built-in color graphics, oriented to running AI languages like DEC's VAXLISP. The machine is a 0.9-MIPS, 32-bit system running VMS or ULTRIX-32M, with 5-MB standard RAM (upgradable to 9 MB), standard 71-MB disk (upgradable to four drives of 467 MB each) and 95-MB streaming tape, floating-point accelerator coprocessor, DECnet Ethernet interface, 19-inch monitor with 1024×864 pixels, MIT's X-Windows, GKS graphics software, and a mouse. The system offers multiwindowing and concurrent tasks. Conventional VMS software applications can be run, as well as AI software, and the workstation is upward-compatible with the rest of the DEC VAX/VMS and VAX/ULTRIX line. VAXLISP can access VMS commands and code written in other VAX layered programs. Networking can be accomplished either through Ethernet or an optional VMS/SNA gateway. At the time of writing, DEC had not included the MicroVAX in the VAXclusters scheme. Also work on providing ULTRIX users with as many integration facilities and symbolic compilers has not progressed as rapidly as it has for VMS.

The expandability (i.e., the ability to maintain excellent response times while adding users), for networked engineering workstations, makes them especially suitable for applications expected to grow. Apollo networks of over 300 machines, all sharing resources and data have been developed at such companies as Caterpillar Tractor (Peoria, Illinois) and Apollo itself. The competition between Sun's Network File System (NFS) and Apollo's Remote File System (RFS) for inclusion in future versions of UNIX can be expected to increase. The RFS design goes deep into the core of the operating system, making it more transparent than NFS. Much progress in network operating systems can be expected in the next few years. As expert systems tend to be highly CPU-intensive, they are an area well-addressed by the internetworking of multiple hosts, a problem that has been tackled most thoroughly by the workstation vendors.

The reasons for employing engineering workstations for expert system projects are as follows

• The need for a high-productivity UNIX-based software development environment, which could be for tools (KES, ART, KEE, etc.) or languages (C, LISP, etc.)

• The need for fast-response-time, high-resolution color graphics, in either development and delivery or both.

• The need to integrate the expert system with existing M-CAD or E-CAD tools that run on engineering workstations.

• The need for expandability, where users can be added without degrading response times, which is important for CPU-intensive jobs.

• The need for compound systems with workstations, LISP machines, and traditional hosts in one network. In such an environment the workstations provide the best man-machine interfaces for most jobs.

## 6-7. ON THE USE OF GENERAL-PURPOSE COMPUTERS

Although there are good reasons for employing LISP machines or engineering workstations for developing expert systems, the current industry trend is to employ conventional computers for the delivery stage. In spite of the new low-end models of LISP machines targeted at the delivery-vehicle market, the sales of IBM PCs and DEC VAXs have been dominating the expert system production environment. It is interesting to look at the use of general-purpose computers for expert systems applications in two lights, first from the perspective of research organizations, and secondly from mainstream MIS and CIM shop floor perspectives.

From the research point of view, specialized hardware systems for expert systems applications provide fast and efficient development and delivery environments. Using the same vendor for development and delivery platform precludes many porting complications. As well as eliminating application porting, it is also simpler to deal with fewer vendors—preferably only one. Connecting machines in a single vendor environment can be considerably simpler than with multiple vendors. LISP machines do still have a reputation for being slow, expensive, and difficult to integrate with production environments. Although these shortcomings are being worked on intensively by the vendors involved, the user marketplace is tending to move even faster.

Researchers are recognizing that new trends in the AI and expert systems commercial markets are causing a broadening of special-purpose computers through added coprocessors, new compilers, expanded interfaces, and advanced networking capabilities. The capabilities for running AI or expert systems programs on conventional general-purpose machines have increased dramatically in the last few years. The transfer of AI/LISP/expert systems technology into the mainstream of computer processing is currently reaching fruition.

The advantages for using general-purpose computers are obvious: computer professionals are familiar with them; there is a large installed base running the traditional software packages of business, research, and government; they are usually less expensive; communication interfaces between different types of machines are plentiful; and software packages are well established. There are also disadvantages, however, primary of which is the need for large amounts of direct-access RAM and CPU capacity. The earliest expert system programs, usually written in LISP, were interpreted on conventional computers and were thus notoriously slow. In subsequent years, however, specialized compilers and the porting of expert systems written in AI languages to languages like C have resulted in much faster, efficient code.

From the MIS and CIM shop floor perspective it is interesting to look at the marketplace patterns of Fig. 5-3 for expert system shells and Fig. 6-3 for symbolic programming languages, showing what environments are favored by which products. Basically the languages are dominant on specialized LISP machines, engineering workstations, and UNIX computers. The shells are dominantly available on the IBM PC with upward portability to the DEC VAX, expecially to VAX VMS, but also to VAX ULTRIX. The languages show the machine inclinations of the research world, and the shells indicate the leanings of business and industry.

Figure 6-3 leads to one of the most interesting conclusions of this book, namely that, although IBM has generated excellent business through its fostering of more expert system shell vendors on the PC than any other machine, it is in danger of losing this business to DEC's VAX series. Acceptance of the IBM 9370 series, announced in late 1986 and competing directly with the VAX line, is likely to be crucial for IBM's continued success in this market. As applications expand, the limitations of the PC as a delivery vehicle are being met, and users are looking around for larger compatible platforms. There is now a rush of vendors porting their PC shells over to the VAX. Products now available on VAX VMS, as well as the PC, include XSYS, GURU, RuleMaster, KES, TIMM, ESP/Advisor, and INSIGHT. Although admittedly a few of these were ported to the VAX first, the expert system shell porting trend is dominantly away from the PC and toward the VAX. In addition to VMS, there is a strong and accelerating trend in favor of VAX UNIX, be it in the ULTRIX or Berkeley 4.3 forms. KES, ART, RuleMaster, and GURU are examples of products available under VAX UNIX in additon to VAX VMS.

The expert system shell market makes an excellent probe to test the current state of the entire MIS and CIM software market. Older categories of software, such as WP and DBMS, are available for a wider

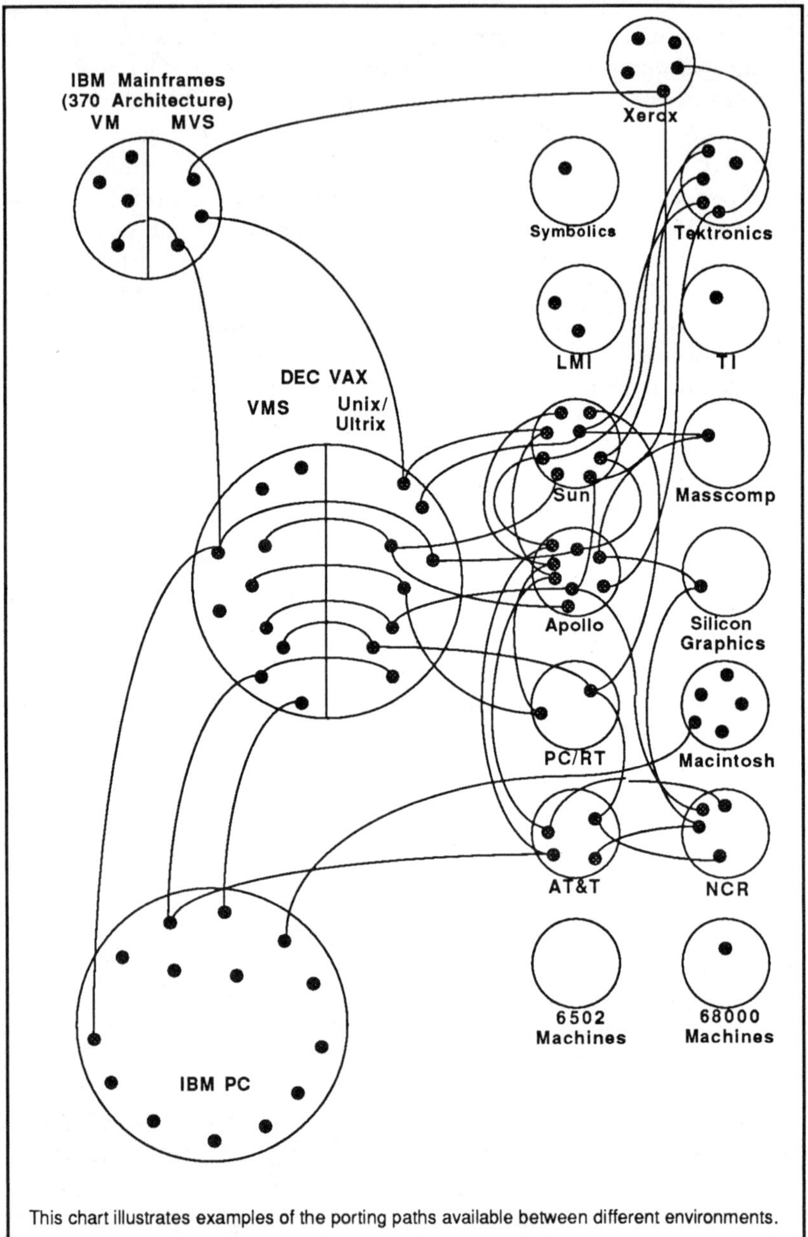


This chart illustrates examples of the porting paths available between different environments.

Fig. 6-3. Symbolic programming languages porting paths.

spread of "obsolete" environments, but in the shell arena the vendor trend to select winning hardware is clear. Software vendors have become a lot more particular about which hardware environments they support, due to the failure or difficulties of many hardware vendors in recent years (e.g., Pixel, Osborne, Gavelin, Syte, Storage Technology, Synapse, Auragen). Spreadsheet and WP microcomputer packages show the older pattern, where they are spread out over five categories of machines: BASIC, CP/M, MS-DOS, UNIX, and Macintosh/SMALLTALK-like. Microprocessor-based implementations, even of multiuser, workstation, and AI products, fit into six categories, where LISP systems are appended on the end of the previous five. The pattern, even though somewhat blurred, is of two 8-bit categories, two 16-bit ones, and two 32-bit ones. In the field of minicomputers, the older DBMS market shows a pattern of almost as many operating systems as vendors. Newer software product releases, however, show support of UNIX for almost all minicomputer vendors. Although most UNIX implementations started on 16-bit machines (68000-based or PDP-11s), the trends have established UNIX as the standard 32-bit operating system for micros, minis, and mainframes. At the mainframe end of the market, uncertainties on operating system trends are slowing down expert system porting moves. Supporting IBM's UNIX (IX/370) would not be so difficult, but the degree of future promotion of IX/370 in favor of MVS or VM is unknown. Even established IBM installations are unclear as to whether to favor VM or MVS. Certainly MVS is the popular environment for large machines, and it can be run under VM for a considerable price in CPU cycles. For IBM customers who have MVS on the mainframes and MS-DOS on the PCs, there is uncertainly over the desirability of introducing a third incompatible operating system (VM) with a radically different internal architecture just to support a mid-sized range of machines (9370s).[3] Customers who have done broad long-range planning are leaning toward UNIX as a common platform for micros, minis, and mainframes, and quite a few are seeing DEC VAXs running UNIX as the first zone to introduce the long-range plan. As will be covered in Chapter 8, DEC's machines seem to connect to IBM systems more easily than IBM systems connect to each other. Project managers looking for robust, expandable expert system delivery vehicles with a future may well be satisfied by investigating the industry trend toward DEC VAX and similar UNIX machines interconnected with IBM PCs and other single-user microcomputers.

Whatever the viewpoint, problems with conventional machines for expert system work do, however, still remain. PCs and PS/2s are still slow, especially when the knowledge bases are large, and the size of the knowledge base is often limited by the machine's RAM. Stand-alone expert systems on a dedicated machine, for development or delivery, are one thing, but a time-sharing situation in a multiuser environment is another. Some programs, such as OPS5, have a loading factor more equal to that of a similar-sized FORTRAN program and do not degrade multiuser performance as much as a LISP program would. What will and will not work depends strictly on application and usage.

An 80286-class PC or PS/2 may be adequate as a stand-alone delivery vehicle for such limited applications as a turbine vibration-analysis expert system. One of these units could be installed at each functional location within the corporation. A sales-forecasting expert system to serve a corporation may be better positioned on a centrally located dial-up access mainframe. The degree of expertise distribution needed, coupled with the most reasonable and cost-effective software tools for accomplishing the task, can greatly influence the decision of machine types.

## 6-8. REAL-TIME AND EMBEDDED EXPERT SYSTEMS

Most of the early expert systems applications were aimed at solving consultative-type problems, often involving an interactive session between the end user and the expert system. For many real-world applications, expert systems must be able to function as an integral part of a sophisticated computerized system that is not directly interacting with a human. Some applications, such as that of hospital patient-monitoring systems and process-control systems, must be able to perform their analyses based on continually arriving data and impart their expertise in the form of adjustments to the display signals to technicians, adjustments to fluid flows, or adjustments to any one of the control parameters in the process through servomotor mechanisms.

Process control has a number of problems well-suited to expert system solution. One such is the issue of alarms. If an incident occurs on a continuous-process chemical plant, then it tends to trigger a large number of alarms in rapid succession. If the alarms are not handled intelligently the control room can rapidly become a loud distracting environment where the operator cannot focus on the incident. The reason too many alarms can occur at once is that numerous sensors, for such measures as temperature or pressure, are positioned all over the plant. Each sensor has its own acceptable minimum/maximum levels and may be triggered in isolation to alert the operator to the start of any minor incident. Many sensors are needed to provide a fine granularity of resolution. The way to use production rules to limit the number of concurrent alarms is to get the expert system to look for patterns of triggerings. For example, if the flow rate from a vessel drops to zero and the pressure in it keeps rising, then instead of triggering two alarms the expert system can warn the operator that the outlet has probably become blocked. The pressure in input pipes will also rise, but once the nature of the incident has been identified, these new alarms can be sent to the operator's screen, but inhibited from sounding klaxons. The probabilities of different scenarios can be calculated by the system, based on hundreds of input signals, and presented to the operator in the order of likelihood. The expert system can also be looking for operators errors in interpreting the situation and taking corrective action. Of course, all these incident patterns will have to be obtained from experienced operators and from an analysis of past problem situations, but the use of expert systems in process control can increase safety, quality, and yields.

Two real-time expert system building tools (PICON and Advisor) have been previously discussed. PICON by LMI (written in C and LISP- and MAP[4]-compatible) runs on the dual processor Lambda/PLUS machines with a 32-bit LISP processor for the rule-based system and a concurrently active 32-bit MC68010 processor for monitoring and controlling process parameters. Even with this distributed architecture, PICON is usually installed in conjunction with an existing process-control machine, such as the Honeywell TDC 3000 (Minneapolis, Minnesota). PICON allows over 20,000 different parameters to be monitored in one system, together with knowledge bases of many thousand rules. The expert system is often best employed as a supervisory machine that can read the other hosts and advise the operators, but not directly alter the plant settings. In the Lambda machine the Multibus interface is used to connect multiple machines, and an optional Ethernet connection is available. These Ethernet and Multibus interfaces provide excellent routes to connect the LISP machine as a slave processor from the direct digital-control machines. The real-time monitoring in PICON is accomplished through LMI's RTIME module, which is written in C and is available independently to link any expert system to time-varying data (RTIME runs on Lambda/PLUS machines). The architecture is shown in Fig. 6-4. Run-time versions of PICON implemented in Common LISP are offered in quantities of $12,000 for a range of computers running Common LISP. It should be understood that a system need not be designed to be real-time and embedded at the same time. Also real-time or embedded systems need not have the authority to act as independent agents, or at least if they do it is important to contain their authority within very safe limits.

The Advisor Design System by UMECORP (Ultimate Media Corporation) has been discussed in Chapter 5. It allows embedded expert systems to be developed on a number of microcomputers (e.g., Apple,

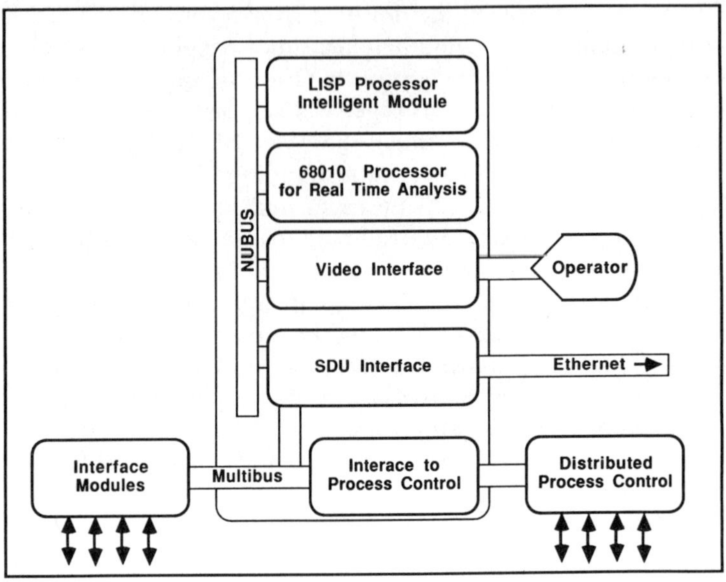


Fig. 6-4. The PICON architecture for rule-based process control.

Amiga, Commodore, IBM). Knowledge bases can then be transported to either of UMECORP's delivery tools, Knowledge Engine (KE) or Expert Controller (EC), for real-time field deployment of rule-based advisory or electromechanical control programs. The products can support anywhere from 4080 to 12,240 rules, depending on the model. The Expert Controller is an extension of KE with a BASIC language controller and an EPROM burner with single-byte, selectable programming used to convert rule bases in RAM to firmware and also to copy operational systems. Whereas Advisor expert systems running on a microcomputer have a throughput of 250 rules/second, the specialized CMOS KE and EC boost that throughput to 5000 rules/second. These systems were designed to both simplify and expand the control capability of many industrial programming-logic controllers, such as those of Allen Bradley, Gould, or General Electric. Using either serial communications or local-area networks, KE and EC can be used to interconnect and control a range of products from laboratory instruments to micros, minis, or mainframes.

Embedding allows a developed expert system to be incorporated as a module within another system. For instance, the KES shell tool (Software A&E, discussed in Chapter 5), which is written in C, can access any of the library of C functions. Conversely, the expert system can be consulted by C-supported programming languages. Most products running under UNIX can generally be embedded by employing UNIX functions, rather than anything provided by the shell vendor. Such systems might be used as a query front end for a database, for intelligent electronic mail sorters and filters (including the circular file), expert-controlled PBX voice-activated call dispatchers, PBX filters to prevent unwanted calls, automatic automobile diagnostic systems, automatic fault-tolerant analysis in computers, and so on. Even such mundane tasks as billing the clients using a multiuser expert system can be accomplished in this manner. The embedded code can either be part of a larger software system running on a general-purpose computer or it can be placed in firmware and employed in a dedicated electronic circuit. The list of potential applications for such embedded systems, from small to large, is limited at this time primarily by imagination, not technology.

At this point in the commercialization of expert systems technology, only a few of the available products are packaged in embeddable form. Also, there are very few real-time systems such as PICON or Advisor available for use. These limitations severely restrict the field for tools in this area, but it is likely that more vendors will be bringing forth relevant products in the next few years. The newer high-power microprocessor chip sets will open new layers of cost-effective possibilities. It is likely that just as microprocessors have been embedded in all kinds of consumer and industrial products, ranging from washing machines to cars, so small expert systems are likely to be found increasingly in such products as gas pumps, ATMs, industrial programmable controllers, and stereos.

## 6-9. AN EXAMPLE OF A SINGLE-USER, MS-DOS/VMS CONFIGURATION

Two example expert system configurations are briefly outlined in this section and the next. These configurations have been developed in the authors' work, and thc decision-making rationale is provided to underscore the strategy theme of this book. The decisions described are oversimplified, but they do bring out some of the key decision points in the process. Due to current market trends, both examples are based on conventional hardware, rather than LISP or workstation vehicles. Many possible solutions exist to each problem, and the ones presented are not necessarily the best or only solutions; rather they are viable solutions. Readers should also not treat these models as solutions that they can apply directly to their application problems. It is the authors' experience that almost any configuration can be made to work given the right engineering team; however, without the correct skills, almost anything can fail. What is needed is an appropriate engineering analysis of each problem as it arises without relying on other people's worked examples.

The application for the first case study is a catalog-selection system for identifying the optimum electric motor to match a specific job. Retail and wholesale outlets for electric motors exist in most large cities, providing several hundred candidate sites to install this expert system product. Each outlet has hundreds of motor products on sale, and if the appropriate expertise is not available many potential purchasers do not know which model best matches their needs. Such innovations as permanent magnet motors, based on the new permanent magnetic materials, make the set of products a continually shifting base to work with. By delivering the correct expertise to the point of sale, the system should be able to close more sales in a shorter time and thus sell more units, resulting in higher profit margins with a significant return on investment.

In this case study a third-party engineering group has identified that an expert-system-based motor selector would be a profitable service to sell to the many outlets across the country. A probabilistic inference mechanism is needed because

- There are several requirements to each motor application, each one having a weighting factor, or probability, associated with it.
- The ability of any one motor to meet a perfectly defined need is typically never 100%; it is usually a matter of a certain probability of fulfilment.
- The suitability of a motor for a job is never decided on the basis of one need, but rather depends on a set of pros and cons. Each pro or con can have a weight factor associated with it.
- The different motor manufacturers rate their products in different ways, so that comparative information is always partial.

The multiple dimensions of uncertainty and volatility mean that this problem cannot be easily solved with algorithmic computing. A heuristic expert system is a much better match. The solution approach was to be able to ask the buyers a flexible series of questions to identify their needs and their relative importance. The expert system needed to operate on a comprehensive and up-to-date database of facts about electric motors. Part of the engineering company's job was to continually research the electric motors on the market and maintain the fact database. As most buyers do not have much time to wait, it was important to be able to complete a consultation in under 5 minutes. In addition there had to be less than 30 seconds of delay between the buyers agreement to use the system and the system's first question.

After defining the application, the engineers had to select the hardware and software tools for the different aspects and phases of the system. What was needed was a relatively simple rule-based expert system shell, with probabilities, a database interface, a high-level language interface, efficient execution, and a low run-time price. The hardware approach adopted was to employ an IBM PC/AT at each point of sale, together with a larger host in a central location. A consultation would be a stand-alone affair on the PC, but weekly or even daily updates of the local knowledge and database were necessary. As the engineering company was familiar with VAX VMS products from its electrical engineering work, there was a desire to use the existing VAX 8200 on the central site. The plan adopted was to do development, maintain the central motor attribute base, and distribute data over phone lines, all on the 8200.

Several MS-DOS-based expert systems could have been used on the local sites, but one was wanted that also ran under VMS. The short list at this stage could have included GURU, XSYS, INSIGHT 2+, RuleMaster, KES, or TIMM. KES was selected mostly on the subjective judgment that Software A & E's commitment to and experience with database integrations was ahead of its competition. A comprehensive relational DBMS was desired, and it was decided the most flexibility would be obtained by integrating a stand-alone product with the expert shell. GURU was rejected because of the perception that the natural language, spreadsheet calculator, and business graphics were unnecessary expenses and also probably used up too much RAM and disk to allow for optimal database and inferencing work. INSIGHT was ruled out because it was judged that the company did not have a track record with large systems and that its metastrategies and high-level language interfaces were not crisply implemented. RuleMaster's induction approach was decided to be too cumbersome for this simple application, where the number of motor examples ran into the hundreds and was constantly changing. Radian Corporation's experience with database integrations was judged to be small, and the tool's ability to be called from external routines was questionable. With TIMM and TIMM-PC the compatability between the two products was unclear, primarily due to General Research's dependence on FORTRAN; VMS FORTRAN is an extremely rich implementation, though IBM's PC FORTRAN is a more limited version. TIMM also employs the same induction strategy that was rejected for RuleMaster, is expensive due to its inclusion of frame-based reasoning, and had an undesirable licencing scheme for the application in hand. XSYS was the second choice after KES, but one of them had to be selected, so XSYS was rejected because its LISP basis caused slow execution times. Vendors reading this case study will want to justify why their products should have been used, but KES should be seen as *a* solution, not *the* solution.

The point of sale configuration chosen was a standard IBM PC/AT with MS-DOS 3.1, 640KB of RAM, 1.2MB floppy, a large disk capacity, and a Hayes 2400bps modem. The selected drives had the largest capacity available at the time of the evaluation (140 MB—from Emerald Systems, San Diego, California—manufactured with Control Data Corporation, Minneapolis, Minneapolis), had a good reputation for reliability, and were accessible under MS-DOS. For the database, dBase II was attractive because of its corporate standard status, but it did not have a high-level programming interface, nor could it run under VMS. Oracle from Oracle Corporation (Menlo Park, California), however, was selected as it is a leading RDBMS that runs under both the VMS and MS-DOS operating systems. The data communications product Oracle Link, from Oracle, was also built into the system to allow files to be moved between the PCs and the VAX.

One of the more interesting tasks was developing a uniform set of interfaces for the end user. Three sets of modules existed in the system—those from KES, those from Oracle, and those of the high-level custom programming needed for data-entry validation, management of non-table records, and complex algorithms for mathematical calculations. Unfortunately, this variety created undue confusion for the user. Three different syntax styles were needed, and the screen prompts would vary from module to module. The problem was solved by creating a custom screen-handling system that overlay all the KES and Oracle modules to provide a uniform, standardized interface.

## 6-10. AN EXAMPLE OF A MULTIUSER UNIX CONFIGURATION

In the second configuration model, the application is law enforcement resource allocation. When a "911" emergency call is received the police department has to decide

- how many police officers to dispatch
- the type and number of vehicles to be used
- any special equipment to be taken

Information concerning each emergency situation builds up over a short time, and decisions have to be made quickly. Law enforcement costs have been rising in recent years, creating the requirement not to send too much coverage. A second reason for being economical in coverage is to preserve forces for possible concurrent incidents. If not enough support is provided, however, then a breakdown in law and order can occur, with serious repercussions. Incident "symptoms" often conflict with each other, making algorithmic decision making problematic. Almost always the available information is only partial, but decisions have to be made, so the unknowns have to be inferred. In addition, descriptions of symptoms arrive in vague terms that have to matched with possible synonyms before commencing inferencing. Certain "diagnoses" fit into routine categories of handling, but others have to be treated as special cases and decided by human experts. Referring to Chapter 3, it can be seen that much of this application is highly suitable for expert system implementation. One of the elements of the police dispatcher system design was to be able to filter out exceptional situations for manual special handling. For more routine cases, the expert system was designed to act as an advisor to allow junior officers to make resource allocation decisions.

To support a citywide police department, it was decided that a multiuser configuration with a shared database was essential. Keeping track of the demographic variables and other facts associated with each incident is central to the system operation, so one common database was needed. Each telephone operator was equipped with a terminal to enter and query the database and expert system. The procedure was to first enter the known facts by relaying questions over the phone to the caller. Usually the first 911 caller would provide only a few key pieces of information, so additional ones would have to be added by subsequent on-site police reports. Many emergency situations would be awaiting further details at any one time and thus would be paused in the computer. Each initial decision to allocate resources is known as an *incident*, and additional allocations to the same incident are called *incident extensions*.

Several viable software/hardware configuration paths for developing this expert system/database exist, so three of the stronger options are outlined prior to a discussion of the one adopted. Besides meeting the basic design specifications for the law enforcement expert system, a key consideration in the analysis was the capability for expanding the number of users. In this case study, demand for the system grew steadily to take it way beyond original planned figures, due to ever-increasing levels of user acceptance and then reliance on the expert system.

The first of three configuration groupings is a set of UNIX-based computers. At the low end of the spectrum, IBM PC/ATs run the XENIX System V (Santa Cruz Operation, Santa Cruz, California) operating system. Applications written under this system can be expanded up through the line of DEC VAX machines from the MicroVAX II on up to the VAX 8650, all running DEC ULTRIX, which is another version of UNIX System V. The common denominator in this expansion path is the UNIX System V operating system with portability up the machine line.

The second approach to expandability is based on IBM PC/XTs or ATs running MS-DOS in a local area network configuration. Sharing of data and resources, including the same hard disks and printers, can be managed by specialized server equipment, such as provided by Novell (Orem, Utah), IBM (Raleigh, North Carolina), Xerox (Dallas, Texas), or Ungermann-Bass, Inc. (Santa Clara, California). The servers need to perform the necessary "record-locking" functions to coordinate access and update of the centralized database although this feature is not always available. Distribution of knowledge bases is a further extension that is not a widely established practice, although TI in conjunction with Apollo has made some important advances in this area. In this approach inferencing is done locally using down-loaded or cached knowledge from the centralized knowledge base.

The third alternative path is to expand up to IBM mainframes with their custom operating systems, notably VM or MVS. The software tools, either shell tools or languages, to focus on for this path are those that are available on IBM PCs and are directly portable to IBM mainframes. A primary justification for this path is the extensive large-organization acceptance of IBM mainframes. A second reason is this application's demand for up to a 100-plus user system, which could potentially grow to 1000 or more users. Choosing this line may be influenced by a desire to keep the knowledge base centralized, rather than distributed on a series of smaller DEC MicroVAXs or IBM 9370s. As an example of appropriate tools, the Aion Corporation expert system shell tools described in Chapter 5 have been specifically designed for the IBM line from PC to mainframe. Aion presents an attactive approach, assuming the shell tool provides the necessary knowledge representation, inference, interface, and other capabilities needed for the application.

Of the three alternatives, the PC network is the most limited in terms of expansion. When up to 20 nodes of the network are accessing the disk server, performance generally degrades dramatically. As a rule of thumb, 20 users is the maximum, and 10 is probably a more realistic figure for a PC-based local area network system with simultaneous database usage. If LAN users are not accessing the same files, then it is often possible to have 200 or more stations on a multiple server network. Loadings for LAN-shared knowledge bases are less well benchmarked. The UNIX growth path also has its limits. The VAX 8650 should be able to service over 50 users, but under certain application loadings with many database products, such as PROGRESS from Data Languages Corporation (Billerica, Massachusetts) or Informix from Informix Software, Inc. (Menlo Park, California), internal control structures or other limitations can exhaust system resources with only 30 users.

The IBM 370 mainframe (e.g., 4300, 3030, 3081, 3090) path is able to support 100-plus users with fairly heavy concurrent disk usage, but the investment in system programming and hardware is substantial. The VM operating system can be run on an IBM PC/370, which would allow a low-cost entry point for migrating up the line, but most corporate mainframe users are employing and prefer MVS/XA. The smallest machine that runs MVS/XA is the IBM 4381, with a configured price of around $500,000. A scaled-down version of MVS/XA, notably MVS/SP, is able to run on the IBM 4361, which is available for about half that cost, but functionality is reduced, and there is no guarantee that the resultant expert system will run without modification under MVS/XA. The necessary development machine for producing a production environment with 100-plus users, therefore, may demand a half-million dollar investment. The UNIX entry development equipment costs for such a machine as the PC/AT running XENIX, in contrast, are often under $10,000. Although mainframe development is more expensive, if the design strategy is handled correctly, such systems can grow to 1000 or more users.

One alternative to such large development investment costs, which still maintains the large system target, is to develop on one system, e.g., UNIX, and port to another, e.g., MVS/XA. Figure 6-4 provides a block diagram detailing this translation approach. Certainly if an upward compatible PC to MVS tool, such as Focus or Aion, is used in the development, custom translators are not needed. More commonly, certain tools were selected in the past because they ran in the UNIX environment, and it was only later discovered that there was a need to service over 100 users, which is usually beyond the capability of UNIX. Certainly IX/370 running on IBM mainframes can support over 100 users, but, as stated earlier, most large-volume organizations favor MVS/XA. If such a move from UNIX to some larger environment, such as MVS, is needed, then the UNIX tool YACC can be resorted to (Fig. 6-5). It is interesting to note that UNIX has the self-referral capability of removing itself, akin to the old saying "it takes a thorn to remove a thorn." For example if an expert system based on the PROGRESS database were developed on a UNIX machine then it could not be directly moved to MVS. The UNIX YACC tool could be employed to produce a compiler/compiler facility to translate the PROGRESS source code into Oracle, for example, which would then run under MVS.

Now that the strategy alternatives have been addressed, the specific selection for this model was based on the UNIX path. Because the number of users was originally to be kept small, IBM PC/ATs were

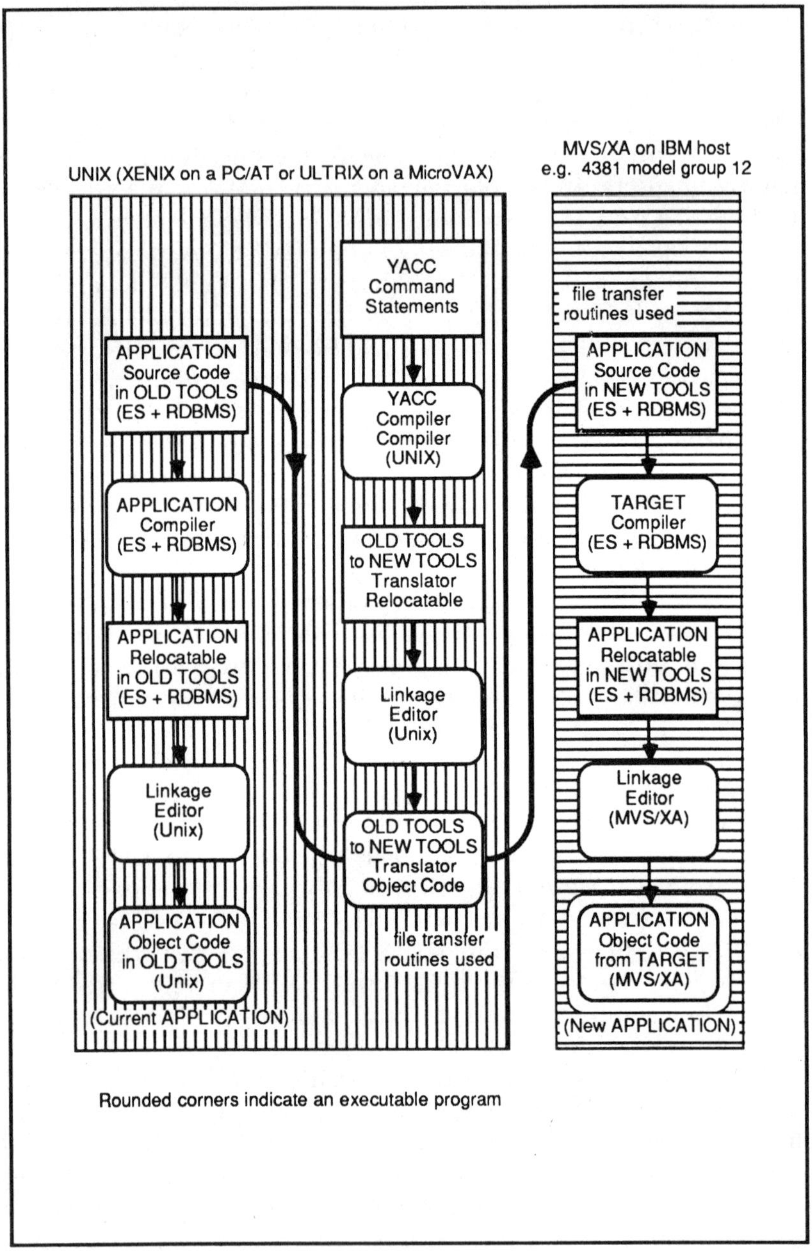


Fig. 6-5. A Unix-to-MVS expert system translator.

chosen running Santa Cruz Operations XENIX (Santa Cruz, California), as it was perceived to be a smooth-running multiuser operating system with good support. The prototype was built with Radian's RuleMaster, due to its running under UNIX, the provided database interface, and the excellent high-level language interface. Silogic's Knowledge Workbench was also considered, as it runs under UNIX and has a database interface, but due to its PROLOG basis it could run only a 68000-based machine. It was possible to put a 68000 coprocessor on the PC/AT, but this created complications with other software requirements. Another possibility was to used Altos or Plexus 68000 machines, but this option was rejected in favor of the RuleMaster strategy on IBM PC/ATs. At the time of the study KES, ART, and GURU were not perceived to be established UNIX products, unlike the two main candidates. The development team was originally hired as a threesome, due to the three-user limit of the AT, but when compile times were observed, two more ATs were purchased.

Using RuleMaster, any relational database manager that matched the application requirements could be used. Both Informix and Unify from Unify Corporation (Sacramento, California) were considered, and Informix was choosen. The prototype was developed and tested, and seven months later was moved into live evaluation. During the bedding-in period, the validation routines, the limited screen formatting options, the menu style, and the long file-closing time of Informix proved not acceptable. The appearance of the screen lacked finesse and would have been much improved by a product, such as Aion, which offers color screen management. Special escape sequences from within XENIX were finally used to achieve the color and formatting desired. On the side of performance, 4 MB of RAM were needed to obtain a reasonable response time, particularly during the development phase when there was switching between multiple concurrent processes. As the application was developed the police-dispatching rule set was refined to remove many of the probabilities from its inferencing, to allow it to follow and enforce a more rigorous set of policies. The system was extremely popular, so a plan was made to rewrite the prototype for a larger DEC-based UNIX environment.

As a consequence of these various factors, it was decided that different tools were needed for the production system. The two main complaints against RuleMaster were the programming complexity and the cumbersomeness of its database interface. The conclusion was drawn that this expert system configuration would be too complex for novice programmers, so the decision was made to copy the functionality of the RuleMaster/Informix programs into a fourth-generation language, PROGRESS, for the production system. After two years of operation, the number of users grew even beyond the capabilities of large UNIX systems, so the MVS/XA translator described above was employed to handle the growth.

## 6-11. A CHECKLIST FOR A FULL CONFIGURATION

We will complete this chapter with the following checklist. The list identifies different properties of the knowledge software, the central machine, the machine room, and the system as a whole that go to make up a viable configuration for a production expert system. If any one of these factors is not thought through and properly considered it can prevent the whole configuration from working. Even if most factors have been analyzed in detail, the addition of a new subsystem has the consequence that all configuration considerations must be reviewed in this new light. A few aspects may not be influenced at all by the new subsystem, others may need a 10–30% increase in allocation, and still others may need doubling or tripling in size.

A sensible approach to sizing is to estimate the output volumes expected from the system as it grows. The necessary input volumes to support these output figures can then be calculated. Successive steps of elaboration and iteration should follow to cover the system internal and external considerations to create the total production system. The process is akin to an architect's designing a building. A architect has to account for many factors, ranging from the client's needs and budget to the local climatic and geographic conditions, the availability of different building materials, and the local building laws.

### Knowledge-engineering product properties

- Product name
- Manufacturer name
- Address and telephone number
- Date product was announced/released
- Product price
- Number of installations
- Proven applications
- Manufacturer size
  - income
  - number of employees
  - year founded
- Product runs on what hardware
- RAM needs

- Runs on what software (operating systems)
- Written in what language/compiler(s) needed
- Disk needs
- Other machine requirements
- Rule representation strategies
- Response time (rules/second)
- Fact-representation strategies
- Other knowledge-representation strategies
- Other fact-representation strategies
- Rule or fact capacity
- Metarules or other metalevel structures and strategies
- Management of fact uncertainty
- Management of rule unreliability
- Sensitivity to rule sequencing
- Chaining (forward and/or backward)
- Other inference mechanisms
- Knowledge-acquisition methods
- Induction/learning by examples
- Use of mathematics/use of special logic in inference mechanisms
- Explanation facilities (How and Why)
- Help facilities (contextually accessed)
- Tools for editing and maintaining knowledge-base facts and rules
- Effects of editing knowledge base on response time
- Style of user interface (e.g., natural language, icons, popups)
- High-level language interfaces
- Graphics interfaces (e.g., ability to show contours)
- Database interfaces
- Screen and report generators
- Other systems this product works with

**Central host properties**

- MIPS size
- MIPS allocation to different tasks at different times
- RAM size
- RAM map of allocation
- Disk capacity
- Disk map of allocation
- Disk seek time
- Disk number of spindles
- Real to virtual ratios (for different tasks)
- Hardware arithmetic capability
- Float-point accelerator

- Number of Unibus (or equivalent) slots
- Map of unibus (or equivalent) slot allocation
- Number of RS-232 (or equivalent) ports
- Map of RS-232 (or equivalent) port allocation
- Number of users supported given the broad system loading
- Number of tasks supported given the broad system loading
- Number of parallel ports
- Map of parallel port allocation
- Interrupt rate capability
- I/O bandwidth capability
- Terminal type and details—applicability for graphics
- Tape backup provisions—number of drives, speed, capacity
- Printer type and details (especially ability to print and stack large volumes neatly)

### System and machine room properties

- Insurance—fire, theft (and when on other sites)
- Air conditioning, capacity, constant humidity for paper stocks
- False ceiling for A/C
- False floor, with tools for lifting sections
- Electrical power, volts, amps, overload protection, lightning protection
- Fire/smoke detection
- Water detection, under floor
- Fire-extinguishing facilities
- Square feet needed for machine room and service areas
- Layout of machine room and service areas
- Ducting and layout for information cables
- Quantities and types of information connectors, ducts, and cables
- Ducting and layout for power cables
- Quantities and types of power connectors, ducts, and cables
- Security systems to prevent unauthorized access to machine room
- Furniture/stands for printers, terminals
- Book shelving for manuals
- Quick-look-up holder for frequently used manuals
- Racks for tapes, disks, printouts
- Storage facilities for supplies: sheet paper, roll paper, tractor paper, ribbons, inks
- Microdisks, hard disks, tapes
- Fireproof safe for backups
- Off-site provisions for backups
- Alternate site for disaster recovery and plan

- Operator skill level
- Operator training plan
- Operator numbers
- Operator shifts
- Operator callout availability
- Ordering procedures for stocks/running materials: roll paper, tractor paper, ribbons, inks, microdisks, hard disks, tapes
- Work-flow routing for output handling, e.g., mailing sacks/paper supplies/franking
- Franking machine, refresh procedures
- Constant operation considerations—which machines can be up for 8, 12, 24 hours per day
- Issues of shutting down at night—allocation of time for system startup. Is there enough processing time during the day for summarizing report data, or should these tasks be run at night?
- Plan and timing for backups
- Uninterruptable power supply (UPS) adequate for host
- Length of time the UPS needs to cover
- Dial-up terminal access (with adequate security) for software service
- Separation of development and production environments for robustness
- Strategy and equipment for transferring data and code between environments
- Mean time between failures (MTBF) and mean time to repair (MTTR) for the different pieces of equipment
  Required availability
- Desirability and cost of having any "warm spares" available
- Maintenance contracts and types for the different pieces of equipment
- Fault isolation and escalation procedures in the event of a system failure
- Expansion plans for the different dimensions in which system constraints may arise
- Delivery time and costing for expansion items, giving tradeoffs for having any expansion items ordered ahead of time (If an expansion item has a 120-day delivery time it is sensible to predict ahead of time when to order it, rather than wait for the day that lack of capacity halts the system)
- Design of adequate background-processing messages (e.g., via UNIX MAIL) to system administrator to protect robustness of unattended nighttime tasks.
- Of course, the items in this list depend on the application at hand, so any match to a selected application will be only partial.

## 6-12. MAIN POINTS: SPECIALIZED HARDWARE AND PROGRAMMING ENVIRONMENTS FOR EXPERT SYSTEMS

At this stage of the life cycle the project team should have gained a familiarity with the application and the tools. It may be thought that a one-sentence description each would be enough to identify these two decisions. What is needed, however, is a detailed analysis and writeup containing

1. All the aspects, features, and boundaries of the application to be developed, and
2. Complete hardware and software configurations, with adequate sizing calculations covering each system dimension, for each step from prototyping, to development, to initial production, to expansion and evolution.

A detailed project plan and budget are usually necessary for the creation of (1) and (2). Although some observers might comment that several life-cycle phases have been completed and yet no implementation has started, the old adage "well-begun is half-done" applies. What the project manager has to do is set up the right initial conditions. Like diving, if the correct angle is taken, then gravity, or the enthusiasm of the project team, will do the rest. Key points to know during this phase are

- Environments contain many tools of a flexible nature that can be used to speed development or be built into the application.
- Expert system development tools with one or two main modules are better suited to well-structured and contained applications.
- There are many dialects and extensions of LISP, some of which tackle object-oriented programming and graphics, making LISP a powerful environment for developing symbolic systems.
- UNIX and MVS/XA also provide powerful environments that can match LISP, PROLOG, or SMALLTALK for certain applications.
- The need for flexibility is the primary reason for selecting a symbolic programming language over an expert system building tool.
- The need to handle elaborate symbolic knowledge structures with high programmer productivity is a second key reason for using LISP.
- Although SMALLTALK itself has not been a major commercial success, object-oriented programming structures are included in a large number of successful products.
- Object-oriented programming is highly applicable to the graphical representation and communication of changing, complex knowledge structures.

- Natural language tends to impose a narrow bandwidth on man-machine interactions, which makes its implementations slow to use.
- If an application is to be developed in LISP or a similar language then the buyer should carefully evaluate the opportunities presented by specialized fast-execution LISP machines.
- If the expert system application requires interfaces to engineering systems, graphics, expandability, or fast response times, then engineering workstations should be investigated.
- The use of general-purpose computers tends to permit easier expert system integration with existing non-AI applications and hosts.
- General-purpose machines can be slow when executing expert systems, due to MIPS limitations, and also run out of RAM capacity.
- The scope of real-time or embedded applications should be strictly limited to increase the chances of success.
- Special tools are recommended for embedded or real time expert systems.
- The use of nondisclosure agreements abounds in the industry, so it is difficult to present real-life case studies.
- The many aspects of the knowledge tools, the central host, the machine room, and the support structures have to be thoroughly thought through for success.

## FOR FURTHER READING

Miller, R. K. (1986). *Computers for Artificial Intelligence.* Madison, GA: SEAI Technical Publications.

## NOTES

[1] For details on SMALLTALK, see *SMALLTALK-80: The Language and its Implementation* by Goldberg and Robson (1983), and *SMALLTALK-80: The Interactive Programming Environment* by Goldberg (1984).

[2] Although specific prices are given here, which will quickly become outdated, the relative pricing patterns are the important point.

[3] The announcement and long delay before shipping of OS/2 has further confused the market.

[4] Manufacturing Automation Protocol.

# Chapter 7
# Knowledge Capture and Codification

## SECTION HEADINGS



## OVERVIEW

The issues of knowledge capture, entry, and refinement in the expert system are elaborated in this chapter. The overview of knowledge-engineering strategies and skills required to select an appropriate application presented in earlier chapters is expanded and refined to include more detailed tactics for extracting knowledge. The first eight sections present high-level strategies for recognizing and gaining knowledge. The remainder of the chapter provides more practical tips for debriefing experts, developing and refining codified knowledge, and defining the hardware and software limits of the system.

## 7-1. KNOWLEDGE CAPTURE AS A KNOWLEDGE-ENGINEERING SKILL

Knowledge capture can be fascinating subject. This area is where the mystery of human knowledge, that elusive, subjective phenomenon structured in mans' consciousness, is transformed into a machine-comprehensible set of knowledge-representation structures and inference techniques. There is a temptation to dive right in and begin knowledge acquisition immediately, but it must be appreciated that knowledge capture is at the midpoint of the expert system development life cycle, not the beginning. For the software manager eager to implement his or her first expert system, the advice is to start with the preliminary life cycle phases—selecting a suitable application, identifying the expert system building tool features needed for the application, choosing building shell tools and support environment aids, and planning for the total system development life cycle (Chapters 3–6)—before focusing on the process of knowledge capture. The application problem should be carefully analyzed to see which problem features can be handled by commercially available tools and which features must be custom-built using symbolic programming languages, long before the knowledge-capture phase begins.

The knowledge engineer or the project manager will invariably perform a cursory knowledge analysis and evaluation during the application-selection phase of the life cycle. It is suggested that the process of detailed knowledge extraction wait until the preliminary work of carefully defining problem scope, feature analysis, and hardware/software selection, has been completed. These life-cycle phases could be performed in parallel, but that entails high risk, for plans tend to evolve and change. If the application problem has not been carefully defined, evaluated, and characterized in advance, it may be discovered that the problem is too complex to be captured in a set of logic-oriented rules or structures. Perhaps the desired shell features are not yet available in commercial tools. When the actual time and cost commitments become clear, the comptroller may decide to postpone or cancel the project. The finished expert system could be an excellent demonstration as a stand-alone entity, but it may be incompatible with existing production systems and therefore could become worthless to the company. Any one of these problems could invalidate the extensive commitment already made by the knowledge engineer and experts. Strategy changes can also invalidate the tool-dependent perspectives used for knowledge capture.

Careful planning and analysis of the entire expert system development process from conceptualization to integration with existing production hardware/software. This approach will minimize effort and waste. Building a successful production expert system requires much more than a knowledge engineer sitting with an expert and extracting chunks of knowledge at the rate of one rule per hour or day. Enthusiastic project managers and fledgling knowledge engineers should avoid

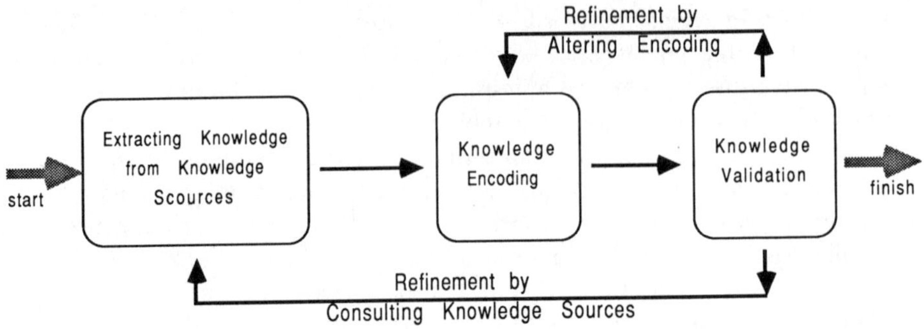


Fig. 7-1. Stages of the knowledge acquisition cycle.

the urge to launch an entensive knowledge-capture venture until the initial planning, evaluation, and documentation are completed.

Knowledge capture can be seen as a cycle within the overall expert system development life cycle. The steps of the knowledge acquisition cycle move from extracting knowledge from the relevant source or sources, to encoding the knowledge in the chosen scheme, to testing or evaluating the knowledge, and then back to extracting further knowledge, as shown in Fig. 7-1. The knowledge base is gradually built up through incremental addition and refinement of knowledge. This can be a long and laborious process, and both knowledge engineers and the experts must be patient as the gradual implementation scheme develops.

When the knowledge engineer is ready to proceed with the task of knowledge capture, he or she will primarily use standard systems-analysis techniques coupled with some new ones. As expert systems technology becomes more pervasive, the title *knowledge engineer* is likely to be subsumed by the title *systems analyst*. The concepts of knowledge engineering should become second nature to systems analysts as they gain proficiency in using commercial expert system building tools. Familiarity will rise as expert systems technology becomes one of the standard software development tools alongside such things as database and spreadsheet programs. The distinction between the knowledge engineer and a system analyst is already minimal in borderline expert systems. Borderline systems include those where the knowledge is essentially already captured in the form of recorded rules that must merely be automated. The leap from a handful of experimental "research" expert system of the 1970s and early 1980s to potentially tens of thousands of commercial expert system applications is the result of a highly successful transfer of technology. The job of the expert system developer (assuming a problem of appropriate type, scale, and difficulty) has been reduced from extensive, tedious, low-level LISP-like programming to the use of high-level development framework structures. For a suitable application, the knowledge engineer should focus on extracting, codifying, and entering the knowledge in the given structural framework. Knowing LISP is no longer a prerequisite. The expert system building shells make the technology viable for large-scale commercial use.

The skill of knowledge engineering, as both an art and a science, requires a keen insight and understanding of human thought processes and human nature. This observation indicates a potential area of education and training useful for making systems analysts proficient in knowledge engineering. Learning the new styles of symbolic programming, with knowledge representations and inference mechanisms, is a matter of switching domain areas rather than adopting new skills or capabilities. Knowledge representations can be seen as a form of data structures, and inference mechanisms as an approach to control structures.

In addition, the knowledge engineer must have a good deal of the psychologist dwelling within. The knowledge engineer has to enjoy working with people, their ideas, and their ways of viewing the world, as well as problem solving in the application-specific domain area. She or he must be able to extract the essence of the expert's knowledge and successfully formulate it into machine knowledge. Inevitably some individuals will be better than others at performing this aspect of the knowledge-engineering task. Some systems analysts, with proper training and education, will be able to make the leap. Others may not have an affinity for the process. In between is a spectrum that is often eased by retaining external consultants.

For some systems analysts, these skills are not new. The human interaction and psychological skills are familiar to analysts who have worked on large multifaceted system design across a broad range of departments within an enterprise. Projects of this type require that the analyst interview departmental coordinators and then decipher the viewpoints and needs expressed by each department. The analyst then seeks to define a system core with interfaces appropriate to all the departmental approaches by analyzing the mutiple needs and viewpoints, until a common set of specifications can be generated. The specifications are then tested and analyzed with feedback from the various departments. This refinement cycle continues until the system is complete. Understanding the various ways humans think, communicate, and act is essential for successfully completing such projects.

Knowledge acquisition can be a difficult task and may become the bottleneck in the development process. The difficulty depends to a great degree on the accessibility, or readiness, of the knowledge. The time and effort required for knowledge acquisition will be minimal if the knowledge is already formulated as knowledge structures (e.g., rules or structure diagrams) in books or manuals. At the other extreme, if no attempts have ever been made to codify the domain knowledge, then the knowledge-acquisition phase could be extensive. Task complexity can increase if the experts in the field have not standardized their knowledge. As indicated in Fig. 3-1, the "easier" applications are those at the more concrete, better defined end of the continuum. Such distinctions have to be identified when selecting an application.

Knowledge acquisition can be further complicated by the differences between an expert's introspective view of his own knowledge and the problem-solving techniques or tools he in fact actually uses. As noted in Chapter 2, the conscious, or aware, portion of the human mind is the tip of the iceberg of human consciousness. The actual mechanisms for storing data, information, and knowledge are not consciously known to the human mind and the introspective recognition of strategies used may be inaccurate or incomplete. According to Dreyfus and Dreyfus (1986), humans performing at the level of expert problem solvers are not consciously aware of "rules" guiding the problem-solving process. The rule-oriented stage was left at the level of "competence," and most human experts solve problems spontaneously and intuitively without conscious access to "how" the deep-level solving is being done.

It therefore becomes the challenge to the knowledge engineer to exercise skill to extract from the expert's speech and action the essence of the domain knowledge and represent it in machine form. Experts are good at generalizing from their problem-solving experiences, but they are usually not so good at recalling the exact problematic situational data that gave rise to the generalization. Even having the expert verbally speak the problem-solving protocol as the process proceeds leaves gaps in the knowledge. The gaps arise because the expert is not consciously aware of all the actual mental processes during the introspection. Usually an expert has some kind of unconscious internal model employed in problem solving. Complications occur, however, as several different models may be used for different kinds of problems, i.e., familiar versus unfamiliar problem categories. Sometimes the expert will revert to analysis from first principles rather than using heuristics. Intuitive components of the human thought process become intertwined with the logical in common-sense knowledge and reasoning, qualitative and inexact reasoning, and temporal and spatial mental models. None of these features can be easily expressed in current expert system technology. Their influences on the application must be filtered out or replaced by other logical or structural mechanisms that are available in expert systems technology. All these complexities of the hidden human thought process challenge the knowledge engineer. It is necessary to see through the thoughts, actions, and explanations provided by the expert to capture the essence of the problem-solving data, its features, and their interactions. Making the unmanifest manifest or binding the unbounded is the true skill of the knowledge engineer.

As noted earlier, well-codified bodies of knowledge can expedite or in many cases almost eliminate the knowledge-acquisition process. The knowledge engineer may not spend most of the knowledge-acquisition time observing or interviewing experts, but instead may be reading texts on the domain area that contain the rules of the area. Manuals used in business or industrial settings are often good sources of knowledge. Analyzing case studies regularly provides insights into the mechanics of problem solving. These materials tend to be used in conjunction with knowledge from human experts within the broad process of knowledge acquisition. Knowledge engineering may also require extensive time by the knowledge engineer alone analyzing the information from different sources and creating potential models of the domain's knowledge. The general guideline is to cross-reference as many sources of knowledge as possible to identify as objective and complete a set of rules as is feasible within the budget.

## 7-2. IDENTIFYING THE EXPERTS FOR THE PROJECT

The policy of assigning experts and other key personnel to software development projects or aspects thereof is well established in commercial and industrial settings. It is useful if one or more people from the user area spend all their time as members of any project team for the project's duration. Structuring appropriate relationships when several companies are involved in one development is more complicated. Generally speaking, virtually all developments will employ components from third parties, so multiorganization management structures must be established. Even if the domain expert is within the same corporation, departmental policies may be very different. Requests for time should be made formally and contractually documented. If there is not a formal and contractual commitment for the expert to spend a specific number of hours on the project, then it is to be expected that he will always have more pressing tasks to do. It is just as essential that contractural agreements are obtained for the services of experts, as it is for the services of knowledge engineers, analysts, programmers, and project managers. If the expert's time is not available as and when needed in the development of the system, knowledge acquisition can become a bottleneck for the entire project.

Generally speaking, the initial stages of knowledge acquisition should be limited to one or possibly two experts. For clearly defined fields experts may be abundant, and it is the responsibility of the project manager to choose the best representative to work with the knowledge engineer. Too many experts can be an early warning that the application is not suitable for implementation. Certainly if the experts do not agree with each other, that is an omen for problems.[1] Often there will be more than a handful of experts nationwide, so it is possible to research the options and try to pick the most knowledgeable and communicative one. Key considerations here are the willingness and availability of the expert to work on the project, the clarity of the expert in verbalizing problem-solving techniques, and the personality matches between the expert and the knowledge engineer. The knowledge engineer and the expert will be working closely together over an extended period, so a good match is mandatory. It is the job of the project manager, knowledge engineer, and other members of the team to keep the expert enthusiastic and interested in the project. One of the best ways to accomplish this is to allow the expert to be actively involved in the development all the way through the life cycle. Involvement should continue into hands-on testing, evaluation, and refinement of the prototype and development systems, but not details of the technical implementation. Another key to maintaining the expert's enthusiasm is to do the groundwork of Chapters 3–6 thoroughly, so that major problems and glitches are not uncovered during the knowledge-capture and codification phase.

The primary expert should be the main source of knowledge for knowledge-base development in projects starting from the human-expertise perspective. Certainly the expert may cite many other sources of knowledge that can be used to support and enlarge on his own, but still the primary expert is the guide. It is a good policy to use only one or possibly two experts at this point to allow depth to be developed in the knowledge base. Too many experts tends to create a base that is broad and shallow. Other experts in the area can be used in the later testing and evaluation phases to ensure that the system has sufficient breadth as well as depth. Employing a single primary expert tends to remove expertise conflicts in the early stages of development. For example, the better defined areas of expertise (e.g., medical diagnosis, fault-tolerance testing) might have rules that could be agreed upon by a group of experts. If there are 100 rules that encompass the totality of the domain knowledge, it may be found that any single expert uses only 50 of them. Furthermore, each expert might use a different 50-rule subset due to completely individualized approaches to solving a given problem. Starting with one expert at least gives a coherent view even if it is partial. Matching partial views tends to be a lot harder in the early stages of analysis before the knowledge has been formalized and tested for accuracy. An additional reason for a single primary expert is apparent for less well developed bodies of expertise: it may be difficult for a group of individuals to come to a consensus on the actual body of significant domain facts and heuristics. In loosely defined domains the degree of expertise overlap could be very small.

As noted in Chapter 3, the range of potential expert systems applications is very broad. The definition of an "expert" varies from field to field as well. For some applications, the experts are not those who have been problem solving in an area for many years. For instance, an expert system used to perform diagnostics on a new microcomputer may rely on the expertise of a specialized group of individuals: the engineers who designed and built the system. Because the computer is based on a new-design architecture never before produced, there will not be diagnostics experts with years of experience available. Such "expertise" may have been developed in the last six months, although the deeper rules governing its structure may have been built up over a decade of schooling.

It may be tempting for project managers to attempt to combine the positions of the domain expert and the knowledge engineer for certain applications. This might be possible if the expert system task is to debug large-scale software-development projects. The software engineer responsible for previously developing a manual or partially automated debugger could serve as both the expert and the knowledge engineer, provided proper instruction in knowledge-engineering technology is given. This dual-role scenario, however, should generally be avoided. Remember that the problem-solving software engineer, when functioning as a technical expert, uses a broad range of not-well-understood capabilities stored in the recesses of his consciousness, including intuition, common-sense knowledge, and multidimensional spatial and temporal models. When he dons the knowledge engineer's hat, however, all this internal knowledge representation must be localized into rules and knowledge structures. Few people can play both roles well for the same project. Observation and discussion tend to be a better approach to making the unmanifest manifest than one-person introspection. It is usually difficult and possibly frustrating for one person to function in both modes. Both depth and breadth of the knowledge base may suffer. It is much better to separate the two functions into two different individuals.

Finally, it is important to emphasize the significance of management commitment to the expert's involvement for the entire duration of the development project. It is difficult to estimate accurately the resources needed for expert system development, so time and cost overruns are the rule rather than the exception. It is therefore crucial that middle and higher level management continue to support the extended time commitment of the project's experts as necessary, or otherwise the final product could be ineffective, if not a failure.

## 7-3. KNOWLEDGE IS THE BASIS OF ACTION— LOOK FOR ACTION TO LOCATE KNOWLEDGE

Expert system problem-solving capabilities can be useful in many different application areas. In Chapter 3, 10 problem categories for expert systems applications were noted: interpretation, prediction, diagnosis, design, planning, monitoring, debugging, repair, instruction, and control. Each of these categories represents a process to be performed, implying actions to be taken by an expert. Each action taken by the expert is based on some internal structure of knowledge of the situation at hand.

Where should the knowledge engineer focus attention when searching out chunks of knowledge? A good heuristic is to look to the central core of action, the most *dynamic key decision points* that influence the entire operation. The key focus should be on the *process*, rather than on the static data entities related to the process. These key points of high activity are often where the business's profit is made or lost. They also tend to be where tempers flare and stresses are generated, e.g., when the computer crashes, the drilling bit sticks, the research plan is finalized, or the commodity is traded. These high-value, high-risk, high-stress points often represent the hub or central entity of the entire enterprise. When actions occur at these key action vortexes, they send reverberations throughout the rest of the enterprise. Failure of an insurance company's central mainframe can bring the activities of tens of branch offices and hundreds of agents to a standstill. A repeatedly sticking oil rig drilling bit can cost the oil company hundreds of thousands of dollars per day and delay the influx of crude oil necessary for generating the entire company's profits. These central entities are critical points in the corporation's profit-making machine.

Without the proper guidance and direction, the knowledge engineer can be distracted to secondary or tertiary areas of the domain knowledge. Typically this implies inordinate time spent capturing passive "data" rather than on dynamic "knowledge." For example, an oil tank may have hundreds of fixed attributes, such as its height above sea level or its color, but the real essence of the business is moving oil in and out of that tank. Without the movements no money is made. Knowledge tends to be associated with transitory profits and losses, rather than with static investments in capital equipment. It is no surprise that the first expert system shells were rule-based, a design geared to the capture of action.

Static data are important, but the knowledge engineer should seek to capture them dynamically, because they influence profit making. A set of "frames" without associated dynamic procedural processes are simply data structures. An excessive focus on capturing and entering static data tends to result in storing facts that have no influence on the specific events, rapidly become out of date, and never get used. In one case study, a company hired 34 full-time data-entry personnel for 3 months to enter the domain data believed to be vital for an expert system. The rules for the system had been developed, and the final data entry push was seen to be necessary to meet the development schedule. Something was wrong, however. If the rules were general-purpose knowledge-bearing structures, why was so much supporting data necessary? The primary problem was that the knowledge chunks (rules) were not generalized (written with variables) and did not focus on the key dynamical properties of the system. Hence there were far too many extraneous rules requiring specific knowledge-base facts. The second problem was too much attention directed to entering all possible cases of data information, rather than having this information entered interactively—as it was created—as the system was used. The overall result was an inefficient expert system with slow response time, based on excess rules and large quantities of inappropriately stored information.

The point of this section, to focus on action, can be seen as a part of a larger *knowledge-action-achievement-fulfillment* (KAAF) cycle. As well as looking for action, it can often be helpful to ask the expert what is fulfilling about his or her job. When does satisfaction arise? What are the events and situations leading up to that experience? If the action is based upon valid knowledge it probably leads to fulfillment, but if it has a partial or incorrect basis then frustration and stress can result. Taking in all aspects of the expert's experience associated with the events in this cycle can help locate knowledge chunks.

The central hub of action, the most critical or vital part of the application problem, should become the first area of investigation for the knowledge engineer. From this well-established central core, the knowledge engineer can then analyze ever-widening aspects of the problem and establish the relationships and interactions between the central core and increasingly more peripheral activities. Chunks of knowledge will be organized around conceptual objects and their interactions, as shown in Fig. 7-2. Task-subtask, part-whole, and causal relationships should be analyzed through diagrams and flow graphs. If the process diagrams easily, it may be a good match for frame-based

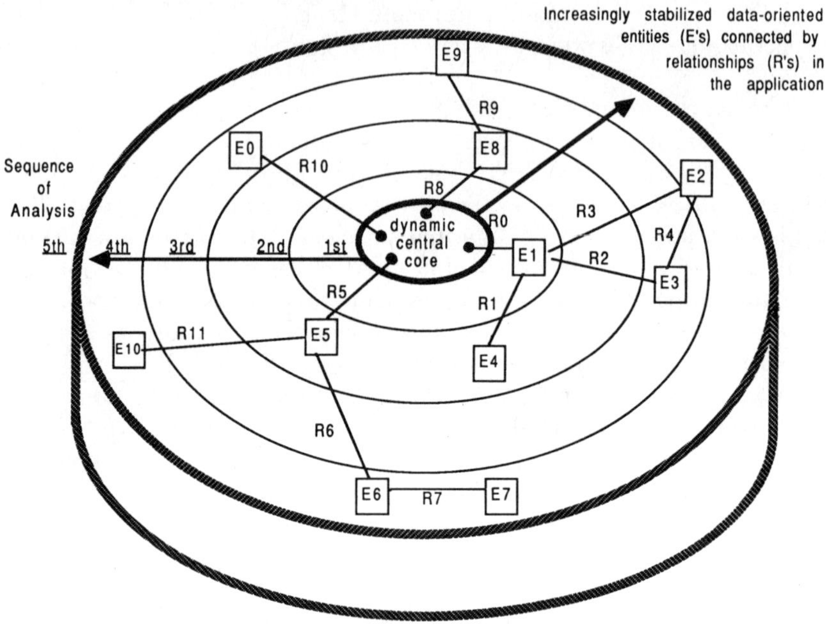


Fig. 7-2. Priority scheme for capturing knowledge.

representation schemes. Complicated processes should be carefully modeled, including all the information that constrains the processes. Information flowing between the parts of the system should also be determined. Knowledge may be separated into problem solving, explanation, and justification. The overall line of reasoning to be performed should be carefully determined.

Even in the early stages of knowledge capture, the knowledge engineer should be alert to extracting material to be used for explanations and justification of inference chains. The engineer should seek to use descriptors and identifiers that will allow the experts to understand the chunks of knowledge in machine form and allow the system to be self-explanatory from the onset.

## 7-4. ALERTNESS CREATES INSIGHT—THE KEY TO CAPTURING KNOWLEDGE

Knowledge capture is creative. Steps of the knowledge engineer's activity encompass periods of gathering information, formulating hypotheses, incubating, gaining concepts from insight, integrating into knowledge organizations, formalizing and evaluating the organizations.

Mental clarity is a central requirement for the knowledge engineer and is necessary to efficiently draw out and formulate the domain knowledge. Insight, alertness, and mental clarity combine to generate the necessary creative environment.

Maintaining mental clarity requires that the knowledge engineer and expert avoid getting overly fatigued during knowledge acquisition. It is not uncommon for management to structure a 2-week-long, all-day-every-day, intensive knowledge-debriefing schedule to save time. Such ongoing sessions tend to strain both the knowledge engineer and the expert and produce marginal results. It is still possible that a number of the knowledge chunks for a system could be extracted under these conditions. The resultant knowledge, however, is mostly shallow knowledge similar to the driver education rules for driving a car. The rules alone do not make good drivers. It is the experience of working with the rules, applying them, and assimilating them into experience that tends to uncovers deeper knowledge structures. Knowledge-base rules must be carefully assembled and refined over a period to develop the fine-tuning necessary for the final system.

It is suggested that the interview sessions be held not more than 2 hours per day to avoid straining both the knowledge engineer and the expert. This schedule keeps both parties fresh for quality interactions and gives the knowledge engineer time to understand, develop, and codify knowledge chunks between sessions. This type of balanced approach of rest and activity produces the best results. Sessions should be recorded on audio or video tape, obviating note taking and allows the knowledge engineer to focus deeply on the strategies used by the expert during the session. The details can be obtained by reviewing the tapes as the knowledge chunks are pieced together after the session.

Maintaining restfulness and alertness also aids the knowledge engineer in focusing on the generality of chunks of knowledge, rather than getting locked into the more superficial details. Knowledge engineers need to think with a great degree of scientific abstraction. Trained scientists usually start their knowledge acquisition by observing real-world, empirical evidence and then formulating abstract generalized models to characterize the phenomena. Hypotheses can be generated and tested that either verify or disprove the model-based hypotheses.

The term *knowledge scientist* may be a better descriptive title than knowledge engineer for this type of work. It takes insight to characterize and code in machine form the masses of perhaps unrelated data and heuristics obtained from the domain knowledge sources. As noted earlier, knowledge engineers also function somewhat like cognitive psychologists. They must be able to synchronize their thinking with the thought processes of the domain expert to extract the essence of the knowledge, in whatever form the expert perceives it, and translate it into a machine-viable framework. The only magic available for this process is maintaining clarity and alertness, so that insight and creativity can generate the effect. New knowledge essentially comes from inside the knowledge engineer rather than from outside. Several hours may be spent sitting listening to the domain expert, but only later, when there is time for quiet reflection, does the new understanding, the new knowledge, dawn in the knowledge engineer's awareness. Much of this knowledge-capture process should be viewed as a process of absorption, relaxation, and reformulation of knowledge structures. In the final analysis, it should be appreciated that the knowledge engineer's clarity of mind is the main resource in getting the job done.

With the advent of expert system building shells, the knowledge engineer's effort has shifted from a balance of system design, programming, and knowledge extraction and codification toward a more abstract framework of knowledge extraction and codification. Within the next few years, the system development functions may very well be taken directly under the wing of the traditional systems analyst, and knowledge extraction and codification may fall into the hands of less computer-technical personnel. In this sense, the knowledge engineer of the future may be more psychologist and less computer scientist.

## 7-5. RULE PERMUTATIONS CREATE NEW RULES

Once a knowledge engineer has discovered a powerful knowledge rule, it often generates many other important rules as permutations. This phenomenon is quite prevalent in mathematics and physics, and it applies even to less well defined application areas. In mathematics, theorems, lemmas, and corollaries partake of this permutation phenomenon. In classical physics, Maxwell's four equations provide the foundation for all electromagnetic theory. These four equations generate hundreds of secondary equations when electromagnetic forces are allowed to interact with themselves and with materials in such areas as optics or fluid mechanics. Some ancient cultural traditions ascribe the unfolding of manifest creation to the permutations of the interactions of fundamental, primitive elements at the basis of nature. Quantum mechanics follows this pattern: it has three underlying vacuum state operators for creating, maintaining, and dissolving entities. The powerful technique of working with *knowledge primitives* is one way to generate a full complement of knowledge-base rules.

It is important to spell out all the permutations and combinations, because most expert systems are not skilled in deducing them from first principles. Due to their inability to work with deep knowledge, expert systems have a difficult time reasoning from first principles. The realistic approach for knowledge-base construction, therefore, is to encode all the actual rule forms that are needed in detail, rather than attempting to infer all the knowledge necessary. Such an approach also improves response times, as it decreases the needed CPU cycles, at the expense of disk and RAM.

Fortunately, the knowledge engineer does not have to attempt to extract every subtle nuance of a general rule from the expert. Once the general form of the knowledge chunk is established, the knowledge engineer can generate many of these rule permutations and combinations and then submit the results to the expert or experts for validation.

A simple example of a rule that can be used to generate a specific rule class is rule 2 of Fig. 4-2

IF the card has been entered, and
the account is not valid
THEN return card and print receipt

The rule expresses a basic routine to be followed in the case of an error, that is, end the processing sequence and print a receipt noting that an error has occurred (and if possible the type of error). This rule can be used as a template to generate other error-handling rules, resulting in the end-of-sequence processing (e.g., invalid access code (rule 3), requesting more than $200, requesting more money than the account contains). Rule 2 can also be seen as one of the exception-handling rules for the expert system, as discussed in the next section.

In opposition to the strategy of generating new rules by permuting old rules, it is sometimes prudent to collapse rules into a more simplified form while refining the knowledge base. Two rules of the form

IF *a* and *b* THEN *c*
IF *c* and *d* THEN *e*

should be collapsed into

IF *a* and *b* and *d* THEN *e*

if condition *c* is not used in the premises of other rules. The approach known as *induction* is one method of condensing rules. Compiling expert systems with induction will perform such compressions if they find that nowhere is condition *c* used in the premise of other rules. Various other types of compression can occur in induction modules, but many knowledge engineers prefer to leave things intact, so that audit trails are clearer and maintenance is easier.

## 7-6. IDENTIFYING THE RULES FOR HANDLING EXCEPTIONS

In standard data-processing computer systems, it is well-known that approximately 80% of the software code of a system is used to deal with 20% of the situations, i.e., exceptions, that can arise in the system. In many cases, expert systems are exception handlers; they diagnose problems, troubleshoot circuits, look for blood infections, and so on. Even in these systems the 80/20 rule still applies, and much effort is spent on portions of the system that are seldom accessed. The main-line cases should be carefully isolated in the domain knowledge from the specialized chunks of knowledge needed to handle the exceptions. By developing the main line first, a knowledge backbone is created upon which the exception conditions can be structured.

One technique useful for analyzing the activity of problem solving is DeMarco's bubble diagram methodology (DeMarco, 1979). These diagrams are patterned after demand-driven *data-flow* software architectures. Each small, or atomic, activity of the application is represented as a circle, and arrows are used to connect the circles much like a flow chart. In addition, the actual information passed between the activity circles is annotated near each arrow. DeMarco's approach is an excellent tool for developing a temporal/spatial layout of the problem-solving model. A simple example for the Automatic Teller Machine example of Chapter 4 (Fig. 4-2) is shown in Fig. 7-3.

This type of mechanism assists the knowledge engineer in breaking out the nonsequential steps of complex processes. The knowledge engineer can collect all the various views from the different knowledge sources and lay out one general framework. Subtle hunches, nuances, and feelings projected by the expert can also be incorporated, creating other links or expanding and filling in greater levels of detail of the model. Exceptions in problem solving will usually be found as loop areas, where an activity can be repeated. For example procedures for handling most items of inventory may be handled by one sequence, but for dangerous items, such as explosives, multiple cross-checking loops hanging off each other may be identified. The basic structure of an exception commences with an identifying fork and follows with negative-feedback loops to cover each level of exception procedure that should be adopted to bring the situation into order.

Exception handling should be limited in expert systems to two or three levels of concurrent exceptions. This constraint provides a means for achieving uniformity and consistency in exception handling. If the expert system is inundated with a greater number of exceptions, the system should inform the system's user that specialized attention is

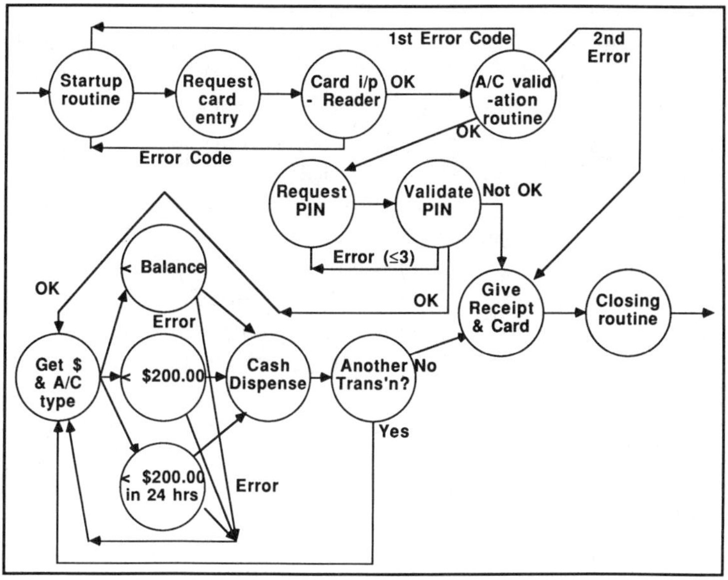


Fig. 7-3. A bubble diagram for the ATM example of Fig. 4-2.

needed. Manual special handling of the strangest cases allows a more cost-effective focus of development resources on the main line and routine exceptions.

## 7-7. REFINING KNOWLEDGE THROUGH ADDITIONAL RULES

Knowlege-base refinement is usually accomplished through either of two modes: modifying the current chunks of knowledge or creating new chunks of knowledge. In the first case, additional conditions could be added to rules' premises, certainty factors could be adjusted, or the rules could be rewritten to reflect a change in the knowledge model. Modifications to the knowledge model often reflect a new understanding of a more refined level in the expert's thinking. Sometimes, however, it will be necessary to add new chunks of knowledge to produce more sophisticated organized knowledge structures capable of capturing subtle nuances in the expertise. This style of enlargement could mean the addition of new rules, new slots in frames, new frames, new self-acting objects, and so on, depending on the system's knowledge-representation architecture.

Refining the body of expertise by adding new knowledge chunks is a common practice. The prototype system is usually developed incrementally, starting with a minuscule subset of the knowledge (a small set of rules). Once the feasibility of the implementation has been established, the knowledge engineer moves onto the full development system and increasing degrees of knowledge are incorporated into the system. In this incremental development, newly added knowledge tends to strengthen the depth and breadth of the knowledge-base facts and heuristics while also creating new inference paths and refining existing paths. For example, Aldo in a Box started with 50 rules and was eventually completed after the addition of 100 more rules. The Automated Teller Machine (ATM) example presented in section 4-2 could easily be expanded by supplying additional rules for multiple attempts at entering the access code before shutting down, or looping to extract more money (possibly from another account) after completing the transaction, or not returning the card if the user has had three unsuccessful attempts to enter the valid access code. Rule 4 of Fig. 4-2 causes the release of cash if the user has been validated and the amount required is less than $200 and less than the balance in the specified account (checking or saving). This knowledge chunk can be further refined by specifying an additional condition stipulating that the sum of all withdrawls from the specified checking or saving account in the last 24 hours must be less than $200. A second approach would be to add this knowledge as a new rule of the form

IF the user has entered the requested amount and the account type (checking or saving) and the sum of all requests for this account and account type for the last 24 hours is less than $200

THEN the total amount is all right

Rule 4 would then be modified to include a condition that "the total amount is all right" in the premise. In this simple example, it might be easier to modify rule 4 directly to include the "total-amount" validation. In other situations, the rule set may remain more comprehensible by adding the additional rule.

Frequently the knowledge engineer will build the prototype system based on a limited model of the domain knowledge. The limited model usually contains many simplifying assumptions. As the system is developed in more detail these simplifying assumptions will typically be replaced by more data and knowledge-organization structures, so that the system can achieve its accuracy performance goals. For example, if the expert system needs to model the functioning of a transistor, the gross level starting point may be simply a digital on/off switch. The next level of understanding is that the transistor is an analog amplifier needing a 0.6-volt bias to turn it on and move it into its linear range. A more detailed model of the transistor will map out its transfer characteristics as a series of curves with near-linear and grossly nonlinear regions. Further refinements, for such areas as high-frequency work, require more refined models based on such things as stray inductances and leakage capacitances. If the transistor is used as a component in a digital computer simulation, the first on/off model may be sufficient. If it is part of a diagnostic testing expert system for military avionics components, however, refinement to deeper models, deeper laws of nature, will probably be required.

Another incentive for adding new knowledge chunks or rules is to enhance the predictive accuracy of the expert system. It may be that several inference paths lead to a specific goal state. Due to fact uncertainties and rule unreliability measures, one goal may be reached with various degrees of certainty. If three branches of the inference tree reach a particular goal with certainty levels (0.5), and two additional branches reach the same goal with certainty (0.85), additional rules can potentially be used to increase the certainty levels of the first three branches to bring them up to the same level as the other two branches. Even when all routes are yielding the same accuracy, it is often possible to add new conditional clauses to existing rules to refine their triggering. Some shell tools support developer-defined "preconditions" for rules, which must be satisfied before checking of rule premises begins. Decreasing the uncertainty of conclusions is one of the main goals to aim at when refining knowledge bases.

As was true for creating new rules by permuting existing rules, the knowledge engineer should always be on the watch for rules that can be collapsed into simpler more compact rules that perform the same function. Whenever new knowledge chunks are being added to the knowledge base or current knowledge chunks are being refined, any affected rules should be analyzed for potential combination. The tradeoffs here are between knowledge-base clarity and response time of the system. In some instances a greater number of rules makes the knowledge base easier to comprehend for both the knowledge engineer and the expert, but, depending on the inferencing mechanisms, too many rules can also adversely affect the system's response time. The decision to include special-case rules in addition to their more general parent rules depends on difficulties in deducing the special-case rule. Things that can be inferred easily and quickly should usually be left out of the knowledge base. Knowledge that would require extensive deep reasoning to deduce from general rules are best written out in advance as special cases. A key part of the knowledge engineer's job is to balance these different concerns.

## 7-8. VERIFYING CORRECTNESS OF KNOWLEDGE AND REMOVING CONTRADICTIONS

The mass of domain data, heuristics, and knowledge structures in the knowledge base developed over weeks or months of work is useless unless the knowledge is accurate and free of contradictions. In many application areas, the degree of uncertainty involved dictates that a system will always be unable to manage 5–10% of the problems. Some of these problems will be identified by the exception-handing rules, and others may be noted by a human overseer when the results look suspicious. Just as testing and debugging a traditional, large-scale, complex, software engineering project can be the most exhausting and exaspirating phase of the system development, verifying the knowledge and eliminating contradictory statements can be one of the most challenging tasks awaiting the knowledge engineer. For this reason it is wise to advance one step at a time and test the validity of each step before proceeding on to the next.

In expert system building shell tools, the domain-dependent "expert's knowledge" and the domain-independent "inference knowledge" are separated in the knowledge base. This separation is one of the great advantages that the expert system technology presents over traditional programming environments. Rules, objects, network nodes, and frames can be reviewed and analyzed with the aid of specialized editors without searching through masses of irrelevant information, including the inference procedures. *Rule trees* display the possible paths of inference for a system (e.g., see the screen picture from Knowledge Craft in the photographs section of this book). The structure-based knowledge architectures (networks and frames) provide a medium for organizing and displaying related domain knowledge, which greatly helps validation. If these types of interactive facilities are available in the development tool kit, the experts associated with the project can have a direct hand in analyzing data correctness and the appropriateness of inference chains. Outside experts can also be invited to participate in the validation process and will often uncover "holes" in the knowledge overlooked by the on-site experts.

Rule validation should start when even the very first rule set developed in the prototype system is available. Each time new rules are added or old rules updated, the system must be checked for contradictions and evaluated by the expert. Knowledge validation should be a continual process occurring in lockstep synchrony with each step of the knowledge acquisition.

Knowledge base faults, or bugs, come in various forms. The simplest errors result from typing mistakes when the data were entered. Other categories of errors include faulty characterizations of chunks of knowledge, references to the wrong variables, improper or inadequate inference rules, ineffective inference strategies, and errors in the test sets run through the system. A good, strong, systematic systems-analysis approach will usually turn up the sources of the problems in a reasonable time. Myers's *The Art of Software Testing* (Meyers, 1980) is recognized as authoritative on these types of traditional software-engineering techniques. The most difficult expert system testing problems can arise in assigning certainty values to data and realiability ratings for rules. There may not be any "errors" in the methodology used, but the inference chains still may not produce the desired results. Then new combinations of ratings must be tried until the desired results are obtained. In some situations, this testing may be a process of trial and error.

Even though rules can be easily added to a rule-based system as the system develops, the knowledge engineer cannot just add rules at random, for several problems can occur. For example, suppose the following rule is added to an existing knowledge base

IF *a* AND *b* THEN *c*

This rule looks innocuous by itself, but suppose the knowledge base already contains a rule of the form

IF *a* AND *c* THEN *b*

hidden in a little-used rule tree somewhere in the remaining 800 rules of the knowledge base. Now if facts (*a* and *b*) or facts (*a* and *c*) become true, the inference engine could go into an infinite loop firing either one rule or the other as the data items *b* and *c* are continually recreated. This can occur if the scheduler does not check for such looping or limit the number of times a rule can be fired in a single inference path. One way to avoid this problem is to use backward- rather than forward-chaining if possible, but in turn this approach can unearth other types of problems.

The following forward-chaining rule provides a less obvious example to illustrate this point

IF the pressure in tank *x* is greater than 100 lb/in.
THEN the pressure in *x*'s predecessor is greater than 100 lb/in.

In this case the rule is recursive and could be problematic. Suppose there are 10 tanks in a sequence containing chemicals in various stages of refinement. The knowledge engineer may want to represent the logic that if any one of the tanks in the sequence (except the first) has the specific pressure condition satisfied, then the immediately preceding tank also has the condition. Suppose also that the intent is that this transfer can happen only for one step, i.e., if tank 6 has the condition, then tank 5 also has, but not tank 4. The rule as written, however, could be recursively applying the condition from tank $n$ to tank $n - 1$ all the way back to tank 1 where $n$ is the first tank satisfying the condition, depending on the handling of the variable $x$ in the inference chain. Backward-chaining recursive rules can cause similar problems. This points out that even the use of simple, uncomplicated rules can cause testing or validataion difficulties.

One final example illustrates the problem of introducing contradictions into a valid and consistent knowledge base by adding a new rule. Assume the system contains the following three rules

1. IF *a* THEN *d* or *e*
2. IF *c* THEN not *d*
3. IF *b* THEN not *e*

Now suppose the following new rule is to be added

4. IF *a* and *b* THEN *c*

If facts *a* and *b* become true, the rule chain 4 → 1 asserts that *d* is not true, whereas rule 1 asserts that either *d* or *e* is true, and rule 3 asserts that *e* is not true. These types of contradictions, of course, can be introduced just as easily by modifying existing rules. Some shell tools, as noted in Chapter 5, offer truth-maintenance or knowledge-base-maintenance software to help test for and elmininate such contradictions. Removing contradictions should be done at each stage as the system develops, for sorting out the contradictions in 500 rules at once can be very challenging. The concept of collapsing rules, as noted earlier, can also be helpful in the verification, validation, and conflict removal processes by simplifying rules and reducing the number of rules.

## 7-9. SUMMARY OF KNOWLEDGE-ACQUISITION HEURISTICS

Various strategies for extracting, codifying, and refining knowledge have been presented so far in this chapter. In this section, practical, detailed techniques for acquiring knowledge are recapitulated. Inputing knowledge structures can be greatly eased by the use of *intelligent editors*. These editors use restricted natural-language interfaces to assist in syntactic checking of entered knowledge structures, ordering rules, designing explanation and justification of inference paths, rule compilation, constructing libraries of test sets, automatic running of tests, displaying inference chains, and so on. Most of the newer shells on the market have intelligent editors, but the earlier tools tended to rely on operating system editors or word processors. The intelligent tools are invaluable aids for streamlining knowledge acquisition, regardless of the knowledge source.

There are three primary sources of expertise for an expert system

- **Books or manuals**—The knowledge here may range from general textbooks about the topic area to technical manuals containing the actual codified set of rules or chunks of knowledge for the project that must be entered into the system.
- **Case studies or test sets**—The knowledge engineer's job here is to study the problem-solving protocols and develop creatively the knowledge structures and suitable inferencing techniques.
- **Human experts**—The knowledge engineer must work closely with the selected experts to develop the domain knowledge in a machine-usable form according to the representation architectures of the selected expert system building tools.

An expert system program can acquire the domain expert's knowledge in four ways

- **Programming**—At the lowest level, the knowledge is coded directly into the chosen programming language. This would occur when a system is being built from scratch using LISP, PROLOG, or one of their derivatives.
- **Intelligent knowledge editors**—The expert system grows as the intelligent editors assist in transferring knowledge from the knowledge engineer or expert to the machine.
- **Learning from examples**—Examples are presented to the system through a natural-language interface, and the system generates rules based on analysis of the examples. A more general case of learning by examples occurs when the program records and analyzes inference chains, while problem solving to attempt to generate new domain rules (e.g., collapsing rules, noting contradictions). These records are best reviewed by a human engineer before any new rules are included in the knowledge base.
- **Discovery**—Discovery is the most experimental type of learning, and it has been used in some research systems. Here the expert system monitors the problem solving or its own activity (a form of self-knowledge). New domain rules can be generated, or general problem-solving strategies can be adjusted to allow the system to evolve.

These latter types of adaptive learning systems are the furthest removed from commercial expert system building tools of today, but are on the horizon for future tools of greater power and robustness.

The following points summarize the activities a knowledge engineer performs in extracting the corpus of expertise from a human expert

- **General familiarity with area**—This step usually involves anywhere from a few days to a few weeks. The knowledge engineer reads widely in the application area, studies selected trade press or technical articles, looks at samples of the problem-solving task, and begins to converse intelligently with experts in the field as the learning process continues.
- **Determine problem scope**—The knowledge engineer decides tentatively what the expert system should and should not be able to do. Plans for various stages of incremental implementation can also be devised. This step refers to the issues of Chapter 3.
- **Identify problem concepts and their interactions**—The knowledge engineer now focuses more closely on the major concepts or components involved in the application. As this conceptualization stage proceeds, linkages between the concepts emerge as a framework for organizing the knowledge developed. Gross organization and strategies are the primary focus, and rudimentary models based on simplifying assumptions are generated in preparation for working with the expert or experts.
- **Debriefing techniques**—The stage has been set for extracting knowledge in detail from the expert or experts assigned to the project. The knowledge engineer seeks to identify concrete characterizations of the data required for the problem-solving task, the strategies involved, what constitutes a solution, what is an adequate solution, whether the problem can be decomposed into subproblems that can be solved independently, and what kinds of knowledge are needed. These points can often be drawn as a tree, with its starting and ending nodes being the first identified. Satisfactory explanations and justifications of the reasoning path and documentation of the procedures and strategies used are also investigated. Documentation may be internal to the organization or may be derived from external sources. Several different types of interaction between the knowledge engineer and the expert are possible. It is strongly recommended that all sessions be recorded on either audio or video tape for later analysis.
- **Problem description and discussion**—The knowledge engineer interrogates the expert. The expert is asked to describe the problems solved and discuss the details of the problem-solving strategies. Such phrases as *if . . .*, *then . . .*, *while . . .*, *whenever . . .*, *during . . .* should be watched for as the basis of rules. Experts may dwell for a long time on points later deemed irrelevant and quickly skate over essentials because

they believe them to be obvious. The knowledge engineer has to refine the knowledge model and fill in gaps, both by asking questions during the sessions and by analyzing the tape recordings afterward.

• **On-site observation**—The expert works through typical problem-solving sessions while the knowledge engineer observes without interrupting. If appropriate, the expert can narrate the problem-solving protocol while solving the task. The knowledge engineer notes both the strategies and techniques revealed, together with gaps in understanding not covered by the expert's verbal cues. Ill-defined or intuitive aspects are marked for later discussion. A variation on this theme involves the same kind of protocol observation, but with problem samples supplied by the knowledge engineer rather than random problems from the field. These sample problems should be carefully constructed by the knowledge engineer to reveal the breadth of domain data, knowledge structures, and strategies used by the expert. This technique can help to fill the gaps in knowledge described above.

• **Analyzing accidents to improve on existing models**—In many fields, especially in manufacturing and transportation, analyzing accidents can reveal a great deal of knowledge. Asking experts how the accident could have been detected a little earlier, how it could have been forecast, and how it could have been avoided often uncover many special rules of thumb. Complex accidents can trigger most of the exception conditions in a set of rules, which, with normal cases, would take thousands of examples to even begin to cover.

• **Development, refinement, and validation of the rule set**—At each stage of the knowledge-acquisition process, from prototyping through the final stages of development and testing, the knowledge engineer includes the experts in the evaluation loop of the expert system. The knowledge base is refined, new knowledge is added, the validity of the knowledge is ascertained, and contradictions are removed incrementally.

It is worth repeating that the knowledge-acquisition process can be greatly shortened if the domain knowledge has already been encoded in some form, such as a procedures manual, and is ripe for automation. These types of delivery vehicle expert systems applications are very accessible and can be rapidly developed. For these application areas, the knowledge-acquistion bottleneck does not exist, and expert system implementation is essentially equivalent to providing a software-engineering solution for any traditional problem. The advantages of using an expert system shell, of course, are the high level of abstraction and the ease of encoding, testing, and delivering the product.

## 7-10. PORTING FROM DEVELOPMENT TO TARGET SYSTEMS

It is a simple but important point that porting knowledge bases often cannot be avoided and that this can give rise to certain knowledge-engineering problems. Large expert systems are usually created through several stages from prototyping, to development, to production. As these stages tend to be best implemented on different classes of hardware with different sets of software tools, it is often difficult to avoid extensive porting. Porting of scientific FORTRAN code, to, say, perform Fast Fourier Transforms, may be relativly simple, but moving knowledge bases from one environment to another is not so well established.

Prototyping can be done on any available machine, assuming the selected expert system building tools will run on it. Due to integrity considerations, neither prototyping nor full-scale development should be done on machines currently operating in the production environment. If the integrity of the production machine is not of the utmost importance, then exceptions might be made in special cases, as for prototyping, which typically involves only light to moderate use of the hardware.

The AI symbolic processing machines outlined in Chapter 6 tend to provide ideal development environments. The cost of such machines (around \$50,000–\$200,000), however, typically rules them out as machines of choice for prototyping. If the goal of prototyping is more to test application feasibility than to evaluate tools, then prototyping can proceed along a less expensive, although temporary, path. If AI machines are already available, or a company has a long-term interest in purchasing one of the LISP-oriented machines, then these high-speed machines with well-developed support environments often provide the optimum prototyping solution.

For most first-time expert system developments, the prototyping machine, given suitable building tools, can be a relatively fast personal computer, such as the higher end IBM PC-class machines. The IBM PC/AT has become a popular protoyping vehicle due to its wide availability in corporate environments and the number of MS-DOS tools on the market. It is possible that the PC/RT also increases its position in entry-level knowledge-engineering applications. The target machine may be expected to operate in a large multiuser environment. As discussed before, there are many ways to provide shared access to common pools of knowledge and data. The older approach is to operate terminals attached to a shared host, and the newer style is to adopt a distributed architecture with multiple workstations and servers connected over a local area network. The degree of success of the application and its marketing to the targeted audience should determine the number of users and the style of distribution.

The use of three different machines (i.e., prototype, development, and target) during the expert system development life cycle demands either portability of the expert system development shell and supporting tools or rewriting the system. Because the purpose of the prototype system is usually to determine the suitability of both the application problem and the selected software, it is desirable that the expert system shell (if found to be suitable) should be able to run on the development machine as well.

Making the transition from the development machine to the target machine may be more complex. The finished expert system may exist as an isolated workstation accessed only by one or a few qualified users. More likely, however, the finished system will have 10–100 users on large minicomputers or mainframes operating in a multiuser environment. Even if the system has only a few users, it will probably need to be integrated with the corporation's other production systems. As a consequence a number of factors tend to place production expert systems on conventional hosts. Project managers may find that the expert system, once completed and tested, has to be rewritten in a language native to the conventional host, i.e., a nonsymbolic language such as C, for both compatibility and speed.

When knowledge bases are moved from one system to another, perhaps from an expert system shell to a high-level language, or from a symbolic language to an expert system environment, incompatibilities can arise. The closer the two knowledge representation schemes, the fewer the differences. Even if the representations are identical, however, problems can arise from different inferencing strategies. In the more flexible systems, metarules are designed to be able to correct for variations in inferencing techniques. Patching up incongruities in the knowledge base, however, can mean returning to the first principles of knowledge engineering as outlined above. Basically, extensive testing has to be done after any porting operation, and any faults identified have to be isolated and corrected. Turning off sections of the knowledge base until an erroneous chunk is found is a proven approach to track down the sources of error. Correcting errors may be simple, but it depends on understanding the idiosyncracies of each knowledge representation scheme and then finding means to modify the destination behavior to match that of the source. One approach that can be used by software houses retained to port knowledge bases is to construct the translators as requested, but contractually agree that the correctness of the result can be established and corrected only by the client's domain experts and knowledge engineers.

## 7-11. DEFINING EXPANSION LIMITS

One of the initial jobs of the knowledge engineer is to define the scope of the expert system application. Policing these limits is another matter, and it has to be done continually to preserve a development's chances of success. At the outset it should be established that the nature of the application allows it to be placed within firm and manageable boundaries. In addition these boundaries should be described in writing, clearly and in detail. If the application is allowed to grow in all directions, it will tend so to fill up with shallow knowledge as to have no value. Creeping developments also tend to exhaust their machine resources, while making serious capacity planning impossible. Even within boundaries, it is good to create sub-boundaries, so incremental development and phased release of function is possible. Some applications, such as Aldo in a Box, MYCIN, and PUFF with its 100 or so rules, are fairly well fixed in size. Other applications, such as XCON, which started at 500 rules and has evolved to over 3000 rules, may continue to grow. XCON's growth is due to the continual addition of new products to the DEC line. Each time new rules are added for a new product, they are carefully partitioned from the existing rules of other products, making incremental expansion easy. XCON can be viewed as comprising several loosely connected subsystems, one for each product type. Compile-time pruning of large rule trees is valuable to keep the number of subsets of rules, and therefore the number of rules, available for any given session to a minimum. If 3000-plus rules were used at once, the effect on response time would be disastrous.

The basic guideline is to define the limit of the original expert system very carefully, but also to allow for the inevitable expansion that occurs in all successful software systems. If large-scale expansion is necessary, the large system should be partitioned into distinct subsystems, as noted above, or several distinct expert systems should be developed. Spreadsheet analyses for the multiple dimensions of capacity planning (see the last secion of Chapter 6) are valuable in this respect, so that the need for increased resources can be predicted. Even if the growth path follows a markedly different time scale from that of the first analysis, the actions at various trigger points still tend to be valid.

If the original conception is too broad a knowledge base implementation will often run into problems. Instead of building one large system, building several smaller ones is often wiser. A benefit of several small systems is parallel rather than series development. Whatever method is adopted to dissect a large problem into small ones, it is important to start with a coherent architecture that can accommodate all the parts. In computer-integrated manufacturing especially, starting with a solid architecture is one of the keys to success. The two basic architectural rules are: decreasing the coupling between modules to a minimum, and making each module do one and only one job. Once the modules are clearly defined, the star architecture with a central message switch and a central respository of facts is a proven approach for success. Whatever knowledge-engineering architecture is adopted, it is vital for expert systems that boundaries be defined ahead of time and that they be policed as the project continues.

## 7-12. MAIN POINTS: KNOWLEDGE CAPTURE AND CODIFICATION

The discussion in this chapter can be summarized in two metalevel points. First, knowledge capture requires a special set of human-understanding skills not always in the repertoire of systems analysts. Second, many of the aspects of establishing, codifying, testing, and verifying knowlege-base rules are similar to standard analytical techniques. For additional information on applying traditional software-engineering practices to the development of expert systems, see Martin (1987) or Richard Walters (1986). The main points of this chapter are

- It is best to start with only one expert, but additional experts are invaluable for testing purposes.
- If an appropriate expert cannot be found for the project, it is wise to proceed no further.
- Books, operations manuals, courses, and many other materials can provide useful background that hastens knowledge acquistion.
- It is important that the selected expert and selected lead knowledge engineer work well as a team, because they will have to spend a lot of time together.
- It is not wise to attempt to have an expert be his own knowledge engineer—the two roles require different psychological and thinking patterns.
- Most domains have a "central entity," a dynamic, key decision point influencing the entire operation, which has to be recognized to provide the hub of the knowledge base.
- The formula that knowledge is the basis of action is one of the ways to identify where knowledge resides.
- Looking for the areas that provide the expert's fulfillment is another way to establish focal points of knowledge—as can be expressed with the formula: knowledge-action-achievement-fulfillment.
- It is important to spell out the permutations and combinations of existing laws as completely new laws, because most expert systems are not good at deducing from first principles.

• Often as many as 80% of the rules in a knowledge base are needed to handle just the 20% of situations known as exception conditions.

• The most frequent approach to refining the conclusions reached by an expert system is to commence with the addition of more conditional clauses to existing rules.

• Further rules will often be indicated by the refinement of existing rules.

• Graphical tools to display rule trees and the activity of the inference engine as it traverses the tree are powerful for debugging.

• Many specific heuristics to be used during knowledge capture are detailed in the chapter (refer to the subheadings of section 7-9).

• One powerful heuristic is to discuss how previous accidents occurred and how they could have been avoided.

• Analyzing sample problems submitted by the expert, and also ones submitted by the knowledge engineer, is a useful approach.

• Porting from the development machine to a larger target machine can require rewriting the rules in a different syntax, which requires extensive retesting.

• It is vital for expert systems that boundaries be defined ahead of time and that they be policed as the project continues.

## NOTES

[1]One approach is to the use *agreement* between experts as a measure of appropriateness for certain conclusions given certain facts. Working with one expert to define the conclusions, however, is still the best approach.

# Chapter 8
# Integrating Expert Systems Into MIS and CIM Environments

## SECTION HEADINGS



## OVERVIEW

Thus far in the expert system development life cycle, the construction of the *stand-alone* expert system has been discussed. For many applications, however, the expert system has to be integrated with the rest of the enterprise's production systems before it can benefit the corporation. Integrating expert systems into the two main currents of commercial environments, management information systems (MIS) and computer-integrated manufacturing (CIM), are discussed in this chapter. Experience has shown that expert systems have to be coupled with accounting, real-time sensors, alarms, database management systems, graphics displays, reporting facilities, and other system interfaces to be productive and profitable. Process control is one of the leading CIM applications of this new technology. The use of expert systems as intermediate junction points to connect other software systems is also covered. A common barrier to integrating traditional systems is that the output of one system must be manually mapped or translated before it is passed on to the next system. Expert systems can help bridge this gap. Advice on common pitfalls in integration and how to avoid them is the final topic of discussion.

## 8-1. A CASE STUDY—BILLING FOR CIM SERVICES WITH A LINK TO MIS

An an introduction to this chapter, it is appropriate to start with a worked example relevant to virtually every expert application. This example concerns accounting charges to users of a multiuser expert system for the system's activity. Every transaction that passes through an expert system, resulting in some recommendation or conclusion, costs money to process. Who should be charged, and how should it be billed? A central accounting principle is to associate expenses with revenues as closely as possible, so that profitability can be monitored and maintained. Basically, if an expert system does not bill its users specifically and exactly, costs are not controlled and profitability is undermined. This section analyzes the need to integrate many expert systems into the MIS accounting function. Because production knowledge tools are expensive to develop, there is a strong incentive to recapture the investments through careful and automated billing.

The three main approaches to expert system billing are (1) per actual transaction; (2) potential use; and (3) per client fee, independent of the number of covered items or actual use. Most fielded applications to date have used option (3), and as a consequence expenses have often exceeded revenues. In most cases, to make a production expert system economically viable, it will have to be employed by more than one covered item, user, or department, and as a consequence a per transaction billing algorithm (approach (1)) will be beneficial. Even if all the users belong to the same large corporation, there is still a strong trend within such organizations to allocate specific costs to individual profit centers. Most human experts have hundreds of clients, and mechanized experts are generally no exception. In fact automation often allows the expert's knowledge to be relayed to an order of magnitude more clients than was previously possible. Consequently the billing mechanisms for automated expertise tend to far outstrip their predecessors in complexity.

Most organizations investing in production-scale expert systems have already implemented stand-alone computerized accounting. In the early stage of the production knowledge system's life, it is not uncommon to find the transaction data keyed once into the expert system and then again into the accounting package. Such rekeying is not only time-consuming and therefore costly, but also creates errors and delays. The request to provide an on-line link between these two environments often takes just a few minutes to surface. Especially in the face of expansion, manual rekeying can rapidly become too time-consuming and thus unmanageable.

Integrating accounting functions with the expert system, however, is usually more involved than just extracting a file from one system, transferring it, and merging it with the other system. Take, for example, a CIM expert system that provides third-party diagnostic services for steam turbines in chemical plants nationwide. Such a service could employ a central host with 30 terminals to allow junior technicians to answer telephone queries. Chemical plant engineers with faulty turbines would call in with their problems and go through a 10-minute question-and-answer session with the central host, mediated by the junior technicians. Given the right knowledge in the host and the right measuring tools on the plant sites, accurate conclusions could be reached rapidly, saving the end user many hours of tedious work. Such an expert system billing requirement could well be handled by a contractual arrangement whereby each plant pays a per turbine fee for covered turbines. Whether faults arise or not, the billing would occur monthly, resulting in a stable income for the system developers.

For example, in this billing system a fee of, say, $1.25 is be set for each covered turbine per month, plus an additional fee of $0.55 for signature-analysis (a signal-processing method for diagnosing turbine faults) services. The question then arises as to exactly how many turbines are to be covered per client per month. Central hosts in this type of expert application tend to hold fixed data on each covered item, so that repeated calls from the same client can be easily tracked, without the need to ask the same simple questions, "name/address/turbine type," time and again. Whenever coverage for new turbines is added, the system must be informed, perhaps by a standard form, and the new data must be keyed into the database. Each chemical manufacturer may have several plants, so the system must be able to cater to several policies per company and several turbines per policy. The number of covered items per month can be subject to additions or deletions, all of which affect the billed amount.

In the early days of such a system, it would not be uncommon for the service company to ask the turbine owners to calculate their own amounts due and pay them monthly. Even though such flexibility may sound financially foolish, it would be appropriate in an environment where a partnership of manufacturers had commissioned the project and set up a separate business unit to handle it. Also in the early days, when no closely coupled accounting package was available, such an approach could be the only option available.

Given the above considerations it is expedient for the service company to implement a new integrated billing system. Both the accounting and expert systems need to know the number and demographic details of the covered turbines. Much of the information needed for billing, however, does not logically belong in the expert system (and much of the information for fault finding is not needed by accounting), so to keep the two separated, a two-way communication link is needed. A sound design would be to keep track of covered turbines per plant, per client in a *special accounting data base* (SAB). Additions and deletions would be submitted directly to the SAB. The basic demographics of every covered turbine would regularly be extracted from the SAB and passed to the expert system base. Activity per turbine could then be taken from the expert system base, tagged to the broader demographics in the SAB, and used for billing each month.

Once such a data-maintenance system was in place, there would be no worry of receiving mismatched calls, where the demographic data did not yet exist in the database. Mismatched calls are likely to occur from clients who desire their new turbines to be on the service, but have not yet submitted their subscription applications. Prior to establishing the billing system, what to do with mismatched calls would still be a question. A typical early-days policy would be to service mismatched calls anyway and hope that their billing would be handled by existing contracts. With the billing functionality established, mismatched calls could be rejected, preventing dollar losses. Any toll-free phone service tends to receive numerous false calls, and the ratio of calls that result in genuine revenue to ones that should be rejected can be as high as 2 to 1.

Rejecting mismatched calls also encourages clients to submit their coverage updates earlier. Any debates over the actual starting date of policy coverage would be avoided by such an approach. Clients would tend to submit their additions as soon as possible, to guarantee coverage, but deletions could take a lot longer to be noted. Such a pattern of reporting would be to the system developer's advantage, as the billing would be increased by additions and not decreased by nonsubmitted deletions. Subsequent credits could be added to the billing algorithm later, to offset late notification of deletions. In the meantime, however, the developer would gain the interest from the difference and have improved cash flow.

This billing system can be implemented on top of a "textbook" accounting system, with one additional database detailing the covered items. Transaction-activity data can be extracted from the knowledge base to feed billing, and demographic data can be moved back into the expert system from the accounting portion. A special screen would be needed for entering the increases and decreases in coverage, and a special report program would be necessary to print the actual invoices. Showing the increases and decreases by plant is beyond the capacity of invoicing modules of most packaged accounting programs. All invoice totals and payees are subsequently entered automatically into the accounts receivable journal. By billing the clients for an exact dollar amount on the day the month ends, payments would be received earlier than the previous approach, and the overall cash flow would be improved. In addition, the old approach of expecting the clients to calculate their own bills could result in underpayments and even missed payments. Investigating the cost-effectiveness of such an integration of accounting with the electronic expert should be considered mandatory for most large applications.

This case study on the coupling of accounting functions into a manufacturing expert system is intended to demonstrate that integrations are frequently unavoidable. A mature expert system may well become a hub surrounded by five or six subsystems. One sound approach to such connectivity problems is to allow only file-transfer mechanisms to pass data between systems. The different modules can be arranged in a star, and file transfers invoked at the end of each shift. Many alternatives exist for integration architectures, but the key is to pick one approach and follow through with it.

## 8-2. A SUCCESSFUL EXPERT SYSTEM IS SELDOM A STAND-ALONE PRODUCT

It is important to understand that a well-conceived and designed expert system incorporates the elements of success. If the application has been carefully selected; the best tools for the job identified; and the knowledge gathered, entered, and tested; then the system should be capable of performing as a specialized expert in less time and at reduced cost. Of course, things can go wrong, but if the steps outlined in this book have been followed, there is every reason to believe that the system will be a success. The popularity of such well-structured expert systems can quickly cause original single-to-few-user designs to expand to large-scale multiuser systems. A number of organizations that have ventured into expert system territory have found that managing growth becomes their main concern. A transformation occurs. Initially the shell-based tool is a tiny subset of the organization's total computing facility. Later the expert system comes to dominate the computer environment, and preexisting systems become organized around it. Such restructuring of "driving and

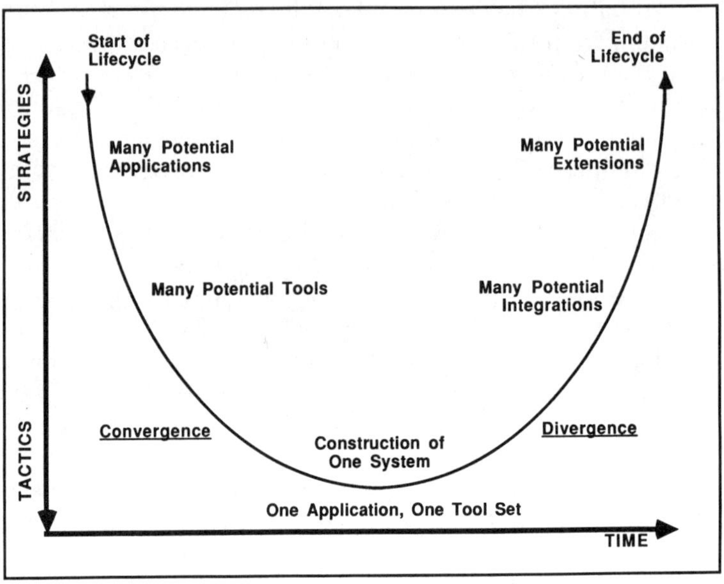


Fig. 8-1. The inward and outward strokes of expert system development.

driven" departmental computing functions can result in a greate deal of integration work.

The critical feature for the success of such complex software installations is the integration of the new expert system with other software packages in use or planned. This system requirement is indicated in the alternative view of the expert system development life cycle shown in Fig. 8-1. In the initial stages of the life cycle, broad strategies are employed to scrutinize potential application fields. Eventually, candidate applications are evaluated and one is chosen. The relevant tools are researched, tool and machine sets are chosen, and the building of the expert system proceeds using the recommended tactics. The life cycle can be seen to start with broad strategies, come down to detailed tactics in its middle sections, and then return to generalized strategies in the later stages. This chapter outlines strategies, key considerations, and components for integrating the finished stand-alone product with other hardware and software components of the production environment.

Experienced system administrators tend to be well aware of the complexities of integrating a new piece of hardware or software with other elements of the computational systems. A network of different software applications often requires constant uploading and downloading of information, from raw data to final management evaluation reports, between subsystems. The network components may range from planning devices to central processing for the job, to accounting and evaluation. Each aspect of the network must be interfaced, either in software or hardware and software, with other appropriate network nodes performing the remainder of the functions.

Highly specialized machines tend to be required for complex integration of diverse systems. For instance, Honeywell's TDC 3000 (Minneapolis, Minnesota) represents the state of the art in integration of distributed process-control systems. Similarly in the management information systems (MIS), Tandem Computers (Cupertino, California) has a solid track record for integrating the variety of distributed components in banking money-tracking systems. Apollo Computer (Chelmsford, Massachusetts) has established one of its niches as integrating different mechanical CAD, CAE, and CAM applications into a cohesive whole. Of course, all these integrations require extensive software, but starting with the right hardware can transform an impossible task into one that is merely complex. These interfaces are sophisticated, for each of the connected computers in a multivendor environment operates on a different set of principles with different design goals, and different nonstandardized tactics are employed to accomplish these diverse goals. Multivendor environments tend to be inevitable in anything other than the smallest businesses, as no one vendor covers all the bases. It may be corporate policy to standardize on IBM, but other markets have different leaders. For example, Tandem excels at fault tolerance, Computervision at computer-aided manufacturing, Apollo at computer-aided design, Wang at word processing, and Cray at large-capacity number crunching. To integrate expert systems into these already complex environments, one more set of goal strategies and implementation tactics must be interfaced with the existing computer systems before the expert system can become a useful element of the production environment.

The expert system begins as a generic shell that can be tailored to fit the needs of the application. This horizontal, generic capability is sacrificed as the system acquires its highly specialized, vertical knowledge. Information and results must be transferred from the expert system, and appropriate inputs to the expert system must be provided. In the latter case, critical data must be funneled into the system. Many multinational corporations have the policy of centralizing MIS and not distributing it to remote sites, especially when they are located in Third World countries. As a consequence communications lines are needed to connect the central host to terminals and small machines on the remote sites. If policies were more flexible, certain integrations could be avoided. But centralization usually aims at saving money in other ways.

To avoid pitfalls, finished expert systems should be incrementally

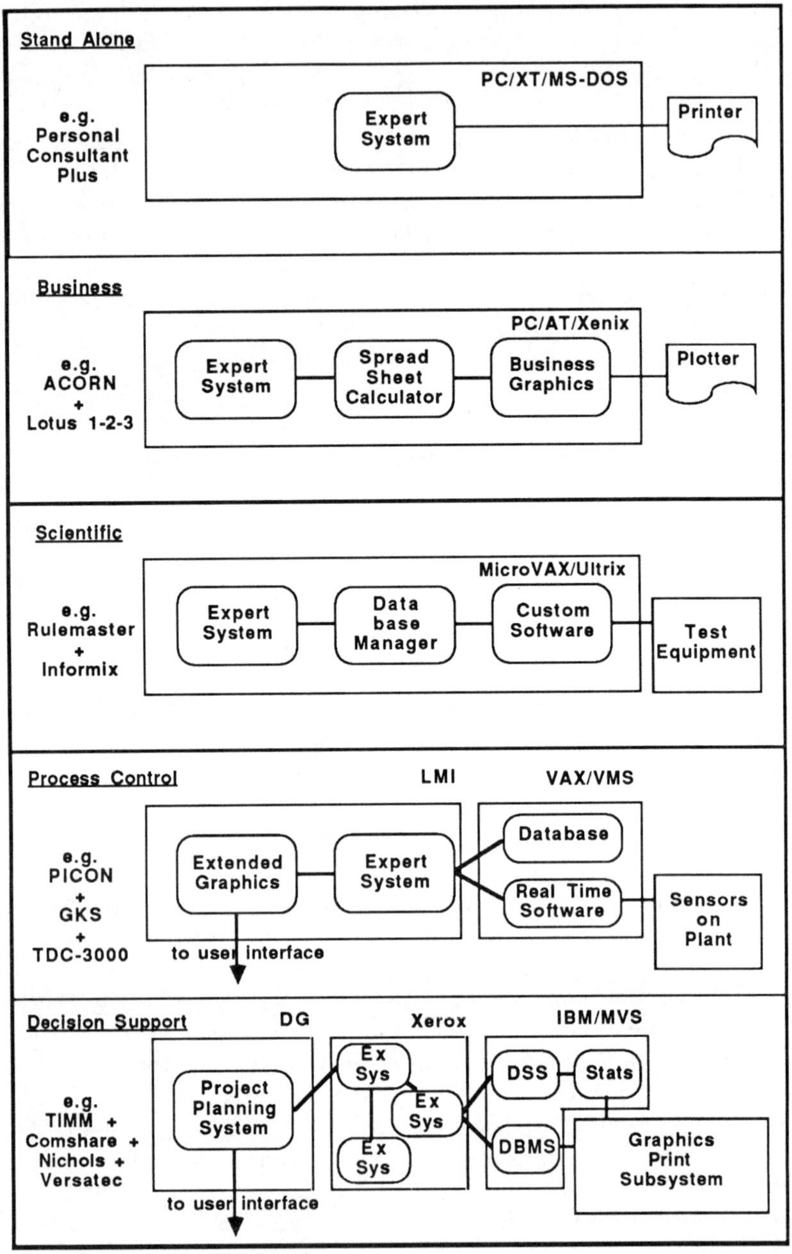


Fig. 8-2. Examples of expert system integrations with other software production systems.

integrated into the mainstream of other computer systems and peripherals in the production environment. In the beginning, it may be useful to manually transfer inputs to and outputs from the expert system as its capability is tested by real cases. As links to other parts of the distributed system are initiated one at a time, the real test cases can provide further verification that the overall system is producing the expected results. The degree of integration needed by the expert system in an MIS or CIM production environment ranges from a completely stand-alone PC/AT level microcomputer to expert systems deeply embedded within other applications. Figure 8-2 shows six different examples of integration based on production environment requirements.

The highest level of integration is found in embedded systems. The classic example of such expert systems, as indicated in Fig. 8-2, is the process-control system. The control computer controls input and output from the process being monitored in the form of sensors and servomotors, respectively. The monitoring expert system is usually located on another minicomputer, and the two computer systems may share a common database. Another highly embedded integrated expert system is an electronic mail server. This expert system sorts all electronic mail, routes messages, and prioritizes and classifies mail, to eliminate junk mail from flooding the mail network. This application is embedded in both a database system (storing of mail) and a communications systems (sending, routing, and receiving mail).

The next two sections continue in the examination of the rationale and philosophy for integrating the new expert system into the production environment, before more specific techniques are discussed in the remaining sections. The main point is that interfaces must be defined and implemented between all related systems in the production environment. Not all of them may be automated, but these interfaces should be as clean and simple as possible. FORTRAN common blocks are one method for sharing data between subroutines, but the interface is undisciplined and error-prone. Expert systems interfaces work better if they are like UNIX pipes, where data flow from one processing operation to another sequentially. Message-passing protocols are one of the most sophisticated levels of integration, but for most applications file-transfer mechanisms provide a good tradeoff between simplicity and power.

## 8-3. THE NEED FOR KNOWLEDGE-BASE INTERFACE STANDARDS

Integrating a new expert system with existing production systems is one concern. A second concern revolves around the breadth of an expert

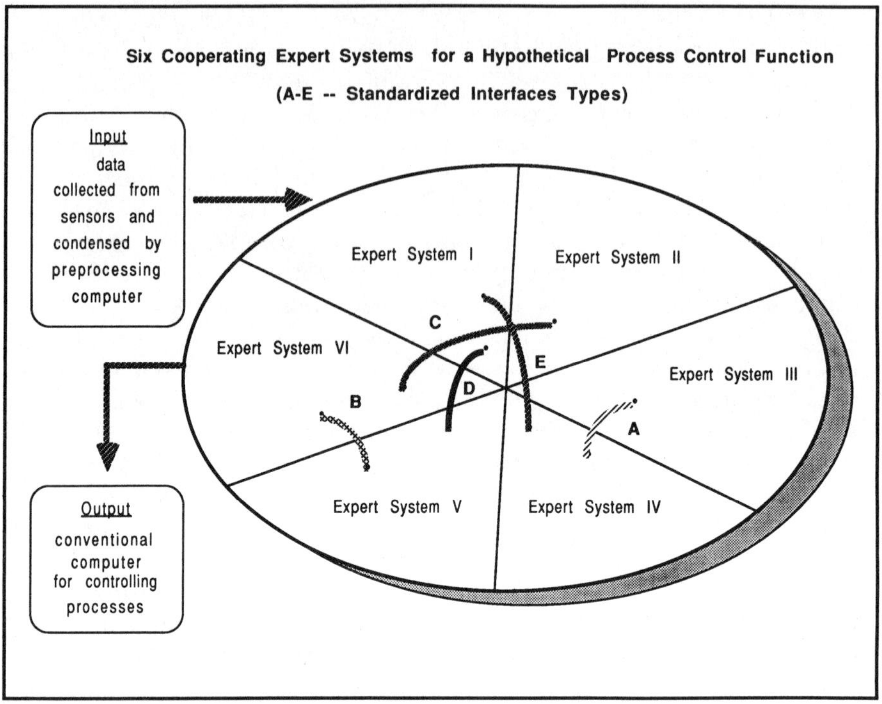


Fig. 8-3. Developing standardized modular expert system interfaces.

system application, which, as noted in Chapter 3, is generally quite limited. It is quite understandable that several expert systems, each tackling one aspect of a complex problem, may be developed either simultaneously or over some period. Integrating half a dozen or more expert systems over time into a production environment, as shown in Fig. 8-3, raises the issue of expert-system-to-expert-system interfaces. An example of such integrations arises in automated stock trading consultation. Each stock or category of stock operates under its own set of rules and could be implemented as a stand-alone expert. Connecting different classes of stock to automate portfolio management is much more complex. There are times when it is valuable to move investments out of one industry, such as steel mills, and transfer the money into another, such as high technology. In this situation two expert systems have to bid against each other to gain control over the funds. Each system in such a development scheme should be carefully designed and developed in modular form with clearly defined interfaces with other modules. This scenario, not so far in the future, presents a solid design challenge to the overall system developer.

At this time, modular design, testing, and integration of expert systems is hampered by the lack of *knowledge-base interface standards.* Certainly it is possible to build stand-alone experts, but the industry standards for creating hooks for later integration with other knowledge bases are yet to mature. Low-level hooks, common to other disciplines, are available, but high-level knowledge interfaces are another matter. The expert systems technology is in the same position as traditional computer standards of a few years ago; each individual manufacturer's products are distinct and are not designed to easily interface the products of other vendors. This individualistic approach, as a marketing ploy to keep consumers purchasing within a single vendor's or group of vendors' product lines, slowed the widespread use of home and business computer systems for a number of years. In contrast the open architecture of IBM's PC allowed it to capture the markets of dozens of closed-architecture vendors. Attempts are now being made to provide industrywide knowledge standards in a mutually cooperative effort by computer vendors, large and small. The seven-layer Open Systems Interconnect (OSI) model, now quite widely accepted, addresses general networking requirements by outlining standard functioning protocols. It is practical to establish knowledge protocols at layers 6 and 7 of the OSI model and implement them on top of such lower-level industry standards as TCP/IP and X.25. One of the powers of the OSI model is that it allows different layers of the cake to be slid in and out without affecting other layers. For example, the same knowledge standard could run as easily on top of XNS as it could on DECnet, Domain, or ECMA protocols. The Corporation for Open Systems (COS, Vienna, Virginia), founded in 1985, is one of the promising large-scale efforts to actually implement the entire OSI model. Even with the cooperation of most of the major hardware firms in the COS venture, however, it is likely to be several years before open-protocol knowledge standards are in effect.

It is expected that the cooperation lesson will be quickly learned by expert systems vendors, and that standardized interfaces will be available in the not-too-distant future. Al machine vendors are already moving in this direction. Symbolics (Concord, Massachusetts) offers software networking products that link its computers to IBM machines via SNA, and DEC hosts via DECnet and to others through TCP/IP Ethernet. Symbolics machines can be accessed at the file-transfer level by Apple Macintoshes running ExperLISP and ExperLINK from ExperTelligence (Santa Barbara, California). Connecting IBM PCs to Symbolics machines can be accomplished with Gold Hill Computer's (Cambridge, Massachusetts) GCLISP CHAOSNET. Similar software networking products are offered by Flavors Technology (Amherst, New Hampshire) to connect LISP Machines, Inc., computers with Gould machines. An LMI/Flavors cooperative marketing agreement has been forged for the Flavors Bus-Link product which is a 32-bit asynchronous bus link permitting LMI Lambda AI workstations to assess Gould superminis in real time. Such an approach provides a fast method of attaching a powerful UNIX mini to a LISP machine. Many more products like these can be expected in the near future.

Standards are needed to extend the expert system's sphere of influence, ranging from the intramachine level, to the departmental level, to the corporate level, and finally to the level of the entire industry. For now, however, the computer systems administrator must attempt to develop a series of knowledge-base standards and interfaces suitable to his department or corporation. The system administrator must review the corporate plan for expert systems development in this light. OSI application layer (layer 7) message-passing standards are well established in other industries (e.g., transactions of electronic banking, handling insurance claims, tracking merchant ships). For expert system interconnection, however, messages should be able to relay both facts and heuristics, so object-oriented programming languages may be more suitable. In MIS circles it has become standard to exchange spreadsheet templates along with spreadsheet data, so that the figures can be manipulated and used at the destination. Similarly, if bodies of expert system data are to be meaningful when delivered, certain heuristics must be coupled with facts. The internal communication protocol between objects with SMALLTALK is one candidate for knowledge-base integration standards. Such formats must be developed by the system administrator as part of the design specification of the overall expert system project.

Guidelines are also needed to sequence and prioritize the interactions between different expert systems and modules. Integration with other components of the production environment could benefit from the transaction-processing approach of *data-flow* environments. This approach yields automated strategies, policies, and procedures for coordinating and controlling the flows of information in a distributed-systems environment. If the system is distributed across several departments, policies for use of the whole system and responsibilities for maintaining each department's aspect of the system must be detailed. One weak link in the production system can result in the entire system being shut down.

A related concern, as expert systems become more strongly connected with other components in the distributed computer system, is the contamination of any one part of the system by other parts. Strict procedures for data reliability and integrity must be established and adhered to, whether the contamination is caused by faulty knowledge in the expert system or by another part of the system (e.g., a data-entry-sensor monitor) that provides inaccurate or inconsistent data to the expert system through a poorly designed interface. This domino effect has been one of the prominent barriers to the deployment of expert systems in CIM environments. By employing extensive testing and by keeping the expert system to an advisory role, rather than having it act as an independent agent, faults and their repercussions should be minimized. Fault-tolerant hardware is likely to become the basis of more and more CIM configurations, but at the current time the two leading fault-tolerant-hardware vendors, Tandem and Stratus (Natick, Massachusetts) support no expert system shells.

The system administrator must seek to balance the elements of flexibility and stability during the phases of expert system integration. Many MIS departments have literally hundreds or thousands of procedures for managing every phase of software engineering from concept formation to full integration with other systems. Many of these rules can be used directly in expert system administration, but others cannot. Such procedures have evolved over years of trial-and-error software-development projects. If the entire set of rules were used during the initial development stages, every piece of software would tend to be too highly overconstrained and would never be completed. Flexibility must be encouraged in the initial stages of development, and this should be reflected in the standards manual. As the standards are evaluated, tested, and revised according to the needs of the department, the degree of enforcement can be increased to establish greater stability within the shop, which in turn results in higher quality products. At later stages, once highly developed multilevel complex structures are developed, greater stability will be required.

Knowledge standards are needed to ensure that modular integration is done professionally, reducing the need for maintenance and patching. The general guiding principle is to keep the degree of integration as low as possible to avoid greater interface complexities while still satisfying the total production system requirements.

## 8-4. KNOWLEDGE-BASE ADMINISTRATION

As the effects of knowledge bases spread into more sections of the organization, it becomes increasingly important to keep the central core orderly. Administration that preserves order will spread order, but a lack of attention will permit entropy to grow in the knowledge base and spread to the different divisions of the enterprise.

Standards for maintaining and increasing the *internal structure* of a knowledge base are required to complement the ones for interconnecting it with other systems. Generally, expert system knowledge bases exist in a perpetual state of evolutionary growth and refinement. Procedures must be developed for defining, adding, and testing new aspects of knowledge in the creation and evolution of production system. Just as with database systems, knowledge-base integrity and reliability are key issues in a production environment. These procedures needed for knowledge bases can be modeled after database administrator rules, for expert system knowledge bases and database systems share many characteristics.

A specialized coordinator is needed to facilitate maintenance and continued development of knowledge bases in a production environment. The *knowledge-base administrator* (KBA) plays essentially the same role in the management of the expert systems knowledge bases as a database administrator (DBA) does for traditional databases. The differences here, as with the knowledge engineer and the systems analyst, are primarily related to the peculiarities of the domain, rather than overall management and organizational strategies. The knowledge-system standards and policies defined by the overall system developer must be successfully implemented and actualized by the KBA. Policies and procedures usually have to be defined or modified as the knowledge base continues to evolve.

For example, the KBA must carefully control the addition of new rules to a rule-based system currently functioning in the production environment. Two versions of the expert system—development and production—should be maintained, preferably on two separate machines. The new rules are incorporated into the existing rule set, and the complete set is tested and debugged, all in the development version. If the production expert system answers clients' insurance questions and resolves disputes, it will typically be in use only from 9 A.M. to 9 P.M. EST. The prime time for testing the new knowledge-base version on the production machine will be from 9 P.M. to 9 A.M., while the machine is not in use. If the new version does not test out on the new machine, it should go back to the development machine for further analysis, but this movement obviously must not interfere with the production machine's availability at 9:00 the next morning. Employing the UNIX Programmer's Workbench tool Source Code Control System (SCCS) permits detailed tracking of versions and modifications to knowledge bases. SCCS has been implemented in a number of other environments, such as VMS, where it is provided by DEC.

Such procedures are not new to MIS environments, but they must generally be applied more rigorously in expert system technology. One new rule added to a knowledge base could result in a machine crash losing the data of tens of transactions. These effects could happen with any software, but whenever a new expert system update model is installed, the risks tend to be greater, as the technology is new and not so universally understood. Thorough testing of each new knowledge release is vital.

In addition to training one or more KBAs, programmer analysts must be trained in the skills necessary to implement the expert system tools. The night-shift machine operator who has worked only with traditional DP tools cannot be expected to put new versions of the knowledge base into action without appropriate training. Expert systems, being heuristic, do not always behave in the same ways as other more traditional software tools. Specialized skills are needed to deal with the unique characteristics and peculiarities of this software.

The KBA's activities span the same range of functions as the DBA. These functions are well established in DP circles and include monitoring and policing knowledge integrity and reliability, sign-on and access permissions, and so on. Just as the DBA relies on a data dictionary, so it is wise for the KBA to establish a knowledge dictionary. A simple list-management program, such as Microsoft File on a Macintosh, is all that is needed to track a few hundred rules. If the knowledge base expands to over a thousand rules or is schema-based, a relational DBMS is more appropriate to handle the complexity. These functions become more critical as the degree of integration of the expert system with other production systems increases. Unreliable or inaccurate responses from the expert system cannot be tolerated in most production systems where the expert system is in the critical data flow path. It is the knowledge-base administrator's job to see that such malfunctions do not occur or are minimized.

## 8-5. INTRAMACHINE AND INTERMACHINE INTEGRATION

Two aspects of integration, discussed as one matter so far, are best treated with different strategies. The two aspects are integration within a machine (intramachine) and integration between machines (intermachine). From an end user's functional view, it usually makes little or no difference which machines the various software units are located on. From an implementation point of view, however, these distribution questions have major effects. At an introductory level it is simpler if the different modules to be connected are all situated on one machine. In more complex systems, however, matters can be simplified considerably if discrete functional units are localized on specific and appropriate machines. The rule, as with modular programming, is to keep linkages between modules as simple and brief as possible. As a consequence it is wise to keep the "strength" of each module as high as possible, which means that all aspects related to one function should be kept in the same module. If each module does part of all the jobs, integration is difficult. What is needed is a clean knowledge architecture, laid out at the beginning of the project, which is then followed for all integrations. Clean interfaces also speed development as they allow different programmers to work in parallel.

Knowledge-base standards should apply equally to software systems coupled with the same machine and to those existing on different machines. Traditionally, more clearly defined and more numerous standards have been developed for networks or intermachine connections. Within a machine, shared database management systems are the most widely accepted means of integration, ahead of pipes, message passing, file passing, common blocks, blackboards, and cut and paste. Call/return structures could be included as another approach to such integrations, but these are better reserved for program modules within the same subsystem. Too close a degree of coupling, as provided by calls or commons, can open up larger possible windows of contamination than is necessary. Databases work well for structured and static data, but they are not so good when the nature of the data is not known in advance. Real-time systems, with their tendency to large amounts of volatile data, tend to find DBMSs too slow. Some RDBMS products allow certain tables to be transparently fixed in RAM, allowing crucial data to be assessed in real time. Even if everything cannot be placed in RAM, buffers and caches, if intelligently used, can make up for many deficiencies. Within the RDBMS world, the most standard interface is Structured Query Language (SQL), as supported by IBM, Oracle, Informix, Pacific Software Manufacturing Company, and others.

One of the newest approaches to expert system integrations is the blackboard approach, where a number of independent actors, such as SMALLTALK objects, communicate by writing and reading to a shared area. If rules are established to clearly govern who has what type of control of a blackboard section at what time, the approach can work quite well. More traditional approaches are file and message transfers. UNIX pipes, for example, follow this traditional style, and in almost all cases the ASCII sequential strings of data are passed via disk to maintain integrity. In these different examples data integrity is invariably traded for speed, so application-specific decisions have to be made.

Integration between machines can employ wide, local, or bus area networks. The longer distance the communication link covers, the slower it tends to go—attenuation of signals is an elementary law of physics. Links may be parallel or serial, and bus connections tend to be the only ones that are serial due to the wiring complexities. In the bus realm there are many proprietary and a few industrywide standards, including Multibus (IEEE Standard 796), H-P bus (IEEE Standard 488),

S-100 (IEEE Standard 696), Multibus II, Versabus, NuBus, STDbus, Q-Bus, Unibus, VAXBI, IBM PC bus, IBM AT bus, and Apple II bus. Most AI machines employ Multibus, Versabus, Q-Bus, VAXBI, or the IBM PC/AT bus. Local area networks (LAN) follow the same pattern with the three main industry standards, Ethernet (IEEE 802.3), IBM's Token Ring (IEEE 802.4), and General Motor's (Warren, MI) Token Bus (IEEE 802.5) with the Manufacturing Automation Protocol (MAP)—developed by GM and the Technical Office Protocol (TOP)—developed by Boeing (Seattle, Washington). Most AI systems seem to be focusing on Ethernet, with the Department of Defense (DoD) standard TCP/IP for higher levels. Gold Hill for example provided TCP/IP hardware and software to link its GCLISP product running on the IBM PC with the Symbolics 3600 family, TI Explorers, Intel iPSCs, DEC VAXs, Sun workstations, and many others. Xerox favors XNS over TCP/IP for its LISP workstations; it can be connected with VAXs, PCs, and other vendors with equipment from 3COM (Mountain View, California) or Bridge Communications (Cupertino, California). In the wide area network (WAN) arena there are even more options, and those favored for AI work are still to be clarified by the industry.

Intramachine integration is not necessarily easier to perform just because the two or more software programs are residing on the same machine. The key to success is clean, standardized interfaces from established vendors. What may start out to be relatively straightforward intramachine couplings can very quickly evolve to couplings between various machines. Enhanced data-maintenance subsystems may start their life on the central host, but as they grow, it will frequently become expedient to off-load these separable modules onto additional hosts. A large VAX can easily become surrounded by supporting MicroVAXs. IBM hopes that the 9370 will introduce the same pattern of growth into System/370-architecture-based corporations. These integrations tend to be inevitable in successful expert systems as the demand for and capabilities of the system increase. Data-processing departments generally have well-established procedures for software engineering, but less well defined rules for integrating software packages, particularly so across machines. For this reason the KBA has to be particularly alert as interfaces spread from within one machine to reach out to other pieces of hardware.

## 8-6. INTEGRATING EXPERT SYSTEMS WITH DATABASE MANAGERS

Sharing data between an expert system and a traditional DBMS is probably the most fundamental and frequently required system collaboration. Although the expert system's knowledge base and the database of traditional MIS records remain separate, the expert system's knowledge chunks or rules often need to be tied to specific fields in a database. If the organization has developed "subject" or corporate databases intended to be the master source of specific classes of information, the expert system developers can get into trouble for developing their own private data stores. A widespread approach to maintaining the integrity of subject DBs is to spin off read-only files for specific applications. If the expert system needs to update these local files, then someone must decide who has the master copy of the data. It can be expedient to lock portions of the subject database, rendering them read-only, until the modified portion is merged with the whole. Nighttime batch runs, to spinoff files and then merge back updates, can be preferable to allowing the expert system on-line access to such crucial data. Comprehensive validation routines are more easily built into batch runs than they are into on-line systems, due to the time constraints of not keeping users waiting.

The issue of logging demographic variables to speed transactions and avoid frustrating users is common to a large proportion of expert system applications. If the machine has to ask for every aspect of the user's name, address, telephone number, perhaps credit status, and so on, for each transaction, then the process is slowed to a snail's pace. Today's users expect a corporation to know their details if they have been given once. It is certainly a pleasure to phone Xerox for photocopier service or Avis to rent a car, given one's phone number, and be referred to by first name from then on.

Maintaining a store of situation-specific facts can often be an application necessity, rather than just a client-oriented luxury. Take the case study example of an expert system designed to assist a personnel officer in matching current employees with new job openings within the company. The rules in the knowledge base need to access information about the company's current employees from the personnel database to perform their analysis. Calls to the database manager from the inference engine should be able to locate all employee records with the appropriate qualifications. Subsequently each employee's record can be screened in detail by the expert system to select the likeliest candidate. Usually no one person is right for the job to the exclusion of others. Instead, several candidates are likely, none of which is absolutely perfect. As a consequence the promotion aspect of the system has to use its heuristics to make tradeoffs. The link between the DB and the expert system, however, is the fundamental ingredient for the system's viability.

Various interactions are possible between an expert system and a database. Any time the expert system needs basic data for the inference process (e.g., for variables in rules), the database supplies the facts.

Conversely, it may be desirable to store results produced by the expert system during an inference process in a database. To keep integrations with other systems to the simplest level, it is desirable to (1) filter these connections through a shared database, and (2) keep the number of variables passed each way to a minimum. An automobile insurance expert system, for example, may deduce the compensation for crash victims and store the result in the claims-management database.

A third style of database-to-expert-system interaction is where the DBMS is executed prior to the inference engine to collect demographic and billing information. Once the ground facts have been accumulated, control is passed to the inferencing mechanism. Human experts often work in this fashion with a receptionist to take down basic information, to save the expert's time. As with computerized expert systems, the human expert often does not work well with tedious details such as name and address, so a division of labor is appropriate.

Take the example of an insurance company with a dial-up expert system used to analyze and route life insurance claims. Customers of the system must first supply all the necessary facts, which takes 2 or 3 minutes. It then typically takes another 1 or 2 minutes to process each session once the base information has been supplied. On average these operators have a 3-minute break between each call. In designing this application, the engineer has to address such questions as: How many consultations can be completed in a working day? If the system has a capacity of handling 200 consultations per day with the CPU working at full capacity, how many terminals or workstations should the company install? Given various growth rates of consultations, when will additional compute power be needed? Given the growth of transactions, when will the database exceed the current disk capacity, necessitating new purchases?

In these large systems, the scale of the experts system's operation is much like that of large-scale DP organized around transaction processing (TP). The basic information for each customer (e.g., company, social security number, address) should be stored and recalled, rather than ask repeat customers for the same information again and again. Standard MIS TP procedures and systems are needed to ensure proper handling and interleaving of queries, storing of intermediate results, and so on. A common requirement for many large production expert systems is to learn, usually with human help, from previous transactions presented to the system. Thus there is a need to log transactions in a database and parse them later with compound inferencing mechanisms. Recorded case histories may be required to further refine or optimize the rule base or to determine the frequencies of problem classes being presented to the machine. If it is known where the expert system is spending most of its time, then attention can be placed there to optimize performance and save money. The fixed data and the conclusions of each session, minimally, must be saved for such analysis. Most expert system shells do not provide facilities for storing and recalling more than the immediate query inference chain, so database managers plus custom programming must be employed.

Some of the expert system building shells discussed in Chapter 5 provide more support for database interfaces than others. RuleMaster and Knowledge Workbench provide ways to interface with database managers, and GURU and ART (Inference Corporation) incorporate relational database managers directly. dBASE III databases can be accessed from such shells as ACORN, Aion/PC, INSIGHT, GURU, and Expert Edge. Other shell systems provide more open-ended hooks, usually through the high-level-language interface, to a variety of databases. As noted in Chapter 5, some of the tools are more restrictive and require sepialized hardware. The Knowledge Workbench system, for instance, requires a Motorola 680X0 microprocessor-based machine, so any associated database program would also have to run on that hardware. A distributed system is an alternative where one end of the link sets hardware constraints that are too limiting for the other end. LISP machines tend to be, by definition, hardware-specific, so integrations to databases frequently require intermachine integration. In such cases it may be advantageous to dedicate a database machine, such as a Britton-Lee or Intel unit, to database management functions.

Multitasking operating systems tend to provide an ideal environment for implementing expert system to database links. Such operations as closing a set of database files can consume a full 30 seconds or more. In an on-line transaction-processing mode, a 30-second delay can constitute far too high a percentage of a 4-minute consultation to be acceptable. Multitasking allows the user of the expert system to return to useful work while the operating system manages the more mundane tasks. Intellicorp's KEE connection is designed to accomplish this task by allowing KEE programs to access main frame databases directly. At American Express, a charge verification system developed by Inference Corp using ART and a combination of Symbolics and Sun hardware allows hundreds of users to access the system simultaneously.

As discussed in this section, many different approaches to database integration exists. The demand for these integrations should not be underestimated. Vendors offer many specific products in this area, as detailed in Chapter 5, but choices should be based on the needs of the application, not on the strengths of sales pitches.

## 8-7. INTERFACING GRAPHICS WITH EXPERT SYSTEMS

Graphics subsystems or interfaces are often another crucial extension of real-world expert systems, especially in the CIM environment. Although English phrase input/output techniques work well for certain expert systems with limited data communication between the system and the user, more complex knowledge and information interchanges are often better handled with graphics displays. Applications that appear to be simple enough to use natural-language communication soon grow in sophistication. After even a little growth the knowledge and data structures become so complex that only through graphics or diagrams can the successfully and rapidly be communicated to the user.

An example of such a graphics expert system extension is the requirement for activity reports. These reports show the nature and kinds of conclusions the expert system is reaching and provide the basis for inferring the system's continued cost-effectiveness. Frequently expert systems grow to service multiple-user departments or organizations and thus enter the realm of business contracts. As is standard, each contract has a limited term, perhaps 1 year, and thus every time the anniversary date arrives a sales task is necessary to get the renewal contract signed. Earlier expert systems frequently had their roots in research environments well-insulated from the hard commercial realities of prospecting and closing client contracts. In today's production applications, however, the job of proving cost-effectiveness to the client is up to the expert system department, and thus sophisticated tools are needed. Operations that must be addressed by such an expert system marketing extension include

1. Track the cost to the client of adopting the expert system recommendations. (These are the billed dollars.)
2. Know the client cost if the expert system recommendations were unavailable.
3. Deduce the savings to the client. Basically (2) minus (1).
4. Track the cost of pulling a transaction through the expert system. (These are raw costs to the computer department.)
5. Calculate the actual cost-effectiveness for each client's usage.
6. Inform and convince the client of return on investment.

Activity reports may not immediately appear to be a graphical matter, but when it comes to communicating something as complex as expert system cost-effectiveness to close a contract, hard-copy color graphics can be hard to surpass. It has been found that printed color graphics reports quickly convince customers and prospects of the benefits of the expert system. In short, the color graphics printouts are a powerful sales tool. Even though such high technology might seem to be overkill for the job, it really does help close deals. The task of communicating complex knowledge structures is difficult enough, but when time is limited and the recipient is new to the business, the investment in a graphics print subsystem (GPS) can be highly cost-effective. A GPS is a matter of benefits within benefits within benefits.

Such graphics print subsystems could, for example, be implemented using Versatec Spectrum equipment hung off an ULTRIX MicroVAX II. The main expert system might run on a high-end ULTRIX VAX, with the two hosts connected via DECnet Ethernet. A monthly process is needed to extract activity and recommendation data for all clients whose starting anniversary date (i.e., contract renewal date) falls in the current month. Extracting facts from the knowledge base involves a mapping from the knowledge domain into the data domain. Representation structures have to be simplified, or flattened, during this translation. After this step comes a lengthy analysis and summarization process that takes over a day to execute. The result is the numeric data summary file. Following these first two knowledge-oriented layers of software are several additional layers that transform the numerical data into graphical images. The total steps can be detailed as follows

1. Extraction from knowledge base of activity and recommendations (for anniversary clients),
2. Mapping from the knowledge domain into the data domain,
3. Numerical data analysis and summarization process,
4. Numeric preprocessing of graphics quantities (especially of scaling and truncation factors),
5. Scheduling of specific reports to be printed,
6. Routing of specific reports to a selected printer,
7. Graphics manager creates tables and graphs,
8. Color separation into four prime colors,
9. Device driver to send separated data out of the CPU,
10. Raster processing in a stand-alone, dedicated CPU (maps vector graphics into raster graphics),
11. Electrostatic printing of raster images.

For applications such as this one it is wise to employ an expandable bank of printers to handle growth. Print requests are directed to the next free print queue by the router program. Provisions are necessary for adding (or deleting) printers from the configuration as the system grows. As color printers are slow and expensive, it is desirable to buy only as much capacity as needed at any one time. Candidate letter-size, hard-copy, color print vendors include Versatec (Santa Clara, California), Calcomp (Anaheim, California), Seiko Instruments (Santa Clara, California), Printacolor (Norcross, Georgia), and Tektronix (Beaverton, Orgeon). A number of low-cost, PC-based color printers are also available, but for a production environment the rated monthly capacity is a crucial issue. If the maximum capacity is exceeded, the reliability decreases dramatically. The above-mentioned five machines are marketed as robust, high-capacity production-application printers.

The above GPS is only one approach, and computer graphics can be integrated with expert systems in a large number of ways. At the simple end of a continuum, only soft-copy, simple business graphics is needed. The easiest way to accomplish this interface is to purchase an expert system building shell tool with this built-in capability (e.g., GURU or Aion). At the other extreme, sophisticated hard-copy graphics capabilities requiring specialized hardware are needed. These packages may run on the same or different machines, and the interfaces, even if very clean, tend to be rather complicated. The Aion/MVS program is of interest, as it is built on IBM's Graphical Data Display Manager (GDDM), which can save some work in certain applications. The more complex applications will often require not only specialized graphics software but also custom creation of the graphics driver to connect the necessary hardware to the expert system.

Although the trend to building certain graphics facilities into the main shell is clearly identified, it will be a long time before they are powerful enough to handle arbitrary soft and hard applications. The activity reports example discussed above is a situation, like accounting, that applies to a large range of production systems. For adequate flexibility to meet production user requirements, it is usually necessary to implement graphics functions with special-purpose tools developed for the job. It should be possible to save a certain amount of work by buying off-the-shelf graphics components, but much of the mapping and integration software will have to be custom-developed.

## 8-8. INTERFACING OTHER CLASSES OF SOFTWARE TOOLS WITH EXPERT SYSTEMS

Databases and graphics packages have been singled out in the previous two sections to indicate some of the important considerations for integrating expert systems into production environments. Both database and graphics capabilities are high on the list of potentially needed interfaces, and they may become necessities for most production MIS and CIM expert systems in the near future. In this section, interfaces with other classes of MIS and CIM software products are surveyed.

Generally, the principles for integration are essentially the same as those noted above for databases and graphics packages.

Some required interfaces may be quite simple and mundane (as in the case of simple business graphics). Others may be more exotic and complex. The simplest cases may involve only moving ASCII information from one point to another. The more technically challenging interfaces will require several stages of processing across carefully designed layers of interfacing software and hardware. One key to success is that if the problem appears to be too complex, then add more layers of software, where each level implements one simple stage of transformation.

Figure 8-4, adapted from two previous technical publications, outlines the three primary tool sets used in the MIS and CIM environments. Although commerical and industrial applications cover many classes of software, there has been as increasing consensus to narrow the number of tools in use to a few basic flexible types. These tools can then be configured by specifying parameters and integrating to form an almost unlimited variety of applications. For each of the three categories—decision support (the lion's share of MIS), mechanical CAD/CAE/CAM, and electronic CAD/CAE/CAM—six tools are identified. Database management and graphics, like most of the tools listed under decision support, apply almost equally when embedded in CIM. These two were covered in the previous two sections.

Turning now to interfaces with spreadsheet calculators, it can be broadly stated that they are similar in many ways to datbase connections. Information for variables may be drawn from spreadsheets, or inference results may be written back to the spreadsheet. Even if the expert system is working as a slave to the spreadsheet to make calculations more intelligent, the basic mode of operation is as described above. GURU presents one of the more comprehensive attempts at an integrated product. A database manager, business graphics package, and a spreadsheet calculator are integral parts of the total expert system support environment. During inference, information stored in data tables, a spreadsheet, or another rule set (i.e., other than the one in use) can be accessed. Consultation results can be stored in the database or moved to graphs, or alternatively reports can be generated. Information from an expert system can be requested in the spreadsheet, such as the best alternative action for a current cell value. Lotus 1-2-3 interfaces are found in a number of expert system products, including ACORN, Aion, and Expert Edge, although the degree of flexibility varies from product to product.

One practical example of linking spreadsheet facilities with inferencing is in cash management. Large corporations have dozens, even

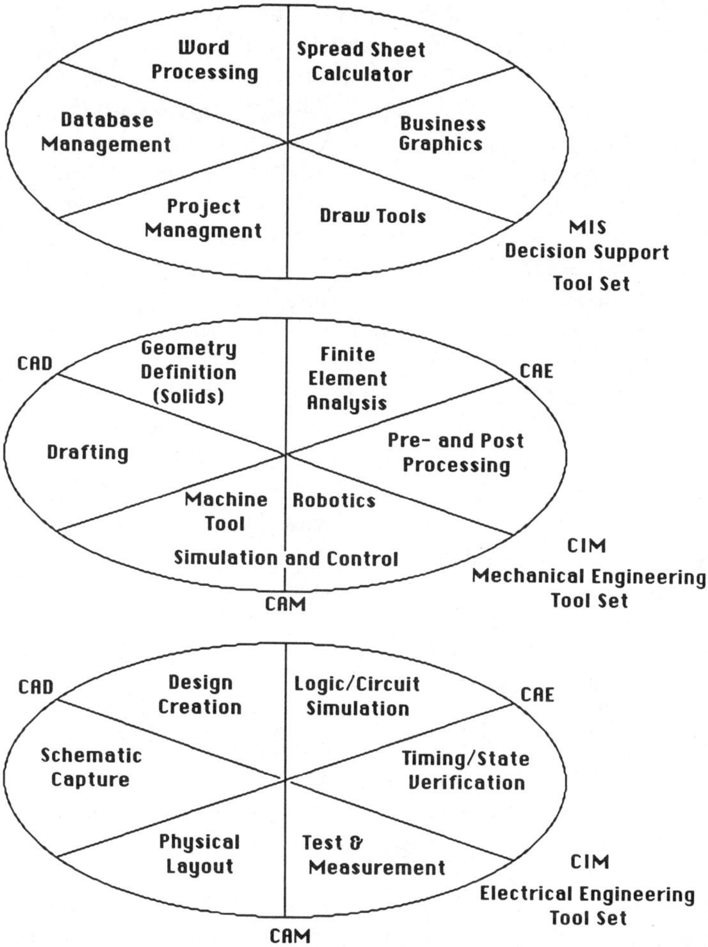


Fig. 8-4. Management Information Systems (MIS) and Computer-Integrated Manufacturing (CIM) tool sets.

hundreds, of bank accounts, which must be constantly juggled to maintain liquid funds for cash flow, while maximizing interest earned on unused finances. The trend is for such a system to be implemented on a microcomputer that dials up a variety of remote bank hosts to obtain account balance information. Knowing which checks have actually cleared and which are still outstanding is vital to keep float to a minimum. Once the spreadsheets are loaded with up-to-date information, the treasurer traditionally studies the financial position and initiates wire transfers to move static funds to higher interest positions. Juggling over 20 bank accounts, with thousands of daily transactions, requires not algorithms but heuristics. Although cash management is a necessity of almost all corporations, once the number of bank accounts has grown beyond a handful then only a highly skilled treasurer with many years of experience can do the job properly. If an expert system is tied into the spreadsheet, however, and it is loaded with the correct rules, then it can point out wise transfers to the treasurer and save considerable time and money. Some of the expert system's work will be to scan the sheet for patterns, while other parts will dwell more on inferencing with bottom-line results. Most spreadsheets have some method of moving data in and out of them (such as DIF created by Visicorp, SYLK pioneered by Microsoft, or variants on plain ASCII). For an interactive cash management tool, file transfer is not enough, because it is desirable to have both the spreadsheet and the expert system concurrently active. Transferring files from *A* to *B* back to *A*—the only possibility in a single-tasking environment—simply cannot provide the desired concurrency. Developers stuck with a single-tasking operating system, such as MS-DOS or CP/M, often end up writing OS extensions to handle multitasking. Even in the multitasking situation the internal code of the spreadsheet must be accessed to make a concurrent tool. It will require a skilled programmer to decode the spreadsheet data strctures and make them accessible to an intermediate module. The UNIX sockets and message queues are powerful methods of interprocess communication that can surpass the basic pipes mechanism for sophisticated integrations. Another approach is to use a low-end Xerox LISP machine, where MS-DOS can be executed along with the LISP environment. In this situation the traditional PC tools, such as Lotus 1-2-3, can still be used, but deep inferencing can be added through concurrent LISP processing.

Project planning interfaces usually can be built to function in a similar "data-stream-in, data-stream-out" mode. For example, an expert system that performs manufacturing resource planning (MRP)/job shop scheduling may need to consult a PERT chart for relevant path features. As timing considerations become increasingly important in automated manufacturing, it is likely that project planning tools will be integrated into more systems. Just as time manufacturing and flexible manufacturing cells are both time-critical operations, so intelligent scheduling is important. Many CIM systems are driven by MRP, and many MRP packages involve scheduling algorithms. What is likely to develop is the connection of MRP packages to sophisticated third-party project planners and the ability to drive both with expert system rules. The task of sequencing a series of machine tool operations is another that is attempted in various embedded pieces of CIM software, but would be better handled with a proven semiautomated project planner. Adding expert system rules to automate these linkages allows proven modules to be coupled with new application areas and at the same time saves reinventing the wheel.

The final tool, the word processor, often has interfaces established with other tools in the business tool set. These interfaces need to be extended to the expert system as well. Generally, these interfaces are one-way: from the graphics, database, spreadsheet, project planner, or draw tools to the word processor (e.g. MS-Word on the Macintosh). Information in the form of graphs, mailing lists, financial reports, planning charts, or drawn figures are passed to the word processor for inclusion in various types of documents. Similarly, results from an expert system consultation may need to be included in reports. Even this type of simple *text merge* can become quite complicated. A case study insurance consultation system produced written letters declaring results to various third parties influenced by the decision. The three main types of letters (by destination) quickly evolved into 30 different variations depending on the type of consultation results. In this case, the problem was not as simple as downloading the information from the expert system to the word processing/printer system. The UNIX tool NROFF was still the primary formatting facility, acting like a word processor, but more flexibility was needed in driving NROFF. The problem was solved by partitioning the letters into clauses, and the clauses were released from the expert system shell according to the inference route and the consultation results. These variable clauses were then inserted into various NROFF templates to provide complete letters. Having solved the letter content issue, the next difficulty was printer output speed, which was solved by adding multiple print queues and additional hardware. After that a new layer of issues arose regarding quality control. Keeping a few dozen letters looking neat and clean is manageable by hand, but when the volume grows into the hundreds, additional software programs were needed to scan for errors and list letters by category.

In Computer Integrated Manufacturing (CIM) applications, tool sets fall into two main categories: mechanical engineering and electrical engineering. Mechanical engineering can encompass structural, civil, and architectural engineering and cartography with the same basic set of tools. Electrical engineering tools are becoming flexible enough to handle digital and analog domains in discrete or integrated and low- or high-current forms. Each category, mechanical or electrical, contains tools used for computer-aided design (CAD), computer-aided engineering (CAE), and computer-aided manufacturing (CAM). Currently the mechanical tool set is in wider use than the electrical tools.

Mechanical CAD is primarily concerned with solids modeling to capture any geometric form and drafting to render the geometric designs on paper. Mechanical CAD applications demand higher resolution graphics than E-CAD, as it displays true-to-life images. Electronic CAD works with symbolic images and can therefore use graphics displays with lower resolution. While an engineer is putting a geometric or circuit design together, he must work within a vast number of constraints. Costs have to be contained. Only parts with an acceptable delivery time can be used. The parts must fit together such that manufacturing assembly and testing is facilitated not hindered. The engineer cannot be expected to have all these constraints in mind at all times, so a concurrent expert advisor can be of value for maintaining quality. As most designs go into a local or central database as they are created, the expert system can access the design data via the database without interfereing directly with the design tools. Workstations, such as Apollo and Sun, offer multiple operating system windows, so that concurrent tasks can be viewed at the same time without necessitating program alterations in the applications program code. Quite a number of CAD/CAE packages take advantage of the windows, especially on Apollo machines, so some of the prerequisites to expert system integration are already in place.

The domain of mechanical CAE tools covers finite-element analysis (FEA) in such areas as structural (static or dynamic), thermal (convection, conduction, radiation, or internal heat generation), fluid flow, and magnetics analysis. Pre- and postprocessing systems are used to define elements and display results. Graphics is a critical tool in CAE, due to the engineer's need to understand complex data structures. Getting the geometric data in and out of these systems is a primary concern. Dividing the pure geometric forms into finite elements is another problem area where expert systems are becoming valuable. There are many ways to dissect one part into elements, and picking the right method can lead to superior results in a fraction of the execution time. As most of these decisions are heuristic, rather than algorithmically based, expert systems can help. Boeing Computer Services in Seattle, Washington, has a sizable department devoted to applying expert systems in engineering, and providing assistance in FEA use is one of their successes. The Boeing innovation advises users of Georgia Tech's GT STRUDL FEA program on such matters as mesh generation and optimization.

The main functions in CAM are controlling machine tools and robotics. The software systems are primarily used for simulation and control programs for machine tools or robots. Other functions, such as hole drilling, welding, assembling parts, spray painting, and routing materials throughout the production line, are also included under CAM. Often islands of automation have been established in manufacturing plants, but computers are needed to make these units more flexible and to link them. Attempts at flexible manufacturing have often been hampered by the need for white-collar workers to make the constant but simple decisions needed to connect these islands. Such decisions tend to be heuristic-based, so traditional software structures have not been successful in bridging the gaps. Teknowledge and the Carnegie Group are two vendors that have been focusing on CIM integrations as a profitable application for expert systems technology. CAD/CAE/CAM integration is further discussed in the next section.

## 8-9. USING EXPERT SYSTEMS TO INTEGRATE OTHER SOFTWARE SYSTEMS

Most of the integration applications described so far have been based on information being channeled to or removed from the expert system. It was found to be necessary that other software systems in the production environment be linked to the expert system via specialized (and, ideally, standardized) interfaces for these information flows to occur. There is, however, a second integration perspective that is relevant to certain more advanced configurations: the expert system is used to link other systems in the production environment.

A good example is the integration of a solids modeler with a machine tool system to create three-dimensional physical renderings of designs.[2] In this application intelligence is needed to (1) map the design from the format of the solids modeler into the often radically different representation scheme used by the machine tool, and (2) to formulate an optimum machine tool path. The cutting process, which is basically described by the tool orientation and velocity at each point in time, can be optimized in many ways. A good path does not contain crashes, does not wear the tool too much, does not overload the motors, provides an acceptable surface finish, and does not take too long.

The internal representation of the solids modeler may take two forms, either boundary-value equations or constructive sequences of how the part is built from geometric primitives. In either instance, surface vectors indicate which parts are hollow and which are not. Machine tool programs, however tend to use older representation approaches, namely surface or wire-frame modeling. Cutter path formulation still requires solid geometric information, but in most existing tool programs this information is supplied by the machine tool expert and not by the geometry-creation process. Formulating tool paths is traditionally done from drafting diagrams, to which the human expert adds considerable world knowledge before results can be obtained. Current programs on the market that attempt to integrate solids with machine tooling tend to start with full geometric descriptions and then compress and summarize them to make them fit the more limited descriptions handled by the tool program. As a third step in this sequence of more going to less, the expert has to reconstruct the "more" using his world knowledge. Creating solid models from wire frames tends to require considerable skill, although some expert automation has been achieved at Lehigh University with POLYGON.

Even if the M-CAD/CAM software preserves solid geometry all the way through its different stages,[3,4] considerable expertise is needed in optimizing the tool path. The various CAD companies centered around Cambridge University in England have been pioneering smart solid-to-solid transfer systems. Several American CIM vendors, namely Computervision (Bedford, Massachusetts), Evans and Sutherland (Salt Lake City, Utah), CIMLinc (Elk Grove Village, Illinois), and Prime Computer (Natick, Massachusetts) have picked up powerful solids-to-tooling programs from Cambridge companies. What is needed next is further intelligence applied to tool-path optimization. Tool-path-determination programs do exist, and some of them, such as Intergraph's (Huntsville, Alabama) provide more optimization than others. If we are to attain machine tools that can run unattended all night, the addition of expert system rules to such programs is desirable.

Two examples of embedded expert systems for CIM use are AutoDesk's (Mill Valley, California) CAD Camera and Daisy Systems Corporation's (Mountain View, California) Testability Analyzer. The CAD Camera is an interesting product, as expert system rules allow it to be simple yet powerful. The product takes raster information from a camera and transforms it into vectors. The main application is taking existing pencil-and-paper drafting diagrams and moving them into AutoCAD where they can be electronically edited. The Versatec Raster Processing Machine mentioned above performs the inverse operation of moving vectors to raster form. To do its work CAD Camera is built around a number of expert system rules that look for standard vector patterns. Not just straight lines, but such other primitives as arcs and circles can be rendered into their AutoCAD forms once recognized by the automated expert. When customers report deficiencies in the program, such as its early tendency to represent one long vector as a series of smaller connected ones, another rule can be added to the system and the problem cured. In this application the expert system is linking a digital camera with a simple CAD program. Users of the system do not see that any expert system is at work, but the overall effect is that images are successfully transformed.

Examples of using expert systems to bridge other classes of software can be found in the MIS areas as well. MIS software might be responsible for condensing data-base personnel information or financial-analysis information into summary reports. The summary information is typically analyzed manually by a manager for particular trends and patterns, which are then often rekeyed into the system to allow sales to be enhanced or manufacturing production increased. In the marketing area, for instance, suppose an enterprise is ready to release a new product, but needs to examine existing customer profiles to determine which current customers are likely buyers for the new product. In an ideal world, the sales database could simply be queried for all previous clients satisfying a given set of specifications. In the real world, however, the indicators of likelihood of purchasing tend to overlap and contradict. Probabilities, sophisticated statistical analysis, and logical inference by the sales manager are necessary to provide judgments with any depth of validity. This prospect qualification is a prime application for an expert system. The system should not only qualify prospective product purchasers, but also perform the central function of linking marketing software and statistical analysis software systems. If the statistical analysis program is allowed to intelligently parse the database, it can first identify the patterns behind past purchases and then apply the criteria to select prospects with high compound certainty factors. The expert system, rather than the human expert, becomes the integrator of the overall MIS system.

## 8-10. POTENTIAL PITFALLS AND HOW TO AVOID THEM

During integration, many previously hidden problems come to the surface, because real-world testing is occurring. Integration can be as complex and expensive as all the preceding phases put together, so considerable planning and attention are required. In this section seven of the common potential pitfalls are touched upon, together with recommended ways to avoid them.

1. Pitfall: Knowledge Bugs. The expert system is basically excellent, but knowledge testing continues to uncover more and more small but unforgivable errors.

   Avoidance. It is best to pick a narrow application and move just one slice into production, rather than attempting to implement a large slice all at once. Phased releases of function also tend to keep users happy, as they get results sooner and their learning curve is not so concentrated. Extensive testing of each step of functionality should commence early in the life cycle. Paper-and-pencil desk testing tends to uncover more bugs in less time than machine testing and should therefore precede machine testing.

2. Pitfall: Supporting Functions Needed. The hub of the expert system functions well, but before it can be put into production it requires several other modules, e.g., data migration from a previous system, enhanced data-base maintenance, activity reporting, and transaction accounting.
   Avoidance. Employ skilled analysts or consultants to identify the necessary suppporting modules as early as possible, so that a headstart can be gained on their design and implementation. In this typical situation it is wise to move the central hub into production anyway, while keeping volumes low, and to use manual handling for the supporting functions.
3. Pitfall: Creeping Featurism. As the system is being developed different members of the team add more and more features. A retrospective analysis of the project plan (if it exists) shows that time is being spent on tasks not originally allocated, and thus the project is running late.
   Avoidance. A functional specification must be written in advance and enforced, to describe the boundaries and content of the application to be implemented. During analysis it is essential to separate "must haves" from "WIBNIFS" (wouldn't it be nice if . . . ). Implementing WIBNIFS is one of the best ways to slow down development and destroy an expert system's cost-effectiveness. Any new vital features that are accepted must be edited into the functional specification.
4. Pitfall: Inadequate Tools. Just when serious progress is being made in implementation and integration, an insurmountable problem is met, and team members suggest changing the tool set.
   Avoidance. Certainly many tools may be inadequate for some jobs. The first step is to qualify the job in advance. Second, if a high-level language interface is available with access to a multitasking operating system, there is almost nothing a skilled programmer cannot accomplish. A general approach, however, is to thoroughly research the options, prototype the application with one or more tool sets, and have a plan for evolving through more than one tool set as the application grows.
5. Pitfall: Lack of Computer Capacity. The steps leading to putting the expert system into production are proceeding well, but suddenly the computer runs out of RAM, MIPS, disk, etc.
   Avoidance. Capacity planning should be done from the very first step of the life cycle. These plans, preferably based on a series of linked spreadsheets, must be continually updated to reflect new understandings. Allocation of resources should be continually

monitored, and care should be taken not to give away resources that will be needed later. MIPS needs and the number of accesses to shared disk servers are two of the more difficult, and therefore problematic, areas to estimate.

6. Pitfall: Interfaces do not work. Development is proceeding well until it is found that there is no reliable way to connect the expert system to the production environment. Either the products do not stand up as advertised, or software integrations are more complex than anticipated.
   Avoidance. File-transfer integrations are easier to implement than real-time ones. Narrower transfers with fewer variables sent less often are simpler to perfect. The number of vendors in the inevitable multivendor environment should be minimized. The various options for integration products should be thoroughly researched before purchases are made. Interfaces should be tested with simple transfers before complex ones are attempted. If a software transform does not function correctly, then (1) redesign the software and if needed, (2) add more layers.
7. Pitfall: Excessive Downtime. Too many crashes occur, and when they happen the windows of contamination are too large, resulting in many faulty data that have to be replaced. When hardware faults are suspected the vendors involved point at each other, saying it is not their fault.
   Avoidance. Change control procedures (e.g., with SCCS), coupled with testing, are the best approach to avoid crashes. Transaction-processing design, so that each atomic update is either 0 or 100% written to disk, helps reduce contamination. The design should keep newly captured data in RAM for as short a time as possible before placing a copy on disk. Modular design, with clean, narrow bandwidth interfaces and redundant integrity validations between modules can also help limit contamination. Fault-tolerant hardware can also be a good investment for many CIM applications. Building custom diagnostic programs is of value to track down and isolate faults. Try to obtain hardware support from a single source, such as Control Data Corporation, which will maintain other vendors' equipment in addition to its own.

Any or all these different pitfalls can cause projects to exceed their money and time budgets. The ability to explain to management what went wrong and why it should not happen again is a key to success in these latter life-cycle stages, as will be discussed in the next chapter.

## 8-11. MAIN POINTS; INTEGRATING EXPERT SYSTEMS IN MIS AND CIM ENVIRONMENTS

Integrating expert systems into mainstream environments, although specifically addressed in this chapter, has been made practical by the many points established throughout the book. If good software-engineering principles have been used at each stage of the life cycle, the expert system can be as well behaved as many traditional programs. Attempting to integrate an experimental prototype that addressed only a small portion of the necessary issues into a high-volume production system is to ask for problems. Some integrations can be simple if the design is crisp, but many require the kind of complexity discussed in the example of the Graphics Print Sybsystem.

- For an expert system to pay for itself, it usually has to become an integral cog in the company's production systems.
- Frequently the inferencing portion of an application needs support from such directions as database management or other existing software systems before it can become useful.
- The three main approaches to expert system billing are
  —per actual transaction
  —potential use, depending on the number of items (e.g., turbines bines) covered or insured through the system
  —per client fee independent of any other factors
- A robust integration architecture is to place the expert system as the hub of a star, with the subsystems each connected by one narrow bandwidth link around it.
- Successful expert systems tend to grow, with both expansion in their own knowledge bases and increases in the number of connected systems.
- There is a remarkable lack of industry standards for interconnecting knowledge bases. As a consequence, integrating several expert systems is frequently difficult.
- Many third-party products are growing up for the interconnection of LISP computers with general-purpose machines.
- Knowledge-base administration (KBA), following the pattern established for data-base administration (DBA), is a vital function for maintaining the integrity of production expert systems.
- The majority of techniques for integrating expert systems into mainstream environments are non-Al approaches (e.g., wide, local, and bus area networks).
- The SMALLTALK message-passing approach allows SMALL-

TALK systems to communicate transparently with a variety of other machines.

- Blackboard architectures are another expert-system-specific approach, where a number of independent actors communicate by writing and reading to a shared area.
- A subsystem for providing hardcopy graphics to show the activity of an expert system may require over 10 layers of hardware and software to map results from the knowledge base onto paper.
- Expert systems provide good opportunities for integrating other classes of software systems, e.g., coupling machine tools with solid modelers or finite element analysis with solids.
- Expert systems also make good advisors for using complex programs, such as those employed for structural engineering analysis.
- This chapter concludes with seven common pitfalls, together with ways to avoid them.

—knowledge bugs
—supporting functions needed
—creeping featurism
—inadequate tools
—lack of computer capacity
—interfaces do not work
—excessive down time

## NOTES

[1] R. T. Fertig and R. G. Bowerman, 1985, *The Software Revolution,* New York: Elsevier and R. G. Bowerman and R. T. Fertig, 1987, *Engineering Workstations: Technlogy and Application Trends,* New York: Van Nostrand Reinhold.

[2] Fully integrated 3D solids modeling systems with complete world models describing all possible surfaces of objects and their potential interactions are still in the area of Al research.

[3] R. G. Bowerman, 1985, "Drafting Links up with Solid Modeling," *Machine Design,* vol. 57 no. 20, September 12, 1985, Penton/IPC, Clinton, OH.

[4] R. G. Bowerman, 1985, "Solid Models Define Finite-Element Geometry," *CAE Magazine,* vol. 4 no. 8, August 1985, Penton/IPC, Clinton, OH.

# Chapter 9
# People Roles in Creating the Production Expert System

## SECTION HEADINGS



## OVERVIEW

This chapter addresses two points: the life cycle phase of moving the integrated tested system into production, and the people roles involved throughout the life cycle. People roles are especially important in this last phase of successful implementation. During this move to production risks are at their highest, so senior management approval and smooth team interactions become more crucial than in any of the previous phases. The human-relations issues are equally important as the technical issues in bringing the expert system into production. Project-organization tips for management are outlined. The job roles necessary for successful completion of the project are reviewed. Expert system development managers have to coordinate and interleave computer technical staff, domain specialists, senior managers, end-user departments, and consultants. Commitment from management to follow through once a project is started is central to success.

## 9-1. STAFF REQUIREMENTS FOR DEVELOPING THE PRODUCTION EXPERT SYSTEM

This chapter continues with the theme of installing the expert system in the real-world production environment after it has passed integration and testing. The technical issues of interfacing the new expert system with other existing software and hardware were outlined in Chapter 8. In this chapter, the human resources involved in various stages of the development of the system, especially the last one, are summarized and the final acceptance and use of the system are examined.

Most software-development life cycles end with the completion of a stand-alone system, but expert systems tend to require continued attention for integration, maintenance, and evolution beyond those needed by the stand-alone system. This final phase is usually more complex than installing standardized software, such as a turn-key accounting package. The custom-built expert system should be treated like a research and development tool (even if it is well-polished) that is now ready for field-testing. This approach demands continued efforts on the parts of the technical staff and the end users to see that the transition from the quiet development state to the fast activity of the corporate environment is smooth, efficient, and effective.

Although the technical aspects of bringing the expert system up to full operational power can be intricate, the people-related issues are even more complex. One reason for the complexity is the increased number of in-house and external personnel involved. A second is the continued reliance on the experts who are the ultimate authorities of the expertise embodied in the system. A third, and key, reason is that the amount of risk usually involved in new and complex expert systems development is considerably higher than for traditional classes of software.

Management commitment is one of the most important requirements for the success of the production system. As noted before, the subtle differences between the expert system development and development of more tried, tested, and proven software technologies demand that management take a different perspective on the expert system development process. There are risks involved. Projects do run over budget. Time schedules do get extended. At any stage along the development life cycle projects may become cost-ineffective and need to be abandoned. The researchlike nature of large expert system developments, even with the aid of sophisticated development tools, presents the genuine possibility that badly managed costs can grow to exceed forecast revenues. Projects can be failures for technical or budgetary reasons. Managers must accept the fact that expert systems technology does not produce instant, snap-together products and therefore must deal with the development risk wisely and patiently.

The duties of a number of the key personnel in expert system life cycles have been outlined in previous chapters. The roles of the knowledge engineer, the domain expert, the overall system designer, and the knowledge-base administrator have been discussed in detail. Figure 9-1 depicts a typical organization structure for these and other key personnel for an *in-house* expert system project team. The domain operations personnel maintain the day-to-day activity in the domain application area, such as handling the routine claims in an insurance company. They will eventually become the end users of the new system. The domain area manager oversees the operation activities of both the human expert and the day-to-day operations. The comparable structure on the software development side consists of programmers, knowledge engineers, an expert system development manager (the project leader), and the corporate software development manager. These two separate divisional entities report to the overall production manager or vice president who correlates and unifies the two divisions' activities.

Independent consultants may be significant adjuncts on both sides of the structure. Domain consultants can assist domain experts in identifying and delineating their specialized knowledge, and expert system building consultants are often indispensable in planning and guiding the

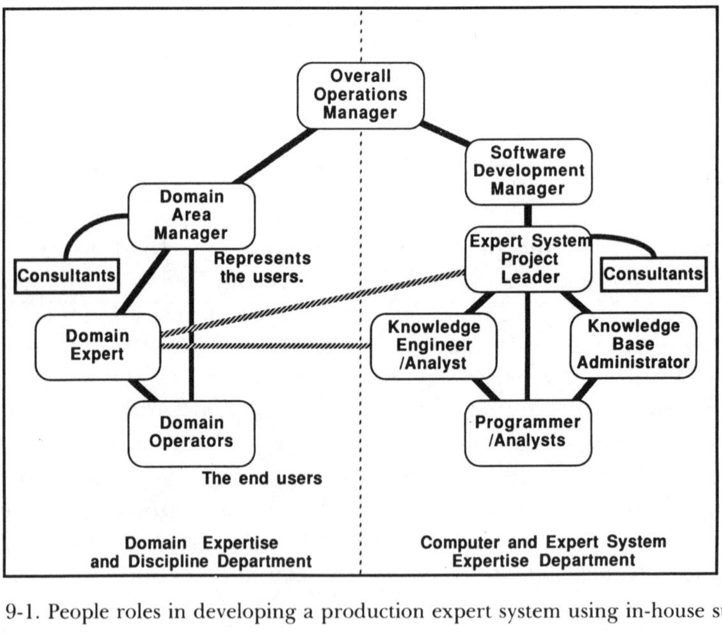


Fig. 9-1. People roles in developing a production expert system using in-house staff.

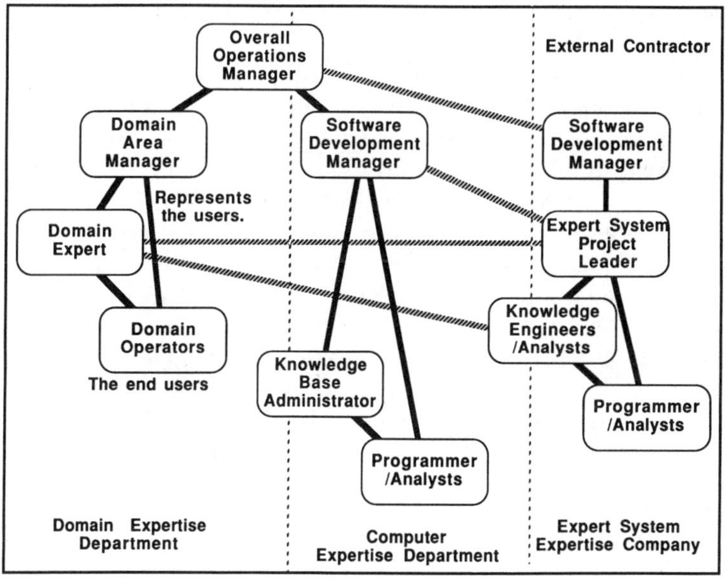


Fig. 9-2. People roles in developing a production expert system using external contractors.

development. Figure 9-2 shows an organizational diagram for development of the expert system by an external contracting or consulting firm.

In expert system development, technical staffing roles are more complex than in traditional software engineering projects, so they must be attended to more carefully. Setting up a conventional database system requires specification of the problem, designing, implementing, and testing the system. Once the system is developed, there is very little need to converse with the original contributors who gave the system its shape. Relational database management (RDBMS) technology, for instance, requires only that the designers specify the fields to be stored and the types of queries that will be needed of the system. Expert system development, in contrast, is not so simple. Even though there is a standard technology underlying the shell tool, the domain knowledge supplied by the expert is anything but standard. Rather than simply specifying fields and query types, the actual structures of the knowledge must be custom-designed by the knowledge engineer. Certainly it can be argued the RDBMSs are flexible, but in contrast it should be understood that expert systems, especially multiple knowledge-representation ones, are considerably more flexible. The commitment of the domain expert is extensive throughout the entire development life cycle and continues beyond installation as the system continues to evolve. Knowledge is far less static than data. Management cannot arbitrarily replace the expert during the development cycle. There may not be another qualified expert available anywhere. Even if other experts can be found, they may have different mental-conceptual knowledge organization patterns not completely consistent with the first expert's framework. (Recall that if an expert system works best with 100 rules, a single expert may only use a subset of 50 of those rules in his or her work.) The same is true for knowledge engineers on the project, once they have begun to develop specialized insights into the domain's knowledge organization. The main point here is that it is not as easy to change personnel in an expert system project as it is in a traditional DP project.

These points in certain ways simply summarize the essential thrust of this book. Expert system development is externally almost identical with traditional software-development projects, but there are subtle differences that make the difference between success or failure.

## 9-2. THE ROLE OF EXPERT SYSTEMS PROJECT MANAGERS

As noted before, expert systems are not plug-in software programs, which can be ordered by a purchasing department and installed 3 months later by a junior operations worker. Word processors and project management tools, in contrast, tend to be fitted into such a category. Certainly expert systems, like spreadsheets or database managers, are empty vessels needing to be filled. The fluid nature of the contents, however, makes managing knowledge-based products more difficult. Expert systems are at the other end of the spectrum from plug-in programs—in the area of custom-built researchlike software projects—and are far removed from the concept of turn-key systems. Expert systems are, in addition, only partially complete when the development has been completed. The finished expert system must then be coaxed out of the isolated development offices into the real world of the production environment. These two primary features of putting expert systems into practice demand that appropriately adjusted management perspectives be employed by administrators of the project.

Unlike traditional software programs, expert systems must be continually guided by management from initial conception to complete integration into the production environment. Initially domain managers may have to convince upper level managers that the development is necessary, but they will not have all the costs to demonstrate economical viability. Almost by definition, only the domain experts will be able to define the details of their application, so that costing requires both divisions; systems and domain. The application itself must be jointly agreed upon by the domain area personnel and the system developers. Budget projections must be drawn up and cost-accounting-evaluation procedures established. The development teams must be established, hiring or relocating personnel as necessary, and contracts with consultants must be drawn up as needed.

Other managerial functions are less obvious but equally important. The political environment of the corporation must be carefully tested to see that the introduction of the expert system will not be unacceptable or violate established policies. The word *policies* sounds pleasanter than *politics* and tends to smooth discussions in this area. Policies should be established to cover such issues as who will be responsible for controlling the system if it crosses over existing organizational (e.g., departmental) boundaries. If the knowledge base contains confidential or sensitive material, will top-level management allow the domain staff to use the system when it is completed? Some policies are often informally stated and enforced, but formalizing them in the knowledge base could be difficult or embarrassing. If the system renders judgments on the effectiveness of employees or departments, its results could affect future appropriations to departments and upset many departmental managers. Will the junior operators resent taking on responsibilities that used to rest with the expert? Will nurses, for example, find it stressful to adapt to using a computer instead of consulting a human doctor? These are some of the policy-sensitive issues that project managers will have to deal with.

Project managers must also assume the role of marketing the system to potential users. In one large industrial environment, production workers stymied the development of expert system projects, for they felt their jobs were being jeopardized. The targeted end-user group must be carefully educated to both the potentials and shortcomings of the expert system to alleviate job security fears. The end-user group must also fully understand that even the most successful systems are limited in scope, need help in handling exceptions, and do not always give optimal or correct results. The need for common-sense checks and balances of expert system results must be carefully explained to domain users. The users of the expert system must have at least some natural enthusiasm for the system, or no amount of management pressure or incentives will make the installation work. Part of the problem of enthusiasm surrounds the issue of establishing the authority and creditability of the system. Doubts about the new technology can be tackled by getting system endorsements by the domain expert and by getting the human expert to assist in training programs for end users.[1]

The four managers shown in Fig. 9-1 for in-house projects are the overall operations manager, the corporate software development manager, the domain area manager, and the expert system development manager (the traditional project manager). The overall operations manager oversees the main two-way split in lines of responsibility, i.e., between the software-development department and the domain-knowledge department. The corporate software development manager is responsible for all software development in the enterprise and must be alert to the special needs of the expert system development. The expert systems development or project manager is next in line under the head of software development. The project manager has responsibility for the actual implementation and for ensuring that resources are channelled to the knowledge engineers and programmers as required. This manager also maintains contacts with the domain manager on the other side of the development team and coordinates the work of outside consultants.

The overall operations manager, the domain area manager, and the software development manager, who are all senior executives, have to be sensitive to the specialized needs of expert system development. In working with more tried and tested technologies (e.g., databases or accounting systems), senior management takes responsibility only for the initial tasks of organizing the project, evaluating resource needs, and approving the schedules and budgets. In most traditional technologies, once the initial planning and budgeting have been completed, the higher level managers are not involved further. The next contact they have with the development team, other than periodic progress reports from the project leader, will be when the finished product is delivered. High-technology projects, like expert systems, however, demand ongoing involvement and commitment from senior management. This involvement means continually assessing project success potential, coordinating resources, and providing visible commitment to finishing the project despite potential time and cost overruns. Schedules do stretch out, and time and cost budget overruns are the norm rather than the exception in expert systems developments, due to the uncertain and variable nature of the problem. Management may be called in on the grass-roots level at any stage of the project to help solidify the uncertain territory inherent in the project's development. In traditional software disciplines, the project leader handles most of these "umbrella" functions, protecting the project team members from outside influences and uncertainties. In knowledge engineering, although the expert systems development manager is the formal project leader, many of the umbrella functions have to go to more senior levels of management. All these guidelines can be seen from the perspective of risk management; it is fortunate that expert systems projects generally have large paybacks to make up for the uncertainties involved.

Continual commitment and support represent one end of the spectrum of management's responsibility. The other end concerns the ability to know when to cancel a development and cut the losses already incurred. This *pull-out point* could occur at any stage of development, from prototyping to middevelopment to the final integration into the production environment. Ideally, technical feasibility, such as problem tractability, is determined early-on, during the prototyping stage. If, however, 500 rules have been developed and integrated into an expert system after 18 man-months of work, and yet there is no glimmer of actually having captured a substantial subset of the domain knowledge, technical feasibility could possibly force abandonment of the project. Interface or integration difficulties of the types described in Chapter 8 could also break the success of a project even at that late stage. The crucial issue in the success of the expert system project, as pointed out in Chapter 3, is choosing an appropriate application problem with a manageable level of difficulty, but a high enough yield to justify the development. The two key issues are technical viability (e.g., number of knowledge chunks, interfaces required, ability to codify knowledge, acceptance of the system) and cost viability. One approach to risk management in this environment is to start more projects than are expected to be supported to completion. The expenses incurred in obtaining good data on the insurmountable complexities of five problems often allow a sixth to become cost-effective.

What are the financial parameters that should bring about project cancellation? If the expense of the system outweighs the expected cost benefits, then development should be aborted. Unfortunately, the experimental nature of expert system development does not always lend itself to clear benefits-accounting until the system is up and running in the production environment. Two commonly used models in system management planning and accounting are known as *cost-benefit monitoring* and *capacity planning and monitoring*. These tools work equally well for expert system development.

Cost-benefit monitoring, usually done on spreadsheets, provides a technique for continually accessing the relationship among three elements; the development cost to date, the projected overall cost, and the estimated benefits. The project life cycle, with extensions for actual production, is broken down into small task steps, each with a cost or benefit. These dollar figures are based on different expenses that could occur and on the cost benefits that could accrue (i.e., ways the system could save or earn the corporation money). Often a task will have several cost elements plus several savings or earnings. These cost-estimate breakdowns should be revised monthly or quarterly, as new financial data becomes available. The bottom line is either a payback period or a return on investment, and after that comes a single spreadsheet cell that says "go" or "stop."

For the oil refinery steam turbine vibration analysis expert system used in previous examples, these production money savers might be: (1) outside maintenance is no longer needed; (2) fewer large parts need replacement, due to more frequent inspections; (3) decreased inspection and maintenance labor time is needed; and (4) increased computerized inspection results in less downtime. Indirect benefits may also be identified, but frequently these are intangibles and more difficult to characterize in dollar amounts. One example might be a reduced work load for the personnel manager—freeing more time for other activities. Another example of an indirect benefit could be the attraction of the production expert system to potential employees. The brightest, highest caliber college graduates tend to seek work environments that use the latest high-technology tools. Increasing the corporation's prestige and prime-employee-drawing ability are indirect but tangible benefits that are difficult to evaluate in dollars.

Cost-benefit data elements should be combined using probabilities of event occurrences. Note that these probabilities are handled by the cost-benefit monitoring spreadsheet, not by the expert system itself. For the steam turbine diagnostic expert system, there are a number of ways that the turbine can break down and affect the corporation. Some of these events, such as simultaneous breakdown of all steam turbine pumps at a refinery resulting in total loss of production income, are given extremely high cost estimates and very low probability of occurrence. Direct costs (such as salaries) are given a definite (probability-1) assignment. Indirect costs, such as the total loss of corporate product and income, have their own probabilities. As the project develops, the probabilities of such catastrophic events occurring approach zero, and their net effect in the equations is effectively eliminated, and then an indirect cost benefit accrues from reducing the potential of such occurrences.

At the beginning of development, data for the real costs and perhaps even for potential cost benefits are sparse. Projections dominate the spreadsheet at this stage. As the project progresses, the spreadsheet can provide more accurate assessments of the cost benefits of the project as real data replace the projections. Suppose the equations contain 20 candidate costs ranging across several orders of magnitude. Perhaps 6 of these costs are ruling the equations at the initial stages of development. As the development continues, however, the dominating factors may change. At project completion, a completely different set of 4 factors may be dominating the cost analysis. If the planning tool was not used, the project could have been cancelled after its initial basis was disproven, but if track is kept of all the potential benefits, certain cancellations may be avoided. A general rule of thumb for managers wishing to sell expert systems development to their superiors is to "maintain a lot of fat" to preserve cost-effectiveness ratios. If the model starts by indicating a 2:1 return on investment, there is plenty of room for erosion down to a 10% profitability figure. If, however, the model maker permitted only a 10% figure to start with, there would be little room for project slippages and cost overruns. As expert systems are a new and successful technology, good implementations (i.e., ones that follow the type of guidelines presented in this book) can often obtain many times the return on investment possible from traditional tools tackling the same application problem. The situation is akin to mining where a mineral bed has been known of for a long time, but only now have the tools become available to extract the ore. In this analogy the mineral bed may be oil refinery, oil loss problems, or health care costs, and the ore extracted by expert system tools is dollars.

The second tool, capacity planning and monitoring, operates under similar principles, but with resource analysis rather than cost analysis as the primary objective. Much has been said about tracking disk, RAM, CPU, MIPS, and so on in Chapters 4, 5, 6, and 8. As is true for the cost-benefit analysis, no all-purpose spreadsheet template exists, as each expert system application is different. What is needed is consultants or other engineers who have a broad base in computer and business matters to draw up appropriate spreadsheet models for the application at hand. Just as senior management should pay regular attention to the cost-benefit model, so also should it monitor the deployment of system resources. Expert system implementations have a greater tendency than other classes of software to consume excessive resources and to expand their needs suddenly in some particular direction. Certainly capacity planning feeds into the cost-benefit analysis, but instead of looking only at the financials, these computer constraints can give better early warnings of problematic areas.

## 9-3. THE ROLE OF KNOWLEDGE ENGINEERS AND PROGRAMMERS

The primary duties of knowledge engineers for an expert system development project have been highlighted throughout the book. The job has been presented as similar to, but subtly different from, the traditional role of the systems analyst. This "expert in expert systems technology" must function both as a systems analyst to design knowledge structures relevant to the problem and also as a codifier of the human knowledge extracted from the domain expert. The knowledge engineer must be multitalented, able to communicate effectively with the domain expert; extract the relevant chunks of knowledge from interviews, procedure observations, books and manuals; codify this knowledge in a machine-acceptable form; and verify the knowledge through continual testing and refinement. The knowledge engineer and the domain expert should work well together as a team and thoroughly enjoy the knowledge-development process.

One of the first things managers who are building a team will notice is that experienced knowledge engineers are in short supply and hard to find. As can be seen from the product comparison matrix in Chapter 5, the total number of expert system tools sold is roughly estimated at under 2000. Most of the tools for which sales figures are not released are very new, and volumes can be expected to match their peers who do announce figures, with 15 to 50 units. Certainly the main volume leaders, ESP/Advisor, Expert Ease, and Insight could bolster these totals with 5000 or more units if one is flexible about definitions. From the perspective of estimating the number of knowledge engineers, expert shells that do not handle uncertainty are not strictly to be classed as expert systems. Even giving a conservative upper limit, the total is still under 5000 units sold. From that figure all the packages that have been purchased for curiosity or experimentation should be removed from the count. Some packages may have been employed by several people, but some knowledge engineers will have worked with several packages. Probably under 25% of the purchased shells have been put to enough use to qualify the developer as a knowledge engineer. DuPont Corporation is reported as having 500 knowledge engineers by Level Five Research following the sale of a corporationwide INSIGHT license. The bottom line for someone trying to recruit skilled knowledge engineers is that there are probably under 2000 candidates to choose from worldwide. Contrast this figure to Bank of America's employment of 2000 traditional programmer/analysis in San Francisco alone.

Even inexperienced university graduates with some training in this direction are snapped up into corporate or industrial/research positions immediately. This shortage of knowledge engineers is likely to continue into the foreseeable future, as expert system developments begin to proliferate throughout industry. Obtaining knowledge-engineering help from expert system consulting firms becomes one of the most reasonable alternatives. The other conclusion is that all work that can be delegated to analysts and programmers should be, saving the knowledge engineer's time for work that needs his skills. Another emerging trend, as noted in Chapter 7, is the likely division of the non-computer-technical-knowledge-acquisition responsibilities from the implementation-oriented systems analysts' and programmers' functions.

Where are the engineers today? A system developer cannot just advertise in a newspaper for 6 experienced knowledge engineers and receive 50 qualified responses overnight. It would be very rare to find a team of skilled engineers who have worked together on expert system projects, except for project teams at a few select universities, research institutes, large corporations, or consulting firms. Most knowledge engineers who are not independents or consultants can be found in one of two places. The first is a comfortable position in a large corporation that is investing in expert systems technology, such as Boeing, Harris, Westinghouse, or DuPont, where all the resources desired by the engineers are at hand. The other place knowledge engineers gravitate is small entrepreneurial concerns. These concerns offer little comfort, as the risks are high, and there is no padding between the engineers and the competitive world. Knowledge engineers in large corporations tend to move from employer to employer, even as frequently as every 6 months, to gain increases in compensation and standing. Start-up companies, however, retain their knowledge engineers longer, but even they lose their engineers if major projects meet with failure and funding dries up. Thus the knowledge engineering market is volatile.

As in any software-development project, the too-many-chiefs-and-not-enough-Indians syndrome can occur in expert systems. There is a need for programmers and analysts to back up the knowledge engineers and experts. Programmers are needed to take the specifications generated by the knowledge engineer (or systems analyst) and do the actual coding in the expert system building tools. This programming work, although not described in detail in this book, is expected to occur during the knowledge-capture and codification phase of the life cycle. The usual analyst-programmer teamwork approach is applicable here. Programmers will need training in using the tools selected for the project and thus should attend appropriate vendor classes. If the programmers are from the traditional DP schools, they will need additional training in the principles of AI prior to training with specific expert system building tools. Fortunately, the burgeoning interest in AI has resulted in an increasing availability of collegiate AI courses offered by university computer science departments. Recent computer science college graduates (undergraduate or graduate) are likely to have had at least some exposure to AI programming techniques and methodologies.

Figure 9-1 shows the expert system development teams clearly divided into two camps: the application problem domain team and the expert system software development team. In some situations it will be tempting to try to combine the roles of knowledge engineer and domain expert. This option might occur if the domain expert has some computer background, or if the knowledge engineer has some previous experience with the domain problem area. It is a rare individual, as discussed earlier, who can perform both jobs well at the same time. On the domain side, expert-level problem solving is basically holistic and intuitive. On the knowledge engineering side, the process is one of deep analysis and synthesis of knowledge structures, often using suitable computer-oriented models that have little resemblance to the expert's own introspectively perceived patterns of problem solving.

Expert system tool vendors sometimes use their product's "high-level user interfaces" as a selling point for the package. Advertisements claim or suggest that users can build their own expert system without prior knowledge of expert systems technology, AI, or even traditional computer practices. They suggest that domain experts can create their own rules, program them into the system, test the results, and rapidly produce full-scale production systems. This approach may be possible for less complex applications, but it can fall far short in producing a real-world production-quality expert system. This same end-user-as-computer-specialist approach has not been overly successful with fourth-generation programming languages (4GLs). Although 4GLs have been accepted as productivity boosters for MIS work, MIS heads have now abandoned earlier vendor claims that these tools can be employed by unskilled end users to develop applications. Certainly end users can attempt to develop part or all of a software system, but the background for good, sound programming practices and software-engineering techniques is usually missing. Systems developed by end users were found to lack the robustness to last for more than even a few months, before data integrity issues brought the program to a halt. Untrained users do not generally see the need for standards, data integrity, backup files, and validation procedures for data entry as central elements of a solid, professional software system. In addition, thorough software testing procedures to prove program correctness are far beyond the capabilities of the casual end user cum designer of a system. In the same way, untrained domain experts cannot be expected to understand the underlying symbolic-representation structures of knowledge engineering tools without the appropriate base-level computer science and AI training.

Programmers play a vital role in expert system development, as in any software development project. Although expert system shells require considerably less programming than a project written in a symbolic, fourth-generation, or high-level language, extensive programming can still be expected. The type of programming involved is writing key words and operators out in the various command languages of the tools employed. Writing out expert system rules, inferencing control structures, setting parameters to determine chaining and probability protocols, and interfacing with the other tools can use up thousands of lines of code. Operating system shells and integrated databases can also consume a few thousand lines of software in production expert applications. It should be possible to remain with under 10,000 lines of software, which may be an order of magnitude less than writing the same functionality from the ground up, but that is still an appreciable amount of code. A viable approach is for the knowledge engineers to direct the analysts and for the analysts to direct the programmers. Usually the programmers do not need knowledge skills to join the project, as knowledge engineers must. The programmers need to be willing to learn and should display a commitment to making their software work, irrespective of technical difficulties. In these new technology projects it is inevitable that a variety of barriers will be encountered. What is needed is an engineering team that is used to breaking boundaries and finding solutions to seemingly intractable problems.

## 9-4. THE USE OF CONSULTANTS

Two potential classes of consultants for expert system development were shown in Fig. 9-1. The first and most obvious class represents the expert system building experts. The other class of adjunct consultants can benefit the project by aiding domain experts in the exposition and development of the corpus of domain knowledge. Because knowledge engineers are so few, many of them do not stay long with one employer or client, but rather are independent, servicing several clients through consulting services.

The value of using external consultants in large-scale, high-risk business ventures has been well documented. It is generally agreed that a consultant's ability to proceed directly to the heart of the problem is well worth the extra cost to the corporation. Consultants all have their specialties, so the key is finding ones that match the needs of the situation. In addition to the specific skills, quite a few consultants are flexible generalists within, say, the area of advanced computer systems ranging from micros to minis to mainframes. In general, the more nonstandard a project is, the more it pays to use the expertise of knowledgeable consultants, rather than expending time and energy of corporate officials to try to gather the full-time employees needed to start a project from scratch. The researchlike or near-experimental nature of expert system developments definitely fits this pattern. Currently available in-house, high-technology software experts without expert systems training will not be able to provide the necessary knowledge and guidance. The subtleties of knowledge engineering and expert system development are not apparent to the uninitiated, and mistakes in the development process can jeopardize the entire project's success. It is better to avoid this scenario by wisely engaging professionals with demonstrated capabilities for advice and construction.

A common question asked by executives is where to find competent consultants. Good consultants are expected to be well-established in their field and recognized by the industry for their skills. Many computer consultants are found through recommendations from other computer professionals who themselves have reached leading positions in the industry. People at the top of the computer profession are frequently asked to recommend a good consultant for this or that situation. In addition to personal recommendation, there are other more objective ways of finding the needed consultants. A good approach is to create a card file of expert system specialists from the trade press. Authors of articles or books, people who speak at conferences, those who give courses, and those mentioned in other articles are often subject to requests for consulting services. The buyer should look for people who appear to think consistent with the buyer's viewpoint. Sales representatives and other company representatives, at such forums as trade shows, are usually asked where knowledgable individuals can be found to support the products they are selling. A common attitude of executives buying consulting services is that they want the best. They wish to know who is at the top of the computer profession in this area and then how can they be contacted.

A caution with respect to the sources of expert system consultants is that many of the candidates are university professors who have been researching knowledge-based systems. The difficulty is that they may not have as much exposure to commercial production environments as is desirable. Although these consultants have an expressed interest in seeing the corporation's project succeed, they often have a strong subconscious commitment to their personal research interests. The main thrust of basic research-oriented work is to publish the results of new knowledge development. The publish-or-perish pressure can cause the consultant to focus more on the basic research and remain insulated from the applied elements necessary to see the corporation's project succeed. It is the responsibility of the project manager to ensure that the corporation is not sponsoring the professor's own research project at the expense of addressing the production environment's needs.

One further point on the sources of consultants is that because expert systems technology is so new the engineers with hands-on production experience tend to be found in small companies rather than large. As was mentioned earlier, knowledge engineers tend to exist in either comfortable positions in large corporations or in entrepreneurial positions in start-up businesses. Those available for hire are almost exclusively the ones working in the small companies, companies that tend to be either product- or service-oriented. To illustrate the small company point, observe that the vendor that has sold the most expert system shells, Level Five Research, has probably not exceeded a cumulative gross income of about $330,000 on shell sales since its conception in 1984. The figure is estimated from approximately 3500 sales of its early product, which cost under $100. Certainly for such a software house, which now has grown to 10 employees, the prospects for the future appear excellent, but from the broad view of American business these products and related companies are still in their infancy. Most other expert shell vendors selling smaller volumes at higher prices, such as Radian, Silogic, and California Intelligence, still tend to come in with gross revenues of under $500,000, apart from a few exceptions, including Inference Corp., Teknowledge, and LISP Machines. Those corporations, such as General Research and Teknowledge, that appear to have larger revenues than is to be expected from their software sales generally earn them by selling consulting services. Even these, in the scale of American business, are classed as small businesses.

Expert system building consultants can provide a number of valuable services for clients, ranging from preliminary application-feasibility analysis to complete expert system building and installation. Consulting firms can usually supply knowledge engineers to work in-house within the corporation if desired. Another consulting pattern is to visit to find out the problems and then visit again later to present the solutions. Because more help is often needed in the start-up stages of the development lifecycle, consultants can be employed to fill in the knowledge and personnel gaps of these appropriate times. In addition, expert system work may be sporadic within a corporation rather than continual as in most DP developments. Corporations may thus avoid the overhead of supporting permanent knowledge-engineering staff without continuous project work by using consultants. Consultants can also function as advisors and provide training in using expert system building tools if necessary. Getting consultants to train in-house staff is one excellent way to preserve the investment.

Whereas consultants are a near necessity for any serious development project where the corporation does not have the properly trained personnel, consultant advisors in developing the structure of the domain knowledge can also be a boon. These consultants may be particularly important for domain areas where the knowledge has had little codification to date. Specialists can assist the company expert in mapping out the regions of the domain knowledge and thereby greatly reduce the concentrated efforts of the knowledge engineer and domain expert. These domain specialists should not be expected to have the specific knowledge-representation schemes in mind, but will work on the overall generic structure of the knowledge.

A final topic concerns mistakes most commonly made by executives purchasing consultants. In other words, how can the executive protect himself from risk? One of the best safeguards is the "salami purchase" strategy, where one "thin slice" is bought at a time. The suggested approach is to start by signing consultants for a 5 or 10-day fixed-limit contract, basically to evaluate how well they perform. Do not sign a 3-month or open-ended contract without experience of the consultant's skill. It is quite common for knowledgeable buyers to retain two or even three consultants, unknown to the other consultants, to work on the same project. Such parallel studies have the powerful effect of increasing the objectivity of the findings. One of the most highly desirable consultant qualities is objectivity, so it is wise to check that the selected individuals are not associated with a particular computer vendor or value-added reseller. Having a series of short contracts, say of 20 working days each, each with specific goals, is an excellent way to get value for money. Consultants who are not objective can be quickly identified in this way and their effect on the project removed without the need for any embarassing contract terminations or morale-damaging confrontations. Studies that are allowed to drag on, especially ones that evaluate too many alternatives, tend to waste funds and not yield the crisp results needed. The short trial study tends to work better than the formal request-for-proposals (RFP) with their resultant canned proposals full of "boiler plate" paragraphs pulled off word processors. Many large consulting houses tend to be good at writing polished proposals, but these corporate efforts give little indication of the skill of the individual to be retained. A common trick in these canned proposals is to use the good résumés to get the job and then switch to less experienced consultants to do the job. Many of the good smaller consulting firms, in contrast, are too busy servicing their existing clients to write detailed proposals. These busy people can best be evaluated via recommendations or by retaining them to perform a short trial study. As a concluding piece of advice, true for any field, it is best to retain busy professionals, not those who appear to have plenty of unoccupied time.

## 9-5. MANAGEMENT STRATEGIES TO RELATE TECHNICAL STAFF AND END USERS

The project personnel tree of Fig. 9-1 contains the technical computer staff on one side and the domain expert plus potential end users on the other side. The figure has been purposely drawn in this forked way to illustrate the gap existing between the two branches. The knowledge engineer's role is to bridge the gap between the two camps—those who know primarily about computers and expert system technology on the one side and those who know primarily of the domain knowledge on the other. These two different groups often have different world views and speak different languages based on their backgrounds. Most computer projects have some communication gap, where systems-analysis techniques are the bridging vehicle, but with expert systems the need to go into such domain detail makes the gap wider. Clear communication across the professional barriers is essential for the successful implementation of the system. It is the job of managers to ensure that powerful, effective communication techniques are being used.

Verbal communication has its limitations in this scenario. The two groups speak languages native to their disciplines, and the common intersection of their technical verbal-based knowledge areas may be quite small. Written communications may not be much better for similar reasons. Even if a standard format for presenting and discussing the knowledge is used, reading lengthy reports in another discipline's language can be ominous. The end result is that such writeups are often read either superficially or not at all. Management must accept the challenge of finding ways to promote and enhance communication. Typically this involves the use of diagrammatic or graphical display aids that transcend language and conceptual barriers.

The different diagrams found throughout this book provide examples of more graphical modes of communication. Although there are various structured approaches to systems-analysis diagrams from such authors as Yourdin, DeMarco, and Martin, in expert systems it is often best to make up diagrams as the need arises. The basic need is to get the facts from the expert's head and place them on a white board where they can be discussed and analyzed. Diagrams may take many forms, such as maps, professional drafting layouts, architects' plans, finite element meshes, relational tables, and networked schemas. The need is to find the appropriate diagrammatic mechanism that can be mutually understood and works for the domain being discussed. Figure 9-3 provides an example of a common interface accessible to both sides.

Another useful technique for removing the barriers between the two personnel divisions is to allow them to temporarily switch roles. This approach has already been suggested for the knowledge engineer, who will most likely spend time reading in the general domain area and then the specific problem application. The next stage of familiarization often includes casual conversation with those working in the field, including the experts and their staffs. Finally, the knowledge engineer is ready to pursue the interviewing and debriefing process as required. In this way, the knowledge engineer gains a basic understanding of the field and

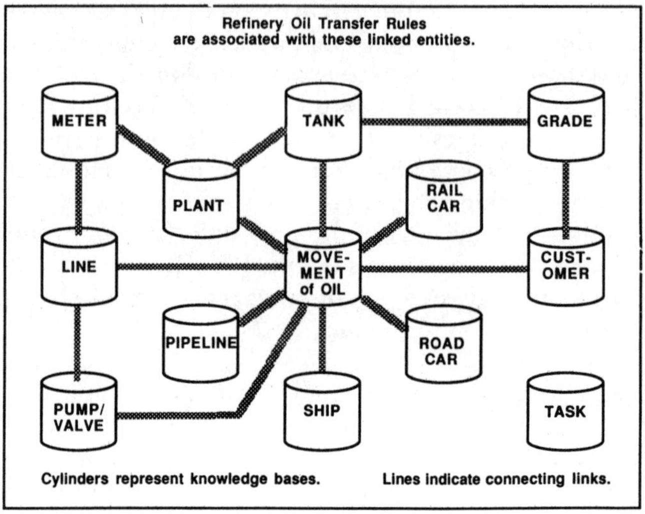


Fig. 9-3. A sample diagram comprehensible to both sides of the organization.

how knowledge is organized within the field. This shallow expertise is used as the basis for drawing out and codifying the deeper aspects of the domain knowledge. At a less involved level, the same kind of introduction to the discipline for the expert system development project manager can be invaluable. It is suggested that this manager spend at least half a day observing the domain experts in action to gain a better understanding of the problem-solving protocols.

On the other side, the domain experts and operations personnel can benefit from a short introductory course in expert systems technology and development. This education will help make formal the chunks of knowledge and also generate a realistic set of expectations for the benefits and capabilities of the system. End-user evaluation of prototype systems also provides them with experience and training before the production system is ready for use. Although exposure to prototypes is valuable, the users should be provided with good "running" software employing debugged interfaces and not be burdened with technical details beyond their interest or understanding. If this point is not adhered to, the exercise, with so many potential benefits, can turn into a disaster that alienates the potential users.

Role reversal is another powerful means of integrating the two diverse factions of the expert system project personnel. It can break down barriers to communication and knowledge through direct experience. On large technical projects it is not uncommon for the project manager to set up workshops to develop team communication skills in the early phases of the project. The result is smoother human interactions and a more productive development environment.

## 9-6. HANDLING EXCEPTIONS IN THE ON-LINE ENVIRONMENT

The narrow range of knowledge incorporated into expert systems means that problems will arise that the systems cannot handle. In such cases, the system must be robust enough to identify these situations and notify the system operator that special attention is needed. This special handling requires that the user of the system be capable of making the proper judgments of what should be done about exceptions.

The expert system for police car dispatch, discussed earlier, illustrates a standard approach to manual special handling for exceptions. The basic formula is that analysis too complex for the system is singled out for "chief of police review," that is, review by the chief of police or a group of officers acting on his behalf. Even more serious cases have higher levels of referral. Another class of exception handling results in a "second opinion" request by the expert system if the program knows that it is about to reach a not-too-firm or dubious conclusion. Second opinions play the vital role of bringing human expertise into play in complex situations that are beyond the capabilities of the machine. Even if the machine becomes quite refined, there is still a moral and legal issue that someone somewhere has to take responsibility and be responsible for the machine's actions.

For each special case the expert system is notifying the system user that the attention of the original expert is needed. This requirement is typical for many real-world expert systems. The expert system will be able to manage 90–95% of the cases presented, but the other 5–10% must be referred to the expert. If the original expert is not available, then it is common to allocate a team of deputy experts to provide judgment. It is vital that managers carefully establish procedures for handling the exceptions, such as how to reach the appropriate expert in times of need. These procedures are particularly relevant when time is critical or life is in jeopardy (e.g., a patrol car dispatcher or a hospital admission approver).

One of the key restrictions of expert systems technology, as noted in Chapters 1 and 3, is the difficulty in error discovery in the logic of the domain knowledge. The development team cannot anticipate every possible query that will be submitted to the system. Some requests will not be handled gracefully, perhaps even moving the software into an endless loop or other failure condition. Just as in the case of straightforward, algorithmic data-processing systems, the development team or software company cannot be expected to test all the myriad conceivable test cases. Even a 1000-line computer program can have more paths from its input to its output than there are stars in the skies or seconds in the life of the universe. Even if the software engineers were somehow able to perform one test every second, the universe does not exist long enough to allow all the tests to be completed. The combinatorial explosion that governs software branching and therefore testing means that any piece of software still has innumerable untested pathways, and therefore possible bugs. Expert systems are no exception to this rule.

The custom-built nature of complicated and sophisticated production expert systems makes verification of software even more difficult than with DP programs. In the expert system scenario, a further source of bugs is that the initial knowledge supplied by the human expert may be in error. A system built with some faulty knowledge premises is not likely to always infer valid results. Knowledge engineers cannot be held responsible for these conceptual errors if the fault lies in the expert's perception of what the knowledge is. Due to these various reasons, human checking of any result that appears to be the slightest bit strange is advised. Allowing expert systems to act as independent agents, especially if their peripherals could in any way be dangerous, is therefore also not advised, except within the most limited and contained environments.

The system operators must be properly trained to deal with the unavoidable exception conditions. The approach may be as simple as entering additional data into the system and restarting the analysis, or it may require consulting a senior staff member or an actual domain expert. Whatever the specific expert system is, operators must be trained to handle exceptions quickly and efficiently according to the demands of the application area.

## 9-7. FROM THE DEVELOPMENT LAB TO THE PRODUCTION ENVIRONMENT

As noted in the overview and in Chapter 1, the current chapter also covers the last stage of the life cycle: putting the completed expert system into production. Advising on this last phase is really quite simple: If no mistakes have been made in earlier phases, there is almost nothing to do. If mistakes have been made, they will tend to surface at this time, and the consequence is that some piece of the work will have to be redone. It is also true that unnoticed changes in the environment while the product was being developed can result in some reworking. Communication, as mentioned before, is therefore key. The system under development should constantly be tested against recent real-life situations throughout the life cycle, first on paper and later on the computer, to avoid subsequent mistakes with demoralizing consequences.

More specifically, if the machine passes all the rigorous integration-phase tests, it should be expected to stand up in the production environment. Training, documentation, and establishing operational procedures to surround the production system are the three main tasks of this phase. Training and documentation should follow the same approaches as for conventional software, and procedures, notably those for exceptions, have been discussed above. Ideally the system has been designed to be self explanatory, with "How," "Why," and "Help" provisions, geared to novice and skilled users. Certainly if the user interfaces have not been designed to be easily understood by the operators of the system, further training will be needed. Gentle introductions, without the full pressure of a production environment all in one day, is the best approach.

*Phased release of function* is the technique that has been advocated to cope with many of these problems. This technique allows the domain expert and the end users to have continual exposure to the system as it develops. Some of the tested prototypes should be released for limited use in the field. This technique also facilitates feedback from users and managers, which can help to optimize the system design, especially as the needs of the company change or are perceived in a deeper light during the software's development. The phased release plan also serves another important function for the technical development personnel: it helps them to focus their attention both on the development-laboratory setting and the real-world-production setting. Such an approach avoids an ivory tower isolation where the knowledge becomes disconnected from its organizing power. By emphasizing communication and sequential unfolding of function the system's knowledge base can become the company's organizing power.

One final user benefit to add to all the many words of advice presented so far is to present a bottle of champagne to the first operator to process a genuine live inquiry on the system the day it goes into production. If the system is used by telephone operators handling telephoned inquiries from remote clients, those minutes waiting for the first call and the imminent opening of the bottle can be a very exciting time.

## 9-8. MAIN POINTS: PEOPLE ROLES IN CREATING THE PRODUCTION EXPERT SYSTEM

The essential point for the start-up phase of expert system development is that any task that has not been done properly in the earlier phases will simply have to be done correctly now. As many previous expert system developments have occurred without life cycles or methodologies, it is understandable that their start-up phases were long and drawn out. This chapter could have detailed such approaches as field-testing, beta-site testing, live testing, production testing, and parallel running, but in our experience, if efficient methodologies are used in the earlier phases, many of the later complexities can be avoided.

- The primary theme of this chapter is to provide project organization tips for all phases of the life cycle.
- Genuine test cases freshly taken from the production environment should be submitted to the expert system regularly—at every stage of the lifecycle.
- Although the technical issues of bringing an expert system into production may be intricate, the people issues tend to be more complex.
- Senior management may view laboratory research as a low-risk activity, but as soon as the system impacts production it becomes the center of many people's attention.
- Management commitment means sticking with the project when time and cost overruns occur—as long as the total investment is still cost-effective.
- Cost-benefit monitoring should be performed monthly or quarterly to ensure that the development is still going to be cost-effective.
- Capacity planning and monitoring are valuable for detecting the early signs of increased risk, which, if allowed to grow, can get out of hand and jeopardize the project.
- The expert system project manager has to bridge the gap between the domain expert's area and the computer professional's area.
- Executives above the project manager should give more attention to expert system projects than to traditional software developments, as there are more unknowns and risks involved.
- Skilled knowledge engineers are in short supply. There may be as few as 2000 worldwide.
- New computer science graduates usually have at least some exposure to expert systems techniques and methodologies.
- A support group of programmers and analysts should be on the project team to make best use of the knowledge engineer's and expert's time.
- Outside consultants provide a valuable option for knowledge engineering tasks. Many of the expert system experts are not available to hire as employees, but are willing to work as consultants.
- Full-time experts will often have to be allocated to a production expert system to address the special exception cases that come up.

- Phased release of function lowers the risk of putting expert systems technology into production.
- A bottle of champagne presented to the operator who handles the first live consultation the day the system goes into production is a good way to boost morale and make the users enthusiastic about the system.

## NOTES

[1] An elaboration of these points is found in David Prerau's article "Selection of an Appropriate Domain for an Expert System", *The AI Magazine*, Vol. 6, No. 2, Summer 1985, pp. 26–30.

# Chapter 10
# Conclusions and Future Trends

## SECTION HEADINGS



## OVERVIEW

Should an expert system implementation commence now, or is it better to wait for more sophisticated technology? Much depends on the application, but an informed decision demands familiarity with projected future trends. Key trends and factors that are expected to influence near and more distant future expert systems technologies are outlined here. These concepts range from continued linear developments in the expert system tool market to new futuristic AI paradigms, perhaps based on technologies of consciousness. The immediate future topics covered provide practical guidelines for the expert system developer who is considering applications now or in the next few years. Weaknesses in current products and future enhancements indicated by vendors provide a window into the immediate future. Medium-future trends draw from extrapolations of today's product and implementation patterns and analysis of current A1 research fields. These changing technology patterns, forecasts, and suggestions are provided as an aid to decision making for putting expert systems into practice within traditional MIS and CIM computer science frameworks.

## 10-1. WAIT FOR BETTER TOOLS OR LEAP NOW?

The detailed "immediate" future is usually easier to forecast than a detailed "distant" future, for as the vision is projected further and further ahead, extrapolation based on current and near-future events and predictions becomes much more speculative, philosophical, and abstract. This limitation is particularly true of the search for more intelligent machines, because the field is developing so rapidly and innovations yet to occur could drastically alter detailed projections. The trends of the more distant future, although not easily extrapolated from current science and technology, contain a type of expected certainty concerning the directions intelligent machines will take. Although the ends are fairly clear, the means are open to speculation. The first chapters presented a pragmatic overview of the managerial and technical strategies necessary to implement expert systems. This final chapter presents a series of short, medium, and longer term forecasts and speculations intended to point out a few of the key future trends for expert system and AI technologies. Some of the points discussed will be obvious, others will require a little more extrapolation, and some are relatively futuristic, provided as food for thought for the imaginative.

The organization of this book has been to start with higher level or more abstract descriptions, more into the details in the middle, and then return to the whole at the end. Starting and ending with the "big picture" allows the reader to view the parts in the context of the whole.

The discussion in Chapter 1 began with a description of expert systems technology, its capabilities, and its current limitations. The philosophical exposition on the nature of intelligence and consciousness presented in Chapter 2 outlined the fundamental difficulty in making machines intelligent. These two chapters compared expert systems technology development with the concepts of human knowledge. Chapters 3 and 4 began the "inward dive" to increasingly concrete levels of detail. The application selection process was seen in the light of capabilities and limitations presented earlier, as well as in respect to specific tool selection characteristics. Chapter 5 came right down to "street level," with an analysis of the actual tools on the market, and Chapter 6 started the move outward again by stepping back to look at the whole of the expert system configuration. The remaining three chapters continued the "outward stroke" in the direction of higher level advice for capturing knowledge, integrating the expert system into the production environment, and procuring personnel to develop and maintain the system.

As noted in the opening pages of the book, many of the topics discussed deviate very little from standard professional software development practices. Points presented in the book's discussions, however, bring out those variations in standard software engineering practices that are peculiar to expert system development. Any one of these special features of expert system development could cause problems for the system developer if overlooked.

This final chapter completes the picture of the whole based on the knowledge of the detailed parts. This final review of trends is vital to the decision maker, for it assists in culturing the broadened style of awareness needed for strategic planning. Project planners need to know not only what will happen in the next 1–5 years, or 10 years, but also what could happen. The word *could* is important to plan for possibilities.

At the outset, the expert system developer or project manager faces the task of deciding precisely the right time for implementation. If the tools needed for an application are available, implementation can proceed directly. What to do when all the tool features needed are not available when planning is another question. On the one hand, virtually any constructs within reason can be programmed from the ground up using one of the AI languages, but the costs may make such a custom development prohibitive. On the other hand, shell tools may be available with 50, 70, or even 95% of the features and interface capabilities needed. When should one proceed and when should one wait for better tools to appear, for that missing feature or two to be added? This, as the seasoned software manager knows, is a complex question without an easy answer.

The most fundamental managerial skill is to be able to sit back, objectively view all the information relevant to a project, and make an informed decision or judgment. The manager must be in charge of "the big picture", i.e., all the influences on a project, to make effective decisions. The number of uncertainties at this point in expert systems development makes this a difficult task. The manager's dilemma is knowing exactly when to make the informed decision, deciding that it is based on sufficient research and appropriate weighting for other time and scheduling constraints. Once the decision has been made, a key to success is to enter into action on the basis of the decision and leave the decision-making phase behind.

Tracking an emerging technology is one of the most valuable techniques for knowing when to implement that technology. New product features, as well as entirely new products, are continually appearing on the market. The new feature needed for an application could appear at any time, perhaps next week, or it could take a few years. For an expert system development project scheduled to begin in 2 months, strategy and tool decisions must be made now—they cannot be delayed any longer. A general planning strategy is for the manager to schedule and conduct the research phase according to a deadline. At the deadline the manager chooses equipment and software and appropriates budgets based on actual or availability. If a piece of hardware cannot be delivered by deadline, it should be replaced with another, perhaps less adequate, product that can be delivered. If a sales representative telephones a week after deadline offering the latest version of the hottest new product on the market—he claims it meets all the specifications for the application and will be displayed at the next Comdex or AAAI convention—the manager should not be swayed. Politely ask for product information for the files, but stick to the original plan. If the offer is not rejected, new product/feature releases can cause the project to be delayed again and again. This situation is the reality managers face in dealing with emerging technologies, particularly in the expert systems field. Even a manager flexible enough to adapt to a vendor's change should be aware that the corporation and staff are probably more rigid.

Establishing deadlines is one way to manage the uncertainty associated with emerging technologies. Firm decision making is needed to avoid halfhearted implementations with inappropriate tools, on the premise that better tools will come along and rescue the project. The only payback on an expert systems investment is a finished, production-environment product that meets the design specifications for the application. The product is worthless if it is 99% completed, but cannot move into the production environment until one new piece of technology is released. Incremental modular development should be coupled with phased release of the product into the final environment, resulting in an increasing return on investment, leading up to a full return upon full completion. There will always be vendors who have not answered requests for information or who will be showing their latest and best products at the next trade show. A successful project demands action here and now based on informed decision making. Flexibility is a virtue only up to the point of decision; after that it is a hindrance to project development and completion.

Long-term planning for scheduling when expert systems developments should start may include projections for 2 to 10 years into the future. This type of planning is a fundamental aspect of business strategy and has to make do with projections, extrapolations, and speculations. For example, in an oil refinery management knows the process control system controlling a bank of distillation units will be depreciated and considered paid for at some set date and will need to be replaced. Additionally, enhancements to adjoining equipment can also require upgrading the plant-control system in 5 years. The distillation units themselves will decrease in reliability over time, and before that occurs expanding volumes and new environmental protection laws may force replacement. Another factor involved in the planning may be that the engineers familiar with the current system are nearing retirement. A new group of employees will need to be hired, creating the need for a means to attract skilled engineers, plus a way to capture the current knowledge and communicate it to the new employees. These various factors, correlated on a project planning spreadsheet, might indicate that the optimum time for replacing the control system will be, say, 4½ years in the future. To meet this installation date, the implementation will have to start in, say, 3 years, and the research phase for software products must commence in 2 years. Although some specific computer could be a prime hardware choice if the replacement were to occur next year, by 1993 this equipment will, of course, be made obsolete by more functional, cheaper machines.

For a project of this size that is expected to grow to over 60 engineers in 3 years, it is wise to allocate one engineer even at the current time. The job of this one is to start tracking technological developments and planning the development. In this initial planning, from the best the engineer can do is realistically extrapolate from the current state of technology to forecast what is likely to be available in 4 years. Insight and wisdom are needed to project the potential state of a more mature technology further in the future. An appropriate approach is to describe the functionality of the system design that will be shopped for at the appointed time, without concern for the actual internal implementation in that "black box" product. For example, it might be dictated that some expert system functionality should be employed to capture the skill of the current operators and pass it on to the new employees. Valuable work on protoyping the current knowledge structures could commence long before it is known what technology is to be used for the final process control system. The project manager must be prepared to keep monitoring the development of the various technologies over the next 4 years to see if the elements for the proposed systems materialize and which vendors come closest to fulfilling the design specifications. Whether to wait or leap now depends on the nature of the application, the pressure for immediate implementation, the cost-benefit analysis, the current state of the technology, and the anticipated near-future improvements in the technology described by vendors.

## 10-2. THE IMMEDIATE FUTURE FOR EXPERT SYSTEM DEVELOPMENTS

The need for project planning based on an analysis of future trends is clear. This section outlines several indicated immediate future trends.

Most forecasts below are linear extrapolations of the data presented in earlier chapters.

### Anticipated extensions to existing classes of expert system building shells

The capacities of expert system shell building tool sets are likely to become richer and support wider ranges of applications. Generally, even the simplest of tools can be expected to become more sophisticated and rich, in terms of function and facilities offered.

To put this trend in perspective, consider a hypothetical, stereotyped, worst-case, early (circa. 1982) shell tool. This tool has a software limit of some 200 rules, but only 100 rules or fewer are performance-acceptable. It employs a simple IF/THEN (no ELSE), rule-based representation scheme without supporting compound or complex rule organization. Inference is by backward-chaining only. No induction or learning by example is supported. The tool cannot handle probabilities for fact uncertainty or rule unreliability, nor does it supply even the simplest mathematical functions, e.g., arithmetic capabilities within the rule conditions. The system developer is not provided with a high-level language interface or other means for connecting to data bases, graphics, or even standard ASCII files. Without even internal source code for customization, programmer productivity is restricted to the minimal functionality provided by the program. Communication with the program by the developer or end user is through very limited text phrase conversation, for the program does not have a natural language or graphics processor. Screen interaction is by line-by-line scrolling only, with no full screen or windowing display available. No on-line help is available. Functionally the program limits the developer with the appearance that it compiles its rules, but the actual implementation uses slow rule interpretation. The system is single-user only, with no way to expand to any form of multiuser environment.

Fortunately, this worst-case scenario is fiction, although some of the very earliest expert systems tools were subject to many of these shortcomings. This hypothetical example illustrates the fact that any one of these limitations could result in the demise of an expert system project. When today's developers use a more advanced tool and encounter one of its limitations, they feel that the higher quality tool is almost as primitive as the stereotype just described.

The best-case scenario, however, is easy to infer from the discussions of Chapters 4 and 5. This ideal tool set offers multiple integrated representation/inference schemes, interleaving of system- or user-defined search strategies, multiple system-defined and/or user-specified schemes for managing uncertainty, access to sophisticated libraries for mathematical or other standardized functions, integral data base manager, integral spreadsheet, integral high-resolution/high-functionality graphics, interfaces to many third-party products, an open architecture with multiple high-level-language interfaces, color full-screen displays with unlimited windowing, pop-up or pull-down menus, icons, incremental compilation, and so on. A vast number of utilities are contained in the ideal to support development of all the special features needed in the expert system, from user interfaces to developer interfaces.

How do these generalized development trends translate into the immediate future of expert systems tool capabilities? Certainly, the expert system building tools will continue to become more sophisticated. Although smaller, single-purpose tools will always have a place, tool sets with multiple representation/inference schemes are expected to become the standard. Because the object-oriented, abstract-data-type formulation offers a highly general structuring scheme, more object-based tools are likely to appear with predefined data types for rules, frames, access triggers, networks, and so on. Such a rich variety of primitives should give the system developer and programmer the greatest flexibility, particularly when coupled with an open architecture that has predefined high-level language, graphics, and data-base interfaces. Access to source code and the capabilities of developer-defined modifications to the source are already providing extensive programming capabilities within tool sets. Facilities to track customer modifications and then reapply them to the next release of the software can be expected. Support tools for such jobs as knowledge capture, knowledge structuring, and knowledge debugging, are likely to increase, with the concept of an AI development environment extending onto conventional machines as well as the LISP computers.

Specialized modules will probably become increasingly available for such tasks as simulation, multiple viewpoints of a particular problem, time-domain analysis, data-driven blackboards for complex reasoning systems, and hardware/software for real-time information processing and response. The necessity of migrating expert systems up and down machine/operating system lines should result in more machine-line compatible tools. Standardization across machine lines (e.g., Common LISP, Common LOOPS) should continue to enhance the integration of highly sophisticated expert systems into complex production environments.

A number of the potential expert system shell features outlined in Chapter 4 have yet to appear in commercial expert system shell products. These features included such things as separate models for inference and explanation, which address such queries as "How do I answer that question?" with a more elementary interaction to match the consultation to the user. Another feature is that few of the tools discussed in Chapter 5 offered extensive metalevel capabilities. For the most part, metalevel capabilities were restricted to hierarchical rule ordering or techniques for conflict resolution when multiple rules were simultaneously ready to be fired. There are also other complex behavioral capacities associated with "self-awareness" that are central to intelligent behavior, based on the ability to learn and adapt to the operating environment. Metarules can be set up as one form of self-referral mechanism, but others are expected to be developed. Examples of such capabilities include dynamic self-monitoring of performance and resultant adjustment of representation implementation schemes, search strategies, reasoning methodologies, or possibly hardware architecture configurations to enhance performance. Libraries of implementation schemes, search schemes, and software-controlled hardware configuration settings are likely to become increasingly used in *metaexpert systems*, which control the overall operation of the expert system. Factory automation robots are a prime target for such systems.

### Knowledge-base-to-knowledge-base integration standards

As knowledge-base-to-knowledge-base integration standards emerge, "intelligence modules" will likely become more prevalent, standardized in structure, and organized into libraries for efficient use. With this standardization, expert system building should become quicker and more efficient, and the potential for linking several expert systems (each with limited breadth) into a single integrated system with a wider knowledge capacity should be enhanced. The interlinking of knowledge-base modules may give rise to multifaceted distributed knowledge-base systems along the lines of the large-scale distributed databases of today. Knowledge-base administrators (KBAs) will enforce order in these large systems, and knowledge-engineering, implementation, and maintenance standards can be expected to become more established.

### Passive advisors evolving to become more active agents

Another important trend is the development of increasingly "active" versus "passive" expert systems. The passive systems are more of the class of expert assistants, which generally advise human experts, and the active, or independent-agent, systems are projected to be directly participating in dynamic or interactive processes without human intervention. A chemical plant process-control system without a human operator lies at one extreme of independence. Such a system would perform its expert analysis of the process-control environment and then automatically adjust as necessary. Another example might be a financial portfolio manager expert system that automatically buys and sells stocks and commodities via modem according to the rules of its knowledge base.

### Computer-user interface becoming more tolerant of errors

Expert systems can be expected to make computer systems smarter, that is, easier to learn and use for both novices and professionals. Making computers more accessible to inexperienced users should result in a deeper penetration of computer technology into different areas of society. Machines may be more tolerant and accepting of user errors such as misspelled and inappropriate commands through the incorporation of small embedded expert systems in the interfaces. The potential uses for such microexpert systems have just begun to be tapped and will probably follow the supply-driven development pattern of other technologies.

### Intelligence added to consumer and industrial products

As expert systems are developed at lower cost and embedded in firmware, the supply-driven capabilities should catalyze an incredible range of applications. Expert systems will not solve all problems, but they do present a new paradigm for adding intelligence to current microprocessor-based devices, ranging from washing machines to photocopiers to servocontrol devices in planetary exploration systems to corporate knowledge bases.

### Embedding small expert systems in software products

Individualized, isolated embedded microcomputer applications represent one end of the spectrum of potentialities. At the other end are highly complex, integrated, large-scale computer systems. As expert systems turn from more passive to active roles, the level of complexity of computer-computer interactions increases. As a first approach in countering this increased complexity, intelligence interfaces or front ends have been added to to existing software packages. The majority of the business software existing on the market aids the manager or executive in organizing and coordinating relevant managerial information.

For instance, PC-based, personnel-tracking programs provide menu-accessed file and command structures for executive work history, performance ratings, and potential future positions, allowing the personnel manager to make accurate and up-to-date decisions on succession planning and relevant training. The decision-making power, however, still lies in the hands of the human user. Such is the case with most data base products, spreadsheet calculators, and planning and productivity tools. At the current time, these tools have essentially no intelligence. With an intelligent expert system front end, however, the personnel succession planner program could become an intelligent assistant to the manager, doing much of the groundwork and offering more informed decision-making choices. At the next level of intelligence, the system might be able to actually make some of the decisions by itself.

Although it is not likely in this example, in other applications the machine could perform the intelligent function completely, without the aid of the human. A higher level of intelligence in the succession planner may result in the expert system going deeper into the decision-making process by actively querying other corporate personnel or encyclopedic knowledge bases.

### Large-scale expert systems with host-to-host interactions

High-level computer-to-computer interaction may become more common as intelligent active agents in each machine engage in dialogues. This desired functionality could be captured in the style of object-oriented programming, where the computers are the objects interacting via import/export message passing. This type of expert system, for instance, could be authorized to automatically purchase semiconductors from vendors under a precisely defined set of market and inventory rules. Similar expert systems might be used for automating stock market investments or managing pension funds, where portfolios must be balanced between high-yield but risky stocks, bonds, and commodities and low-yield but stable offerings. Stock exchanges, such as the New York and Hong Kong exchanges, are currently highly automated (the New York exchange is one of the largest users of Tandem fault-tolerant hardware for the tracking of transactions), so further automation can not be ruled out. The next logical step will probably be introducing active intelligent agents into the trading process. Trading may even evolve to allow direct expert-system-to-expert-system exchanges.

Another prime application area for distributed expertise is airline reservation systems. In a travel agency, an expert system request will be made to find the fastest and least expensive route to a destination by directly accessing the airline computers. The airlines could handle information requests with an expert system that seeks to satisfy the requirements of the request while maximizing local route or global operational parameters, such as seat occupancy, number of flights, flight or ground personnel, or a variety of other direct or indirect costs. In this gamelike scenario, the expert systems "play" each other to optimize the benefits.

### Corporate knowledge bases

The large-scale expert systems noted above will require extensive distributed knowledge bases. In the case of the airline reservation system, existing centralized *subject* or *entity databases* will mostly likely be extended with intelligent expert systems front ends. The combination has already been described by the term *intelligent database* (e.g., Oracle Corp.). The next logical step, moving into the latter 1980s and early 1990s, will be the development of large-scale *corporate knowledge bases.* Whereas the subject, or entity, databases organize files of static information only, the large-scale knowledge bases will provide an opportunity for codifying and storing the strategies, policies, and other bodies of relevant knowledge guiding the corporation in symbolic form. Such corporate knowledge bases may become intimately related with the success of the corporation, for there is a strong correlation between the degree of knowledge available and the success of an action in the business community. The difficult job of documenting the corporate knowledge in rule or knowledge-chunk form should result in greater automation of corporate functioning, saving the creative energy of the managers for specialized, expansive, and more rewarding work. The potential for improving research and development, manufacturing, market research, product positioning, and sales should be significant with the aid of large knowledge bases to enhance the decision-making power. Such expert systems incorporating corporate knowledge (e.g., planning strategies, marketing strategies, sales strategies, goals, staffing, manufacturing, product histories, customer histories) might even be used for the mutual benefit and profit of competing companies. Some large bodies of generally applicable knowledge, e.g., scientific knowledge, are becoming available for purchase, and markets for commercially available specialized knowledge bases are already opening.

### Preloaded knowledge bases sold as turn-key systems

Key representations and strategies originally programmed in the AI languages of the 1970s were crystallized into standard high-level expert system building shells in the early 1980s. Prepackaged capabilities for representation/inference schemes could then be loaded with the domain-specific knowledge from the expert to create the custom expert system. Logically, two further stages of development can be inferred — "semicustomized" expert system shells and fully developed "turn-key" expert systems. The semicustomized shells can be defined as those tailored to a particular commercial problem area where there is a considerable amount of standardization and carryover of expert knowledge, such as accounting or law. Only a portion of the final domain-specific knowledge has to be supplied by the buyer, greatly reducing the development time and cost. This pattern, in effect, presents another view of the modular development theme.

The completed turn-key expert systems, however are ready to go when purchased. In essence, they are similar to on-line data base query systems, except that they have been developed with the expert systems technology and can therefore offer capabilities for more in-depth, rule-oriented knowledge. Several examples, as noted in the opening pages of Chapter 1, have already come to market.

### Movement of expert systems onto conventional hardware

On the hardware side, porting expert system shell tools to general-purpose machines running such languages as C is greatly enhancing the availability of expert systems technology in conventional production environments. Currently C tools tend to incur a penalty of lost flexibility, lost ability to create symbolic extensions, and the absence of graphical, debugging, and productivity tools, but these deficiencies are likely to be remedied as the number of conventional machine developments and delivery installations increases. The availability of multiple specialized processors for LISP functions, database processing, array acceleration, and other functions in the forthcoming generations of computing hardware should result in hybrid computing environments for mixed symbolic and numeric processing. The mix may occur either within a single cabinet or spread as servers across a local area network, allowing the intermixing of conventional and symbolic machines or workstations. Knowledge servers are likely to become increasingly widespread.

The support base for the broad infusion of expert system technology into commercial and industrial environments is becoming increasingly well established and solid. Continuing hardware developments (e.g., RISC machines, massively parallel processing machines, neural network co-processor boards, and so on) should help support the expanded functional capabilities. With these technological advances, the level of "intelligence" associated with expert systems hardware and software can be expected to continue to increase. Roughly, this translates into an increased emphasis on the "what" rather than the "how" element of knowledge acquisition and use for developers and end users alike.

## 10-3. CURRENT AI RESEARCH AREAS

The expert system builder was admonished early in this book to avoid attempting to capture expert knowledge based on the deeper qualities of human consciousness. The codification of logical heuristics for various types of human problem solving is approachable with current expert system technologies, but the more complex and subtle aspects of the human psyche are as yet unknown and therefore cannot be modeled with existing AI technology. As noted in Chapter 2, true "knowledge," as it is known to humans, is a subjective phenomenon based on an intimate experience of the subjective knower, the object known, and the process of knowing. The concept of "knowledge" used in knowledge-based systems is much more restricted. Machine knowledge is equated with the organization of symbol structures representing concepts and mechanisms for performing "deductive reasoning" via traversal of symbolic inference networks. The primary application of knowledge-based structures described in this book is in terms of "shallow" structures of knowledge based on empirically generated heuristics, rather than the "deep" knowledge structures that would be generated from first principles, that is, axioms or laws of nature specific to the field.

It quite probable that an increasing number of expert systems in the future will be based on deep axioms or laws of nature, once these laws are discovered for each field of knowledge. This development should result in a deepening of the contents of commercial knowledge bases, but certainly not to the degree or quality of knowledge known in the human experience.

Human knowledge is often associated with the concepts of *wisdom* and *intuition* as well. Wisdom is seen as a type of spontaneous application of deep human knowledge based on broad comprehension and understanding arising at the right place in the right sequence of time. Wisdom can therefore be seen as a spontaneous by-product of the correlation of deep human intelligence with the environment the human is acting in. Likewise, human intuition is quite probably the result of various independent but interacting subconscious processes operating on some subtler levels of the brain or mind. Asynchronous opportunistic processors occasionally input packets of subconsciously processed information to the conscious mind through some unknown mechanism. The value of intuition, as with wisdom, is in the interrelatedness of the state of a person's mind, desire or intention, and an environmental situation. Possibly some kind of asynchronous, opportunistic, parallel blackboard architecture based on various knowledge sources could emulate some type of limited "intuition" a decade or so in the future. Concepts such as Minsky's "Society of Mind" (1986) may lead the way. It is not so likely, however, that such a mechanism will give rise to anything like the kind of intuitive flashes that humans experience. It is not easy to conceive how these properties, uniquely and subjectively human to this point, could be instilled into the current paradigm of expert system technology now or in the forseeable future.

The ability to learn from experience is also central to the concept of human growth and intelligence. Machine learning, however, is a scarce and highly specialized commodity in current applied and research programs in spite of its central position in the concept of an intelligent machine. At best, even in research systems, most machine learning in AI programs can be best described as *deduction,* rather than the type of *inductive* process associated with learning new skills, new strategies for doing things, that is at the core of human nature.

The demand for real machine learning can be seen on every level of application. As an example, consider the issue of integrating knowledge bases. In cancer research, for instance, different facts are known by various laboratories around the world, but connecting the facts to form a single unified understanding is yet to come. Part of the problem is that each institute does not know all about the advances being made in the various other laboratories. It would be beneficial if a shared knowledge base could be created to further the cause of eliminating cancer. The steps might be to establish local knowledge bases for each site, then connect them with knowledge-standard interfaces. The next step of making partial stores more complete, by transferring missing data from one site to another, however, is not so easy. To transfer the missing knowledge from one cancer research knowledge base to another, the expert systems on the machines would have to be able to "learn" the appropriate knowledge. It might be thought that learning could be as simple as copying any missing or modified rules, in the same way that master files in a DP system are automatically updated after the day's transactions.

To date, however, learning has not been successful through such elementary mechanisms, and most expert system shell tools offer little in the way of even rudimentary learning devices. The two exceptions are learning rules from examples (a very limited form of induction) and certain types of metalevel learning for optimizing performance. It has not been possible to create general-purpose learning modules, for the learning process in humans is not yet understood. Learning, like so many other human abilities, appears to rely on human consciousness capabilities beyond anything available in today's machine. Human learning involves ingesting raw sensory data, pattern matching and correlating data with previously learned knowledge, concept forming, generating associative networks of knowledge in memory, and so on. Expert systems and AI systems in general are woefully lacking in this dimension of generalized learning, making them inflexible and unadaptable. One has only to look at the computer's ability to recover from mistakes, internal or external, to be reminded of this lack.

Although learning is one of the most fundamental characteristics of intelligent biological entities, it is one of the least understood. Whereas the simplest of organisms appears to learn through processes of simple adaptation to stimuli, the complex, high-level, cognitive learning functions used by humans are not well understood. There is suggestive evidence that human learning could not proceed at all without some archetypal forms within human consciousness. These forms or structures of consciousness allow external sensory data and internal thought processes to follow specific patterns that result in an orderly perception of the world and its functioning. Without such blueprint "frames" of knowledge, which as yet are not understood, humans would perceive total chaos. The structure of the nervous system, and in particular the brain, supports such a structuring of knowledge and learning experience.

A goal of AI research into learning has been to imitate this sensory-type learning and to produce systems that can perform higher level learning of new constructs and rules. Applications areas abound that cry out for anything from simple to complex learning. For example learning could be employed by expert systems for analyzing the testability of electronic circuits. A simple learning task might include remembering which circuits were not easy to test and automatically incorporating that information into the next design version. The same thing could be done with expert systems on the level of repairing electronic circuits. As faults are uncovered in circuit boards, patterns for weak components or designs could be stored and automatically incorporated into later inferences.

Automated program generation is another example area that could gain from simple machine learning. Mathematically provable correct programs can be generated in some areas, such as screen design and database interfaces, but automatic program design has not proven itself to be a solution to the complex programming required for advanced computer systems, embedded systems, or real-time systems. Program code automatically generated from specification in these areas could be enhanced during an initial "training period" where an expert system diagnoses and perhaps fixes bugs. The expert could also be used as a continuous run-time module that would allow the program to continue learning and fixing later surfacing bugs.

Another not too complex learning example is an integrated circuit chip manufacturing system. Typically there are hundreds of different parameters for gas pressures, doping quantities, and so on, that the designer tries to optimize. These rules could be adjusted by dynamic monitoring of the parameters and yields by an expert system that can learn new rules and dynamically incorporate them into the system's operating set. This theme has already been expanded in terms of metalevel monitoring of an expert system's performance and dynamic readjustment of software and hardware configuration parameters for system optimization.

CIM processes for connecting a number of machines for a production or assembly line process could benefit from learning. This connection process might include various different software and hardware systems for managing task, ranging from materials handling and distribution, to assembly robots, to welding machines, and even to accounting. An expert system is needed to design and continually redesign the line configuration for optimizing changing work loads. One serious problem in these automated designs is the data contamination on surrounding parts of a system when one of the machines has a problem. The window of contamination, that is, the extent of the area affected by a fault, needs to be continually minimized for each segment of the line, which may entail learning new strategies for organizing the line beyond those originally supplied by the system designer.

A similar situation can be found in distributed network operating systems work. Initially operating systems performed extremely rudimentary functions. For instance, even the early versions of MS-DOS and UNIX did not have graphics, data base, or local area network interfaces. Gradually these features have been added, giving rise to rich tool sets and environments where machines can be linked to machines in any number of ways. The original configurations of such multifunctioned operating systems can be set by a systems programmer, but continual system optimization demands an automated procedure that can perform dynamic analysis and reconfiguration after an optimum configuration has been learned from "experience." The TIMM/TUNER expert system for tuning VAX/VMS has already been mentioned, and the YES/MVS product does the same for MVS environments. One early operating system, IBM's DOS/VS in the 1970s was repackaged as DOS/VSE for the 1980s with the CICS teleprocessing monitor and DL/1 database manager. A relatively simple combination like this could be used to enhance systems programmer productivity, but considerably more complicated learning expert systems enhancers are going to be needed in the future.

The potential for deeper understanding in AI is almost unbounded. Only the very surface level of human capabilities has been captured in the current "logic-oriented" state of expert systems technology. At this time various research issues under investigation in AI and cognitive science could have practical implications for commercial expert systems technology in the next few years. These include work on

—neural modeling and neural networks
—cognitive models and mental modeling
—common-sense knowledge and reasoning
—default reasoning
—reasoning (learning) by analogy
—learning by examples or observation and discovery
—qualitative reasoning and simulation
—non-Boolean logics
—belief systems
—truth-maintenance systems
—metaknowledge capabilities like self-referral
—language translation understanding
—the role of intention, desire, and emotion in cognitive processes

A review of research issues in AI can be found in Nilsson (1983). Michalski (1986) provides an overview of the primary issues of machine learning from both the AI and cognitive science perspectives.[1] The interested reader will find a wealth of AI research information, particularly in the area of machine learning (e.g., see Holland et al., 1986 and Langley et al., 1986 for discussions on machine induction and discovery), for this one process is so centrally important to many aspects of AI and expert systems development.

The non-algorithmic computing discipline knows as *neural networks* (also known as *artificial neural systems (ANS)* and *neurocomputing*) offers promise for immediate advances in machine learning. While AI researchers have focused on logic and repetitive algorithms for reasoning and sensory problem-solving, neural network researchers were examining multi-processor, distributed, computing systems modeled on known mathematical principles of adaptive learning in brain physiology (e.g., see Grossberg 1982). A few layers or slabs of highly interconnected simple neuron-like processing elements (PEs) have been shown to learn patterns adaptively (e.g., acoustical signals, speech, visual) by repeated exposures to training samples. These networks can then perform complex pattern matching and classification and are particularly robust when input signals contain noise (see Rumelhart, et al., 1986, and McClelland, et al., 1986, for a discussion of these topics). Special co-processor hardware boards, such as the Hecht-Nielson Neurocomputer Corporation (San Diego, California) ANZA with network specification language AXON, are now appearing on the market and can be accessed via function calls on a PC/AT host. A number of the difficult AI problems that have defied solution through logic and deduction may be solved by neural networks, allowing integrated logic and complex sensory-like or associative memory processing in hybrid expert system architectures.[2]

Deeper machine knowledge, with its associated deep reasoning and inferring from first principles and laws of nature, along with wisdom and intuition, have been singled out as the areas of market-pull that also contain some promise for new expert system technologies. Other topics, such as common sense knowledge, have been even more of a stumbling block for researchers searching for explanatory mechanisms. General Motors, for example, in its work with Teknowledge, Inc., to create automobile diagnostic systems, has repeatedly run into common sense as a developmental barrier. Because cars are such an essential part of American culture expert diagnostic systems are needed. For the same reason, however, automobile expert systems are difficult to build. Mechanics have imbibed so much "world knowledge" of the cars they repair, they employ many levels of interwoven common sense reasoning. Although GM has invested heavily in Teknowledge's knowledge-engineering abilities, it may be the 1990's before automobile diagnostic systems are seen in at the dealerships. Other applications, such as American Express's credit authorization expert system, which have been selected to not require common sense or learning, can be expected to have wider production success in the near future.

## 10-4. HARDWARE ADVANCES INSPIRED BY THE DEMAND FOR FASTER MACHINES

The possibilities for expert system applications with current tools seem to be virtually unlimited, even given the infancy of the present commercialized technology. Unfortunately, however, many of the most needed applications are impractical or infeasible today, not because of expert systems technology limitations, but because of limitations in machine and processor speeds. Machine performance is creating a crisis in all industries, for applications in all fields are demanding information-processing speeds that cannot be met with today's technology. High performance demands an extremely high bandwidth of information and communication between the machine, the user, and other machines. Graphics, color, and complex knowledge structures used in expert systems tax the limits of current hardware and can make many applications impractical due to machine limitations.

The specialized LISP processing machines do offer higher symbolic processing speeds, but the well-entrenched conventional computing environment has drawn implementations away from LISP machines to run in fast languages, such as C, on traditional machines. The benefits of increased speed (C over interpreted or compiled LISP running on conventional machines) and portability are tradeoffs for the potential loss in programmer productivity tools and increased difficulty in programming complex knowledge structures. LISP therefore might be used for building the system, but it may then be ported. The anticipated increased use of conventional machines over AI machines for experts system work may severely limit the applications that can be developed. For the development of complex systems in AI languages requiring subtle and complex knowledge structures, specialized development environments with an array of programmer productivity tools and extremely fast performance based on specialized hardwares are demanded.

As noted in Chapter 6, specialized LISP chips, such as those under development at Texas Instruments and Xerox, could ease this processor crunch when installed in traditional machines. An increasing number of hardware vendors (e.g., Hewlett-Packard, LISP Machines, Inc., Britton-Lee, and Intel) are making a variety of specialized processors specialized for such functions as database, control, and CAD available as coprocessors. Specialized LISP machines are still likely to be used in networks to handle the expert system processing. The Xerox 1185 and 1186 AI workstations (the Dove models) are now offered with MS-DOS coprocessors. IBM PC/RTs are also being linked to IBM mainframes or 9370s for more processing power via layers of Ethernet, SNA, and Courier.

Distributed processing is one method to attempt to cope with the MIPS crunch, but many applications will still have to wait for more processing power. Reduced Instruction Set Computer (RISC) machines offer some promise, but the anticipated speed benefit is expected to be limited to a factor of 2 or 3 times current speeds. Another promising alternative is parallel processing machines.

The human brain has often been viewed as the ideal model for massive computations. The brain, however, is formed of very different "hardware" from today's digital computers. The brain is a massively parallel computer, while most computing machines are still in their serial infancy stages. The neuron, the basic element in the brain circuitry, is a highly sophisticated biological electrochemical computer in its own right. Although the processing speed of the neuronal element is only on the order of milliseconds, compared with nanoseconds in the fastest of today's computers, this speed deficit is amply compensated for by an interconnection scheme that appears to link each of the $10^{10}$ neurons to any other brain neuron in not more than five synaptic junctions. The fanout from a single neuron is on the order of $10^4$. Much work has gone into modeling such neural circuitry, on the level of both individual elements and functions the circuitry performs as a whole (for instance, see Anderson, 1983 or Baron, 1987).

With the widespread availability of elementary processors in chip form, research has been moving ahead in developing parallel processing architectures based on simple or complex processing elements and a variety of interconnection schemes. Most machines are still of the SIMD (single instruction multiple data stream) type. Here a single instruction is transmitted to all the processors in the array-type network. Each processor works on a part of the data using the same instruction. MIMD (multiple instruction multiple data stream) machines, which come much closer to emulating the brain's style of functioning, are still on the drawingboard.

Some of the current, large-scale parallel processing machines include the Connection Machine developed by Thinking Machines Corporation (Cambridge, Massachusetts) (see Hillis, 1985, 1987), the Massively Parallel Processor (MPP) designed by the Goodyear Aerospace Corporation (Akron, Ohio) (see Potter, 1985), the Distributed Array Processor (DAP) developed by International Computers Ltd. (England), the Butterfly from Bolt, Beranek and Newman, Inc. (Cambridge, Massachusetts), and the Cosmic Cube originating at California Institute of Technology (Pasadena, California) and now being marketed by Intel Corporation (Santa Clara, California).

The Connection Machine, for instance, has 65,536 processors, and the MPP has 16,384. In MPP, the processors can communicate only with their nearest neighbors, which severely limits certain types of processing where the effects need to be propagated more generally. Even though MPP can do 6.5 billion basic operations per second, key bottlenecks occur at the front end trying to get that much information into the computer. Current advances in 2D holographic light processing of information, such as in vision, inspection systems, suffer the same problem. The optical, coherent light computers of the future, may solve many of these problems.

The difficulty in parallel processing often comes in attempting to develop on algorithm to run on the machine. Decomposing a problem so that many aspects can be operated on in parallel is still very much an art, and only certain problems seem to have this characteristic. When the problem is suitable, large-scale parallel processing can provide performance beyond any other current computers. Applications in satellite image data can be processed in seconds rather than days. The dynamics of galaxy movements can be simulated. Neural networks have also been simulated with these architectures (see Fahlman, 1979, Rumelhart et al., 1986, and McClelland et al., 1986 for examples).

Most parallel processing software and specialized hardware schemes are still a long way from anything remotely resembling the complexity found in the brain, but they do offer some hope for future expert systems that can pursue multiple lines of inquiry in advance.

## 10-5. INCREASED KNOWLEDGE AVAILABILITY AS SOFT SCIENCES DEVELOP INTO HARD SCIENCES

In the next three sections, we will present final observations relating to the continued development of intelligent machines and the impact such a development may have on our society as a whole. In this section, comments are made concerning the nature of developing bodies of knowledge or expertise. The second section offers a very high-level perspective on the future of hardware systems. The final section of the three speculates on discoveries in the area of human consciousness which may present a new paradigm for developing intelligent machines.

Expert systems are one of the most promising technologies on the horizon for capturing the exploding areas of scientific knowledge as they develop and making them available to others via large interacting knowledge bases. The role of expert systems is expected to increase, in documenting and debugging knowledge structures and then acting as delivery vehicles to allow ordinary people to access and manipulate this knowledge. For example, the GM motivation to move into expert diagnostic tools is that cars are increasing rapidly in complexity, especially in embedded electronics for controlling vehicle performance. Deploying expert systems technologies to handle the mushrooming knowledge and the consequential increasing sophistication of society are a natural outcome of the current trend in the discovery and application of scientific knowledge.

Scientific discovery of new knowledge, from a historical perspective, displays an orderly sequential unfoldment. From the outside, the presentation of new discoveries in scientific journals, textbooks, trade magazines, and the popular press has the flavor of a well-organized, well-orchestrated systematic advancement of knowledge. The appearance is that all the players know their own roles, past, present, and future, in their entirety, and that somewhere at the top a master manager is handing out discovery assignments that scientists then automatically fulfill. The literature shows that each discovery is fully integrated and intertwined with other related discoveries as the synergy created moves the entire body of knowledge of life forward. The timing is also marvelously orchestrated; graphs of the increasing efficiency of solar cells or the increased packing of gates on integrated circuits are remarkably linear. The next step of progress tends to arrive as punctually as the morning commuter train, and implementers frequently bank their all on the certainty of the next step.

On the level of individual research, however, it is not so cut and dried. For every scientific concept that appears as a "discovery" acknowledged by the scientific and popular community, hundreds or thousands of ideas have not panned out. Very few researchers know in advance that they have a winner. So much of the scientific discovery process is trial-and-error experimentation, rather than the well-planned, well-organized discovery path usually presented to the public. When a scheduled discover is needed to continue the smooth curves, the past innovators usually have no idea how to create progress, when suddenly, just at the appointed time, the breakthrough appears in an unexpected form from an unanticipated direction.

There does appear to be some form of "intelligent manager" overseeing the process of scientific discovery and evolution, although this director seems to function in the background, hidden from all but the most perceptive. At the appropriate time in the evolutionary sequence, the next stages of discovery are "seeded" into the collective consciousness, the human thought processes, and the next discoveries spontaneously come forth from the maturation of these ideas. The template of nature driving the evolutionary impulse of developing science and technology seems to project what is to be known next by mankind. Those with the appropriate vision pick up these abstract a priori impulses deep within their minds and transform them into concrete realities that are shared by the collective consciousness as a whole.

If this pattern of the past can be expected to continue into the future, we can expect that the current soft sciences will continue to evolve to become hard sciences as more knowledge becomes available. The less concrete, less precise areas of scientific investigation should become more stable and powerful. Some disciplines within the physical sciences were the first to move in the direction of such maturity. The sciences of mind and social systems, perhaps being more complex, have not yet reached these stages. Progress is continuing, however, and there seems to be no reason to believe that at some day in the future the principles and laws of nature governing the functioning of the mind, whether they be physical, nonphysical, or both, will be as well known as the premises of modern physics, chemistry, and biology are today. In terms of discoveries related to intelligence and intelligent functioning of man and machine, those disciplines involved in the study of cognitive science are likely to lead the way.

The primary impact of this evolution of mankind is the vast array of increasing knowledge in the world. The rate of knowledge progression in the scientific age has been phenomenal. It has been estimated that over 90% of the scientific and technological knowledge enjoyed by mankind today has been discovered in the last 50 years, and that human knowledge now doubles every 7 to 10 years. Futurists and socioscientific commentators, such as John Naisbitt, Buckminster Fuller, and Carl Sagan, each offer different perspectives of the growth of human knowledge. Although it is difficult to quantify, the knowledge explosion is undeniable. The potential amount of new knowledge becoming available as new areas of investigation first become soft, inexact sciences and then move toward hard or exact sciences is almost unfathomable. The key question is: how is the world going to manage this knowledge and put it to good use?

Medicine has had its valid knowledge "gold standard," namely the prospective double-blind crossover method, for just 30 years. This gold standard is being applied at a rate orders of magnitude ahead of any past age to confirm areas of new medical discovery, to areas of medical practice that predated the standard, and old wives tales and folklore. Knowledge, for example, of the adverse effects of smoking cigarettes and the causes of birth defects are undergoing dramatic revisions. From one perspective, these advances can be seen as the increasing discovery of deeper laws or principles of nature. These laws can then be codified into practical, useful, applied bodies of knowledge, perhaps amenable to expert systems applications as discussed in Chapter 3.

Practically speaking, this great explosion and diversification of knowledge, even within one field of specialization, make it nearly impossible for one expert to keep abreast of all developments in the area. This limitation forces an even greater degree of specialization and isolation of researchers and practitioners. Expert systems appear to one of the most promising technologies for capturing the exploding areas of knowledge as they develop and making them available to others via large interacting knowledge bases. This librarian work will require sophisticated integration of knowledge bases, such as those discussed in Chapter 8 and far beyond.

Help in integrating vast knowledge bases should come from standardization. It is expected that within 5 years we shall have base standards (paralleling the direction of the establishment of Common LISP). Multiple knowledge bases with large stores of expertise could then be linked through sophisticated integration techniques probably using something like a gateway expert processor to switch to the appropriate knowledge base for a query. Just as the IEEE 802 committee has worked to standardized local area networks, similar standardization can be expected from organizations like the CCITT, ECMA, ACM, ANSI, and AAAI for knowledge-base design and interface standards.

An additional feature for integrating knowledge of an area may come in the form of national or international knowledge bases. Researchers can not only access knowledge in this base, they can continually add to it. These additions might be accomplished by communicating expert systems, one on the researcher's end and one on the main knowledge base. The expert systems could work out which installation has which information and update both systems to keep them both at full power.

The explosion of knowledge occurring in this scientific age requires that the information age be replaced by an 'age of knowledge.' Applications for expert system development, from small stand-alone systems to huge networks of communicating active agent expert systems, have just begun to be tapped for the current stage of knowledge. Developments based on the expert systems technologies of the future may offer the only solution to the knowledge explosion.

## 10-6. PARALLELS BETWEEN THE DEVELOPMENT OF PHYSICS AND THE DEVELOPMENT OF AI

Expert systems technology is an applied development of AI research. AI research, in turn, depends on computer hardware and software developments and the realization of novel approaches for organizing the characteristics associated with knowledge and machine intelligence. Two central themes for the continued development of AI and therefore expert systems are the advances in hardware due to developments in applied physics and changing viewpoints of objective scientific inquiry based on recent investigations in pure and theoretical physics.

The application of the principles of physical laws has resulted in the increasing refinements seen in computing machinery. The progression of physical discovery since the advent of the current scientific age approximately 400 years ago has been based on the following three points

- the discovery of increasingly deeper laws of nature
- investigation in terms of increasingly finer time scales
- investigation in terms of increasingly finer distance scales

In actuality these three points are not separate, but represent an integrated perspective of the structure of the physical universe. Stated another way, the discovery of deeper laws of nature is found at increasingly more refined time and distance scales. It appears that the laws of nature governing the activities of matter and energy in the universe are layered, and the subtler, deeper laws give rise to more powerful, more universal realities. The layers of classical physics (e.g., celestial mechanics—Kepler, terrestrial mechanics—Newton, electromagnetism—Maxwell) unfolded first, because they were operating on more obvious time and distance scales. The discoveries of subnuclear and quantum mechanical physics during this century describe the inner workings of nature operating at much finer levels. The latest theories in Super Unification of all the laws of nature, such as the supergravity and superstring theories emerging since 1982, cover much finer interactions at the proposed fundamental level of universal creation and evolution itself, the Planck scale ($10^{-43}$ seconds on the time scale, $10^{-33}$ centimeters on the distance scale). A graphical summary of some of these key developments is found in Fig. 10-1.

The application of physical laws of nature in the form of technologies has followed basic discoveries in the field. For computer technology, the

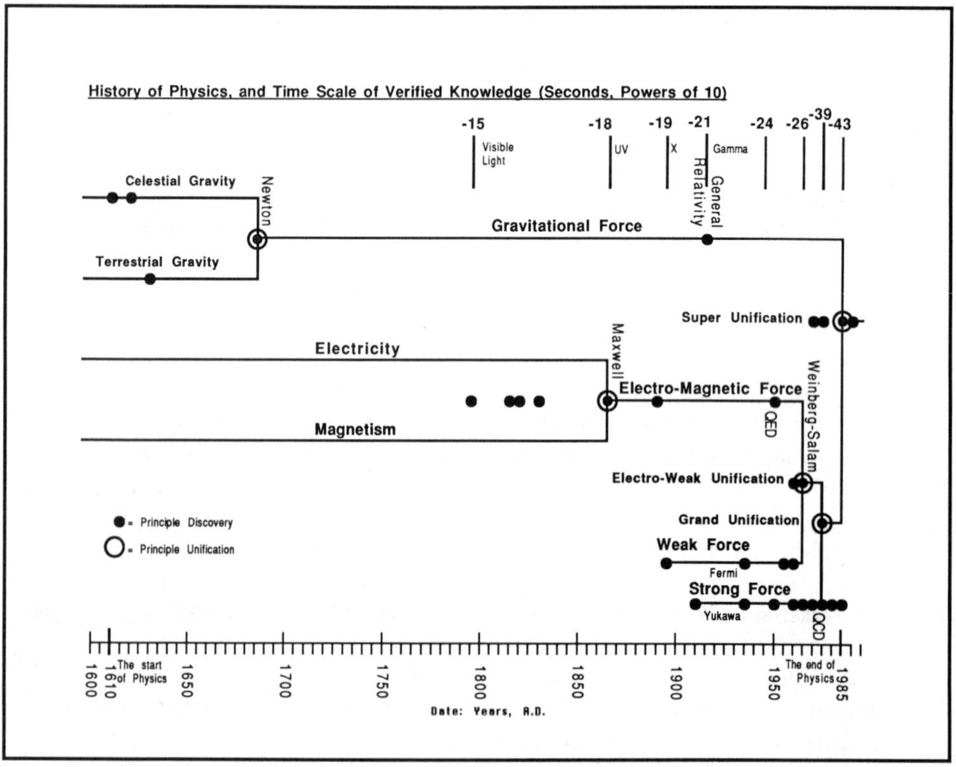


Fig. 10-1. A unification history of physics.

development of hardware has followed a parallel path, based on the applications of physical laws

- the use of increasingly more refined technologies
- increasingly faster machines
- increasingly smaller devices

Historically, computer hardware has progressed through manual devices, electromechanical switches, vacuum tubes, transistors, and large-scale integrated circuits (LSI) to very large scale circuits (VLSI)—microchips with hundreds of thousands of transistors. The shift from the use of the particle nature of physics to the field or wave nature associated with quantum mechanics, such as the MOS FETs (metal oxide semiconductor field effect transistors, such as CMOS), has been central in the speed gains and lower power consumption. Associated advances in materials science have changed the substrate of transistors from germanium to silicon to gallium arsenide. The refinement of the base electrical computer technology and improvements in strategies for numerical and symbolic computing have resulted in speed increases from the 5 instructions per second of the Harvard Mark I in 1943 to 200 MIPS (200,000,000 instructions per second) of the Texas Instruments/Control Data Corporation/Defense Advanced Research Project Agency GaAs microprocessor development scheduled for delivery before 1990. At the same time, the size of physical devices has been reduced from the first electromechanical switches (on the order of 1 meter) to the latest VLSI transistors (on the order of 1 micron). Refining technologies has resulted in approximately eight orders of magnitude increase in computer speed in half a century and shrinking device sizes by six orders of magnitude.

The key point for the future is that to date only the more surface levels of the laws of nature have been captured for use by man's technology. The earliest computer operated on principles strictly associated with Maxwell's four equations of electromagnetism. The computer circuits of today are based on deeper layers of knowledge, particularly in the quantum mechanical (cira 1930s–1960s) derivation of numerical values for the properties of semiconductor materials. The basic substrate for computing remains, however, the laws of nature associated with electronic level. Figure 10-1 shows how, in the years from 1967 to the early 1980s, the four fundamental forces of physics (gravitation, electromagnetic, weak, and strong interactions) have been unified in various theories. The deepest, most encompassing theories of Super Unification, which are gaining some experimental support, strike at the heart of achieving Einstein's dream of a single fundamental force field of nature. How will the technologies of the future, based on the applied values of these much deeper laws of physics, operate? At what speed will they operate?

It is difficult to even begin to speculate on what computers based on these deeper technologies will look like. It is very likely that the entire modality of electronic-based computers will be supplanted by something much more powerful, something much more akin to the fieldlike qualities of the quantum mechanical or unified field levels of physics. Experimental models of light-based, laser computers are being tested today; they have binary switching performed by pulses of laser beams at a rate 1000 times faster than the processors mentioned above. Other optical computing systems under development incorporate hybrid technologies of electronic and laser holographic full-field information processing, where parallelism reached fulfillment in holographic image processing. Recent discoveries in the area of high temperature superconducting materials, just emerging at the time of this writing, bring forth a whole new range of possibilities. Virtually anything is possible for the future.

Hardware-technology development represents only one facet of the future advances expected for AI systems. Obviously, the central concept relating to intelligent machines, the software systems, does not have such a clearly defined path to follow. It would be invaluable if cognitive psychology had completely mapped out the different regions of mental processing to such a degree that implementing these models, in whatever form, could result in the creation of machine intelligence of the *n*th degree. Unfortunately, no such models exist. The real breakthrough giving rise to machine intelligence will most likely be based on different types of information-processing paradigms that can be seen only as science fiction today. Increasing hardware speeds will provide the substrate for the more important discoveries related to machine intelligence, i.e., how to organize the activity of millions of ultrafast, ultracomplex multiprocessor systems to work on a single problem, how to decompose problems into something amenable to massively parallel processing, and so on. Linear developments in technology will eventually effect these changes, but will they really give the ability to produce something more closely related to real intelligence? A new paradigm shift of the type discussed in the next section will be needed to push the development of truly intelligent machines from a path of linear acceleration into hyperspace.

## 10-7. TOWARD A TECHNOLOGY OF MIND AND CONSCIOUSNESS

The development of physics noted in the previous section has been motivated by one principle—man's desire to replace the apparent disconnected diversity seen in life with a more unified scheme. The principle of a law of nature is itself a unifying concept, bringing together all possible observed behaviors under different conditions into one succinct law or equation. The progression of physics outlined in Fig. 10-1 has demonstrated increasing unification of the forces of nature, which by 1920 had yielded just four fundamental forces, namely, electromagnetism, gravitation, the strong nuclear force, and the weak nuclear force. In 1968 the unification of electromagnetism with the weak force, discovered independently by both Weinberg and Salam, reduced the number of fundamental forces to just three. By 1975 various discoveries in quantumchromodynamics were able to unify the strong force with the electro-weak force, termed the *Grand Unification*. In 1982, the *Super Unification* theories started to appear linking gravitation with the grand unified forces, creating a single *Unified Field*. In these theories, one unified field is seen as the source of all the laws of nature structuring the universe from the microscopic Planck scale to the macroscopic scale of the universe as a whole.

Although physics has unraveled some of the great mysteries of physical matter and energy with advances in the unification of the material world into one single field, many physicists have observed that it still leaves man with two universes, not one. As noted by physics Nobel Laureate Eugene Wigner, the unified field of physics does not address the concepts or experience of thought, emotions, feelings, being, or consciousness, or any of a number of other cognitive experiences humans have every day. Obviously, a *science of consciousness* is needed to provide answers to these questions, and this science will probably be subjective as well as objective.

The first step toward bringing these two universes together, as noted in Chapter 2, is likely to be an increasing recognition that a scientific subjective mode of gaining knowledge is possible and can be used to uncover the primary elements of the field of consciousness. Once this has occurred, the next logical step is to find a means for creating a unified theoretical understanding, verified by scientific experimentation, to show the intimate interrelatedness between both subjective and objective phenomena at their common basis.

Physics, of course, is not the only study that seeks to find unifying principles in the various spheres of life. Virtually all scientific studies, soft or hard, can be viewed as attempts to create order out of chaos, understanding out of incoherence, knowledge out of data. There is an innate drive in humankind to understand and know, to make sense of the innumerable events and experiences that assail the senses and dwell in the thought process day after day. Human consciousness is the perceiver, the intelligent agent in these interactions, and it is the desire deep within the human mind to know itself that initiates the search inside and out.

The investigation into what makes up mind and consciousness is proceeding from many directions. Researchers in cognitive science, consisting of such disciplines as cognitive psychology, linguistics, philosophy, and AI, are collectively attacking the problem from their respective angles. Many of the works cited throughout this book aim to address these fundamental issues. Work in the neurosciences, molecular biology, biophysics, chemical biology, and related areas is seeking to establish the physical foundations and correlates for mind and consciousness. Great breakthroughs in knowledge of brain functioning, neurotransmitters, hormonal activities, and other areas, such as decoding DNA and genetic engineering, are changing the way scientists understand physiological functioning and the impact these styles of functioning have on states of mind and feeling. The psychophysiological correlates of higher states of consciousness are starting to unfold in various research areas. Anthropologists and research scholars are reviving the knowledge buried deep in cultural traditions, such as those of ancient China, the Indian Vedas, the Mayan, Incan, Egyptian, and Greek civilizations. Religion scholars are now seeking to identify the neurophysiological correlates of spiritual experiences.

Very likely this trend of psychophysiological study of all aspects of experience-associated human consciousness will continue to be one of the most important areas of scientific investigation in the remainder of this century and beyond. This will have two impacts on the development of expert systems and AI in general. First, increasingly more detailed models of the systems that support intelligent behavior in biological entities will be put to use in machines to emulate intelligent behavior. Accurate theories outlining the fundamental primitives of the basic building blocks of consciousness, as noted in Chapter 2, might go a long way toward creating deeper level symbol sets for intelligence simulation in machines. Second, these deeper laws of nature structuring the consciousness of man will be experimentally verified and harnessed for use, giving rise to newer, as yet undiscovered, technologies of mind and mental potential. If man has to date been using only 5–10% of his mental potential, as has been suggested by phychologists and neuroscientists alike, what will be the impact of development of mental technologies where 20, 50, or 90% are used? How will this influence the concept of an intelligent machine? Advanced civilizations collectively functioning at a much higher mental utilization may not have the need for intelligent machines at all. More likely, they will have the "knowledge-engineering" capabilities to directly link mental capacities to their machines or to directly link laws of nature governing consciousness to machines to produce the effect of real intelligence in computing machines, whatever their "hardware" may be.

Science fiction—flights of imagination you might say. The thought of increasingly more power emulations of intelligence in a machine is plausible; current expert systems are an outgrowth of that trend and can be expected to continue. The Japanese are actively engaged in the development of human-like computers in their new "6th generation" *Human Frontiers* program. Even the concept of linking a human to a computer to transmit intention or knowledge directly by thought is conceivable based on extrapolations of current-day technology. But the actual *existence* of some form of real intelligence somehow attached to or functioning through a physical machine sounds like pure science fiction or, minimally, mysticism. But one has only to think of the descriptions of early science fiction writers, who so accurately described the events to occur 20, 50, or 100 years later, to realize that they can in fact be prophets of the future drawing insights through some window of creative genius (maybe the 50% mental capacity level) that is not realized by society as a whole until later.

The investigation of the science of mind will very likely follow the same pattern the scientific investigation of matter has in the past. That is, the investigation will start with the more surface levels of mind and proceed to finer and finer levels of mental energy and intelligence as the components and internal structure of consciousness become more apparent. The search for unity will likely result in a unified field of all laws of nature governing the phenomena of mind or psyche and the whole of human consciousness. Although this discovery of a unified field of mind or consciousness will be new to Western science, it will not be so considered to the Eastern schools of thought and investigation.

The tie between physics, the objective study of matter and energy, and a science of consciousness, both subjective and objective, is quite strong. Many of the world's top physicists (e.g., Heisenberg, Wheeler, and Wigner) have commented that human consciousness does in fact seem to affect matter on the quantum mechanical level. The debate over the causative agent of the collapse of the wave function, dating back to the thought experiments on Schroedinger's cat, has brought the observer into the process of observation. This unavoidable conclusion prompts the search for a higher level of natural law that unifies the objective unified field discovered by physics with the subjective realm of consciousness. Top theoretical physicists such as John Hagelin, who pioneered the discovery of the *W* and *Y* heavy bozon particles involved in the electro-weak unification, propose that the ancient descriptions of human consciousness and records of experience found in the Vedic literature do in fact describe a unified field of consciousness, which is almost a perfect match the unified field of modern physics. The general premise for such studies of consciousness, as noted in Chapter 2, is that consciousness is not solely a by-product of brain functioning, but has in itself an ontological status of pure existence. It is precisely this realm of pure existence, pure potentiality, that can manifest itself in the forms of objective existence known by modern physics and the subjective forms experienced as the various aspects of human consciousness. Human consciousness has the capacity to perceive and appreciate all the numerous physical layers of life from universal level to the level of Planck's scale, and therefore there are most likely laws of consciousness that function in parallel with the laws of physics on these various levels.

Deep discoveries in the areas of human mind and consciousness could cause a paradigm shift toward technologies that will revolutionize our view of ourselves, our environment, and our ability to fulfill our desires through computing machines. With discovery and application of the laws of consciousness, which might be called the laws governing the mind energies, what we now call true intelligence could become possible in machines from simple computers to actual intelligent robots or androids. Whereas today the brain may be seen as the classical parallel processor running some form of "software" of the subtle energy mind fields, future machines may run pieces of this "software" directly if suitable physical substrates or "intelligence attractors" can be built. Laws of nature may interface directly with machines of the future. These points are presented so the project manager may have a vision of the future AI products and expert systems. These intelligent machines may appear sooner than most of us think.

## 10-8. SOCIAL IMPLICATIONS OF SUCCESSFUL EXPERT SYSTEM IMPLEMENTATIONS

Many great claims have been made for the expert systems of today and tomorrow. In this book, we have tried to balance optimism with a healthy dose of scepticism based on real and hypothetical capabilities of current and future states of the technology. The future for problem solving through expert systems appears bright, at least where the technology has advanced sufficient to handle the application. Even the current state of the commercial market has brought many new problem areas that could not have been handled by the technologies of 5 years ago. The forecast for the next 3 to 10 years consists of a large number of active agent expert systems communicating with each other, connecting large-scale corporate knowledge bases incorporating rudimentary forms of machine learning running on sufficient hardware to support huge bandwidths of knowledge transfer.

As a consequence of future expert systems active advising capacities, more cooperative ventures in business and industry are conceivable. Operations research (OR), in various developments since the mid-1970s, has shown that the odds of losing are less in win-win game plans than in win-lose approaches. The goal of organizations employing OR techniques becomes one of searching through the alternatives and selecting the one with the smallest risks combined with the best chances of winning. In other words, scientific methods have shown that for one group to win another does not have to lose. These game theories have been applied to many areas, such as simulated nuclear war, wherein the conclusion is reached that there are no winners.

Another factor that could increase cooperation is the use of expert systems to organize libraries. Even today, the massive amounts of information available to any corporation make isolated, secretive, competitive moves less possible than in the past. This increasing publication of technical information trends to force a more cooperative strategy among competitors. The push for standards in the computer hardware and software industries, for example, illustrates this trend.

The next generation of huge, knowledge-base, active agent expert systems should be able to function in either competitive or cooperative modes. Corporate expert systems and strategy planners can try to outwit the expert systems of competitors, or the corporation's systems can try to work out situations for maximum mutual benefit. Much depends on the corporation's view of the business community and world.

"Market niches" are important in this regard. An expert system, for example, could simulate the entry of a new product onto the marketplace with minimized cost and without harm to other competitors. Instead of losing $5 million on a test market, $100,000 in expert system simulation could possibly deduce the same effect. Of course, the value of the simulation is restricted by the complexity of the models used, but it is expected that more powerful, large-scale modeling tools will be emerging in time. A step beyond a corporation simulating its own product release would be for different corporations to connect their various knowledge bases to play out a competitive scenario purely within computers. This situation could occur if a number of competing corporations decided to use sophisticated corporate knowledge bases containing corporate strengths, customer base, product-line strengths and weakness, marketing, manufacturing, and distribution capabilities to determine product competition outcomes. For example, several competing companies in the same market could decide that three should continue to sell their lines of laundry powder, because their market niches do not overlap, while the other two would create greater revenues by exploiting lines of related products. Expert systems could work out arrangements most likely to maximize the profits and overall success of all five corporations, based on the facts, strategies, and goals contained in the five individual corporate knowledge bases.

Although many of the short-term forecasts in this chapter appear to be just around the corner, at this time expert system developers are still working to create applications that live up to the often overly optimistic advertised claims. Expert systems must live up to the descriptions in the trade press and the claims advertised by vendors before they will be accepted as a bona fide technology. Another interesting possibility to consider is that in the time it could take more intelligent expert systems to reach wide market penetration and acceptance, a newer technology might come along to perform these intelligent functions. The timetable for developing a true technology of mind and consciousness is not clear, but if and when such knowledge becomes available, the massive paradigm shift will cause previous expert system developments to become less significant as the laws of nature governing real or natural intelligence will be available for harnessing directly. AI is likely to be a leader in bringing forth deeper levels of knowledge. AI has the unique responsibility within the cognitive sciences of not only creating theories of intelligent functioning, but also justifying these models with actual implemented constructions.

As with the development of any significant technology, expert system developments carry with them a considerable responsibility. Knowledge is power, and it can be used for the betterment of mankind or for chaotic or disorderly ends. Such statements have been made for many new technologies, but their truth is ever more apparent as the power associated with the technology increases. Wide use of powerful expert systems brings with it potential hazards, many of which have been clearly depicted by the creative minds of science fiction writers. For instance, the role of metarules in governing the goals and direction of the activity of future expert systems is particularly important. Those setting up very critical expert systems with metalevel strategies should be most careful that the system goals are not altered by the system itself, by other departments, or by criminals. Arthur C. Clarke explored the consequences when a computer based on Isaac Asimov's three laws of robotics (the foundation for humanitarian metalevel strategies) has a contradictory metagoal added to its workings in *2001* and *2010*. In *2001*, HAL is instructed by another department that the ship's crew can be sacrificed if that is necessary to perform the ship's mission. As a consequence of the contradictory goal states the computer malfunctions and must be immobilized. The movie *War Games* involves a similar theme when a young "hacker" gains access to a secret, military expert system and inadvertently nearly triggers a nuclear first strike. The *Terminator* is a third work which explores the theme of military expert systems changing their own meta-rules to the detriment of mankind.

In short, intelligent machine technologies bring great power that can be used for either the benefit or detriment of mankind as a whole. The social responsibility of those designers and maintainers of expert systems, now and in the future, cannot be overemphasized.

Intelligence machines can be put to good use on the level of small localized problems or international problems. It has often been said that today there are no technological barriers to feeding all the world's people. The barriers that remain are politically and economically motivated rather than necessitated by deficiencies in the earth's resources or distribution technologies. As noted for the corporate case above, the expert systems of the future may be able to mediate some of these problems and find unempassioned solutions where all parties involved can benefit.

World-level economic and political planning could help ease some of the tensions between nations. The massive wholesale destruction of life, property, and the unprecedented imbalancing of the earth's ecosphere and biosphere due to radioactive fallout and nuclear winter leaves no winners in a nuclear war. It is possible that future expert systems employing win-win strategies could work out optimum solutions that attend to the best interests of each country. It may sound farfetched, but it is conceivable that a much greater degree of world cooperation and peace could result from the use of highly respected, automated "intelligent mediators." These systems might work for long-range planning of resources and maximize short- and long-term planning goals, so that such problems as toxic waste neutralization and ozone layer depletion do not impair or threaten the quality of life for succeeding generations.

Most certainly, the wide spread fabrication of intelligent machines, whether through progressively more refined degrees of emulation or breakthrough discoveries in the capture of "real intelligence," will alter the way we as people view ourselves and our environment, as well as our life styles. An increasing amount of the busywork of mental processing could be turned over to machines, leaving more time for creative growth and expansion. The elements of human existence that cannot be captured in a machine will help define the deeper essences of humankind. In this way, the intelligent machine may teach us far more about ourselves than we can now imagine.

## 10-9. MAIN POINTS: CONCLUSIONS AND FUTURE TRENDS

- A decision maker has to pay attention to future trends, because this technology is changing so rapidly.

- Corporate strategic planning is identifying opportunities for many expert systems implementations to occur starting in 2 to 5 years.
- Future projects should have an engineer assigned to them in their embryonic stages for tracking technologies and planning.
- Waiting for the necessary features for a project to reach the market may mean waiting several years, or the desired feature could come to market next week.
- Many factors affect the optimal start date for a development.
- The immediate future forecasts for expert systems include

  —anticipated extensions to existing classes of expert shells
  —especially increased metalevel or goal-setting abilities
  —more and improved object-oriented user interfaces
  —knowledge-base-to-knowledge-base integration standards
  —passive advisors evolving to become more active agents
  —computer-user interfaces becoming more tolerant of errors
  —intelligence added to consumer and industrial products
  —embedding small expert systems in software products
  —large scale expert systems with host to host interactions
  —corporate knowledge bases
  —preloaded knowledge bases sold as turn key systems
  —movement of expert systems onto conventional hardware

- Current AI research may yield technologies of tomorrow, although research is a long way from matching humans in such fields as

  —intuition
  —wisdom
  —learning
  —common sense

- Computer science technologies are applications of developments in physics, so the uncovering of deeper, more unified levels of physics should, in due time, give rise to new applied technologies.
- A breakthrough in parallel processing techniques could supply unprecedented quantities of processing power to tackle AI research issues.
- Computer technologies are expected to continue their march into faster and faster levels of physics following the pattern of progressing along the electromagnetic spectrum.
- The goal of AI research is to produce direct technologies of mind and consciousness, that, if realized, would supersede the current simulations.

• New paradigms of research into consciousness, perhaps coupling subjective methodologies with current objective approaches, may enter the domain of AI investigation and technology.

• Expert systems may influence many areas of corporate and economical activity, either to increase cooperation or to increase competition.

• Society can choose how it employs this new, flexible technology, although there are indications that it may be used to identify win-win game strategies rather than the outdated win-lose approach.

## NOTES

[1] Many of the AI research topics involve machine learning in one form or another. A set of collected papers describing many of the learning research issues can be found in Michalski, Carbonell, and Mitchell, (Eds.), *Machine Learning: An Artificial Intelligence Approach*, Volumes I and II (1983 and 1986).

[2] For a review of neural network commercial possibilities, see J. Kimoshita and N. G. Palevsky, "Computing with Neural Networks," *High Technology*, Vol. 7, No. 5, May 1987.

# Bibliography


Aikins, J. S. (1983). "Prototypical Knowledge for Expert Systems." *Artificial Intelligence*, vol. 20, pp. 163–210.

Alexander, C., R. Boyer, V. Alexander (1987). "Higher States of Consciousness in the Vedic Psychology of Maharishi Mahesh Yogi: A Theoretical Introduction and Research Review." *Modern Science and Vedic Science,* vol. 1, no. 1, pp. 89–126.

American National Standards Institute (1980). "*Data Processing - Open Systems Interconnection - Basic Reference Model,*" ANSI Document Number X3S37-80-115 New York, NY

Anderson, J. R. (1983). *The Architecture of Cognition.* Cambridge, MA: Harvard University Press.

Anderson, J. R., A. T. Corbett (1986). *Essential LISP.* Reading, MA: Addison-Wesley.

Bachant, J., J. McDermott (1984). "R1 Revisited: Four Years in the Trenches." *Artificial Intelligence,* vol. 5, No. 3, pp. 21–32.

Baron, R. J. (1987). *The Cerebral Computer.* Hillsdale, NJ: Lawrence Earlbaum.

Bobrow, D. G., M. J. Stefik (1986). "Perspectives on Artificial Intelligence Programming." *Science,* February 28, 1986, pp. 951–957.

Blum, B. I. (1982). "The Life Cycle—Debate Over Alternate Models." *Association of Computing Machinery (ACM) SIGSOFT Software Engineering Notes,* vol. 7, no. 4, pp. 18–20.

Boehm, B. (1981). *Software Engineering Economics.* Englewood Cliffs, NJ: Prentice-Hall.

Bowerman, R. G. (1983). "Relational Database Systems for Micros." *Datamation,* vol. 29, no. 7, pp. 128–134.

Bowerman, R. G. (1985). "Integrating Solids with Drafting." *Machine Design,* vol. 57, no. 20, pp. 46–49.

Bowerman, R. G. (1985). "Solid Models Define Finite-Element Geometry." *CAE Magazine,* vol. 4, no. 8, pp. 34–42.

Bowerman, R. G., R. T. Fertig (1987). *Engineering Workstations, Technology and Application Trends.* New York: Van Nostrand Reinhold.

Bramer, D., M. Bramer (1984). *The Fifth Generation: An Annotated Bibliography.* Hillsdale, NJ: Lawrence Earlbaum.

Buchanan, B. G., E. A. Feigenbaum (1978). "DENDRAL and MetaDENDRAL: Their Application Dimension." *Artificial Intelligence,* vol. 11, pp. 5–24.

Chandler, K. (1987). "Modern Science and Vedic Science: An Introduction." *Modern Science and Vedic Science,* vol. 1, no. 1, pp. 5–26.

Charniak, E., D. McDermott (1985). *Introduction to Artificial Intelligence.* Reading, MA: Addison-Wesley.

Charniak, E., C. Riesbeck, D. McDermott (1987). *Artificial Intelligence Programming,* 2d ed. Hillsdale, NJ: Lawrence Earlbaum.

Clocksin, W. F., C. S. Mellish (1984). *Programming in Prolog,* 2d ed. New York: Springer-Verlag.

Codd, E. F. (1985a). "Is Your DBMS Really Relational?" *ComputerWorld,* October 14.

Codd, E. F. (1985b). "Does Your DBMS Run By the Rules?" *ComputerWorld,* October 21.

Cooper, R. G. (1983). "A Process Model for Industrial New Product Development." *IEEE Transactions on Engineering Management,* vol. EM-30, no. 1.

Cox, B. (1986). *Object-Oriented Programming: An Evolutionary Approach.* Reading, MA: Addison-Wesley.

Date, C. J. (1983). *An Introduction to Database Systems,* vol. 2. Reading, MA: Addison-Wesley.

Davis, D. (1986). "Artificial Intelligence Enters the Mainstream." *High Technology,* vol. 6, no. 7, July, pp. 16–23.

DeMarco, T. (1979). *Structure Analysis and System Specifications.* New York: Yourdon Press.

Dennett, D. C. (1981). *Brainstorms: Philosophical Essays on Mind and Psychology.* Scituate, MA: Bradford Co. (MIT Press).

Dreyfus, H., S. Dreyfus (1986). *Mind Over Machine: The Power of Human. Intuition and Expertise in the Era of the Computer.* New York: The Free Press.

Duda, R. O., R. Reboh (1984). "AI and Decision Making: The PROSPECTOR Experience." In W. Reitman (ed.), *Artificial Intelligence Applications for Business.* Norwood, NJ: Ablex.

Dym, C. L. (1984). "Expert Systems: New Approaches to Computer Aided Engineering." Technical report, Intelligent Systems Laboratory Series ISL-84-2, Xerox Palo Alto Research Center, 3333 Coyote Hill Road, Palo Alto, CA.

Fahlman, S. E. (1979). *NETL: A System for Representing and Using Real-World Knowledge.* Cambridge, MA: MIT Press.

Feigenbaum, E. A., P. McCorduck (1984). *The Fifth Generation: Artificial Intelligence and Japan's Computer Challenge to the World.* Reading, MA: Addison-Wesley.

Fertig, R. T., R. G. Bowerman (1985). *The Software Revolution: Trends, Players, and Market Dynamics in Personal Computer Software.* New York: Elsevier.

Ferris, D. (1983). "The Little Engine That Can." *Computer Decisions,* vol. 15, no. 5, pp. 152–162.

Fikes, R. E., N. J. Nilsson (1971). "STRIPS: A New Approach to the Application of Theorem Proving to Problem Solving." *Artificial Intelligence,* vol. 2, pp. 189–208.

Forsyth, R. (ed.) (1985). *Expert Systems: Principles and Case Studies.* New York: Chapman & Hall.

Gladden, G. R. (1982). "Stop the Life Cycle, I Want to Get Off." *Association of Computing Machinery (ACM) SIGSOFT Software Engineering Notes,* vol. 17, no. 2.

Goldberg, A. (1984). *Smalltalk-80: The Interactive Programming Environment.* Reading, MA: Addison-Wesley.

Goldberg, A., D. Robson (1983). *Smalltalk-80: The Language and Its Implementation.* Reading, MA: Addison-Wesley.

Griesmer, J. H., S. J. Hong, M. Karnaugh, J. K. Kaster, M. I. Schor, R. L. Ennis, D. A. Klein, K. R. Milliken, H. M. Van Woerkorn (1984). "YES/MVS: A Continuous Real Time Expert System." *Proceedings of the National Conference on Artificial Intelligence* (AAAI-84), pp. 130–136.

Grossberg, S. (1982). *Studies of Mind and Brain: Neural Principles of Learning, Perception, Development, Cognition and Motor Control.* Boston: Reidel.

Hagelin, J. (1987). "Is Consciousness the Unified Field? A Field Theorist's View." *Modern Science and Vedic Science,* vol. 1, no. 1, pp. 29–87.

Harmon, P., D. King (1985). *Expert Systems: Artificial Intelligence in Business.* New York: Wiley.

Haugeland, J. (ed.) (1981). *Mind Design: Philosophy, Psychology, and Artificial Intelligence.* Scituate, MA: Bradford Co. (MIT Press).

Haugeland, J. (1985). *Artificial Intelligence: The Very Idea.* Scituate, MA: Bradford Co. (MIT Press).

Hayes-Roth, F., D. A. Waterman, D. B. Lenat (eds.) (1983). *Building Expert Systems.* Reading, MA: Addison-Wesley.

Hewett, J., R. Sasson (1986). *Expert Systems 1986: USA and Canada.* Princeton, N.J., Ovum, Inc.

Hillis, D. W. (1985). *The Connection Machine.* Cambridge, MA: MIT Press.

Hillis, D. W. (1987). "The Connection Machine." *Scientific American,* vol. 256, no. 6, pp. 108–115.

Holland, J. (1975). *Adaptation in Natural and Artificial Systems.* Ann Arbor, MI: University of Michigan Press.

Holland, J., K. J. Holyoak, R. E. Nisbett, P. R. Thagard (1986). *Induction: The Process of Inference, Learning, and Discovery.* Scituate, MA: Bradford Co. (MIT Press).

Hunt, D. V. (1986). *Artificial Intelligence and Expert Systems Sourcebook.* New York: Chapman & Hall.

Jackson, P. (1986). *Introduction to Expert Systems.* Reading, MA: Addison-Wesley.

Kinoshita, J., N. G. Paleusky (1987). "Computing With Neural Networks." *High Technology,* vol. 7, no. 5., pp. 24–31.

Klahr, P., D. A. Waterman (1986). *Expert Systems: Techniques, Tools, and Applications.* Reading, MA: Addison-Wesley.

Kowalski, R. A. (1979). "Algorithm = Logic + Control." *Communications of the Association of Computing Machinery (ACM),* vol. 22, pp. 424–436.

Langley, P., H. A. Simon, G. L. Bradshaw, J. M. Zytkow (1986). *Scientific Discovery: Computational Explorations of the Creative Process.* Cambridge, MA: MIT Press.

Martin, J. (1986). *Fourth-Generation Languages,* 4 vols. Englewood Cliffs, NJ: Prentice-Hall.

Martin, J. (1973). *Design of Man-Computer Dialogues.* Englewood Cliffs, NJ. Prentice-Hall.

Martin, N. (1987). *Software Engineering of Expert Systems.* Reading, MA: Addison-Wesley.

McCarthy, J., P. W. Abrahams, D. J. Edwards, T. P. Hart, M. I. Levin (1980). *LISP 1.5 Programmer's Manual.* Cambridge, MA: MIT Press.

McClelland, J. L., D. E. Rumelhart, and PDP Research Group (1986). *Parallel Distributed Processing: Explorations in the Microstructure of Cognition,* vol. 2: *Psychological and Biological Models.* Scituate, MA: Bradford Co. (MIT Press).

McCracken, D. D., M. A. Jackson (1982). "Life Cycle Concept Considered Harmful." *Association of Computing Machinery (ACM) SIGSOFT Software Engineering Notes,* vol. 17, no. 2, pp. 29–32.

McDermott, J. (1982). "R1: A Rule-based Configurer of Computer Systems." *Artificial Intelligence,* vol. 19, pp. 39–88.

Merrit, R. (1986). "Artificial Intelligence Tackles Industrial Tasks." *The Industrial and Process Control Magazine,* January, pp. 41–45.

Michalski, R. S. (1986). "Understanding the Nature of Learning." In *Machine Learning. An Artificial Intelligence Approach,* vol. 2. R. S. Michalski, J. G. Carbonell, T. M. Mitchell (eds.). Los Altos, CA: Morgan Kaufman.

Michalski, R. S., J. G. Carbonell, T. M. Mitchell (eds.) (1983). *Machine Learning: An Artificial Intelligence Approach,* volume 1. Palo Alto, CA: Tioga.

Michalski, R. S., J. G. Carbonell, T. M. Mitchell (eds.) (1986). *Machine Learning: An Artificial Intelligence Approach,* vol. 2. Los Altos, CA: Morgan Kaufman.

Michie, D. (ed.) (1979). *Expert Systems in the Micro-Electronic Age.* Edinburgh, Scotland: Edinburgh University Press.

Miller, R. K. (1986). *Computers for Artificial Intelligence: A Technology Assessment and Forecast.* Madison, GA: SEAI Technical Publications.

Minsky, M. (1986). *A Society of Mind.* Simon & Schuster. New York:

Minsky, M. (1975). "A Framework for Representing Knowledge." *In the Psychology of Computer Vision,* P. H. Winston (ed.), New York: McGraw-Hill.

Myers, G. J. (1980). *The Art of Software Testing.* New York: Wiley.

Newell, A. (1982). "The Knowledge Level." *Artificial Intelligence,* vol. 18, pp. 87–127.

Newell, A., H. A. Simon (1976). "Computer Science as Empirical Inquiry: Symbols and Search." *Communications of the Association of Computing Machinery* (ACM), vol. 19, no. 3.

Newell, A., H. A. Simon (1963). "GSP, a Program That Simulates Human Thought." In *Computers and Thought.* E. A. Feigenbaum and J. Feldman (ed.). New York: McGraw-Hill.

Newell, A., J. C. Shaw, H. A. Simon (1963). "Empirical Explorations with the Logic Theory Machine: A Case Study in Heuristics." In *Computers and Thought.* E. A. Feigenbaum and J. Feldman (eds.). New York: McGraw-Hill.

Nicolis, G. (1977). *Self Organization in Non-equilibrium Systems from Dissipative Structures to Order Through Fluctuations.* New York: Wiley.

Nii, P. (1986a). "The Blackboard Model of Problem Solving." *The AI Magazine,* vol. 7, no. 2, spring.

Nii, P. (1986b). "Blackboard Systems Part II: Blackboard Application Systems." *The AI Magazine,* vol. 7, no. 3, conference issue.

Nilsson, N. J. (1983). "Artificial Intelligence Prepares for 2001." *The AI Magazine,* vol. 3, no. 4, pp. 7–13.

Norman, D. A., D. E. Rumelhart (eds.) (1975). *Exploration in Cognition.* San Francisco: W. H. Freeman.

O'Connor, D. E. (1984). "Using Expert Systems to Manage Change and Complexity in Manufacturing." In *Artificial Intelligence Applications for Business.* W. Reitman (ed.). Norwood, NJ: Ablex.

Osborn, R. L. (1986). "Online, Artificial Intelligence-Based Turbine Generator Diagnostics." *The AI Magazine,* vol. 7, no. 4, fall.

Pan, J. Y., J. M. Tenenbaum (1986). "PIES: An Engineer's Do-It-Yourself Knowledge System for Interpretation of Parametric Test Data." *The AI Magazine,* vol. 7, no. 4, fall.

Potter, J. L. (ed.) (1985). *The Massively Parallel Processor.* Cambridge, MA: MIT Press.

Prerau, D. (1985). "Selection of an Appropriate Domain for an Expert System." *The AI Magazine,* vol. 6, no. 2, summer, pp. 26–30.

Prigogine, I. (1968). *Introduction to Thermodynamics of Irreversible Processes.* New York: Interscience.

Rich, C., B. Buchanan (1985). *Tutorial No. 9: Expert Systems (Parts 1 and 2).* Conference Tutorial Program, Ninth International Joint Conference on Artificial Intelligence.

Rich, C., R. C. Walters (1986). *Artificial Intelligence and Software Engineering.* Los Altos, CA: Morgan Kaufmann.

Rich, E. (1983). *Artificial Intelligence.* New York: McGraw-Hill.

Robinson, J. A. (1983). "Logic Programming—Past, Present, and Future." *New Generation Computing,* vol. 1, no. 2, pp. 107–124.

Rogers, J. B. (1986). *A Prolog Primer.* Reading, MA: Addison-Wesley.

Rumelhart, D. E., J. L. McClelland, the PDP Research Group (1986). *Parallel Distributed Processing: Explorations in the Microstructure of Cognition,* vol. 1: Foundation Scituate, MA: Bradford Co. (MIT Press).

Samuel, A. L. (1963). "Some Studies in Machine Learning Using the Game of Checkers." In *Computers and Thought.* E. A. Feigenbaum and J. Feldman (eds.). New York: McGraw-Hill.

Searle, J. (1984). *Minds, Brains and Science.* Cambridge, MA: Harvard University Press.

Shortliffe, E. H. (1976). *Computer-Based Medical Consultation: MYCIN.* New York: American Elsevier.

Silverman, B. (1987). *Expert Systems in Business.* Reading, MA: Addison-Wesley.
Simon, H. A. (1981). *The Sciences of the Artificial.* Cambridge, MA: MIT Press.
Stefik, M. (1981*a*). "Planning with Constraints (MOLGEN: part 1)." *Artificial Intelligence,* vol. 16, pp. 111–140.
Stefik, M. (1981*b*). "Planning with Constraints (MOLGEN: part 2)." *Artificial Intelligence,* vol. 16, pp. 141–170.
Stefik, M., D. G. Bobrow (1986). "Object-Oriented Programming: Themes and Variations." *The AI Magazine,* vol. 6, no. 4.
Stefik, M., J. Aikins, R. Balzer, J. Benoit, L. Birnbaum, F. Hayes-Roth, E. Sacerdoti (1983). "The Architecture of Expert Systems." In *Building Expert Systems.* F. Hayes-Roth, D. A. Waterman, D. B. Lenat (eds.). Reading, MA: Addison-Wesley.
Sterling, L., E. Shapiro (1986). *The Art of Prolog: Advanced Programming Techniques.* Cambridge, MA: MIT Press.
Stroebel, G., R. D. Baxter, M. J. Denney (1986). "A Capacity Planning Expert System for IBM System/38." *IEEE Computer,* vol. 19, no. 7, pp. 42–50.
Turing, A. M. (1963). "Computing Machinery and Intelligence." In *Computers and Thought.* E. A. Feigenbaum and J. Feldman (eds.). New York: McGraw-Hill.
Vesonder, G. T., S. J. Stollfo, J. E. Zielinski, F. D. Miller, D. H. Copp (1983). "ACE: An Expert System for Telephone Cable Maintenance." *Proceedings of the International Joint Conference on Artificial Intelligence* (IJCAI-83), pp. 116–121.
Walker, T. C., R. K. Miller (1986). *Expert Systems 1986: An Assessment of Technology and Applications.* Madison, GA: SEA1 Technical Publications.
Wasserman, A. I., P. Freeman (1983). "Ada Methodologies: Concepts and Requirements." *Association of Computing Machinery (ACM) SIGSOFT Software Engineering Notes,* vol. 8, no. 1, pp. 33–50.
Waterman, D. A. (1986). *A Guide to Expert Systems.* Reading, MA: Addison-Wesley.
Wilensky, R. (1984). *LISPCraft.* New York: Norton.
Wilensky, R. (1986). *Common LISPCraft.* New York: Norton.
Williamson, M. (1985). *Artificial Intelligence for Microcomputers: The Guide for Business Decision Makers.* Englewood Cliffs, NJ: Prentice-Hall (Brady Communications).
Wilson, E. O. (1975). *Sociobiology, The New System.* Cambridge, MA: Harvard University Press.
Winograd, T., F. Flores (1986). *Understanding Computers and Cognition.* Norwood, NJ: Ablex.
Winston, P., B. Horn (1984). LISP: Second Edition. Reading, MA: Addison-Wesley.
Winston, P., K. A. Prendergast (1986). *The AI Business: Commercial Uses of Artificial Intelligence.* Cambridge, MA: MIT Press.
Wright, J. R., F. D. Miller, G. Otto, G.U.E., F. M. Siegfried, G. T. Vesconder, J. E. Zielinski (1984). "ACE: Going From Prototype to Product with an Expert System." *Association for Computing Machinery Conference Proceedings,* October.
Yazdani, M. (1986). *Artificial Intelligence: Principles and Applications.* New York: Chapman & Hall.
Yogi, M. M. (1966). *The Science of Being and The Art of Living.* Livingston Manor, NY: MIU Press.
Yogi, M. M. (1967). *Bhagavad-Gita. A New Translation and Commentary. Chapters 1–6.* Baltimore, MD: Penguin Books.
Yourdon, E. (1975). *Techniques of Program Structure and Design.* Englewood Cliffs, NJ: Prentice-Hall.

# Index